W9-BUM-368

*Pretty Modern*

# Pretty Modern

## BEAUTY, SEX, AND PLASTIC SURGERY IN BRAZIL

Alexander Edmonds

Duke University Press :: Durham and London :: 2010

FOR MY PARENTS,

BARNEY EDMONDS AND

JULIE LOVE EDMONDS

© 2010 Duke University Press
All rights reserved
Printed in the United States
of America on acid-free paper ⊗
Designed by Amy Ruth Buchanan
Typeset in Scala and Scala Sans
by Tseng Information Systems, Inc.
Library of Congress Cataloging-
in-Publication Data appear on the
last printed page of this book.

*Only intellectuals like misery.*

*The poor prefer luxury.*

—JOÃOSINHO TRINTA, CARNAVAL DESIGNER

# Contents

# Illustrations

FIGURES

# *Introduction* In the Universe of Beauty

::: **ESTER**

"It's going to rain," Ester says, as we sit down on a concrete step between a row of motorbikes and a sparkling white police jeep parked at the foot of Vidigal, a *favela* in Rio de Janeiro. It's a winter day in July, and the lush vegetation behind us seems out of place in the cool air. It's been a few months since I've last seen Ester, and she starts to bring me up to date on her job search. With one hand I reach around in my backpack for my tape recorder while nervously shooting a glance at two military policemen looking over at us with a bored expression. She tells me she has just completed a course at one of the tiny private universities that have sprung up around the city called "shopping mall colleges." "They are everywhere now, in the poorest peripheries; they even have one in a metro station." Ester took a course in administration at the cheapest one she could find. "My dream is to work with numbers," she says.[1]

Ester is polite and mild mannered, which contrasts a little with her husky voice. At twenty-six, her somewhat resigned manner makes her seem older than women her age I know in the Zona Sul—the wealthy South Zone and home to Rio's famous beaches. Her straight hair is dyed the color of honey, almost the same hue as her bronzed skin. While talking later about a new government policy of racial quotas she describes herself as *morena*, a term that can mean both brunette and brown-skinned. I met Ester through her former employer, Dr. Eduardo, a young plastic surgeon with a private practice in the beach neighborhood of Leblon, an upscale cousin to the now somewhat seedy Copacabana.[2] Ester worked five days a week in Dr. Eduardo's house preparing lunch and dinner for him, his wife, and two small children, before taking the short bus ride back to Vidigal.

Eduardo had told me of a conversation he'd had with her in his house. Ester had finished preparing their dinner and was getting ready to go home when she shyly asked for a word with him. He hesitated, as his wife normally deals with the help. But then Ester added, "It's a medical question. *Quero botar silicone, doutor.* [I want to put in silicone, doctor]." Slightly non-plussed, Eduardo tried to make sure Ester had really thought through the surgery, asking her: "Are you sure that this is what you want?"

She had in fact done thorough research, reading up on prosthetic materials in a *lan-house*, Internet café, and even phoned Silimed, the largest silicone manufacturer in Latin America, which has a factory abutting a Rio favela. Ester had already settled on a midcost model (R$1,500), size (175 cm), and shape (natural), and was able to convince Eduardo in a minute that she was an appropriate candidate. But the surgeon didn't feel quite right about doing the operation himself. Instead, he referred her to Dr. Rafaela, a young doctor about Ester's age who was completing her residency at Santa Casa de Misericórdia, a hospital in downtown Rio that offers discounted cosmetic surgery to what Dr. Eduardo calls the "popular classes."

The sun is getting low in the sky now, almost touching the tops of the red brick shanties built on the highest ridge of the rock face. A Brazilian sociologist friend warned me not to stay in the favela at night. Ester seems to read my thoughts and stands up. I stuff my recorder in my backpack and we start the long climb up. *Mototaxis* whir by us, commuters riding behind clutching bags of groceries. It only costs one real to get a lift from the "asphalt"—what residents call life at street level—to the top of Vidigal. There are no cars except for a few police jeeps, semiautomatic weapons sticking out the windows, and the odd taxi, passengerless—a driver returning home from work. At every turn we seem to pass another bar, beauty parlor, or evangelical church (there are eighteen in Vidigal alone). Ester points to a tiny white façade stenciled with the words "Jesus is Love." "My parents took me there when I was a kid, but now I'm a Catholic." Reaching a bend, we pause to take in a view of the gently arcing beach of Ipanema stretching out under dark rain clouds.

Ester starts chatting again about her job prospects. "I could make maybe 1,500 reais a month as an office assistant, but without 'IQ' [connections] I'll never find one." She shrugs, "I'll just take whatever comes along." Perhaps another job as a cook, where she can earn maybe 700 reais. Or failing that she would even "work with a family," a euphemism for the least prestigious but most common occupation for women in Brazil's favelas: house clean-ing. Later I find out that Ester left school at fourteen to help her mother work as a maid in the Zona Sul.

The first drops of rain smack against the canopy of yellow and green plastic streamers above us—decorations for the World Cup that no one has bothered to take down after Brazil's elimination. People break into a run, and the light squall efficiently clears the streets in a few minutes. I have always loved Rio when it rains: it ceases to resemble other sprawling concrete infernos and seems to emerge in its hidden identity as an urban tropical rainforest. The rainwater drips off the thick leaves of bromeliads clinging to the trunks of old-growth trees, quickly forming a light stream in the cobblestone road. "How good it rained!" Ester says. "*Porque ela acalma o povo* [It calms the people]. They stay at home, lose their will."

Ester points up the hill at a small bakery. "It was here," she says. She is referring to the "problem" last week. "I was taking my kids to school. The police were down there," she gestures down the road, "and the *traficantes* [traffickers] up there."

"What happened?" I ask.

"We just waited for the gunfire to stop." Ester adds with a smile, "At least there is one thing we don't have to worry about here."

"What's that?"

"Getting robbed." The traficantes don't allow anyone from the "commu-nity" to be assaulted. But still there are weekly reports in Rio's papers of *favelados* getting hit with "lost bullets." I ask if she is worried her son might get involved with drugs.

"Not really—he is quiet. It's my daughter. She is only nine, but she is blond with green eyes. Soon, there will be lots of these boys after her. It would be better for her if she were less pretty."

We keep climbing, my rain-soaked τ-shirt clinging to my back, until we come to a tiny bar with folding tables and bright yellow plastic chairs. The walls are lavishly decorated with posters of blonds in bikinis. Perched high on a stack of beer crates, a τv broadcasts the semifinals of the Cup. Ester introduces me now to Jurandir, her *namoradinho*, an affectionate diminu-tive, or perhaps she means "sort of her boyfriend." Jurandir is a couple of shades lighter than Ester, heavyset, with closely shaved black hair and a three-day beard. The son of migrants from northeastern Brazil, he doesn't have the extroverted manner of a Carioca, a resident of Rio de Janeiro. Jurandir's uncle fills two shot glasses for me and Ester from a large bottle of Brahma (small cups keep the beer cold longer). "*Saude* [health]," we say, lifting our glasses. Then Jurandir looks at me and says, "You're going to make Ester famous."

The group laughs, and then I realize that *famosa* seems to connote "promiscuous." I have learned that protesting too much just invites more *sacanagem*, teasing—a Carioca specialty. No one says anything; then Jurandir slaps me on the back. "I was only joking, I am a very ironic person."

Ester explains to the group that I am "writing a story" about her plastic surgery operation. Jurandir's older sister, who later invites us to her home to watch DVDs of a charismatic priest, can't resist a wry comment, "Ester is the *siliconada* of Vidigal."

Ester shrugs her shoulders and says, "I was born bald, naked, and without teeth. Everything else is *lucro*, profit." The group cracks up. *Siliconada*—a slang term for a woman with breast implants—suggests another irony. *Siliconada* originally referred to *artistas*, usually whitish actresses and models. They popularized the breast implant during the 1999 Carnaval, when the nation viewed their surgically enhanced bodies during intensive television coverage of the parades. Calling a darkish resident of a favela a siliconada starkly contrasts the glamorous beauty of Globo TV with the more "humble" life in Vidigal.

It's halftime now, and a conversation has sprung up about family back in Ceará. Most of Ester's friends and her parents originally came from the edge of the *sertão*, an enormous desert plain in the northeast. "Here in Rio it is hard to say that people ever go hungry," Jurandir says.

"But in the interior, sometimes there was no food," his uncle adds. "We came to Rio to work."

Ester says that last year she traveled two days by bus to Ceará to visit her relatives, who raise pigs. "It was so peaceful. But I couldn't earn a living there."

"What did they think of your plastic surgery?" I ask.

"They thought it was cool. I told everyone. Except for my great-grandmother. She had never heard of *plástica*."


::: **RIO 40 DEGREES**

Rio de Janeiro. "City of Beauty and Chaos." *Cidade maravilha* (Marvelous City). Allow me for a moment the pleasure of glossing it. It's a sweltering Saturday afternoon in February, the height of the summer. The sky seems to hang low over a gray horizon blurred in the haze. The heavy scent of frying oil mixes with the lightest of sea breezes. A boardwalk wraps around the Bay of Guanabara, Portuguese tiles arranged in a continuous undulating swirl. All the stations of life are on promenade. A hundred shades of brown and pink contrast with wet nylon in primary colors. Waves slap lightly on the wet sand. Children laugh, their mouths smeared with ice cream. Men from the Favela Surf Club lie out by the break point, bobbing in the not-quite-clean sea. They rise one by one, and for a moment they seem to miraculously stand on the water in a long arc facing the condos and, higher up, the rocky ridge dotted with brick shanties.

Amid the hedonism, there is urban order: tribal divisions, rules of etiquette, rituals of courtship. Closer to the old center, beaches are "popular" and too polluted for the middle class. Children play in the tiny waves, while their guardians buy cans of "stupidly" cold Brahma from Dona Firmina, a hot dog vendor and former maid who pooled her savings for a facelift. Farther south lies the brilliant white sand beach of Copacabana, a former resort for the sick. Sea bathing was once permitted only for the ill, and then only before eight in the morning. But the opening of the art deco Copacabana Palace in 1923 inaugurated a new era in which Rio de Janeiro would become a symbol of tropical cool and sensuality. Now the chic reputation of Copacabana has faded like the pastel colors of its poorly built condominiums. A couple with skin the color and texture of leather come in nothing except thongs and bathing suit for a quick dip. They are irritated by the family next to them, *farofeiros*, they say, who break beach etiquette by eating meat dipped in manioc flour.

Many of the elite, who once lived in mansions built on the cooler, forest-covered hills, now occupy Ipanema and Leblon. Far south from the old city, these narrow strips of land thread through steep rock faces and the ocean. The beaches here too are divided into microhabitats. On the quiet southern end, Ester takes her two kids to play in the sand. Against a backdrop of tropical landscape, *playboys* and *pitbulls* survey the field like generals, their brown smooth chests sculpted by the bench press. Here the custom is to stand, not lie on the sand, the better to see, and be seen. One of these sunbathers, a blond fifteen-year-old, was the muse of the bossa nova classic, "Garota de Ipanema." The most-recorded song of all time according to Internet legend, it extended Rio de Janeiro's reputation for female beauty and grace. A few yards away, and no less interested in the display of flesh, two other tribes gather, the *gais* and *intelectuais*.

Beyond the South Zone, the coastal highway winds through granite boulders to the wilder beaches of Barra. Surf pounds long swathes of sand running parallel to strip malls. This is the land of the *emergentes*, those newly arrived to the middle class. They left murderous and congested urban neighborhoods to live in condos that rise up eerily out of cleared swamplands by the edge of the rainforest. The "city" has come with them as well. Residents of new favelas, such as "City of God," which accompanied the expansion of Brazil's former capital, browse shops in frigidly air-conditioned malls.

The transition from ocean, sand, and rainforest to life on the asphalt is gradual. Bodies generally become more clothed the farther they are from the beach, though occasionally a man, tan and naked except for a Speedo, can be seen on a busy avenue, like a lone figure wandering through an embarrassing dream. Closer to the center the city becomes *decadente*. The Portuguese word describes not luxury but rather a tragic process of decay and neglect. The old neighborhoods in the center, though, show another kind of life in their dying. Tropical vegetation thrives amid rotting infrastructure. In one square, meat warming in the sun is sold from wooden wagons. A man with a stump gives out political pamphlets with his good arm. An elderly man sits alone, absorbed in writing a composition titled "Electricity," printed in the deliberate scrawl of an autodidact. Old friends sip coffee with or without a drop of the sugarcane liquor that is said to "open the appetite."

Night falls, faster in the tropical summer than in more temperate latitudes. The trees line the streets like soft, warm curtains. Maids on their day off begin to go home. Most are dressed in heels and jeans, tan too like their mistresses. One mother goes into the street to pick up her child, who is still young enough to be allowed to kick a ball with the kids who live in the building. The pair stroll hand in hand to the gypsy van that will take them an hour or two through the Saturday night traffic to a suburb with muddy roads and tiny, whitewashed churches, arriving late, but in time for a midnight dance.

Down the block, behind the counter of BiBi Snack Bar, men shout out the names of fruit juices native to Amazônia and Pará. Two teenage boys drink muscle-enhancing *bombas*, while their girlfriends savor a pale green *vitamina* made with avocado and milk. The foursome walk toward Arpoador. Fishermen stand on the edge of the outermost rocks and cast into the darkness. The glowing bobs make a long wobbly arc into the black sky. On one side of the break point a simple gym has been improvised. Men with wiry arms and lean faces politely take turns with the homemade barbells, gumdrops of concrete balancing at the ends. They do neat repetitions on the chin-up bars, the sea breeze drying their sweaty backs.

For those who will go out, preparations begin. Dona Iraci returns home from the funeral of a neighbor, a teenage boy. After a quick shower she heads to a *forró* dance in a tiny square tucked into the winding streets of one of Rio's 700 favelas. Already the rumbling bass of a *baile funk* can be heard mingling with the sharp reports that locals expertly identify as firecrackers or else gunshots. "Down on the asphalt," local bohemians gather in a bar, devouring pork and pineapple sandwiches. One sits alone writing science fiction stories featuring *mulata* cyborgs while others drink shots, sweating into their beards.

As the night progresses, it takes on an apocalyptic feeling. Unlike in New York it is the buses, not the taxis, that are reckless, windows rattling as they careen down the wide avenues. At a thousand parties, conversations break apart at the first chords of a classic by Gilberto Gil or Jorge Ben. Grandmothers and children imitate the racy choreographies of TV dancers. Youth *ficar com*, "stay with" each other, mouths meeting for messy kisses that last a minute or two hours, and then end. Fights break out, entertainment for soccer fans or the thieves who hang out in the shadows of discos. Here they rob drunk gringos stumbling into the streets with a girl who has delicately negotiated a "program." The night too is divided into fiefdoms ruled by the *mulheres da vida*, "women of the life," though many are not women. On one ocean avenue they stand in the glare of the oncoming traffic. Boys in more discrete positions occupy the street behind, while a neighborhood in the old center is the turf of the *travestis*, transvestites, who know better than anyone the pain—and rewards—of beauty. Statuesque—with voluptuous hips and bottoms, and long, muscular legs—these "erotic warriors" (Denizart 1998) stop traffic, or slow it down.

How did plastic surgery—a practice often associated with body hatred and alienation—take root in this city known for its glorious embrace of sensuality and pleasure?

::: **AMONG THE SOCIALITES**

Claude Lévi-Strauss (1973) observed that ethnographers move across barriers not just of culture but of social class. He meant that in leaving their own society they often acquire a *higher* social status. Yet some of my informants are in fact my social superiors. Many are wealthier. More importantly, they have power and glamour, connections to politics and entertainment. I only met Ester in a later period of fieldwork. When I first begin research in 1999, I find myself in a milieu closer to that inhabited by her former employer, Dr. Eduardo.

Soon after arriving in Rio I interview a plastic surgeon, Dr. Adriano, a current favorite among the elite. He seems amused by the idea of an anthropologist hanging around his patients—or clients as he calls them. "Why don't you start where plástica started," he says, "among the socialites." He gives me the phone number of a patient, Tatiana, who becomes my initial guide to Rio's "universe of beauty."

On the phone she says, "You're interested in beauty? Tomorrow, there's a *festa*. We'll talk there." The next day I go to her penthouse apartment in Ipanema, where she lives alone with her two adult children. Divorced from a filmmaker, she works as a publicity director for film and television. Arriving early, or rather not quite late enough, Tatiana greets me with two *beijinhos* (kisses) and then disappears in the bathroom. She emerges several minutes later dressed in a black evening gown. As we go down to her car I ask about her most recent surgery, an operation to "correct" her eyelid (she is a veteran plástica patient). "I was coming back from Angra [a beach resort] and they took a photo of me, and the moment I saw my face I said, 'do I have to live with this?' I called Adriano."

Tatiana is a consummate multitasker. She seems to know everyone in Rio, and spends a considerable part of the time I am with her on her cell phone. As she threads through traffic, she can simultaneously light a Marlboro, chew gum, and—cell cradled under her chin—note down a number. In a smoker's voice, she barks out strings of kisses, curses, and softening nicknames. *Meu bem, querido, puta que pariu* (My dear, love, the whore who gave birth). Every once in a while, she'll turn to me, as if by way of explanation, and simply say "Rio de Janeiro" and laugh. Between calls, she glances into the driving mirror to make sure everything is "in place," as if her features and body parts were the contents of loosely packed luggage, liable to become unsettled.

I ask her how plástica has changed since she had her first operation, a liposuction, fifteen years ago. "Oh it's part of daily life now. It's easier, safer—techniques have improved. And everyone is doing it," she adds. "My secretary is having plástica, because something is bothering her. This is cool. I have the flu so I take medicine. I have a falling breast so I have a plástica. To feel better, to work better, to be in a better mood."

We pull up to one of the condos along Ipanema beach. She is guided into a space by one of Rio's *flanelinhas*, indigents who control much of the parking in the city. We take the elevator up to another penthouse. "Socialite territory," she says, "boring but essential." There is an empty dance floor, a crowded bar, and men in white suits accompanied by young, very tall women. As we move from group to group, Tatiana fills me in on the details—genealogies, philanthropies, and *namoros*, love affairs. And who's "had what" (*plástica*) with whom. People are identified as of this or that family. One man is introduced as the "owner" of Rio's stock exchange. After he refers to the backers of Tatiana's samba school as *bandidos*, criminals, Tatiana whispers to me, "Bandidos? He is the bandido. All his art galleries are for money laundering."

We move out to a terrace. Below, waves come crashing out of the darkness onto the white beach. In the distance I see lights from Vidigal twinkling in the humid night. A middle-aged man comes up to Tatiana. "Let me see the portrait," he says, squeezing her arm. He turns to me and says, "I've known her twenty years, hasn't aged a bit."

"I keep it locked up tight," Tatiana says, smiling at the reference to the Oscar Wilde character who remains youthful while an oil painting of him mysteriously registers the passage of time. Then she quotes another playwright, the Brazilian Nelson Rodrigues. "Nelson said to me, 'Tatiana, only assholes age. Everyone else becomes wiser.' This is very true. If you are super happy, have an active life, and a wrinkle bothers you, why not do something about it? That's different than having *plástica* out of bitterness. Aging is not cool."

Through Tatiana and other contacts, I begin hanging out with a crowd of diplomats' wives, aging TV actresses, and philanthropists. Like many anthropologists, I am surprised by generous offers of hospitality, and fieldwork often takes place over a lunch of grilled fish or chicken. (The traditional meat, rice, and beans do not appear often on the tables of my informants.) Or in the evenings I tag along to *coquetels*, parties to launch *telenovelas*, or in one case, to commemorate a joint *plástica* makeover and apartment redecoration. Talk about plastic surgery flows freely in this milieu. As Gláucia, a self-described socialite, explains, "I want to be younger, logically. I don't know how it is in America but in Brazil, we go to the hair salon and announce, 'Hey people, Monday I'm going to change everything. I'm going to do lipo, eyes, hair.' There isn't that mystery." As my social circle expands over the months of fieldwork, I feel I have interviewed a reasonable number of patients since almost everyone knows someone who has "had something done." Nevertheless I worry that my fieldwork suffers from an irredeemable fault in ethnography: thinness. Can I really do proper fieldwork without observing the practice?

### : : :  THE LIGHT OF HEAVEN CONDUCTS HIS SCALPEL

After receiving a hefty fee for an operation surgeons are understandably reluctant to ask any favors from their "clients." But one day, during my first period of fieldwork, I read a newspaper article about plastic surgery residency programs in public hospitals. Perhaps here in a busy teaching hospital I will be granted permission to observe clinical practice? Through another surgeon I get the mobile number of Dr. Eduardo, the former employer of Ester.

A mutual acquaintance described him as unlike most plastic surgeons, who are "fat, bald, and old-fashioned." When I meet him in his office, he sits behind a brand new iMac, which he uses for communicating via Skype with North American colleagues. In his mid-thirties, he is tall and slim, with salt-and-pepper hair, and dresses in a style that in Rio would be called *moderno*. I explain my dilemma to him. After checking with the director of the plastic surgery ward, he agrees to let me shadow him in his rounds at Santa Casa, a hospital in downtown Rio with one of the largest residency programs in plastic surgery in Brazil.

I leave my apartment just after sunrise. Though it's the tail end of Rio's muggy summer, at this hour the air is almost fresh. The bus makes good time, depositing me at Avenida Presidente Vargas downtown. A few minutes early, I stop at a stand for my favorite snack, a bowl of dark purple slush made from *açaí*, an Amazonian fruit. Housed in an old convent, the hospital takes up a whole city block. Throngs of people pass by its enormous gates, workers, street kids, shoppers glancing down at the pirated goods and candies sitting on makeshift stands lining the sidewalks. One vendor hawks homemade packets of herbs and roots. Among the folk remedies are teas that aid in *cicatrização*, scarring. Inside the hospital, long lines of patients sprawl through the labyrinthine corridors and I have to ask directions several times before I find my way to the thirty-eighth ward, identified with a small plaque on a dirty tile wall: "Cirurgia plástica e reconstrutora, Prof. Ivo Pitanguy."

Accustomed to private clinics, where at most three or four patients sit in icy air conditioning drinking *cafezinho* and reading magazines such as *Plástica & You*, I am not prepared for the chaotic scene I find at the ward.

There are over a hundred patients crowded into dark corridors. A few sit on a narrow wooden bench, fanning themselves with medical exams. Most mill about, striking up conversations with strangers about hospital bureaucracy, or how Dr. Pitanguy is such a "genius." Some discretely lift up their blouses to compare results of past operations. Air conditioning is available only in the operating rooms, and the narrow waiting areas are sweltering. Later I read that during peak times in the 1990s patients camped out overnight to secure a better place in line.

As at private clinics, most patients are female (or children—companions to their mothers, or candidates for reconstructive surgery). But while private-sector patients tend to be, if not white, then *whitish* as you say in Portuguese, here they span the full range of Brazil's famous "rainbow of color terms." With a few it is easy to tell what the complaint is, as the residents in surgery say—a cleft palate, a chest burn, a mangled ear. Most, though, have come for *estética*: the full range of cosmetic procedures, from breast implants to facelifts, liposuction, and nose jobs.

This particular group of patients is ready for their operations, and there is an excited buzz in the hallways. They have been waiting months or a few years in some cases, depending on their skill in navigating the hospital bureaucracy. Some have made more than ten visits to the hospital to have the full battery of health tests, a visit to the hospital photographer, even a required psychological screening. At each step things go wrong: documents are lost, times confused, exams misinterpreted. But today the patients have finally reached the last hurdle before their operation: the *plano cirúrgico*, an exam that serves as a pedagogical exercise for the residents. Led one by one into a lecture theater, the patient disrobes while a senior professor discusses her "indication" with the thirty-five to forty residents in attendance.

A woman hands me her medical files. "Doctor, I'm having a *lifting*," she explains anxiously, "and I want to know if these expression lines will come out?" Notebook in hand, I am easily mistaken for a resident. I explain my research.

"You came all the way from America," she asks, "to study beauty?"

Her friend says, "Well, he's in the right place," pointing at the long line of patients in the hallway. They laugh.

"What do you think of the hospital?" I ask.

"It's very basic," the first woman, Claudia Regina, says. "They give you a list of the drugs you'll need, but you have to get them yourself. You even bring your own sheets—and a bottle of juice, to drink when you wake up from surgery."

A few onlookers have gathered around us. A breast surgery patient, Ecila, adds, "*É isso mesmo* [True]. It's old, and I thought, is it really hygienic? I met a woman with a scar the size of a finger on her breasts. She was crying, and she didn't have the courage to redo it." Ecila notices the anxious expression on Claudia Regina's face. "But it's still a bargain," she adds, "and they have good professionals."

The women nod their heads solemnly. It is one point all agree on—the good name of Pitanguy, the plastic surgery ward's founder. Now in his '70s, he rarely performs surgery in the public clinic, but most are confident he has bestowed his gifts on the residents. We are interrupted as a woman walks out of a consultation room and pumps her fist in the air twice. She shouts, "*Foi liberada!*" (It was approved!).

The small group cheers, "*Parabéns!*" (Congratulations!).

The group breaks up as Claudia Regina pushes her way to the front of a crowd forming around a hospital administrator. She tells me she has an "in" with the hospital staff and hopes to "*dar um jeitinho*" (pull strings), to get a more senior surgeon to perform her facelift. She whispers in my ear, "You see, the doctors here are just students."

: : :

I begin visiting the hospital a few times a week. One day, Bruno, a southerner who has moved to Rio for the residency program, tells me he is to perform a breast lift, his first. "Why don't you come along?" he suggests. As we make our way upstairs to the examination rooms, residents bustle past yelling out greetings in exuberant Carioca slang, "*Fala Bruno! Beleza?*" literally, "Speak Bruno! Beautiful?" We enter a small locker room adjoining the operating room. As I put on a set of green scrubs and plastic bags over my shoes, the icy air conditioning feels like a respite from the waiting rooms. Another resident begins teasing Bruno, doing a caricature of his southern accent. I ask the two residents if there are regional differences in plástica.

"*Claro*," Bruno says. "For example, in the South to get the symmetry right we make a tiny point in the center of the chest. But not in Rio, because there is a greater chance of forming a keloid scar."

"Why?" I ask.

"Because of this miscegenation," the Carioca says. He explains that patients with some African ancestry are more likely to form prominent scars.

"In the South, they're descended from Poles and Germans, and they have big breasts already and so we do fewer implants. In Rio it's very different. The Carioca is *bunduda* [large bottomed] and has smaller breasts—"

The Carioca resident interrupts him. "*Sim*, the Carioca has a more delineated waist and a *bunda* with volume due to the mixture with the black race. And this woman with smaller breasts and a bigger bunda became the model for all women, whites too."

"But even this is changing now," Bruno adds. "Now with the breast craze we're starting to put in more prostheses." Slipping a green cap over his blond hair, he shrugs his shoulders. "*Plástica é moda*" (Plástica is fashion). The three of us now in scrubs, we walk into the operating rooms.

At Santa Casa surgery is performed mornings and afternoons five days a week, all year round. With two operating rooms, each of which can accommodate two major surgeries requiring general anesthesia, and several smaller rooms for minor procedures, residents receive ample "hands-on" experience. A patient lies on the operating table, her body below her waist covered in a green sheet. A resident is stitching up the incisions made in the bottom half of the right breast. Yellow fat bulges from the sutures and glistens in the bright lights. The resident snips off the excess and places it next to pieces of breast tissue. Later a nurse weighs this material (to help ensure symmetry). Not yet used to observing surgery, I start to feel queasy and wander back out to the waiting rooms. There is no cafeteria for the patients, but a vendor, Lúcia, sells chicken pastries from a cooler. "How is business?" I ask, taking a sip of Guarana soda to settle my stomach.

"The patients buy more stuff," Lúcia says. "They are hungry because they aren't sick." I ask her if she has ever considered having plástica.

"Claro, but . . ." she rubs her index finger and thumb together. "But one day I will be rich." She says this with such an air of quiet confidence that I can't help asking how. She is writing a telenovela. "It's about a man who helps animals. It's called "The Millionaire and the Beggars." After I sell it to Globo I'll be able to afford Pitanguy's private clinic."

"What do you want to have done?" I ask.

"*Todas as plásticas* [All the plásticas]. I want to refine the nose, lift everything up, put silicone in the bottom, everything to become young again. Then I'll give the rest of the money to an animal shelter and go to Switzerland."

I ask her why; the answer is so obvious to her that she looks at me for a second, to see if the question is sincere. "To find a husband." She tells me that thirty-two years ago she had dated a Swiss petroleum engineer she had met on the beach at Copacabana. "Back when I was really pretty."

: : :

Many patients tell me they first heard about Santa Casa from a television story on Ivo Pitanguy, who founded the ward in 1962. Owner of a pristine island off the coast of Rio de Janeiro, from which he commutes to his exclusive private clinic, he is as well known in Brazil as his celebrity clientele. But Pitanguy does not fit the image of the slick plastic surgeon who successfully turns the insecurities of the wealthy into a personal fortune. Among the first patients treated at Santa Casa were hundreds of children burned in a horrific circus fire. Pitanguy's reputation for charity work also extends to cosmetic surgery as well, which is offered at "bargain prices" to patients in Santa Casa, a hospital run with a mixture of charity and state funding.

Pitanguy's work in "democratizing" plastic surgery has garnered him a list of awards and achievements to arouse envy in any academic: a handful of honorary doctorates, membership in a hundred professional associations, and over 800 publications. But despite a high profile in the media, unlike most surgeons I met, Pitanguy is given to reflection on his practice. His best-selling autobiography tells of his encounters with Brazilian and European celebrities. Yet his medical publications—with titles such as "Philosophical and Psychological Aspects of Plastic Surgery"—are sprinkled with quotes from continental thinkers—Lévi-Strauss, Foucault, and so on. In these writings, which earned him a place in Brazil's prestigious Academy of Letters, this "philosopher of plástica" (as a colleague dubbed him, perhaps not without some malice) has outlined a distinct vision of plastic surgery.

Emphasizing the "union" of reconstructive and cosmetic procedures, Pitanguy argues that both types of surgery operate not on pathologies or defects, but on a suffering psyche. In this view, the plastic surgeon becomes "a psychologist with a scalpel in his hand"—albeit, surgeons are quick to point out, a more effective one (Pitanguy 1976: 125). Realizing plastic surgery's healing potential, Pitanguy set out on a lifelong mission to make it more accessible, proclaiming to the media that "plastic surgery is not only for the rich. The poor have the right to be beautiful." Over the past four decades, he and other surgeons have worked to realize this notion of a "right to beauty" for all. It's true that demand for cosmetic surgery is growing in many industrialized nations. But Brazil is one of the only countries in the world to take the step of offering cosmetic surgery within an ailing public health system. In addition to Santa Casa, a network of public hospitals run on state and municipal budgets offer free cosmetic procedures.

Since opening his clinic, Pitanguy has trained over 500 plastic surgeons, many of whom have gone on to teach new generations of surgeons. Rio and São Paulo have some of the densest concentrations of plastic surgeons in the world. As these markets have become too competitive, younger surgeons have branched out to cities and small towns around the country. Landlocked Minas Gerais now has a higher rate of cosmetic surgery than the state of Rio de Janeiro (SBCP 2005). With a reputation for quality surgeons, cheap prices, and pleasant beaches, Brazil has also become one of the world's top destinations for "medical tourism."

In the private sector, cost cutting, the stabilization of inflation, and financing plans have made plástica accessible to the middle and lower middle class. Patients can divide their bills into small monthly payments spaced over a period of a year or longer. During the 1990s, the number of operations performed increased sixfold (*Veja* 2001a). A survey of 3,200 women in ten countries found that 54 percent of Brazilians (compared to 30 percent of Americans) had "considered having cosmetic surgery," the highest of the countries surveyed and more than double the average (Etcoff et al. 2004). In 2001, Brazil's largest news magazine, *Veja*, ran a story titled "Empire of the Scalpel," which claimed that Brazil had displaced the United States as the world's "champion" of cosmetic surgery (*Veja* 2001a).[3] As if to confirm the victory, a samba school honored Pitanguy in a 1999 Carnaval allegory: "In the Universe of Beauty." Perched high on a float, the surgeon led hundreds of paraders through Rio's stadium as they danced to the song "No universo da beleza, Mestre Pitanguy," performed by Caprichosos de Pilares Samba School:

> Creating and modeling nature
> The hands of the architect
> Are in the universe of beauty
> Giving men their value with his chisel. . . .
> The self-esteem in each ego awakens
> Plastic beauty from subtlety to perfection
> The light of heaven conducts his scalpel
> Caprichosos sings Master Pitanguy.

Some surgeons, it's true, have privately questioned whether the "popular classes" are suitable candidates for cosmetic procedures. But the majority of plastic surgeons—as well as the media—have been remarkably positive about the growth of plastic surgery. Some news stories cite the international reputation of Brazilian surgeons as a point of pride. Others view the growth of plástica as an indicator of *economic* health, a flexing of

Brazil's consumer muscle. *Veja*—the Brazilian equivalent to *Time*—argues that since the 1994 currency plan made credit more available, plástica has become "integral to the roster of middle class aspirations" (*Veja* 2002). The fact that more Brazilians are having cosmetic surgery, it reasons, simply means that more Brazilians are becoming middle class.

Rising demand, however, cannot be explained simply as a product of prosperity. If cosmetic surgery rates reflect wealth, then they should be lower in the developing world. Yet much richer European countries have per capita cosmetic surgery rates only about a fifth of Brazil's. Moreover, the rapid growth of plastic surgery also overlapped with a period of rising income concentration in the 1980s and 1990s. While an ambitious 1989 constitution guaranteed a universal right to healthcare, the gap between public and private care deepened as federal spending plunged (Biehl 2005: 47). Brazil's favelas have become icons of savage capitalism. How in these circumstances can we understand a "right to beauty"? Why are patients such as Ester embracing a medical technology formerly the preserve of Tatiana and other members of the nation's elite? Why did a security guard at one of Rio's largest prisons seek out an operation termed "correction of the Negroid nose" in a land often celebrated for its racial democracy? And what notion of health allows a public hospital to offer free liposuctions, breast implants, and facelifts to "the people"?

::: **VAIN, VULGAR, AND SUPERFICIAL**

Heroes and heroines in popular narrative traditions are often physically attractive. Their beauty may presage an extraordinary destiny, magical reversals of fortune, or tragic ends. But beauty *work* seems made for the minor key of comedy more interested in human vanity and frailty. If outward beauty often symbolizes inner goodness, beauty practices on the other hand point to moral failings: for example, the rich or stupid trying to avoid aging or genetics or other dimensions of human fate. Moreover, some practices such as plastic surgery are not only disturbing, but also comical. Stories of beauty work—particularly *failed* beauty work—can provoke schadenfreude as the vanity of others is revealed. This becomes tricky terrain to approach as an anthropologist hoping his subjects—in this case, a diverse "tribe" of Brazilian socialites, low-income service workers, housewives, celebrities, and other consumers of beauty—will come across sympathetically to the reader.

I begin thus by mentioning a particular moral field surrounding beauty work, or at least "excessive" beauty work in much of the West. As an anonymous reviewer of my research grant wrote, beauty is "a trivial aspect of the human condition." He or she was certainly right, though I would argue it is also a central aspect of modern selves that reminds us—comically and tragically—that the human condition is sometimes trivial. Cosmetic practices are not only trivial, they are *vain*, betraying a narcissistic concern with the self. When they are seen to display poor or common taste, they are *vulgar*. Beauty work can also seem like a *superficial* realm of experience, centered on surfaces at the expense of self-development. Such moral charges are, of course, deeply rooted in the Judeo-Christian tradition. Yet, within the large range of societies that share this tradition, there are considerable differences. In the United States, judgments of vanity can also be moral and political statements applied to subordinate groups. (Think of the various contexts in which Catholics, "Latins," Native Americans, or women are seen as vain.) To understand the ethics surrounding beauty therefore requires the hermeneutic effort of entering into life worlds with other values, as well perhaps as some self-critique to bring to light tacit assumptions.

Writing about beauty recalls another dilemma: the scholar confronting life as it is lived. The "will to truth" of scholars leads them to look for abstraction, depth, and logic. Beauty is sensual, superficial, and to some extent irrational. Friedrich Nietzsche critiqued the scholarly bias toward depth, and against "appearances." He was writing about philosophy and aesthetics, but his critique is relevant too for sociological interpretations of physical beauty. Attractiveness has a social effect that seems to short-circuit other networks of power. Consider the common adjectives used to describe it: *radiant, dazzling*, or, more recently, *hot*. Smiles *light up* rooms. To acknowledge the almost magical social and psychological power of beauty shifts the ethical frame we use to evaluate beauty work: to pursue something that confers obvious benefits is, after all, rational. At the same time, it hints at a problem in trying to explain the ineffable and ephemeral effects of attractiveness in terms of structures. My hope is that an ethnographic approach will help offset the scholar's preference for "depth" and better grasp a social phenomenon that has much to do with shining surfaces.

It is perhaps easier for us to accept as another manifestation of human diversity the Ilongot warrior taking a human head to relieve grief, or even a Sudanese teenager being circumcised in order to marry, than a Brazilian secretary having liposuction to raise her self-esteem. As plastic surgery becomes staple fare on reality television, and routinized for some, it may seem to us, unlike tribal body modification, all *too* familiar. Nevertheless, I would like to invite readers to approach the topic with the same spirit of generous cultural (but not moral) relativism that ethnographers say is necessary to understand, say, the face painting of the Brazilian Caduveo Indians. It's true that the anthropological effort to contextualize or humanize disturbing bodily practices often applies to more exotic or endangered groups than the Brazilians portrayed here. But I argue that class and cultural differences also influence the perception of medical beauty work, complicating the ethnographer's task of persuasively and accurately conveying aspects of life that in some respects depart from the values (which are also my values) of "erudite culture" (Lehmann 1996).

Vulgar connotes not only poor taste, but also in its etymology *popularized*. Beauty industries have rapidly expanded in the past three decades, as Brazil underwent a transformation into a consumer society with deeply entrenched market stratification. Some surgeons say that the poor, as much as the rich, "suffer from aesthetic defects." Other doctors, though, have become unnerved by poor and uneducated patients. A resident confessed his doubts: "You have patients who can't speak Portuguese well, who haven't been to the dentist. If I were poor I would take care of my teeth before having cosmetic surgery." One European resident was amazed that a patient had to delay a consultation because she couldn't afford the bus fare to the hospital. Such patients may appear to be wasting resources or even undermining the dignity of the medical specialty as they demand "miracles": a magical rejuvenation or else the perfect figures of *artistas*. These celebrities have themselves demonstrated to the public the wealth and power that can be gained through plástica-sculpted forms, provoking debates about the commercialization of sex and medicine. In these circumstances, beauty practices represent to some a pronounced instance of vulgarization—of medicine or else erotic experience. And yet, such moral judgments are not always compelling for the myriad "users" of beauty, for whom sexual desirability and its cosmetic enhancement can have quite a different significance.

When I began fieldwork I saw my field sites as almost saturated with neoliberal irony. Residents in surgery get valuable training in cosmetic procedures within a faltering public health system, and then open lucrative private practices. Patients disfigured by industrial fires and traffic accidents wait in the same hallways along with women seeking *lipoescultura*. The poor are granted "a right to beauty" in a country where other rights are neglected. The final irony, it seemed to me, lay in the samba song "In the Universe of

Beauty." A Carnaval parade—that beloved "folk opera" often celebrated for its roots in Rio's favelas—pays homage to a fabulously wealthy plastic surgeon with a clientele of international celebrities. Was this perhaps just another of those bizarre juxtapositions of Brazil *mundo cão*, "dog world," that have been the staple of magical realism and a local tradition of bitter wit?

My ironic perspective though left me with a feeling of unease. New to Brazil, trying to understand a foreign society, I wondered if I was missing something essential. After all, there is a long tradition of criticizing Carnaval as a collective *fantasia* (fantasy, mask) that distracts attention from exploitation. Such paternalistic views provoked one famous Carnavalesco to quip, "Only intellectuals like misery. The poor prefer luxury." His comment reminded me of the conflicts in Brazil that often surround any invocation of the *povão*, the "common people." After Brazil became a republic in 1889, a central challenge facing elites (they felt) was to define a national identity that would allow it to join the ranks of "civilized" nations. The category of povão played a contested role in the scientific, artistic, and spiritual projects underlying this quest. As an "internal exotic," they invigorated modernist avant-gardes and their later avatars. But often enough, the povão have disappointed elites (Lehmann 1996). Two decades of military dictatorship ended in 1985 with dancing in the streets and a brief moment of hope that a country ruled for most of its 500-year history by a tiny oligarchy would become an open, democratic society finally able to address its massive extremes of wealth and poverty. Shortly thereafter, in 1990, a newly enfranchised population elected as president Fernando Collor de Mello, a Center-Right, corrupt, and telegenic populist. Intellectuals fretted not just that the powerful Globo TV network had engineered the electoral victory, but also that the people had gone directly from illiteracy to massification, "without passing through an intermediate stage of absorbing modern culture" (Mello and Novais 1998: 640).

Seen in the light of a longer history of elite attempts to fathom—and often steer—the desires of the people, Pitanguy's right to beauty began to raise new questions for me. Did the popular embrace of plastic surgery indicate yet another example of the people "misbehaving"? Does class position change the meaning and value of cosmetic practices, or of sexual attractiveness? How could beauty be understood in relation to a longer history of intimate hierarchy as well as a more recent growth of consumer aspirations in Brazil? One question I consider in the following pages then is what beauty *means* and *does* for different social actors. How does it look different through the eyes of an illiterate maid versus a professional, to a secular Catholic versus an evangelical Protestant, to a single mother versus the daughter of a strict father?

For "users" beauty is a realm of praxis: home remedies and techniques of artifice were often passed between generations of women to the disapproval of male clerics, reformers, and doctors (Lichtenstein 1987). Modern beauty practices, it's true, depend on experts and industrial technologies, but their social use can be seen often as a "tactic," a move performed by the weak on terrain defined by the strong (de Certeau 2002). Although on the face of it, we might think that beauty is just another realm for encoding class domination—a function that so many aspects of the body perform (Bourdieu 1984)—physical beauty often impetuously disregards social hierarchy. It is quite obvious that the elite are not always good-looking, even when their privilege thoroughly pervades others aspects of their social person, from taste in photography to table manners. Beauty hierarchies do not simply mirror other hierarchies of wealth or status. Rather, it is precisely the gap between aesthetic and other scales of social position that makes attractiveness such an essential form of value and all-too-often imaginary vehicle of ascent for those blocked from more formal routes of social mobility. While beauty is unfair in that it appears to be "awarded" to the morally undeserving, it can also grant power to those excluded from other systems of privilege based in wealth, pedigree, or education.

From this perspective, I try to understand diverse social phenomena: why working class women enthusiastically negotiate the bureaucratic obstacles of public hospitals to have often minor cosmetic body contouring; why the social fantasy of "entering TV" is widespread in urban peripheries; why sexual attractiveness can be imagined as a means of escaping poverty; and why in the telenovela the beauty of heroines (and actresses who portray them) often acquires a seemingly magical power of challenging social hierarchies. My aim is to constitute beauty as a social domain that has its own internal logic that cannot be reduced to an operation of other forms of power.[4] Rather than view it only as a social construction (I agree with Viveiros de Castro that there are already too many things that don't exist),[5] I find it more fruitful to work from the assumption that physical attractiveness is an objective form of value, if not "possessed" by individuals, then observable within certain social relationships and moments. This approach matches the ethnographic method in being able to bring us closer to the views of actors for whom beauty is shaped by the exigencies of life as it unfolds.

: : :

During fieldwork I often had a feeling of disorientation while moving between different social worlds. One week I would chop onions with a divorced housewife in Ipanema, and then take a bus to the peripheries of
the city with her maid. Another week I might hang out on the set of a
telenovela and then visit an NGO that offers a course in fashion modeling
for "needy communities." I was certainly not always successful in moving
across class gaps. Though I was often surprised by the hospitality I encountered across the social spectrum, it would be naïve to believe that the
friendship that is so easily extended in Rio de Janeiro can dissolve social
boundaries, which are built into the architecture of the city. It would also be
difficult to simply correlate socioeconomic status with the views and actions
surrounding beauty. It's true there were some easily observable differences
between relatively wealthier and poorer patients. A few women at the lower
end of the socioeconomic spectrum did not seem to fully understand—
or else mocked—the "therapeutic rationale" of cosmetic surgery as means
to heal psychological suffering. A patient who has liquid silicone injected
into her buttocks in a beauty parlor (a procedure not considered "safe" by
plastic surgeons) may have different notions of health than the plastic surgeon who styles himself a "psychologist with a scalpel in his hand" (Pitanguy 1976: 125). Other working-class patients, however, spoke in the same
strongly psychotherapeutic idiom used by wealthier patients, praising plástica's benefits for "self-esteem."

In making cosmetic surgery more widely available, surgeons have remarkably defined it as a treatment of mental suffering. Yet as we shall see,
notions such as self-esteem—as well as the body itself—have a history.
Medical and therapeutic techniques have long held a privileged position in
Brazil as tools of governance, exercised by elites concerned with the health
of an unruly and "backwards" population, or sometimes appropriated by
the povão as tools of self-transformation and healing. I thus try to read the
aesthetic defect not only as a psychological reflection of body-image, but
also as a symptom of other forms of distress in the body politic. How does
the surgeons' gift of surgery reflect and break from a longer tradition in
which elites have engineered and treated the suffering of the people? And
what aspirations and anxieties in globalizing Brazil are projected in desires
for this special form of healing?

Plastic surgery cannot thus only be seen as an example of conspicuous
consumption, whereby poorer patients imitate wealthier ones in a bid for

status. While residents living in neighborhoods seen by the middle class as urban islands of barbarism dream of being fashion models, fashion, for its part, often borrows "from the street" (or in Brazil, the favela). And wealthy teenagers emulate national sex icons from humble backgrounds who have used plástica to embody a widely held erotic ideal. Beauty culture is elaborated within a diversified global and national mass media which ranges from the slick products of the Globo TV network to pirated cable, Internet kiosks, and black market CDs and DVDs. Within this symbolic world, a kind of "universe of beauty," consumers in diverse market positions adopt therapeutic, cosmetic, and medical techniques as tools of self-governance. Class and racial identifications can thus be reshuffled as style, beauty, and body practices become widely shared domains of self-expression.

Despite new economic growth in the 2000s, Brazil is a deeply stratified society. While class is often not a stable "identity" that can be used to analyze beauty culture, it is often present in social relationships. For example, some surgeons and wealthy women become amused or perturbed that "even maids" are having plastic surgery. The elite seem to feel something like bathos confronted with women of such low status expending precious resources on a luxury item. The vanity of maids though can also be read in another way. A disturbing Brazilian proverb states: "White women for marriage; mulatas for screwing; black women for work" (Freyre 1986 in Goldstein 2003: 102). The splitting of sexual and maternal roles along class and color lines is perhaps fading as consumer and medical discourses project sexuality as a realm of rights, health, and self-expression. Yet domestic service remains widespread, and the *empregada*, maid, remains an almost archetypical feminine role, one that is ambivalently transmitted across generations. Estimates of the number of domestic workers, who are often not officially registered, vary; one puts it at a fifth of the female workforce (Goldenberg 2000: 109–13). Paid housework is in some ways the opposite of "beauty": chemicals are bad for skin, nails break, and more generally, menial labor carries a strong stigma. It is still seen as women's work, but it is an aspect of femininity often explicitly opposed to other more respectable or eroticized gender roles. The persistence of this level of privatized domestic work points to a class rift running through modern female norms of sexual, maternal, and professional personas. It also suggests that diverse social—and also sexual—aspirations subtly shape demand for beauty work.

In addition to the users of beauty, I also became interested in documenting the "producers." Many studies of Brazil and Latin America have researched oppressed social groups: peasants, homosexuals, favela residents, landless workers, indigenous people, and Afro-Americans (for one exception see Velho 1998). More recently a few studies have addressed this imbalance in Brazil, looking at the middle class and the more prosaic activities of everyday consumption (e.g., O'Dougherty 2002, Owensby 1999). I became interested, however, not just in the middle class, but rather in a tiny entertainment elite.

Anthropologists have long recognized the importance of nonhuman beings on the cultural life of the people they study. Evans-Pritchard described Azande witches as if they exist. Why have anthropologists then generally ignored celebrities, who arguably enjoy an equally central position in the social imagination of the modern world? Moreover, celebrities, unlike other beings endowed with superhuman powers, can actually be interviewed. This group of actors, models, celebrity doctors, pop stars—and their handlers—are specialists in the semiotics of appearance. They might reveal why a black actress can sell Coca-Cola, but only to the popular classes. Or perhaps they'll say what plásticas are necessary to sell one's image so that it can sell lingerie. I want to understand how together with other less visible members of the elite they have defined a vision of the "good life" that is readily absorbed, if often in altered form, by a nation of television lovers.

The prevalence of images of the female body in modernity is sometimes linked to risks of commodification. Acknowledging this point, I might have austerely banned the visual from this book. Instead, attempting to convey the *sense* of social life as it looks to actors, I try to mirror the culture of beauty's visualization of the body in photographs and writing. The glossy images of beauty culture are here presented not just as "texts" to be read and deciphered, but as commodities with social lives. For example, *Plástica & Beleza* is a glossy monthly sold at newsstands next to magazines such as *Vogue*. It mixes photos of nude models with shots of surgeons in tuxedos and grotesque close-ups of deformities. In addition to analyzing the meaning of such images, I found it useful to talk to the ex-journalist who founded it, a chief plastic surgeon in a public hospital who advertises in it, and a single mother who consumes the publication with evident pleasure.

I was only able to write this book when I stopped trying to write a different one. The other one would have been anthropology as cultural critique, the kind of book I have always admired. These kinds of ethnographies have conceptual elegance and political urgency. They are able to marshal the myriad data of fieldwork to unmask ideologies. Yet I have found as I write this book that I cannot in the end resolve all the contradictions of the field.

I have accepted the blurring that comes from shifting between points of view as an effect of one way of doing anthropology. If writing ethnography is often a process of translation, the best translations are ones that do not only betray the source language, but also allow it to *mess* with the translating "language"—in this case the ethnographic text—imposing some of its rhythms and tone. Hence I find that some aspects of the ethos of Brazilian life, as I see it—with its historical pastiche, its delight in impurity and inauthentic hybridity, and even perhaps an inclination toward the lurid and melodramatic—have willy-nilly made their way into my presentation of this research. While one of my models was the documentary film with its tension between authorship and multiple perspectives, the other was the essay: an *attempt*, a journeying together in thought, though one that draws primarily on fieldwork rather than personal experience (Eriksen 2006: 17). Oriented toward ambiguity, it is a particularly good form to think about the position of beauty in capitalism.

### ::: BRAZIL

I'm in a tiny *boteco*. Men spill out into the street holding plastic cups of beer. I sit at the bar, cracked glass smeared with grease from a leg of pork that no one ever seems to eat. A Michael Jackson hit comes on the radio. The man next to me leans so close to me I can smell the *cachaça* on his breath and whispers in my ear, "*Black music* is the twentieth century's soundtrack of joy." Black music—the English phrase is always used in Brazil—signifies North American, not Afro-Brazilian, music. He may be right, yet Brazil has a claim too, along with only a handful of countries, to be part of the vanguard of global pop. Shown in art houses around the world, *Black Orpheus* (1959) captured audiences with its transposition of a Greek myth to a Rio de Janeiro favela. Some viewers complained that the film is not actually Brazilian (the director was French, and the female lead was played by a black actress from Pittsburgh), but it was mainly the soundtrack that became a powerful emblem of Brazil. The strangeness of the lilting Portuguese that seemed not so much sung as whispered over the syncopated African percussion defined a new kind of tropical cool.

Physical beauty, along with samba and soccer, is a cliché of Brazil. As a tropicalist fantasy of foreigners ready to believe in a "world without sin" south of the equator, it runs through five centuries of Brazilian history, from the letters of Portuguese sailors to the brochures of the online sex tourism business. Beautiful Brazil also became a central theme in the burgeoning nationalist imagination in the postcolonial period. While in the nineteenth century the alluring Indian maiden represented Brazilian difference from a corrupt Europe, in the twentieth century the mulata came to symbolize sensuality.

Referring to their long dependence on foreign science and fashion, Wilson Martins remarked that Brazilians have a tendency to "live vicariously their own existence, as though it were a reflection in a mirror" (in Stepan 1991: 44). In the realm of popular culture, however, they learned to like what they saw. In the 1920s, modernist vanguards pronounced an end to slavish imitation of Europe. While Picasso gazed at African masks, Paul Gauguin painted Tahitians, and Josephine Baker thrilled a Parisian public, Brazilian artists and intellectuals slummed it in bohemian quarters in Rio de Janeiro. Here they danced to the new music of samba, an Afro-Brazilian creation that would become inextricably linked to mulatas, Carnaval, and a proudly tropical, mixed, and sensual national identity (Vianna 1999). A new, erotically charged vision of the body politic was thus central to modern Brazil's self-image.

The female body was certainly an object of an elite, patriarchal gaze. Yet women too became consumers of beauty as the colonial patriarchy and later state paternalism faded, and as Brazil developed a flourishing consumer culture. Beginning in the 1960s, Brazil created one of the most sophisticated media networks in the developing world. By the 1980s images of a populace moving toward "glamour and modernity," as the Globo TV network put it, were reaching the remotest corners of the nation, from the arid plains of the sertão to the forest villages of Amazônia (Kottak 1990). Beauty industries can raise the specter of cultural imperialism. Understood broadly to include the technical apparatus that manufactures, enhances, and transmits sexual allure and glamour, these businesses require large capital outlays and advanced technology. Their global growth thus partly reflects Western "soft power" or dominance in popular culture. But Brazilian television—in some ways like India's film industry—became a truly popular medium that cannily blended local traditions with global media and technology into commercially successful products. Brazil's "beautiful game" of soccer, long a proud sign of a *mestiço* national identity, is marketed to world audiences. And plástica-sculpted artistas appear in locally inflected melodramas, which are then enjoyed by audiences from Moldovo to Indonesia. Taking into account the nation's complex position in the global cultural economy, it would be hard to see the growth of beauty industries there as simply an effect of Westernization, much less make the claim that Brazil suffers collectively from "low self-esteem" in regards to its physicality. Global beauty industries do not simply erase local traditions; rather they can create surprising new hybrid social forms and controversies, ranging from the half-comic nationalist grumbling in a debate about "large breast imperialism" allegedly launched by California blonds to the racial consciousness-raising of NGOs that teach citizenship lessons alongside hairstyling inspired by African Americans.

The idea that Brazilians were sensual and beautiful in a distinctive manner that violated the ethnocentric cannon of Europe—and that these traits furthermore were linked to vibrant cultural syncretism and racial conviviality—is of obvious appeal. The celebration of beauty, however, also points to tensions in the nation's quest for a modern identity. Brazil, which imported more slaves than any other country in the world, adopted an image of itself as a land of racial democracy in the twentieth century. When the United States was consumed with the violence of desegregation, UNESCO held up Brazil as the social experiment that refuted "separate but equal." Yet in recent decades, activists, social scientists, and newly democratic governments have attacked this picture of "racial exceptionalism," and shown how darker Brazilians are excluded from a range of social institutions (Telles 2004). Others have responded by affirming a distinct syncretistic tradition and a "sociological intelligence" that deemphasize racial boundaries between groups. Pierre Bourdieu and Loïc Wacquant (1999) go further, even claiming that multiculturalism is a new form of "imperial reason" that exports the North American common sense of race onto a society with a different tradition of envisioning human relatedness and difference.

Cultural aesthetic ideals often seem to mirror larger social hierarchies. With light faces dominating the national media, the charge seems relevant to multiracial Brazil. Yet, the situation is more complex than it appears at first glance. Brazil is often described as having a "folk taxonomy" of color terms, rather than bipolar racial categories. Many people prefer to identify with terms such as *moreno* ("brown" but also "brunette") that refer to appearance, rather than to ancestry. Such terms "politely," as Brazilians say sometimes, avoid a racial classification (pointing to the fact that darker terms have negative stereotypes). They can also have aesthetic and erotic connotations. But unlike in many parts of the world where lightness of skin tone is fetishized, in Brazil *brown* is beautiful. On the other hand, blackness is stigmatized, and European facial features and hair confer social advantages. Tensions between these aesthetic ideals reflect larger ambivalence in Brazil's trajectory toward modernity: a vision of a unique, multihued tropical civilization with a genius for syncretism, and a whitening country, moving away from Africa, and as a surgeon put it, "towards Europe."

Brazil is now on the brink of a sea change in its racial thinking. In the postdictatorship era, from the mid-1980s on, new black movements have scored unprecedented victories with a newly democratic state. Governments and NGOs are reversing official portraits of the land as "mixed," replacing them with multicultural language and policies, including controversial experiments with racial quotas in universities (Htun 2004, Fry 2005). It is not always clear, however, who is black in a country where half the population is estimated to have African ancestry, but where only 6 percent identified as "black" in the 2000 census. In these circumstances, the black movement is counting on a number of "conversions" from other color positions. It must not simply affirm racial pride; it must change the very social perception of race and color. The Brazil case illustrates not only the dilemmas of racial consciousness raising, but also shifts in the nature of identifications in late capitalism.

In the present moment, racial identities are often defined and visualized in consumer culture—a social domain oriented towards "appearances" and aesthetics. Marketing research is beginning to collect demographic data on race and new beauty products are targeting ethnic groups (new developments in Brazil). Black Brazilians are appearing as ordinary consumers on TV. And the larger black culture of the Americas provides positive models of black "glamour and modernity." Together these developments are interpellating the black citizen-consumer. Louis Althusser (1971) uses the term *interpellate* to refer to the way in which ideologies "address" and produce a subject. One example is the shout of a policeman on the street, "Hey you there!" When the hailed individual turns around, he recognizes himself as a subject of the state. I adapt the term to refer to how corporate marketing, state polices, and grass-roots movements are together identifying and visualizing a new kind of black subject. This is certainly not a top-down development, imposed by authoritarian states and multinational corporations; nor again is it only an example of effective social activism. Rather it also reflects the role of consumption—perhaps now the "vanguard of history" (D. Miller 1995)—to shape the political processes of social exclusion and inclusion.

The aesthetic quality of new forms of racial identification, however, has provoked debate about their superficiality, narcissism, and capacity for meaningful social change. Do they represent another "symptom" of a neoliberal economy? Or will the affirmation of market-based black identities help to overcome internalized racism, raise individual and group "self-esteem," and ultimately challenge a long history of white domination? The issue has become crucial in the current moment in Brazil, as global black culture is redefining cool and as poorer sectors of the population are emerging as consumers in one of the most celebrity and media focused societies in the developing world.

::: **BEAUTY**

Judging from its iconography, modern civilization appears to worship female beauty and youth. Many body rituals aim to preserve or improve the body. The stars, superhuman or at least superfeminine beings, are the heroines of our "myths." Public space is saturated with images of the female body. And much of our economic exchange transpires within "Cathedrals of capitalism" (Benjamin 1999), department stores and malls where the commodity on display often acquires its seductive powers from female sexuality. Why this should be so is not immediately obvious. After all, it is has been said we live in a masculinist or logocentric epoch, where left brain thinking dominates and men head military-industrial complexes.

One reason, of course, is consumer capitalism. The discovery that a breast bursting out of a low décolletage could sell ordinary commodities was perhaps belated, but once made, seems to have endless applications. The beauty industry is an economic workhorse. Profitability is high. It thrives in periods of recession. And it reaches even seemingly inhospitable corners of the globe, from Brazil's poor peripheries, where the density of beauty parlors is rivaled only by bars and evangelical churches; to Saudi Arabia, where imported cosmetics are worn beneath the veil. But even outside the "beauty sector" of the economy, images of the female body are the frequent medium of exchange for capitalism's astonishing range of material and symbolic production.

Beauty may be in a sense the ultimate commodity, but we might still ask the question: *Why* should it sell so well? Sociobiologists argue we are "hard-wired" by evolution to be drawn to beautiful people (Etcoff 2000). Attractive traits signal fitness and fertility, and humans are led by inherited sexual drives to respond to them. Unlike most studies in the interpretive social sciences, I do not entirely dismiss such arguments. In fact, as we shall see, there is a surprising convergence between the forces of competition unleashed by markets and those of evolutionary sexual selection. Yet, humans are biocultural beings, and whatever evolutionary mechanisms that work in us are inseparable from the symbolic meanings of the erotic body. And in fact, cultural elaborations of beauty often seem to go "against nature." Saharan Moors admire not slender waists, but women who emerge from months in fattening huts with their bellies covered in rolls of flesh (Popenoe 2003). The Japanese traditionally bound breasts and developed a fetish for the nape (L. Miller 2006). And the European consumptive, cheeks burning with fever, had a beauty that emanated from her proximity to the netherworld of death, rather than from her reproductive potential.

The very diversity of body modification suggests, however, a universal fascination with human beauty. Tribal as much as industrialized societies exhibit, in the terms of Lévi-Strauss (1973), a striking "horror of nature," painting, cutting, scarring, molding, and crushing the body until it takes a suitably beautiful, seductive, or simply human shape. In emphasizing how such practices are part of political and cosmological systems, anthropologists have tended to neglect their aesthetic and erotic allure.[6] Many coming-of-age rituals enhance the bodies of the newly pubescent. Such body modification reflects an interest in beauty that is not reducible to the purpose of group survival. During a time of famine Kalahari tribes use scarce animal fat as a cosmetic skin lotion rather than a source of calories (Turner 1980). Moreover, physical beauty often "translates" well across cultural boundaries. Intense interethnic hatred, which curiously often includes repulsion at the other's body, can morph into erotic interest. Mass media strikingly illustrate the *legibility* of the sexually charismatic body in different regions. The "sex symbol" is, unlike many cultural symbols, able to symbolize the same thing in diverse locales: a seductive, larger-than-life masculinity or femininity.

If beauty sells well, this is not only because it stimulates sexual desire in brains hard-wired to respond to particular physical traits such as slender waists. Images of the female body strikingly target female consumers, rather than (only) provoke male desire. Beauty industries can create bodily alienation, stress, and eating disorders—why then should they continue to flourish? Feminist theories have argued that beauty ideals and practices reflect patriarchal ideologies and inequalities (Bartky 1990, Bordo 1993, Chernin 1981, Faludi 1992, Jeffreys 2005, Morgan 1991, Rankin 2005, Wolf 1991). These critiques vary in their emphasis on the coercive power of men, the profit motive of industry and medicine, and a more diffuse, internalized, and "disciplinary" power, but converge on the point that beauty practices function as a means for the social control of the female body. As Naomi Wolf (1991: 3), perhaps the best-known critic, put it: the beauty myth is "the last best belief system that keeps male dominance intact."

The domain of beauty is certainly unequal, and to some extent reflects larger oppressive structures of modern life. Yet, beauty culture does not only subject women to dominant norms; it also reflects and shapes a particular kind of modern *subject* with diverse aspirations for self-transformation, social mobility, and sexual pleasure and power. So while I analyze the gender ideologies and structures that sustain the beauty myth in Brazil, I also recognize some limitations to this approach. For one, it is difficult to explain the complex behavior surrounding desire and attraction as an exercise of domination. Patriarchy is a near universal. How then can we understand variations across different historical epochs and societies in the significance of sexual desirability? While Brazil's aesthetic ideals reflect European dominance, they also point to a cultural logic of color that celebrates mixture and eroticizes brownness (a "logic" that would not be intelligible in most of Asia). In these circumstances, beauty does not just reflect inequalities internal to society; it also becomes a domain of national or cultural *identification*. Beauty is partly a myth, yet myths are not just falsehoods; they are also stories that are collectively told, a pattern of remembering—and forgetting.

The rise of beauty culture thus reflects the stimulation of new desires and aspirations as older ways of organizing female sexuality and motherhood are transformed. The point can perhaps be made more clearly by reference to non-Western regions. Female beauty often emerges as a key sign of the modern—as lure, moral threat, or even liberation. Whereas communist regimes often see display of the female body as a symbol of bourgeois decadence, in postsocialist China, the sexless Mao suit has given way in just a generation to the myriad variations of global fashion. Such changes in dress are part of larger changes in sexual norms and ideals for women (Farrer 2002). Beauty culture can also become an explosive symbol in local conflicts. In 2002, over a hundred people died in riots when Nigeria was chosen to host a Miss World beauty contest. Clerics called the contest a "sex hazard" while protestors chanted, "Down with beauty" (*The Guardian* 2002). The contestants responded by threatening to boycott the contest after a Nigerian sharia court sentenced a woman to be stoned for adultery. Yet many Muslim women too are becoming subjects in a global beauty industry. Traditional garments—whether seen as signs of piety, the "Orient," or ethnic difference—can be aestheticized and eroticized in consumer culture (Moors and Tarlo 2007, Ossman 2002). These examples suggest that the striking visibility of female beauty in the public sphere can symbolize other conflicts undergone by nations as they become more closely linked to a global capitalist economy.

Many of the processes identified with modernity—such as social engineering, technological innovation, or the emergence of a public sphere—have been seen as male domains. It is also possible, though, to imagine an account of historical change that stresses how the feminine becomes a key emblem of the modern. In this alternative story of the "gender of modernity" (Felski 1995), the dream world of mass consumption can illustrate inchoate shifts in structures of feeling and desiring (Benjamin 1999). Consumption has often been seen as a typically female activity, reflecting patriarchal traditions that located women in the private world of the home. Yet mass consumption brings women into the public sphere, as the *consumer* becomes blurred with the *citizen* (García Canclini 2001).[7] Female pleasures and desires—often seen as dangerous or irrelevant—become integral to social reproduction. The modern consumer possesses a capacity for dreaming and projecting herself into the alternative futures promised by commodities. Beauty industries strikingly tap into this imaginative capacity.

The implications of such changes for any "positive" notion of freedom are difficult to judge. Modernity also poses new risks of commodification, as the life force of sexuality becomes entangled with markets. The commodity has often been used as a metaphor to describe the position of women within capitalism. Marx denounced bourgeois marriage for creating speculation in women's virginity. A transition to a more open market economy can bring a rise in prostitution (Babb 2001). Even where the erotically provocative body has become mundane, anxieties about commodification persist. In many regions (including Brazil) the boundaries between the entertainment, culture, and sex industries are becoming more permeable. Aspects of pornography have gone "mainstream"—from pole dancing to "prostitute chic" fashion to body hair waxing.[8] In the United States, female college students talk about not feeling "porn-worthy" in the eyes of their partners (Kuczynski 2006: 255). In Brazil, the same model may pose in publications such as a woman's fashion magazine, *Playboy*, and *Plástica & You*—a glossy monthly that combines stories on medical revolutions with images of female celebrities. These diverse media genres furnish erotic ideals that shape the body-image of plástica patients. Many emerging forms of sexual exchange reflect a market logic: college students supported by "sugar daddies"; "mail order brides"; sex tourism; and more generally a notion of choice within Internet dating and the "hook-up" (all present in Brazil). In these sexual cultures, based often on relatively transient exchanges — or ones arranged at a distance — attractiveness becomes an exchangeable form of physical capital. Beauty work can be embraced as a means to compete in "markets" of sexual-affective relationships or in uncertain service economies. The *value* of attractiveness — and the beauty work that maintains it — thus reflects larger economic regimes in consumer capitalism.

Many accounts of modernity stress a process of "creative destruction" that undermines older forms of authority defined around tribe, family, and often for women, "nature" (Berman 1982). Medical contraception has fundamentally altered struggles over the control of female reproduction and sexuality. In many regions, including Brazil, new kinds of "elective sexuality" reflect the declining ability of the patriarchal family to regulate sexual relationships (Giddens 1993, Castells 1997). Mass media spread "modern" notions of partnership based in romantic love — or else sexual choice exercised during long periods of the lifecycle (Rebhun 1999).[9] And new demographic groups of women are interpellated as consumers with rights to pleasure (as well as duties of self-care): the middle-aged and elderly, the divorced, the adolescent.

The notion of sexual and reproductive choice is paradoxically accompanied by regimes of medical control. As we will see, plastic surgery is closely linked to a larger field that "manages" female reproduction and sexuality. Many patients say they have surgery to correct changes to the body they blame on pregnancy and breast-feeding. Beauty work can be embraced as a modern technique for negotiating conflicts between maternal and sexual roles. While some women see plástica as a means of enhancing health, others use cosmetic procedures to make minor adjustments in the pursuit of what a plastic surgeon redundantly termed a "more perfect" figure. Driven by a competitive logic, rather than a desire to be "normal," such patients view medical practices as means of erotic body sculpting. These various kinds of intervention constitute attractiveness as a physiological realm defined in the "objective" terms and measurements of medicine. They reflect a biological framing of sexuality — what I call "bare sex" — that breaks from the symbolic and ceremonial dimensions of erotic experience. Such "biologized selves" are emerging during a time of uncertainty and change in sexual-affective relationships. Situating plastic surgery against larger changes in female sexuality and reproduction, I focus on a paradox:

the female body is eroticized, visualized, and commodified—turned into an object of a new sexual culture—at the same time as women become subjects asserting sexual rights and control over reproduction.

I have indicated rather briefly how beauty becomes a "problem" in modernity. In doing so, I have suggested that aesthetic ideals cannot be seen *only* as a reflection of gender or racial subordination. Once we consider broader historical changes—from the expansion of consumer culture to transformations in love and sexuality to the rise of medical techniques of self-regulation—it becomes more fruitful to see beauty as a complex domain of interlocking values and institutions, what Marcel Mauss (1990) would have called, a "total social fact." I explore how beauty can be seen in relation to larger contradictions in modernity: between new freedoms and desires unleashed in consumer capitalism and the constraints on freedom experienced by "liberated" subjects as they are exposed to the hazards of generalized exchange.

:::  **PLAN OF THE BOOK**

The book has two lines of analysis. The first asks how Brazil can shed light on the significance of beauty as a domain of modern experience. I also explore a second problem, taking the reverse approach. Using beauty as a lens, I bring into focus some of the larger tensions in modernizing Brazil, a nation with deep market inequalities and a flourishing consumer culture, with a modern identity based on racial and cultural mixture and a newer strident assertion of identity politics, with a reputation for natural sensuality and high rates of interventionist medicine on the female body.

I have organized the book into three parts (plus a conclusion), each focusing on a major domain of modern experience: medicine and psychology, race and nation, and gender and sexuality. Part 1 tells the story of a new social fact: the remarkable growth of cosmetic surgery in a developing country still in a peripheral relationship to the centers where much of the capital and technologies of beauty were first developed. I examine how a "therapeutic rationale" for cosmetic surgery is deployed in private clinics and in public hospitals that both serve a needy population and provide valuable scientific training to plastic surgery residents. I also situate beauty culture and plastic surgery in relation to larger social transformations in modernizing Brazil, such as the rise of mass media, the search for an authentic national identity, and the importation of medical technologies. Drawing on ethnography in plastic surgery clinics and media production sites, I critically examine the implications of a notion of "aesthetic health" underlying the plastic surgery cure.

The controversial idea that Brazil enjoys forms of racial conviviality and harmony absent in most of the world has dominated Brazilianist scholarship and nationalist elaborations of a modern identity throughout the twentieth century. Since the 1960s, a number of critics and a growing black movement have challenged this view of "racial exceptionalism," arguing instead that Brazilian "racial democracy" is a "myth." Part 2 approaches beauty culture as a sideways "window" onto this controversy, and the changing significance of color in the postdictatorship period as a celebrity and media-focused consumer culture becomes a central domain of identification.

Part 3 and a conclusion bring together the themes of the book, analyzing how gender and sexuality shape the medical practices, market dynamics, and modes of self-governance earlier discussed. Situating plastic surgery in relation to a larger political economy of female reproduction, I show how it is becoming normalized as an aspect of female health. Beauty cultures reflect larger changes in female sexuality and reproduction as they are defined within consumer culture, medicine, and psychology. Drawing on a range of examples—from maids who aspire to acquire cosmetic surgeries, to favela residents who dream of fashion modeling, to single mothers who embrace plastic surgery as a means of erotic body sculpting—I analyze how sexual and class aspirations subtly mingle in beauty culture. I conclude by returning to the central theme of beauty's relationship to social conflicts in modernity.

# PART ONE

# The Self-Esteem in Each Ego Awakens

The luxuriant nature that enchanted early travelers to Brazil still survives
in the massive urban rainforest that runs through many sections of Rio de
Janeiro. There are streets where the transition from city to dense tropical
foliage is so fast that they seem to me like a passage to another world. Our
taxi turns onto one of these roads, winding steeply up from the neighborhood of Gávea into the mist-shrouded green ridge flanking the South Zone.
My friend Hermano is taking me to a birthday party to introduce me to a
*plástica* patient, Preta Gil. After doing a Ph.D. in anthropology, Hermano
left academia and now divides his time between Globo Network in Rio and
Brasília, where he advises the minister of culture, Gilberto Gil, on Internet
policy. Gilberto, one of Brazil's biggest pop stars, was appointed to the post
by President da Silva, becoming one of the first black ministers in Brazilian history.

The party is for Gil's daughter, Maria, who is the sister of Preta. When
we arrive, around thirty people are mingling on the veranda of a villa.
Though we're only a few minutes' drive up from the shopping district, the
only evidence of the city is the cobblestone road curving through a verdant
valley below. It's a humid evening and the air seems thick with *beijinhos*,
perfume, and the sweet caramel scent of *doce de leite*. The women are *produzida*, "dressed up," in high heels, and dance together in a circle to favor-
ites of MPB (Música Popular Brasileira; a lumpy genre that mixes pop, rock,
and traditional rhythms like samba). The men stand in clusters drinking.
It feels like many other Carioca parties, except that many of the authors of
the songs played by the DJ are in attendance.

I recognize a few faces from similar gatherings or else from LP photos.
There is Sandra—Gil's "ex" and Preta's mother—a tough-looking blond
woman dressed in a flowing white dress. Next to her, pale and shy, is Dedé,
the ex-wife of another MPB star, Caetano Veloso. I feel awkward trying to do
"research" here and drift over to the bar. Hermano intercepts me, though,
and introduces me to Maria. I am introduced as the *antropólogo da plástica*.

"*Fala serio*! [Really!] I just did one now too."

Hermano laughs, "What?"

"Ah, a lipo. Here." Maria pats the outside of her thighs, then smooths
down her dress.

"The links are complicated," Hermano explains. "Her ex-girlfriend is here, but she now goes out with that guy, whose ex-girlfriend goes out with . . ." I quickly lose track, but retain the description of Maria, who "*só namora menina*," "only goes out with girls." I am reminded of the surprised reaction of a visiting American friend who went to a lesbian disco and encountered women decked out in the de rigueur Carioca fashion of long hair, high heels, and extra tight jeans. She was disappointed that there seemed to be little "critique of normative femininity" in queer Rio, but I have long since realized that interest in plastic surgery in Brazil cuts across subcultures, identities, and professions. Preta now joins us. I recognize her from the cover of *Raça* magazine, a glossy monthly marketed to Afro-Brazilians. Like her sister she has straight, long hair and light-colored eyes. Though her name means "black," she could fit into a number of color terms in colloquial Portuguese. There are more introductions and beijinhos.

"Plástica?" Preta says, "I already did all of them. I love them. Call me."

The next week I arrange to meet Preta at her condo in a beach neighborhood, where she lives with her father. Preta greets me in the frigid, marble lobby, dressed in a golden velour tracksuit, sleeves rolled up to expose her tattoos. Walking to the car, she explains that her dad is upstairs giving an interview to the *New York Times* on Brazil's innovations with intellectual property rights. Gil has been active in the global open-source movement, making a portion of his songs available for free downloading.

We start talking about Preta's career as a singer as we merge into the line of traffic crawling south out of the city. Her CDs—which blend pop and Brazilian funk—have been a modest success. But with a reputation for spontaneity and straight talk, she has also become known as a media "personality." Today she is going to a rehearsal for a television program that pairs *artistas* and athletes with professional dancers in a ballroom dance contest. Preta has achieved a certain notoriety. "When I launched my first CD, *Preta*, I decided to pose naked on the cover weighing 68 kilos. Naked—no, all you could see was part of my breasts. It was done discreetly. I couldn't believe the reaction. How can a fatty [*uma gordinha*] pose naked?"

Appearing nude in a *Playboy*-type magazine in Brazil is considered to be a normal "career move" for celebrities. The problem was not with her nudity but with her weight. "I don't fit into certain beauty standards, and the public couldn't handle this. But I have the right, because it's my body. It was artistic expression. I have nothing to do with marketing. I'm a daughter of *tropicalismo*, and my idea of life is different."[1]

Preta adds, "Later I discovered there was another reason. Just after the album was launched, my father was made minister of culture." But the biggest problem, she explains, was the fact that she began to "date famous and handsome men."

"How could a girl who isn't thin, who isn't Juliana Pães, who is black, date the romantic lead of a novela?"

"People said that?" I ask.

"It was on the cover of magazines. Brazil is like that."

I ask if the decision to have plástica was related to her career. "No, I did the first ones before I started. I think plástica is becoming banal. For example, I did three, plus three liposuctions. I never messed with my face though. I put in silicone because I wanted to. I had a baby, I breast-fed, and so I had the implants, did an abdominal surgery to take out the loose skin, and had a lipo. This was *bacana* [cool]. It helped me, left me happy."

We're interrupted by her cell phone.

"*Alô*. He was well-endowed?" she says, and begins laughing. I turn my head to look out the window. The highway feels like a parking lot. We're in Barra now, crawling past an endless stream of malls, franchises, and kitsch monuments. In the distance clusters of giant condos seem to shimmer in the haze.

Preta hangs up the phone, explaining, "They do these silly stories and want my opinion. The new Superman's clothes are really tight and his genitals look very big and the studio wanted them digitally diminished. I was going to say, I think it's cool he has a big dick; he is Superman after all. But I've got to watch what I say. And really I never looked at the penis of Superman, or the penis of Batman, or the penis of any other superhero. It's like this every day. Journalists!"

Preta returns to the topic of plástica. "I think *consumo* [consumerism] is the world's big evil. Take my manicurist, she has three kids, her husband's broke, and she got it in her head to have a lipo. It went wrong, and she stayed three weeks in the hospital. She is a woman; she has the right. But it's expensive, and you have to know where to do it. It's the massification of the media. Same as a *favela* kid who wants those Nikes so badly he robs you to get them." Preta is continually interrupted by her cell phone. This time it's her sister.

"*Oi Ju*, are you coming to Church tonight?" She loses reception and then explains that she converted to evangelical Christianity four years ago. I dumbly nod my head as I try to mentally tally this new bit of information with what I know about her life. There is nothing remarkable per se about being a *crente*, "a believer," in Rio de Janeiro. Evangelical Christianity has hit Latin America with almost revolutionary force in the past few decades. It's true that popular Catholicism has long coexisted with other faiths, from the Afro-Brazilian Candomblé to the New Age "Union of the Vegetable." There is, however, a specific politics in this latest battle for souls. The churches are winning converts among the poor, *away* from two ambitious social movements in Brazil: liberation theology and Afro-Brazilian sects. Apolitical, haunted by corruption scandals, and preaching a message of domestic peace, why would an evangelical church attract a member of the entertainment elite such as Preta? Preta's case is even more curious because, as she explains, her whole family "is of the Candomblé world." "My mom, dad, stepmom," she continues. "And I was too. I think it's beautiful, but it's culture, not religion. I mean the *Orixás* [Candomblé deities] do have powers. But I opted for the powers of Jesus."

I ask if she changed her views of beauty after converting, as evangelical Christianity has been quite critical of worldly "vanity." "I don't listen to this. I go to Church with make-up. I went once in a bikini, straight from the beach."

"And no one minds?"

"Neither the male nor the female pastor. Jesus must thank God that at least I left the beach and showed up! I'm very vain; I like make-up, décolletage. No problem."

"Does your church disapprove of plástica?"

"Not mine. The pastor even wants to do it. She even came to visit me in the hospital, while I was recuperating."

I ask Preta if she had any problems with her surgeries. As she talks in more detail, I realize she has more ambivalent feelings than she had at first let on.

"When I had my second lipo I wasn't well, I didn't know where I was going . . . a friend went to do it and I said, 'Ah, I'll go with you!' But I came out of the surgery with a deep depression. After [psycho]analysis and everything, I saw that I had mutilated my body." She explains that she had a series of complications, and a "hole" that needed to be corrected with a third liposuction. "I had a fever, inflammations and infections. You end up in pain, putting in needles, draining the pus, it was chaos. And I came out of that lipo with the same problems, thinking the same things. And I thought, 'My God, I want to be a singer and now I'm here in a bed, liposuctioned, with bad anemia, wounded.'" Then she adds, "But I have the right, if I want to do it."

As Preta talks I think of how plástica often fits into a long therapeutic *process* in which medical, psychoanalytic, and here, even spiritual, notions of suffering intermingle. Plástica was a result of consumerism, she said, but it was also a "right," connected as much to her career as to her experience of motherhood. Her ambivalence, like that of many women, was directed at *certain* operations, not cosmetic surgery per se. Liposuction had become "banal," but she remained extremely positive about her first surgeries—implants and a tummy tuck—"I never had any problems with them. They were perfect, excellent, and I love them."

An evangelical Christian, daughter of one of the most critically acclaimed artists in Brazil, and named "black" by her father in an unusual affirmation of racial pride, Preta is hardly the typical *siliconada*. Yet like many plástica patients of diverse class backgrounds, she said that cosmetic surgery would help her "self-esteem." Ironically, one of the operations that she said was most therapeutic—breast enlargement—is one widely viewed in Brazil as a *moda*, a fashion. It began at a surprisingly precise date: the Carnaval of 1999, the same year a samba school paid homage to Ivo Pitanguy.

: : :

The term *methodological nationalism* indicates how ideologies of race and nation shape the writing of history. In Brazil there is perhaps also a species of "aesthetic nationalism." Of course, the debates over siliconadas are half in jest. Yet only half. After all, it is often through jokes, gossip, and complaints muttered under one's breath that the fantasy life of nationalism plays itself out. From this perspective, we can begin to understand the popular reaction to silicone breast implants. This controversy reflects a particular tradition of fetishizing the female body. But the fact that it was connected to Carnaval, a key symbol of Brazilian identity, points to other issues as well.

In the United States, breast implants provoked an ongoing debate about their safety, leading to a temporary ban by the FDA and the largest class-action lawsuit in American history (Haiken 1997). In Brazil, the health risks of silicone implants were discussed much less, and Brazilian regulatory agencies never restricted their use. Implants, though, did spark other debates: about Brazil's national identity, its relationship to North America, and real versus artificial beauty.

In March 1999, the news magazine *Istoé* exclaims: "So many young women exhibited their 'retreaded' breasts . . . that they soon renamed the samba stadium Silicone Valley" (*Istoé* 1999). Among those parading were some of the most well-known artistas in Brazil: models, actresses, singers, dancers, and television presenters. A flurry of media stories featured the siliconadas, many of them *topless*. (Brazilians use the English word perhaps to express the foreign origins of this custom. Whatever the size of a bikini top—and they are known in slang as "dental floss"—it is still not permitted to remove it in public.) Interest piqued around the operations of Carla Perez. Raised in a working-class district of Salvador, Perez first became known as a dancer in a pop group. As with many female *artistas*, her fame was often credited to possession of a physique that embodied the national aesthetic ideal, even though it was widely known that she had had plastic surgery. So when Perez, known as the Bunda Nacional, "national bottom," got 220 ml silicone implants in time for the 1999 Carnaval, the question was raised whether breasts had become the "new national preference."

Intellectuals, artists, and patients debated whether the implant was compatible with a Brazilian "biotype." Polls were conducted and noted writers consulted. One magazine declares: "Breasts are invading Brazilian daily life" (*Istoé Online* 2000). Plastic surgeons reported a rise in demand for implants, a surprising trend since aesthetic breast *reductions* had long been among the most popular procedures in Brazil (SBCP 2005). The average size of the prosthesis almost doubled from the mid-1980s (*Época* 1999b). A Brazilian anthropologist warned the large breast fashion was another example of the "assimilation of an American standard" (*Valor Económico* 2000). Then the July 9, 2001, Latin American edition of *Time* featured a smiling and siliconada Perez on the cover dressed in a bikini (figure 1). The headline stated Latin American women were "sculpting their bodies . . . along Californian lines. Is this cultural imperialism?" For her part, Perez remarked, "Everyone is accustomed to praise my *bumbum*, but now what I most like in my body are my breasts. I feel more sensual."

Carnaval parades are an outlet for the creativity of samba composers and dancers, a spectacle of cross-class and interracial mixing, a celebration of themes drawn from Brazilian and Afro-Brazilian history. They represent Brazil in the foreign imagination as the locale of the "world's biggest party." And they showcase "beauty": both of the floats and costumes often made in a favela cottage industry, as well as of the dancers. Carnaval is also seen as an expression of national popular culture, archetypically embodied by the *mulata* dancer. In the debates about silicone, the mulata could signify both the tradition of Carnaval, as well as a particular ideal of the female body that emphasized the buttocks, hips, and thighs, and not the breasts—an ideal that the siliconadas seemed to undermine. While a few black activists critiqued the sexualized image of the mulata, most observers instead were

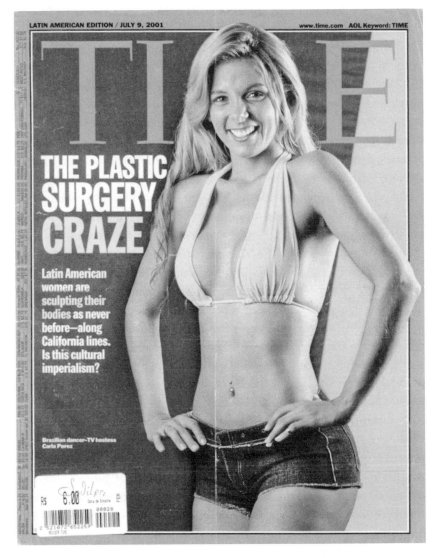

LATIN AMERICAN EDITION / JULY 9, 2001      www.time.com   AOL Keyword: TIME

# THE PLASTIC SURGERY CRAZE

Latin American women are sculpting their bodies as never before—along California lines. Is this cultural imperialism?

Brazilian dancer–TV hostess
Carla Perez

R$   6,00

1. Carla Perez on the cover of the Latin American edition of *Time* magazine.

more concerned about the threats posed by these celebrities to traditional erotic culture.

The appearance of the siliconadas during Carnaval was also significant because they represented other changes in the festival. The Rio Carnaval has become a commercial spectacle with a multimillion dollar budget supplied by the state tourism agency as well as "animal bankers" who run an illegal numbers game. To boost media coverage of their allegories, samba schools began inviting celebrities to take the honored positions as queens and princesses of their parades—roles that traditionally had been held by mestiço women from the neighborhoods, often favelas, that mounted the parades (Guillermoprieto 1990: 49). Some residents of favelas told me they no longer felt like parading because "Carnaval was business now." The artistas were weakening Carnaval's roots in the "community," and besides, they didn't samba all that well. The "Carnaval of siliconadas," as it was dubbed, thus signified other changes in Brazilian society: the eclipse of the samba school's roots in Afro-Brazilian culture, the commercialization of Carnaval and other popular traditions, and hence, globalization and a loss of cultural originality. The controversies over the appearance of the siliconadas can thus be related to a longer history of seeing the national body as a powerful aesthetic and erotic symbol in the ongoing search for a modern identity.

: : :

Why did Ester, the personal cook of a plastic surgeon, save a portion of her minimum wage in order to have silicone implants at Santa Casa? Ester told me that in order to get "medical information" she had bought a copy of *Plástica & Beleza*: a consumer magazine featuring journalistic style stories (paid for by surgeons) next to images of seminude models and celebrities. Is she emulating women such as Preta, Carla Perez, the wealthy patients of her employer, or for that matter, Pamela Anderson, who have made *plástica* a glamorous fashion?

Ester does not have a "working-class consciousness" in a classical sense. Her work is often solitary, cleaning or cooking in a private home. She is not politically active, and participates in many aspects of the same youth culture enjoyed by the middle class. Though she doesn't identify with a proletarian group, she does experience various kinds of social exclusion. When she fills out a job application, she faces the dilemma of either lying about her address, or risking the prejudice she would encounter as a *favelada* (resident of a favela). She dreams of office work, however modest—"working with numbers"—despite knowing her chances are slim. After leaving high school during a moment of "trouble" at home to work beside her mother as a maid, she is now taking night classes, where she studies Portuguese grammar. Sympathizing with my own errors in speech, Ester laughed, "*Nossa!* [gosh!], it's difficult even for us." "Bad Portuguese" is often viewed as a failure of the poor to master the complexities of language, leading some to feel alienated from their own speech. Ester nevertheless dreams of attending university. Yet even with a high school diploma she will be excluded from the "right" to the quality education provided by Rio's free public universities (which generally require private school preparation in order to pass the entrance exam). This is one example of how rights to public goods end up tacitly reinforcing class structure. Another is the right to security. Interrupted by a gun battle while walking her kids to school, she was reminded that this right is often suspended. Barred from the knowledge economy, she also has difficulty entering the lower end of the regulated service economy. Without personal connections or a *boa aparência*, a euphemism for a whitish appearance, or some exceptional quality—stunning beauty, for example—to differentiate her in a tight labor market, she has trouble getting the low-paid but regulated jobs in retail shops "on the asphalt."

Like many women in Brazil's peripheries, she has worked as a domestic laborer where the lived experience of class is often intimate. The apartment buildings where she cooks and cleans are a microcosm of a larger hierarchy. In much of Brazil, apartments have a separate service zone, with their own entrance, where domestic workers do laundry, eat, use the toilet, and sometimes sleep. It's true that since a 1996 law prohibited discrimination in "accessing the elevators," many feel more comfortable riding in the "noble" elevator rather than in the service elevator meant for maids and janitors, or else residents when they are walking their dogs, dripping with sweat, or otherwise "dirty" (Holston 2008: 278). Yet such new forms of social mixing—for example, when Ester came out of the kitchen to speak directly to her boss, Dr. Eduardo—can simply lead to moments of awkwardness.

Ester is not among the poorest of the poor. Unlike some of her extended family in the *sertão*, who struggle at times to put a meal of manioc or macaroni on the table, she eats well. Many of the appliances that once signified entrance into the middle class clutter the small house built from exposed brick where she lives. Class is a blunt concept, and there is certainly no mechanical imitation of the rich. The family eats a lot of ice cream, not because it is a symbol of affluence but because they like it. They are proud of their rooftop garden not because they aspire to the petit bourgeoisie, but because it gives them pleasure. And their DVD player is not (only) conspicuous consumption, but a means toward the spiritual insight they receive from the recorded sermons of a young charismatic priest.

Ester's decision to have silicone implants was thus unlikely an attempt to simply emulate an artista such as Preta or to become middle class. She knows too well the real barriers she faces in attaining this implicit norm of citizenship. Moreover, like Preta, Ester was dismayed by the "consumerism" she says pervades life in Brazil. (Ester is a practicing Catholic; like Preta she converted away from the religion of her parents, who are evangelical.) She was talking about her daughter, who was "so pretty, she must be a miracle of nature." She was concerned that when she becomes older she "will be attracted to a *traficante* [drug trafficker]." I asked Ester if she herself had experienced this as an teenager. "Never. I sincerely would have given all for someone who loved me and respected me. I know girls who say, 'Look at the boy, how cute, he has a *moto*!' And if he sells it, will they stay with the moto, stuck to the seat?"

Also like Preta, Ester stresses the psychological basis of her complaint and the nature of the healing she experienced. Over coffee, she spoke thoughtfully about her operations: "I did plastic surgery not because of physical, but psychological, discomfort. I was married seven years, but to start another relationship you think, will someone like me, accept my defects? This messes with your interior. I didn't put in an implant to exhibit myself, to call attention of men on the street, but to feel better. It wasn't a simple vanity, but necessary aesthetic surgery. A necessary vanity. Surgery improves a woman's *auto-estima* [self-esteem]."

Although like Preta, Ester is a single mother, and has light brown skin in a white-dominated society, in many ways these women inhabit different worlds. Perhaps more important than class boundaries is the "glass screen" that divides the consumers and producers of mass media. Despite such social gaps between them, why then did both women see their operations as a form of psychological healing? What notion of "health" is embodied by a woman such as Tiazinha, "Little Aunt," a sexual icon who has appeared on notebooks marketed to kids with her trademark S&M-themed mask and whip, or by a siliconada TV star dancing in a bikini to the vigorous samba? How did cosmetic surgery come to be seen as a therapeutic practice?

Praia da Urca is a small arc of sand at the foot of one of Rio's main tourist sites, the Sugar Loaf. Nestled in a protected part of the bay, it has small waves and polluted water. It's the end of a muggy Saturday afternoon, and numerous small *barracas* do a brisk business selling beer and snacks. One of these is run by Dona Firmina, a fifty-eight-year-old widow, and her companion, Gilson. She tells me she left her village in the state of Minas Gerais, where she was born to a family of subsistence farmers, because there "wasn't enough food growing up." When she moved to Rio, she worked as a live-in maid, one of the only jobs available to many migrants drawn to Brazil's big cities. After meeting Gilson, who drives a gypsy van, they pooled their savings and bought a license to run the stand.

I first met Firmina at Santa Casa, where she was waiting in line to have a touch-up for a facelift. "My face was awful because I was in the sun so much," she said. Like most patients, she is too poor to afford a health plan, though over the course of three years has managed to save about R$1,300 to pay for the operation. Before having the *lifting*, she had been to a hospital only once in her life, to give birth to her daughter. Later I discover that she is functionally illiterate, though she has learned how to sign her name on medical forms.

"It didn't come out well," she says. She tugs at her left cheek, pulling the skin taut against her cheekbone.

"And how was your surgeon?"

"Oh, he was great. But I was disappointed. I thought I would be rejuvenated, just like the artistas [celebrities]." Firmina laughs at this, and then turns to serve a customer. I ask her if I can take her picture. "Just not this," she points at the hot dogs lying in a syrupy red onion sauce. "It's so ugly." She approves a backdrop of sand and rock face. As I set up my tripod, she takes off her baseball cap and tries to flatten her shoulder-length curls against the sides of her head.

"My hair is really *ruim*," she says. Ruim, "bad," can also mean "kinky" when referring to hair. Unsatisfied, she borrows a comb from a very drunk woman sitting in a beach chair. A small crowd begins to gather, and as I take a few shots a man with a pot belly yells out, "*Olha*, it's the Gisele of Urca." Everyone cracks up, including Firmina, at this reference to Brazil's most famous supermodel. I take a seat next to Gilson, who is drinking a can of beer. He has the manner of an aging *malandro*, the roguish man-about-town celebrated in samba songs. Shirtless, he reclines in a folding beach chair and eyes me a little suspiciously. I buy a beer and raise the can toward him, "*Saude* [Health]."

"Saude," he mumbles. Would he consider having plástica? I ask.

"Me?" he says. "I was born ugly, and I will die ugly."

He falls silent for a moment then breaks into a wide grin, as if suddenly remembering a joke. "But I already had plástica, many years ago."

"What do you mean?" I ask.

"78 percent of my skin was burned. Look." He points to the undersides of his arms, and insists I grab a loose fold of skin. Then he pulls down his shorts a couple of inches to reveal shiny scar tissue zigzagging towards his groin. There had been an explosion at the service where he worked repairing air conditioners, which killed two people and put him in a coma.

"I was lucky. I have a relative in the air force so I went to their hospital. I got an infection and had to stay there a year and four months. I don't remember how many operations I had—they put so much skin on me. You see, I used to play guitar," he says, looking down at the mottled skin on his fist. "My hands aren't so great now. But they fixed up my face well, don't you think?"

Firmina has a lifting for rejuvenation, while Gilson is treated for trauma sustained in a workplace accident. Their two operations represent a major distinction made in plastic surgery between cosmetic (*estética*) and reconstructive (*reparadora*) procedures. They also seem to encapsulate the gendered history of the medical specialty, from the repair of disfigured soldiers to "improvements" of the female body. The distinction though is not just a technical classification, but rests on a broader understanding of what constitutes legitimate medicine—as well as legitimate suffering. Insurance policies and public health systems in many countries only cover reconstructive surgeries, and cosmetic surgery is often seen as a luxury consumer service. This economic rationale reflects a moral understanding of which medical procedures are most necessary.

Yet distinctions between the two types of procedures are not always clear. The same techniques used in cosmetic surgery are used in reconstructive operations. Reconstructive procedures do not only restore functionality; they also improve appearance. And cosmetic procedures, such as reduction of large breasts, can also have functional justifications (e.g., reducing back pain). Moreover, reconstructive operations, like any surgery, carry real health risks, but often do not produce gains to physical health. While some might question the need for Firmina's facelift, including Gilson, she nevertheless felt that it would give her some psychological benefit. Moreover, "normal" unattractiveness and old(er) age can also cause stigma: people judged to have a below-average appearance by others suffer real social and economic penalties (Hamermesh and Biddle 1994). If we grant that appearance can have repercussions for mental health and social functioning (and few doubt that some congenital defects cause "suffering"), it becomes harder to strictly separate cosmetic and reconstructive surgery.

It is just such a gray area that Brazilian surgeons are experimentally exploring. Arguing for the "union" of reparadora and estética, they have successfully promoted a vision of cosmetic surgery as a psychotherapeutic intervention worthy of being offered in a public health system to needy patients. This section tells the story of how surgeons developed this innovative philosophy of health.

: : :

I first met Pitanguy at the outset of fieldwork. Intrigued perhaps by the idea of an anthropological study, he agreed to meet me. That one brief interview helped open doors for me during the months of fieldwork, but I didn't see the surgeon again until five years later. This time we meet at Santa Casa. I am with an American friend, Jonathan, a filmmaker writing a black comedy about expatriates living in Rio de Janeiro. Two of the central characters are a French anthropologist and a British plastic surgeon, and Jonathan is curious to learn more about the world of plástica. Pitanguy, a wine aficionado, has recently seen Jonathan's documentary on the globalization of the wine industry, and gives us a warm welcome.

Pitanguy, a former black belt in karate, seems to have aged somewhat since I last saw him, but his celebrity stature has if anything grown. He's wearing a beige Italian suit, and sunglasses he doesn't remove inside the dark rooms of the clinic. We make up a curious procession: two visitors with tape recorder and video camera; an entourage of five or six surgeons and residents; and a tall man in a dark suit (a body guard). The normally boisterous waiting rooms fall silent as we pass by. I realize the patients, many in awe of Pitanguy's gifts, recognize him from television. Jonathan shoots some footage on his digital camcorder; then the three of us squeeze into a black Mercedes outfitted with twin DVD screens. As the driver pulls out of the hospital, we begin a long conversation about plastic surgery, wine, cinema, and "beauty."

Pitanguy has so much practice telling his story to national and international media that he comes across as a practiced performer. He seems not insincere, but mannered. In Portuguese he could also be said to "have culture." Like many surgeons, Pitanguy has a number of aesthetic interests. A noted lover of nature who created an ecological sanctuary, he also served as president of Rio's Museum of Modern Art from 1975 to 1985. During our conversation, he moves with ease between languages when he feels some phrase from French, English, or Portuguese is more apt. Always ready with a joke, he sometimes speaks more thoughtfully, then suddenly returns his attention to you with a considerate observation. Though I don't see him with women, I imagine that he would be an old-fashioned gallant.[2]

We arrive at Porcão restaurant, where Pitanguy treats us to an unending supply of grilled meats and an expensive bottle of Chilean wine. Looking for insight into the character he is basing on the surgeon's life, Jonathan asks him about a recent award (a national news magazine elected Pitanguy one of the "ten most important Brazilian doctors of the century," placing him in the illustrious company of Oswaldo Cruz, who was credited with eradicating Yellow Fever in parts of Brazil). But Pitanguy waves his hand modestly and says the most meaningful recognition of his work was the Carnaval parade. "As I rode through the samba stadium on the float, I realized the song is a hymn to the benefits of plastic surgery to the human being. The lyrics show that the patient is looking for his own soul, his own divine image. And I thought it was very beautiful when I saw that what I do is comprehended by the people."

Anthropology defines itself so much by its method, yet I've rarely observed others doing fieldwork. Jonathan is doing research too I now realize, though a different kind. Drawing on large reserves of cultural capital from his ties to Hollywood and a European childhood, his manner is both provocative and warmly flattering. It is also simply more effective than my own passive, empathic listening that I had assumed was the normal mode of "research." He manages to draw Pitanguy out, who ranges widely in his reflections, from his experiences in France to an interview with *60 Minutes*. At one point toward the end of the meal, I slip in a standard interview question (now back in Portuguese), "Why did you want to become a plastic surgeon?"

"My father was a general surgeon," Pitanguy begins,

> but I was raised in a very humanistic family. I loved to read everything. When I came to Rio and started working in a public hospital I saw that many of the scars and bruises were not considered so important by doc-

tors. But I saw talking with these patients that deformities are often the most important psychologically. They are like an organic lesion, but in the psyche. Patients whose appearance I improved were often more grateful to me than a patient whose life I had saved. And I realized that people have the right to their own divine image, like their own God, what they think they are.

This insight—that patients suffer as much psychologically from deformities as they do from "organic lesions"—led Pitanguy to work over the next four decades at realizing a "right to beauty."

This project, of course, depended on a reputation as a gifted surgeon and technical innovator. Born in the interior and mountainous state of Minas Gerais in 1926, he claims he has never lost his Mineiro traits of modesty and a contemplative temperament. He lied about his age to enter medical school at sixteen, and used to spend time after classes watching his father operate. But while Brazilian plastic surgeons had already begun performing facelifts in the 1920s, the specialty to him seemed "behind" what was being done abroad. "I went to the U.S. on a scholarship, to Cincinnati, real corn country," Pitanguy told me during our first meeting. "I had a good formation. I later trained in France and England, spent almost five years abroad." Pitanguy's mentors in England were, in fact, two pioneers of modern techniques of reconstructive surgery: Archibald McIndoe and Sir Harold Delf Gillies. Gillies was knighted for his service during the First World War, increasing "plastic surgery's prestige throughout the British Empire" (Haiken 1997: 34). McIndoe, Gillies's younger cousin, became the Allies' leading surgeon during the Second World War (Gilman 1999: 195). Pitanguy's innovations in aesthetic surgery thus run in a direct line back to the foundations of the specialty.

After returning to Brazil, he felt that he wanted to "share with others." Plastic surgery is in many ways still an artisanal practice based on apprenticeship with a master. To emphasize their training with an undisputed master, many surgeons advertise their membership in an organization named the Society of *Ex*-Students of Prof. Pitanguy. These ex-students, some of them now themselves in their seventies, have in turn trained new generations of surgeons, helping spread his methods and "philosophy" as they open up practices around the country, in Latin America, and beyond (Veja 2002, Pitanguy 2008).

Pitanguy has not only taught students his own surgical techniques, but also a distinct vision of plastic surgery that he calls "humanistic" or "anthropological." This vision emphasizes what he calls the "union" of reconstructive and aesthetic surgery. Since both types of procedures heal the psyche, distinctions between them are relative. In perhaps his most eloquent statement of plástica's true therapeutic purpose, Pitanguy writes: "The goal of plastic surgery . . . emanates simply from a transcendent finality, which is the attempt to harmonize the body with the spirit, emotion with reason, aiming to establish an internal equilibrium that will permit the patient to re-encounter, *re-structure himself,* in order that he feels himself in harmony with his own image and the universe that surrounds him" (Pitanguy 1992: 272). In short, the real therapeutic object of plastic surgery is not the body, but the mind.

Pitanguy's style can seem overblown, but it's also based on a psychological insight stemming from his enormous clinical experience: patients notoriously do not have an objective body-image. For Pitanguy, appearance—and literally the skin—is just the outer, visible edge of the self. The skin is both "a principal component of the personality" as well as "a sexual organ" (Pitanguy 1992: 269). For this reason, surgical incisions "go beneath the skin, touching as well the psyche" (Pitanguy 1983: 8). Or more simply, "A plastic surgeon is a psychologist with a scalpel in his hand" (Pitanguy 1976: 125). He thus must also have a gift for compassionately understanding the patient's mental state, the real target of the intervention. This conception of harmonizing "spirit and body" recalls the practices of a well-known Brazilian medium who incorporates a dead German physician in order to perform "spiritual surgery" (Hess 1994). But to reach his patient's internal state, the plastic surgeon, of course, must use a scalpel.

: : :

At the outset of my fieldwork, Pitanguy suggests that I observe an operation. He tells me he has already selected a patient for me, Flávia. "She is pretty and young," he adds, "and I expect we'll have excellent results."

I meet Flávia at the clinic on the eve of her combined liposuction and breast lift operation. She is accompanied by her mother, Bete. Both women have long black hair and bangs, tanned skin, eyes outlined with dark makeup. They tell me they are of "gypsy origin." Flávia, who is twenty-five and divorced, lives with her five-year-old daughter and Bete in Meier. The neighborhood is located in the North Zone, far from the beaches, its hot, traffic-congested avenues lined with low brick houses. She could never afford Pitanguy's prices on her income as a telemarketer, but a member of the staff she knew arranged a steep discount. She says the clinic is the "Mercedes" of plástica, while Santa Casa is merely a "vw bug."

Mildly star-struck with "Dr. Ivo," Flávia is unstinting in praising his gifts as a surgeon. She is also particularly impressed by his ability to "understand her problem," often referring to him as her *amigo* (friend). "It's like he sees so well all sides of someone, what they're needing. As a human being, he puts himself in the place of his patients, to understand their trauma."

I go back to the clinic the next morning at eight. It's a sticky day in the middle of Rio's summer, a downtime for surgeons. (There is a seasonal spike in demand for plástica during the winter, the ideal time to recuperate away from the harsh sun and prepare for the "sand test": the display of the new physique on the beach.) When I walk into the operating room, a resident is taking several shots of Flávia with a digital camera.[3] After the general anesthesia takes effect, the surgeon begins to carefully paint black lines around the sides of her breasts and abdomen. Pitanguy then enters the room in his trademark skullcap with a floral pattern. Following the black lines with his scalpel he cuts out a wedge-shaped piece of tissue. When the triangular gap is closed, the breast is pushed higher up on the chest, creating a rounder, more protruding shape. He also removes the areola, and reattaches it lower down on the breast (a poorly executed breast surgery, he explains, can be spotted by the "too high nipple" that protrudes from a décolletage).

Pitanguy motions for me to visit an adjacent room, where a second team is performing the same operation on a middle-aged patient. More tissue has been removed than in Flávia's surgery, and the operation is not as "clean" — there is blood running down her abdomen, and fat tissue protrudes from the sutures. When I return to Flávia's operation, Pitanguy has moved onto the liposuction. He inserts a metal instrument about a foot long into the arabesque pattern drawn on her abdomen. It takes a surprising amount of mechanical force to dislodge fat from tissue, and I can see her skin undulating from the pressure of the needle beneath it.

Pitanguy seems to complete an entire operation himself only rarely these days, and leaves the two patients in the hands of his medical team. Leading me into a consultation room, he explains, "The second patient is a bit obese, with a large abdomen, with enormous breasts that are inconvenient for her posture. It wasn't just an aesthetic operation. Flávia suffered from a psychological trauma because she's a beautiful woman with a breast that's very deformed, asymmetric and falling. What you are doing is re-constructing or recuperating her self-esteem, which is not superficial: it's deeper than the skin."

Pitanguy formally classified both surgeries as estética, not reparadora. The distinction is still important; for one, at Santa Casa clinic reparadora is free and has scheduling priority (or at least it does in principle; during one visit, the ratio of cosmetic to reconstructive surgery—normally about 50/50—had increased. Patient fees, a resident explained, would pay for renovating the clinic infrastructure). But while the distinction is still used in clinical practice, Pitanguy also stresses that lines between the two types of surgery are blurred.[4] He said, for example, that Flávia's surgery aimed to "reconstruct" her self-esteem, implying perhaps a kinship with reconstruc-tive operations. The second surgery was also "not just aesthetic," because there was some "functional" benefit to the correction of large breasts. Yet even with estética, he recognizes degrees of "need." Pitanguy said Flávia was "young and pretty," and thought it unfair that her beauty should be ruined by "flaccid breasts." Although it is the deformed who most deserve surgery according to the egalitarian rationale of public hospitals, flawed beauty may be a greater stimulus to the charitable impulses of the surgeon. In any event, underlining the healing function of cosmetic operations helps to justify them, even as the *need for justification* reveals lingering doubts about the therapeutic rationale.

Run with money from Catholic charities and some state funding, Santa Casa charges estética patients for basic hospital costs and anesthesia.[5] But at some fully public hospitals, supported by state or municipal budgets, cosmetic surgeries are offered at no cost to the patient. How were surgeons able to extend Pitanguy's "philosophy" of plastic surgery to offer free cos-metic procedures within a public health system serving a "needy popula-tion"?

: : :

The taxi speeds along a deserted avenue at the edge of Rio's downtown, not far from the Sambodromo, a special stadium built for the city's Carnaval parades. A concrete wall along the highway is covered in whimsical hip-hop murals alternating with graffitied slogans denouncing "neoliberalism" and the IMF. A dense matrix of shanties comes into view, sitting a few yards back from apartment buildings almost blackened by pollution. I lean my head out the window and get a glimpse of a favela etched into a rocky hill, one of dozens in the city which, Lévi-Strauss complained, give the bay of Guanabara the appearance of a mouth with missing teeth. "It's Mangueira," the driver says, home to what is arguably the most famous samba school in Brazil. Just past the entrance to the favela, he slows down and drops me at Barata Ribeiro, a municipal public hospital with a plastic surgery ward.

A surgeon at Santa Casa had given me the cell number of a resident at the hospital.[6] Today is the day of the "surgical plan," a pedagogical exercise for the residents, and there are already long lines. I make my way to the examination room and briefly explain my research to the group of residents and professors. One surgeon shakes his head in disbelief. "Only in the United States," he says, gesturing at the meagerly equipped examination room. I laugh along with the others, despite being the target of the joke. The head surgeon and founder of the service arrives and greets me warmly. Dr. Claudio (first names are preferred in Brazil, even with a title) is a slim, affable man with large glasses that seem to cover half his face. Trained by Pitanguy in the 1960s, he founded the hospital's plastic surgery ward over thirty-five years ago. As a resident presents the next patient to the group, Dr. Claudio whispers to me that the first operation had been a success, but that a *retoque*, "touch-up," is warranted because "the important thing is to please the patient." I ask him how he had convinced the public health system to fund cosmetic surgeries. He leads me into a cavernous room where the hospital laundry is done.

"In the past," he says, "The public health system [sus] or any governmental agency only paid for reconstructive surgery. Few surgeons did cosmetic operations; they thought it was vanity. But in fact, there is a great difficulty in knowing what is cosmetic and what is reconstructive. Face, breast, and abdomen are considered estética, although they have psychological repercussions."

"But if sus doesn't authorize cosmetic surgery, how is it funded?" I ask.

"Our strongest argument went like this. The World Health Organization said many years ago that health is a state of physical, social, and mental well-being, not simply the absence of illness. You have to reach health through happiness. We were able to show that plástica has psychological effects for the poor as well as the rich of course. We treat everyone."

"Did you talk to someone in the municipal government?" I ask.

"I didn't do it by talking to anyone—I did it by doing it, and when a doubt came up, an obstacle, we demonstrated, we argued, and we continued to do it, until it was recognized as a necessary thing, a just thing, and a thing done well. . . . Today the majority of hospitals do estética—within the limitations of the lines of patients of course. And so estética was gradually accepted as having a social purpose. We operate on the poor who have the chance to improve their appearance, and it's a necessity not a vanity."

Pitanguy's junior by only a few years, Dr. Claudio is less given to elegant turns of phrase, less driven to systematize his views in medical writings, and possessed of a more modest reputation as a surgeon. But he has also taken his mentor's vision a step further, in a sense to its logical conclusion, arguing that plástica's psychotherapeutic benefits serve a "social purpose" and thus should be offered within a public health system "as a necessity."

Should we view the philosophy of Pitanguy and his students as a clever piece of medical casuistry? Certainly, as we shall see, there are also less "philosophical" reasons for allowing cosmetic surgery in public hospitals: as one surgeon put it, the residents need a "place to practice." But my point is not that plastic surgery is not "legitimate healing." If scientific and state institutions, professional colleagues, and patients view plastic surgeons as healers, then in some sense they *are*. The surgeons' argument for the "union" of reparadora and estética may be self-interested, but it's also true that functional and aesthetic rationales are not easily distinguished. Doing fieldwork made it more clear to me that both types of procedures often leave satisfied and grateful patients. Moreover, Pitanguy's reasoning is not entirely novel. Though Brazilian surgeons are pioneers, they are perhaps only following a historical drift in democratic societies toward the notion that appearance is essential to mental well-being, economic competitiveness, and social and sexual competence. My aim then is not simply to expose the inconsistencies in this philosophy, but also to analyze how it is *productive* of new notions of health as it gains traction in local worlds.

And yet plastic surgery has an ambiguous relationship to health. Located on the border between beauty and medicine, consumer society and public clinics, psychotherapy and erotic enhancement, it's not clear what kind of healing it represents. Surgeons often argue plástica has universal benefits, since "faced with an aesthetic defect, don't the poor suffer as much as the rich?" To understand how such philosophies acquire moral authority and cultural acceptance, however, we must move beyond medical arguments to look at the wider world that shapes notions of suffering, health, and of course beauty. In the pages that follow, I read this philosophy of health in relation to the constraints and opportunities presented by clinical practice, as well as to a history of medicine, the body, and sexuality in Brazil. Unlike earlier forms of state biopolitics aimed at the national population, plastic surgery targets the individual self and promotes an expansive, perhaps even progressive, notion of health as a qualitatively defined state of well-being. Yet analyzing how cosmetic procedures—and the bodies of patients—are made "available" within an ailing, two-tiered health system, I am led to an older question that has haunted Brazil's civilizing and later modernizing projects: How do relationships between elites and the people shape the use and appropriation of metropolitan techniques in Brazil?

:  :  :  :  :  :    WITHOUT TITS THERE IS NO PARADISE

> Here, we import everything. Laws, ideas, philosophies, theories, subjects of conversation, aesthetics, sciences, styles, industries, fashions, mannerisms, jokes, everything comes in boxes on the boat. Civilization is very expensive, what with the customs dues: and it's all secondhand, it wasn't made for us.
> —Eça de Queirós, *Maias* (1870), in Schwarz (1992: x–xi)

In seventh grade I wrote a rather austere essay arguing that all ads should be banned. I liked the glimpses into the adult world offered by sitcoms, but I viewed ads as "unnecessary." That memory popped into my head as I remember my initial reactions to the permeable borders between plastic surgery and Brazil's flourishing entertainment industries. I often felt a mixture of boredom and even disgust watching Brazilian television and tended to neglect media as research material. My hope instead was that in-depth interviews would reveal something like the "emotional truth" of beauty. Later I began to question this attitude. Celebrity culture in a sense thrives on qualities that can frustrate or even mock the values of the scholar: aura rather than merit, bodily rather than mental presence, gossip rather than reason. And implicit judgments of taste—tawdry, artificial, and the like—were perhaps interfering with my understanding of the "universe of beauty." Was my "psychological" focus even influenced by plastic surgeons' promotions of a therapeutic transformation? What if I were to think more like an archaeologist, I wondered, looking more to material objects, which in Brazil often include the flickering images of electronic media, for clues to the values of this civilization? Clifford Geertz's "deep hanging out" (1973), I began to realize, can involve watching a lot of TV.

Attractiveness is often a prerequisite not only for the poor and "good" heroines of folk stories, but also for novela actresses and the sexual aristocracy of supermodels, pop divas, and movie stars. As a technique that promises to turn ugly ducklings into princesses (or working-class girls into media sex icons), plastic surgery often has a fantastical dimension. Surgeons are adored as artistic geniuses with "gifted hands" who seem to perform almost magical transformations. But cosmetic work also points to a dark and comedic side of beauty also present—as the motif of metamorphosis—in many popular narrative traditions. It can evoke the doctor as a Frankenstein figure, a predator-profiteer, as well as the menacing woman-machine; the hubris of human alterations of nature, as well as the moral vacuity behind seductive surfaces. Perhaps this explains the ease with which plastic surgery enters into jokes, paranoia, melodrama, and other phenomena of collective fantasy life.

Silicone breast implants act as a sort of magical object that promise social ascension but that ultimately cause the downfall of the heroine in the Colombian telenovela *Sin tetas no hay paraíso* (Without Tits There Is No Paradise). The drama in twenty-six episodes narrates the story of Catalina, a seventeen-year-old living in an urban periphery known for being a hub of the narcotics trade. Observing the material success of her friends working as prostitutes, Catalina believes having breast implants will grant her entry into a "paradise" she sees in very worldly terms. To obtain money for plastic surgery, she attempts to become a *pre-pago*, a prepaid prostitute contacted via cell phone at any hour by her drug trafficker clients (the slang term *pre-pago* suggests a major theme of the drama: the relationships between commodities and sex). Her plans go tragically awry, and Catalina is raped by her would-be clients. After having an abortion, she eventually has breast implants in exchange for sex with a plastic surgeon. The prostheses, though, turn out to be used and after having a series of corrective surgeries, the story ends with Catalina's suicide.

The novela's author claimed he based the plot on the life histories of women he interviewed in the neighborhood where the novela is set. In a nation where radio stations offer breast implant prizes, and a mayor provided free cosmetic surgeries to public employees, the show was received as social commentary. It set a telenovela ratings record in Columbia and sparked a media debate about the link between prostitution and drugs and the growing popularity of plastic surgery (Goodman 2006). Its success perhaps was also due to its imaginative association between violence and beauty, between sexual exploitation and "normal" consumerism. The talisman of silicone prostheses suggests other fetishized objects as well: drugs, another substance that promises a "magical" gain of wealth and power, but at a deadly cost, as well as the female body itself, commodified and fragmented as it is exchanged for money or medical goods.

In Brazil, too, plastic surgery is often discussed in popular culture. Not only medical marketing, but also a range of media—national news programs, talk shows, Internet blogs, samba songs, telenovelas, pornography, and so forth—are filled with jokes and references to this modern technology understood to be a "Brazilian specialty." Of course, the nexus of medicine and commerce is as old as print capitalism itself. And the marketing exuberance surrounding plastic surgery is hardly unique to Brazil, as I was often reminded when I began writing this book in Los Angeles. Not surprisingly, medical marketing often boosts technical advances and minimizes surgical risks. Rather than view the growth of plastic surgery as only a result of clever marketing, I instead situate it in relation to a larger history of importing global technologies, commodities, and images in Brazil.

I find the figure of the "fetish" useful for thinking about diverse social phenomena that are not obviously linked. The original meaning of the term *fetish* is a "false god." Imported into English from the Portuguese *feitiço*, the word lost favor in anthropological studies of religion because it seemed to be highly charged with Judeo-Christian ideas of idolatry. The notion has figured centrally in social theory, however, perhaps because of its links to both Marx and Freud. Despite differences between the two thinkers, we might say the fetish represents for both a problem in the interplay between objects and persons. For Freud, the fetish appears in his discussion of sexual perversions as an object that displaces desire from a person to a thing and from the whole to the part. Marx uses the fetish as a metaphor to refer to a different kind of "perversion": a misunderstanding of the relationships between human beings and the objects they produce. He argues that capitalism is beset by a paradox: the bourgeois revolution that destroys traditional metaphysical sources of authority is accompanied by a reenchantment of the inorganic world as commodities take on magical properties. Masking their origins in human labor, commodities become a new, particularly modern kind of fetish in the marketplace.

The work of Walter Benjamin (1999; see too Buck-Morss 1989) imaginatively combines Freudian and Marxist notions of the fetish. Displayed in arcade windows, and eventually in luminous electronic and digital media, the commodity belongs to a "dream world" that is absorbed into the consumer's fantasy life. Benjamin was particularly interested in fashion as a characteristic feature of modern capitalism. With its mockery of established authority and planned obsolescence, fashion exemplifies modernity's temporal focus on the present and youth. It also reflects changes in the meaning of women's nature, as the life force of sexuality becomes entangled with the inorganic forms of commodities, clothes, and accoutrements: "In fetishism, sex does away with the boundaries separating the organic world from the inorganic. . . . Fashion itself is only another medium enticing [sex] still more deeply into the universe of matter." For him, fashion also has a special connection to prostitution. Both phenomena suggest that erotic and economic forms of fetishism become interwoven in consumer capitalism: the eroticization of the commodity is the flip side of the commodification of sex. Libidinal drives are directed into inorganic matter, while sexual experience can become shaped by the dream world of mass consumption.

The fetish has other meanings too in Brazil. Elites attacked (and fell under the sway of) the power of the *feitiço*, the idols worshipped in syncretistic and "barbaric" possession cults (Maggie 1992). Many of these practices had a healing rationale, and could be attacked as "false medicine" (Peard 1999: 124). Fetishism, then, can also indicate struggles over the definition of "true" medical and spiritual therapies within a modernizing nation attempting to adapt metropolitan technology to local realities—a meaning highly suggestive for contemporary uses of beauty as well. I draw on these various notions of the fetish to discuss the fragmentation and commodification of the female body, the mingling of sexual and economic desires, and the ethical dilemmas surrounding deep class stratification in Brazilian modernity.

While elites repressed fetish worship, they themselves in a sense fetishized the body politic as they struggled to create authentic popular culture. The question of Brazilian identity would become an almost obsessive concern of the elite in the twentieth century: how would a former plantation society based on slave labor develop the culture, science, and industry necessary to join the ranks of modern nations (an aspiration many felt was justified by Brazil's size and resources)? Merged with that question, or rather hanging over it like a shadow, was the problem of the *povão*, "the common people." Could a national body of assimilated Indians, freedmen, and their half-caste, possibly degenerate, descendants provide the raw material out of which a modern citizenry could be forged?

The question is intimately linked to gender and sexuality. In the course of the twentieth century, brown female beauty and tropical sensuality became important emblems of national popular culture. In Latin America, *popular culture* has double, often conflicting connotations: referring to the authentic culture of the common people, as well as to mass-produced cultural commodities. These two meanings are not always separable. For example, the celebration of samba as an organic expression of Afro-Brazilian syncretism corresponded with the rise of a commercial music industry and radio (Vianna 1999). And avant-garde artworks depicting a mestiço people coexisted with new kinds of fetishisms of the female body within a growing mass media. In a modernizing nation in a "dependent" position in the global economy, popular culture can thus inspire particular fetishisms of technologies, image-commodities, and the female body.

I argue that such fetishized relationships in the contemporary beauty industry recall an older problematic of dependency and authenticity that has haunted Brazil's attempts to establish a modern identity. I aim to bring into relation two objects of study: "Brazil" and "beauty." On the one hand, I discuss how erotic and economic interests in the modern have colored the social domain of female beauty in the twentieth century. On the other hand, I also analyze the class and transnational relationships that underlie Brazil's appropriation of modern medicine, technologies, and media. The "Brazilian body," I argue, does not just exist as a statistical entity in scientific research (defined by percentage of the population with heart disease, obesity, etc.), but also as a historical fact: a body politic traversed by political, economic, and erotic relations reflected in medical technologies.

: : :

A familiar site in Brazil's cities are the small crowds standing around newspaper kiosks, reading about yesterday's murders in the pages of a local tabloid. Step inside and the curious browser finds a vast popular press: from a self-help literature aimed at the autodidact to the range of Brazilian versions of magazines such as *Cosmopolitan* and the *New Yorker*. In the "women's section," one may flip through the pages of *Plástica & Beleza* and *Plástica & Corpo*. These publications have a look (and price) similar to the fashion magazines next to which they are displayed: high-quality "production values" and splashy color photos of celebrities. In a recent issue, the front matter showed a portrait of a smiling Pitanguy, fragments of nude female bodies, and articles with titles such as "Conquer the Bottom of Your Dreams" and "Dress to Kill: Lingerie to Seduce." In the midst of glamorous and sensual images, there were also incongruously clinical-looking shots of scars and stitches, and even grotesque close-ups of decaying gums and teeth.

The jarring images made me think of how the dyad of violence and beauty has often appeared in representations of Brazil. For much of colonial history, "beautiful Brazil," portrayed as a tropical Eden peopled by healthy and alluring inhabitants, was counterposed to European civilization. There was a frequent slippage between the beauty of luxuriant nature and of Indians, between land and women. In fact, the first words written about Brazil, by a scribe on Pedro Álvarez Cabral's voyage of discovery, betrayed a fascination with the beauty and innocence of the local women: "There walked among them three or four maidens, young and gracious, with very black, shoulder length hair. . . . And one was so well made up and so round, and her shameful part (that had no shame) so gracious, that many women from our land . . . will feel shame in not having theirs like hers" (in Parker 1991: 10). Such images—a kind of primal scene in the nationalist imaginary—were an invitation to colonial rule: as the scribe suggests in his letter to the Portuguese monarch, "Saving this people" is the "principal seed that Your Highness should sow in her [the land]" (9). They also became powerful tropes in the political thought of the Enlightenment that would later be imported by Brazilian elites attempting to nudge the new republic toward European civilization.

If Indians were innocent in the colonial imagination, they were also lustful and violent—impulses that took their paradigmatic forms in incest and cannibalism. A "green hell" of disease and bloodlust emerged as the flip side of tropical paradise (Parker 1991: 11). In reality, Brazil's natives, like North America's, were subjected to brutal "civilizing" policies. But Brazilian dealings with Indians—and later African slaves, freedmen, and the mestiço population—also reflected a distinct notion of citizenship that was both "hierarchical and inclusive," James Holston (2008) argues. The United States tended to employ a logic of *separation* in dealing with non-whites. Indians were treated as alien nations, blacks subjected to legal segregation. In Brazil racial others tended to be incorporated *into* the national body. In this model of citizenship, particular notions of blood, race, and soul were used as technologies of governance and assimilation. The body of a slave, for example, could be "read" for signs of docility or strength. This intimate form of bodily knowledge upheld hierarchy, but also reflected more fluid understandings of racial boundaries. The Brazilian state thus "regarded Indianness as a temporary condition" (ibid.: 71), while it tried to "whiten" blacks and mestiços through absorption into the general population (Skidmore 1974). A view of the people's bodies and souls as essentially malleable and plastic material has thus figured in a distinctive political rationality for most of the nation's history.

Histories of Brazil often stress the country's "dependent development." In economic terms, dependency meant Brazil produced a small number of agricultural crops on large plantations controlled by a rural oligarchy. Gilberto Freyre was only partly exaggerating when he declared that "Brazil is sugar and sugar is the Negro" (1956: 36). Adding coffee and rubber, one could tell a complex history of the land by tracing the "social lives" of these commodities (Appadurai 1988). Even after the declaration of the first republic in 1889 and new ambitions for modernization, a São Paulo coffee group soon consolidated its control over the nation's economy (Needell 1987: 17). And it was profits from coffee—fueled by European demand for that perhaps paradigmatically modern drug—that ironically provided the capital that would later initiate Brazil's rapid industrialization (Ortiz 2000: 140).

Economic dependency has often been linked in Brazil to the problem of cultural authenticity and imitation. Roberto Schwarz (1992: 1) argues that "the artificial, inauthentic and imitative nature of our [i.e., Brazilian] cultural life" has been experienced as a "malaise" for Brazilian elites.[7] For the elite of Rio de Janeiro, as Jeffrey Needell (1987) puts it, "civilization *was* Europe" or, more precisely, France and England. In faculties of law or medicine, they learned the scientific fashions of the day: social Darwinism and Auguste Comte's positivism.[8] Belle epoque society danced to European polkas and mazurkas, purged of the more "savage" elements they had been given in the city's popular culture (Rowe and Schelling 1991: 131). And in temperatures that reached 100 degrees in the summer, Carioca ladies dressed in long, full skirts and corsets (Needell 1987: 169–70). Men at least could unbutton high starched collars in neighborhoods such as Lapa, "our little improvised Montmartre in the tropics," which offered more Bohemian pleasures (Caulfield 1997: 93). The desire for Europeanization perhaps reached its most fetishized form in the practice of prostitution. The ultimate adornment for the Carioca gentleman of the belle epoque was the *cocotte*, a French-speaking courtesan (Needell 1987).

These women occupied the top rung of an elaborate hierarchy of prostitution that showed how the idea of "Europe" informed the racial and class dynamics of commercial sex. The *francesas* were distinguished from the less desirable *polacas*, "Eastern Europeans," many of them assumed to be Jewish, who had accompanied the massive waves of immigration to the Americas. *Mulatas* and *pretas* (blacks), ostensibly color terms, in practice referred to sexual desirability and class, rather than skin tone. The "exotic" mulatas worked along with the francesas in Lapa, a neighborhood filled with cabarets decorated with symbols of French erotica. The pretas, on the other hand, worked alongside polacas in the Mangue, a rougher section of town created out of former swamplands (Caulfield 1997: 91). These neighborhoods were also a key site in the "discovery" of samba as a key emblem of modern Brazilian identity (Vianna 1999). Like the later figure of the female artista, these women played crucial roles as "sex symbols" in the consumer fetishism of the epoch. Not only were they the most desirable commodity of all, but working as models in haut couture advertisements they helped sell other fashionable items (Needell 1987: 160). From the beginning of Brazil's modernization project, the female body figured centrally in the markets of exchange created in the encounter between global capitalism and local logics of class and color.

This was the cultural world—insecurely obsessed with Europe, ambivalent about the nation's backward economy and barbaric population—that gave birth to the cultural movement of *modernismo*. Launched in 1922 in São Paulo, this group of artists and scholars redefined the problematic of imitation. Oswald de Andrade's oft-quoted "anthropophagist manifesto" irreverently used the figure of the cannibal to define a new stance toward the foreign (Parker 1991: 16). Rejecting subservient imitation, as well as a xenophobic obsession with purity, de Andrade (1967) announced cosmopolitan culture should be "consumed" to create a uniquely hybrid national art. But were the Brazilian modernists simply following the lead of European avant-gardes, thus remaining imitative? The "primitive," though, was located not outside the nation, in Africa or the Pacific, but (and here was the originality of their logic) *within* the popular culture of the mestiço people. Symbols of syncretism become national patrimony, "barbarous and ours" (Dunn 2001: 16).

A new kind of mystique began to surround the *povão*, the common people. As Jesus Martín-Barbero puts it, "The black physical gesture became the heart of popular, mass culture" (1993: 174). This history has been often recorded. The image of samba coming down from the hillside favelas and into the emergent national consciousness is an irresistible founding myth of Brazilian identity. Hermano Vianna (1999), however, has told a more complex story, showing the role of elite and foreign actors in turning samba into a symbol of Brazil's national identity. Encouraged by visitors such as French poet Blaise Cendrars, a founder of cubist poetry, Brazilian classical composers and elites began to see their "own" popular culture through the prism of European avant-gardes' fascination with the primitive (ibid.).

The modernistas' "rediscovery of Brazil"—as they dubbed it—later proved useful to the populist Estado Novo (1937–45) as it promoted symbols that would affirm national pride (Sevcenko 2000: 96). Once-repressed possession cults such as Umbanda became symbols of integration and cultural syncretism (Ortiz 2000: 132–33). But it was *futebol*, samba, and Carnaval that occupied central stage in a spectacularization of Brazilian identity. Getúlio Vargas, the populist dictator, took to addressing the nation by radio from soccer stadiums (Rowe and Schelling 1991: 138–40). A distinctive style perfected by black and mestiço players, known for its improvisation and daring, elevated the game into a symbol of national cohesion. During the same period, *escolas de samba* (samba schools) based in poor neighborhoods became acknowledged sources of a consecrated national musical expression (Parker 1991: 157).[9] Of course, many nations have looked to folk culture as a source of modern authenticity (Ivy 1995). Yet for the student of twentieth century nationalism, Brazil's transformation of "barbaric" traditions into its official cultural expression still appears remarkable. There is an odd contrast between the national slogan of "order and progress" (taken from Compte's positivism) and a music and dance form that even today thrills audiences with the deafening volume of the drum section, the chaotic screeching of the *cuíca*, and the wild gyrations of the *sambista*.

The gaze on the female body played a crucial role in this search for a modern identity. Paintings such as Tarsila de Amaral's *Carnaval em Madureira* (1924) and Emiliano di Cavalcanti's *Samba* (1925) depicted cultural syncretism and multihued brown female beauty within the demimonde of street festivals and samba bars. Nationalists such as scholar Gilberto Freyre (1986: 63) embraced such images as a subversive attack on the elite practice of imitating European fashions, what he dismissed as "Aryanization." If the futebol player, that twentieth-century icon of masculinity, symbolized Brazil's progress as a modern nation, the mulata samba dancer was his feminine counterpart, a sensual embodiment of mixture as a national trait. Of course, for the modernist artists and scholars reinventing Brazilian identity, the mulata was sometimes the *mulher da vida*, a "woman of the life" who frequented the bohemian bars where samba was enjoyed. The celebration of sensuality in Brazilian modernism also reflected an older patriarchal morality that "split" the categories of mother and sexual being along class and color lines (discussed in part 3). Modern, beautiful Brazil was thus the product of reciprocal gazes between Europeans and Brazilians, as well as between elites and the people. This new, erotically charged vision of the body politic did not simply stem from a dependent position in the global economy, but also reflected an intimate history of domination.

It has often been observed that modernity in Latin America is a future project, a set of *aspirations*. A proverb wittily makes the point: Brazil is *always* a country of the future. The modern is not quite now, but rather a goal that is continuously receding. And indeed the modernists were in some ways out of step with the society around them. In the 1920s, Brazil had a mostly agrarian economy. It was not until the regimes of Getúlio Vargas (1930–45, 1951–54) that an era of intensive, state-led industrialization began. By 1943, Vargas could boast that a formerly "semi-colonial, agrarian" nation was ready to "assume the responsibilities of an autonomous industrial life" (Oliven 2000: 62). Developmentalism reached a peak with the administrations of Juscelino Kubitschek (1956–60) and the military dictatorship (1964–85), symbolized most dramatically by the planning of Brasília. Replacing Rio de Janeiro as the nation's capital, the city was constructed in the form of an airplane in an arid plateau far from the coast. Its streamlined design in the high modernist style became a powerful symbol of a utopian future. But as in other forms of modernism, its vision of "the people" was fraught with contradictions. The laborers who built the city settled in peripheral "satellites" that undermined the planned social integration of the city (Holston 1989). President Kubitschek, who presided over Brasília's construction, also admired the work of Pitanguy. Impressed by this example of medical progress, Kubitschek attended the opening of Pitanguy's clinic in 1962, two years after the inauguration of the new capital.

Developmentalism and modernization were not only political and economic policies; they formed an ethos that permeated Brazilian society during these "years of confidence" (Mello and Novais 1998, Parker 1999: 103). Unlike in Europe, mass media emerged more or less simultaneously with industrialization. In a country with high illiteracy rates, the media played a central role in creating "the imaginary of developmentalism and modernization" (García Canclini 2001: 90). During the 1960s and 1970s, Brazil created one of the largest television networks in the developing world (Skidmore 1988: 111). Established with the support of the military dictatorship, Globo network defined its programming mission as "presenting an image of a populace moving together toward modernity, glamour, and a materially enriched, upwardly mobile lifestyle" (Kottak 1990: 37). A culture industry known for its "export-quality" products successfully linked modernization to a sphere of consumption defined by images of prosperity, technology, and "glamour."

I have so far discussed some contradictions underlying Brazil's quest to become a modern society. The problematic of imitation and authenticity shaped the importation of foreign knowledge, technology, and culture, often frustrating ambitions to create a modern—yet uniquely Brazilian—identity. In this process, the body politic became not only a crucial economic, but also aesthetic and erotic resource (often gendered female), for elite nation-building projects. I have thus tried to minimize boundaries between political and "libidinal" economy, arguing that diverse forms of fetishism underlay Brazil's relationships to the modern. With these remarks in mind, let us turn now to the entanglements between things and people, between technology and sex, and between economic and erotic exchange within the contemporary "universe of beauty."

: : :

Fetishisms of commodities, images, and body parts often mingle in fantasies of personal transformation. Lígia arrives at her consultation holding up a picture of Sharon Stone torn from a magazine. "I want to be plásticafied [plásticazada]," Luanda declares. Public hospitals and cheap private clinics promise both bodily change, and a chance to obtain some of Globo's "modernity and glamour." New slang terms such as *turbinada* and *siliconada* evoke qualities such as streamlined and smooth, while ad copy promotes *moderno* beauty procedures. Cars, oddly enough, often figure in discussions of plástica. Breast-implants are like a "turboed" car, or known in slang as the safety device "air bag." Some patients feel they face a difficult consumer choice: buying plástica or a car. (Cars too are perhaps in Brazil a particularly fetishized modern technology as public transportation is often seen as an indignity for the masses.) Both can be purchased through credit plans, or through consumer associations known as *consórcios* (*Veja* 2001c).

Medical techniques such as plastic surgery can thus be understood in relation to the mystique surrounding progress and technology (Larvie 1997). Maureen O'Dougherty (2002: 130–31) argues that Brazilian consumers are seeking to "take part in a modern world, to provide, renew, and sanctify a spirit of modernity." Such a "spirit of modernity" pervades the beauty industry. A bewildering proliferation of terminology, often foreign or foreign sounding, creates an aura of continual technological advance. News articles herald imported treatments and "scientific discoveries": "A new treatment for stretch marks, discovered in Italy, has just arrived in Brazil" or "Modernity, sensuality, and efficiency now together in one product." To cite just a few of dozens of the pseudomedical treatments on offer: aesthetic ultrasound treatment, infrared therapy, Instant Plástica, Do-in, Sculpteur (a French method), and the "Russian Treatment" (developed by Soviet astronauts to prevent muscular atrophy). In São Paulo alone, the adult education institute trained 50,000 *esteticistas* in such cosmetic services during a five year period (*Veja* 2004). Surgeons stress that they themselves must continually undergo new training to avoid "becoming obsolete, such is the velocity of progress."

The fetishism of technology and progress is often allied with a fetishism of the female body where the fragment—either eroticized or pathologized—stands for the whole. Bodies are visualized, treated, and priced in parts. The ubiquitous "before and after" photos divide the body into closeups of busts, buttocks, and abdomens. Beauty practices also promote the *quantification* of the body. News media define ideals with precise numerical information: the measurements taken of the bust, waist, hips—and in Brazil, the thighs too. Ads target body parts: e.g., "buttocks in the right measurement." Other measurements include clothing size, body fat ratios, percentage of fat liposuctioned, differences between "apparent and chronological age," or years subtracted by a facelift. Media stories give ages in parentheses after the bold-type name, often serving as a deadpan punch line. This face (but!) sixty-one. That boyfriend (and yet!) forty-eight. Those breasts (and only!) R$8,000. Quantitative information provides criteria for comparison with others and with oneself over time, fueling a competitive search for perfection. Such numbers are balanced against price information, creating a kind of calculus for the mutual conversion of body (parts) and capital (which sometimes includes combining surgeries, as in figure 2).

These forms of fetishisms also reflect the erotic visualization of a mixed, popular culture that has pervaded Brazil's search for modernity. The mulata—key symbol of the newly valorized brown body politic—appears in commodified form in beauty culture. A beer that mixes dark and light brews, for example, is marketed in a stylized bohemian samba ambience as "Mulata: The Perfect Mixture." Globeleza is a kind of cyber-cartoon mulata logo for Globo's Carnaval coverage based on a mestiço samba dancer of "humble origins." The Brazilian Society of Plastic Surgeons and state regulatory agencies officially prohibit medical advertising. Nevertheless news media and consumer medical magazines are filled with direct advertising from clinics and credit plans. Some ads have local references to Brazilian popular culture—nods to the Brazilian "national preference" for *bundas em-*

Submeter-se
a duas
cirurgias
plásticas
na mesma
ocasião
é mais
econômico
e seguro para
aquelas
que estão
descontentes
com partes
diferentes do
corpo. Basta
ter certeza do
que se quer
modificar

2. "Combined surgeries: having two plastic surgeries at
the same time is more economical and secure for those
discontented with different parts of the body."

*pinadas* (large, round bottoms) and smaller breasts. One ad quotes a popular samba song:

> Come here my girl
> Come here my heart
> Come here my fine waist
> Come here my pestle waist.

It then announces that a surgeon has developed a specific technique to
mold such "pestle waists" (*Plástica & Beleza* 2001a: 104).

A "dream of consumption," as one ad puts it, plástica has entered into
the popular imagination of the good, or at least, glamorous life. Trying to

grow their business in a tight market, many surgeons simply use images of models in poses and lighting that recall soft porn rather than a medical clinic. Yet even mainstream news media seem to be aware of the power of plástica-enhanced artistas to attract viewers. Some surgeons such as Pitanguy are themselves celebrities and make frequent appearances in news programs, gossip and society columns, and the pages of magazines such as *Plástica & Beleza*. In his busy offices in São Paulo, the monthly's editor, Norbert Busto, explains how plastic surgery transformed his career as a journalist. He tells me he had been working at a general interest magazine that often ran stories on plástica. "Then a surgeon called me and said, 'Look, someone needs to launch a magazine oriented toward this public wanting information about plástica. There isn't anything now, so whoever does it first will have a great chance of success.'"

Norberto leapt at the opportunity, leaving his old job, and investing his personal savings in the project. Initially surgeons were hesitant to appear in a publication with direct advertising. "And so the way we persuaded the doctors was to do journalism and interviews—like you're doing with me now." Norberto adds, "Of course, it's also a form of publicity, because the surgeons pay to appear."

I ask him if the magazine also provides information about risks and complications. "There really isn't much risk because Brazilian plastic surgery if it's not the best is the second best in the world . . . , we lose only to the Americans, nê?" he says, laughing. "Come, let me show you the fan mail!" The magazine promotes surgeons—and itself—through a monthly plástica sweepstakes. Readers write in their "dreams," and the winner receives a free operation. Norberto shows me boxes of letters that he has received with return addresses, not just in São Paulo and Rio, but in remote states such as Amazônia.[10]

The television program, *Antes e depois* (Before and After), has also used plástica sweepstakes to boost ratings. "It was a pioneering idea: to offer plastic surgery to our viewers," explains the show's founder and hostess, Eliana Ovalle. An ex-novela actress, Eliana has luminous tan skin, which she maintains with a rigorous beauty regimen. The half-hour show is broadcast *daily*. Eliana initially targeted her friends, "the elite, the dominant class of Rio." But after two years broadcasting on a local channel in Rio, she realized she could attract a more "popular" audience, as plastic surgery is no longer "for the rich." (I am surprised to learn that Eliana is, like Preta Gil, an evangelical Christian. Apparently, the evangelical suspicion toward worldly pursuits does not extend to plástica. Later it occurs to me that medical modifications

As dançarinas Gal e Rúbia comemoraram de forma diferente o sucesso do novo CD da banda. O entusiasmo foi tão grande que elas resolveram aumentar os seios e deixar o corpo ainda mais bonito. O cirurgião plástico escolhido foi o Dr. Marcus Vinícius dos Santos, responsável pelas formas perfeitas da amiga

**Patrulha do Samba**

# No ritmo

3. "Dancers Gal and Rúbia commemorated the success of their band's new CD in a different form." They pose here with their plastic surgeon, Dr. Marcus Vinícius dos Santos.

of appearance do not normally elicit Christian sanctions against *vaidade*, vanity.) Like Norberto, Eliana proudly shows me fan mail from around the country, stored in large garbage bags in a closet. The next time I see her the show has moved into a professional studio and begun broadcasting to a national audience.

Perhaps the most essential ingredient in the media dissemination of plástica is the focus on celebrities. "Here in Brazil there is no prejudice," Norberto tells me. "The majority of artistas admit [*assume*] having plástica. . . . We promote them and they promote us. It's very important to have them say 'I did plástica. I recommend it. My life changed.'" One article he showed me featured an unlikely model: Debora Rodrigues, a former activist from the radical Landless Workers' Movement (MST). The majority of artistas, though, are drawn from the ranks of Globo's sophisticated star system that feeds its export-quality novelas. Another article in the monthly (2001b: 66) told the success story of two dancers from the Bahian samba group Patrulha do Samba. After Sony launched their first CD, the "girls resolved to make their bodies more sensual and modeled [*delineado*]" with breast implants and liposuction (figure 3).

But not all admire the human coupling with technology and plástica began to provoke anxieties about bodily integrity and the commodification of sex. *Made-in-cirurgia*, a slang term, puns on the association between implants, the United States, and man-made, rather than natural, beauty. Singer Seu Jorge also stresses the artificiality of silicone in a popular samba hit, "Mania de peitão." Over a pared-down samba beat, he sings in a whisper:

> There is no beauty on Earth
> That compares with hers
> But what people don't realize
> Is that this trembling cyclone
> The muse of generation 2000
> Is a scaffolding of Silicone.

The song then addresses this muse directly, accusing her of thinking only of "luxury and wealth," while ignoring the narrator's poverty. "All that you see, you want," he complains. In the song, as in the Colombian telenovela, body fetishism is tied to the commodity fetishism in pop culture. Silicone represents not just artificiality, but also the fantasy of using the body as a vehicle of social ascension.

Not surprisingly, the siliconada, a cyborg-like figure, has entered into the world of cyber-rumor. One blog sounded a macabre tone, wondering if the implant, a potential eco-hazard, should be removed from the body of a dead siliconada before she was buried. The link between surgery and body fragmentation is reflected in darker fantasies. Patients connect plástica with death, or a potential loss of identity, wondering if they will wake up from anesthesia. Nancy Scheper-Hughes (1992: 235) reported a "fascination and horror" with plastic surgery and organ theft already in the 1980s among favela residents. Both practices symbolized a state where "we don't know whose body we are talking to anymore" as well as the vulnerability of the "bodies of the young, the poor, and the beautiful."

Siliconadas became a symbol not just of artificiality, but also of modern sophistication in a national beauty contest. Beauty pageants are remarkably popular events in the developing world where they can function as a "badge of civilized, modern status" (Cohen, Wilk, and Stoeltje 1996: 9). But in Brazil the somewhat dowdy national pageant has in a sense become redundant, since much of the culture industry functions as a de facto beauty contest. Still, the annual Miss Brasil event generates a modest amount of attention. The 2001 winner, Juliana Borges, was dubbed Miss Siliconada after she announced that she had had nineteen surgical interventions. The svelte, liposuctioned, and siliconada Borges drew comparisons with the legendary 1954 winner, Marta Rocha. It was rumored that Rocha had lost the Miss

World competition only because of an "extra two inches in the hips." This loss was invoked as a symbol in a kind of "negative nationalism." Wide hips were viewed as a national biological trait that signified sensual enjoyment: if Rocha lost the world contest, commentators knowingly implied, then the "loss" is the world's—and Brazil's gain. In an interview about Borges, Rocha quips, "With lipo and silicone, beauty is no longer authentic . . . like this, any woman can participate [in the miss contests]" (*Jornal do Brasil* 2001). One could question the meaning of debating merit in a contest based on genetic endowment, but the other point the controversy raised was the loss of tradition. Borges defended herself, saying that plástica was necessary to "compete" with the plástica-enhanced Miss Venezuelas, and that she wanted to "modernize" the beauty contest (ibid.). Her comment suggests how the language of Developmentalism—with its stress on modern technology and the need to be competitive in global markets—can migrate from official spheres to the personal project of physiological improvement.

: : :

Enhancement technologies are provoking a mixture of fascination, hope, and fear in many regions. Francis Fukuyama (2004: 42) has called the ideology of transhumanism—the use of technology to surpass biological limits—the "most dangerous idea in the world." "Techno-optimists," on the other hand, argue that enhancement can solve a range of problems, from aging angst to social stigma. The fantastic quality of such technologies, however, can lead both critics and boosters to isolate them from their social and class contexts. I argue that the ethical questions posed by new medical technologies must also be understood in relation to local market and sexual dynamics that endow them with moral and emotional force. For Benjamin (1999), modern technology is a magical means of assuring prosperity for all, a fetish that obscures class relations. It belongs to a "dream world" in that it activates the fairy-tale-like wish for happiness. But technological progress can also acquire specific meanings in the peripheries of capitalism. Just as the most powerful magic often comes from afar, technologies may gain prestige the further they travel. Viewed as both a miraculous technology and medical luxury, plástica can inspire intense interest among friends, family, and coworkers. After having silicone implants, Clarissa said, "No one in my circle had seen a plástica before. So imagine the curiosity! They came up to me saying 'Let me see! Let me see! Can I touch it?'"

The modernistas ingeniously performed what I see as a particular nationalist "move" that can surface in diverse spheres: "barbaric" and "backward" Brazil nevertheless provides the conditions for a creative adaptation of foreign ideas and practices. Plastic surgeons argue in a similar vein that they have borrowed a metropolitan technology, but have improved on it as they discover its "social purpose," and practice it in "messy conditions" on a non-European, "miscegenated" population. Yet this appropriation, however inventive, also reflects older contradictions underlying the use of modern imports to engineer the body politic, as we will see in the next sections. Meanwhile, consumers continue to vigorously embrace plástica, unsettling a few elite observers who wonder whether the popular classes possess "the culture" necessary to understand this modern medical practice. Such concerns recall earlier debates about the capacity of the Brazilian people to become modern.

I am hesitant, however, to see beauty culture as a symptom of a failed modernity or an improper consumption. Once the science of the "savage," anthropology more recently has challenged the notion that some places and peoples are effectively living in the past. Notions such as "primitive" or "civilization" have become impolite, but a technical and often moral timetable underlies evaluations of regional differences. Modernity, though, is often frustratingly difficult to "locate." Certainly modernity cannot be defined as the surpassing of earlier forms of brutality. Perhaps it can be claimed simply that modernity should be equated with the possession of superior technology. But this response may itself reflect the modern fetishization of technology, which makes it a magical solution for human problems. Brazil, a country with an ambivalent relationship to Western civilization, perhaps illustrates the problem particularly clearly. One of the world's most progressive constitutions coexists with brutal police and drug violence. A theorist of the neo-Marxist dependency theory presided as president over a transition to neoliberalism. And a popular culture with a reputation for natural sensuality has embraced nonclinical, high-tech medical interventions on the female body. Thus the question arises: As Brazil selectively appropriates global images and technology, is it slavishly following fashions and exhibiting its dependency, or is it leading the way to a future where cosmetic-medical practices become normalized within projects of self-optimization and health?

Levante suas
mamas e sua
auto-estima

*Faça uma plástica
de mamas pela
técnica Periareolar*

• Anestesia Local
• Redução de volume
• Cicatriz apenas ao
redor das aréolas
• Aumento das mamas
(prótese de silicone)
• Não necessita uso
de telas para sustentação

Dr. Wagner
Montenegro
*Clínica de Cirurgia Plástica*
Rua Apeninos, 919
Paraíso - São Paulo - SP
Fone: (011) 539-1811
Fax: (011) 574-6204

4. Plastic surgery ad: "Raise your breasts and your self-esteem."

: : : : : :   **A BRIEF HISTORY OF SELF-ESTEEM**

One not-so-subtle ad for a plastic surgery clinic urges consumers to "raise your breasts and your self-esteem" (figure 4). The notion of self-esteem is not just a standard beauty marketing point, however; it also crops up in a surprising range of contexts. In the United States, self-esteem became a central concept in a new political rationality that gained ground in the wake of a perceived failure of government in the 1980s. A task force established by a California Assembly bill, for example, found low self-esteem implicated in an astonishing number of problems: from violent crime to teen pregnancy to chronic welfare dependency (Cruikshank 1996: 232). Having "good" self-esteem was imagined as a form of self-governance in areas where the state in unable to govern.

In Brazil, it would be hard to imagine a diagnosis of low self-esteem offered as an explanation for violent crime. Nevertheless, the term *auto-estima* figures in a range of therapeutic techniques and social movements. Grass-roots activists work to "rescue" the self-esteem of the Afro-Brazilian. Self-help and feminist books offer do-it-yourself techniques for healing this elusive domain of well-being. Self-esteem figures too within Brazil's AIDS program. Public health campaigns aim to raise "consciousness over risk and attitudes and values related to self-esteem" while promoting condom use (Biehl 2004: 108).

From a cross-cultural perspective, there is perhaps a certain weirdness to the notion of self-esteem. For the devout who believe the self must be surrendered, transcended, or even extinguished, the idea that it should instead be "esteemed" might be incomprehensible. The word *self-esteem* in English did not appear until the end of the nineteenth century, and perhaps would not have been intelligible in the religious idiom of an earlier epoch (Ward 1996). Yet, for better or worse, self-esteem is now becoming a *global* notion, useful to a range of social and psychotherapeutic projects. This broad appeal suggests that it reflects other changes in political rationality.

In this section, I begin by outlining a genealogy of self-esteem. My aim is to defamiliarize plastic surgery's core diagnostic and therapeutic concept. Disembedded from its everyday clinical context, it may appear as historically unique as the rationales underlying more exotic bodily practices. After all, we might ask, why should self-esteem matter for a treatment that involves cutting the body? If the plastic surgeon is a psychologist with a scalpel in his hand, shouldn't a patient have psychotherapy, thereby avoiding the scalpel? The laconic answer surgeons (and many patients) offer is that plástica simply works better. Thus a plastic surgeon joked, "What is the difference between a psychoanalyst and a plastic surgeon? The psychoanalyst knows everything but changes nothing. The plastic surgeon knows nothing but changes everything."

In fact, as we shall see, there are striking similarities and historical parallels between these two treatments that target mind-body interactions. Plástica's expansive therapeutic mandate can even lead to difficulties in deciding when surgical intervention, and when the "talking cure," is the more appropriate treatment—a task that some surgeons employ psychologists to perform. There is, however, an important difference between the two therapies: psychoanalysis was notoriously ineffective on the working class, while plástica claims to be a universal cure. Yet while patients from a range of socioeconomic strata say they do experience a boost to self-esteem, we might ask how suffering and healing come to be framed in a psychological idiom in the first place? Some surgeons are concerned with making a "differential diagnosis" between psychotherapy and plástica. Widening the focus away from this technical question, I ask how the therapeutic rationale underlying cosmetic surgery is related to a longer history of medical efforts to heal the bodies and minds of the suffering people, from earlier mental and social hygiene movements to later market-based forms of self-governance?

: : :

While some patients dismiss risks—"plástica is only skin"—observing a facelift makes clear that this is an extreme practice of body modification by any standard. Add to this aggression health risks, the odd mixture of erotic and grotesque in medical marketing, and patient attitudes that range from humble gratitude to a compulsive drive to acquire operations, and it becomes impossible to ignore the question that most plastic surgeons take for granted: Is cosmetic surgery a medical practice?

According to a tautological definition in which *medical* denotes a practice performed by a surgeon with the right training and certification, the answer would be yes. This answer in turn begs the more difficult question that has haunted the rise of the specialty in its modern form: Does the practitioner of cosmetic surgery violate the Hippocratic oath? To justify the risk, surgery must heal in some way. Can cosmetic surgery meet this standard? Due to high risks, all surgery must reckon with a cost-benefit ratio. Yet cosmetic surgery patients must be, by definition, *already healthy*. As the freelance snack vendor who works the plastic surgery ward of Santa Casa put it, patients are "hungry because they aren't sick." In fact, precisely because there is no medical benefit, strictly speaking, they must be in a better state of health than the average surgery patient for whom more risk is justified. Candidates are told to lose weight and quit smoking in order to qualify for cosmetic procedures. Furthermore, if the patient stands to make some functional gain, or suffers from an obvious disfigurement, then the operation is no longer cosmetic, but reconstructive. What then is the name of the illness or disorder that cosmetic surgery cures?

One irony in the development of modern plastic surgery is that in order for it to gain legitimacy as a medical specialty in the late nineteenth century, it had to exclude cosmetic procedures. The term *beauty doctor* referred to a quack, not a plastic surgeon. Indeed, not all of the pioneers of cosmetic techniques were board-certified surgeons, or even doctors (Haiken 1997). Constructionist approaches to medicine have shown that diagnoses can in some cases create "illness" (Hacking 1995). But in the case of plastic surgery, doctors began imagining and experimenting with aesthetic surgeries and other treatments *before* they had properly defined a disorder (Haiken 1997). With cosmetic surgery, it was the illness, not the cure, which awaited discovery.

Plastic surgeons rapidly improved techniques as they gained enormous practice reconstructing the mutilated faces of soldiers of the First World War. Some surgeons soon began to wonder if these procedures could be applied for purely cosmetic purposes. To become legitimate medicine, however, cosmetic surgery had to borrow the conceptual innovations of other disciplines: psychoanalysis and psychology. The psychoanalytic concept of the "inferiority complex" held that deviations from norms of appearance could disturb mental health. More generally, psychoanalytic ideas gave scientific backing to the growing social recognition of the importance of appearance for normal functioning. The inferiority complex eventually blossomed into the more flexible and encompassing notion of self-esteem. First a technical concept in the emerging psychological disciplines in the late nineteenth century, it was popularized in the postwar period, making a journey from "revolutionary to normal knowledge" (Ward 1996: 7; Cruikshank 1996: 232). Self-esteem is important for cosmetic surgery because it enables surgeons to argue they are healing a psychological complaint. In the notion of low self-esteem one might say aesthetic surgery found a treatable condition.

Plastic surgery's debt to psychological concepts is reflected in the close historical links in the early decades of the twentieth century among the medical specialty, psychoanalysis, and psychosomatic medicine. Sander Gilman has called plastic surgery "psychoanalysis in reverse" (1998:13). Plastic surgery heals the mind through the body. Psychoanalysis, on the other hand, addresses the suffering body through the mind. Both treatments share a conception of illness as stemming from subtle interactions between mind and body. They both too emerged as responses to the health problems created by modern weaponry in the First World War. While Sir Harold Delf Gillies — one of Pitanguy's mentors — pioneered modern techniques of reconstructive facial surgery on soldiers in Edinburgh, in a London suburb W. H. R. Rivers, another physician (and anthropologist), developed experimental healing techniques for a new syndrome struggling to achieve medical legitimacy: shell shock (ibid.: 14). Influenced by Freud's ideas, Rivers's work revealed similarities between shell shock and the neurosis suffered by civilian (often female) patients (Gask 2004: 14). Oddly enough, the search for treatments of neurotic illness also led psychoanalysts to the experimental work of plastic surgeons. Some early psychoanalysts believed that the nose was psychically connected to the genitals and thus concluded that sexual disorders might be cured by nasal surgery (Gilman 1998).

These experimental treatments reflected a new view of the subtle relationships between organic and mental disorders. It's true that older forms of medical knowledge also made a link between outer appearance and inner qualities. But arts such as phrenology, which divined character traits from the shape of the head, saw morphology as a sign of *immutable* character. A specialty that viewed physical traits as "true" indicators of moral and psychological health was logically suspicious about the wisdom of altering appearance. Indeed, as Gilman (1999) argues, plastic surgery's ambivalent status as medicine initially stemmed from its potential to alter outward signs of inner qualities such as "blood" or moral condition. Rhinoplasty (at least a successful procedure, a rare outcome) threatened to mask the telltale sign of syphilis. The conceptual innovation is thus to view appearance not as a "destiny" but rather as a *changeable* index of psychic health. Given the democratic promise of this rationale, it is perhaps not surprising that the inferiority complex and self-esteem (as well as cosmetic surgery) should flourish in the New World. It is as if appearance were added, along with wealth and pedigree, to the list of life's inherited injustices that do not sit well with egalitarian aspirations.

Of course, the growth of cosmetic surgery has not been without controversy. A dense thicket of anxieties seem to converge in the practice: the commercialization of medicine, a backlash against feminism, racial alienation, celebrity worship. Yet while there are disagreements about the line separating "vanity" from "necessity," the notion that appearance has a psychological dimension is simply becoming part of cultural common sense—a point that becomes clearer from an historical perspective.

Not only do aesthetic ideals vary over time; so does the degree to which the ugly or deformed are expected to endure their fate. Victorian England viewed surgery on a cleft palate as cosmetic. The implication was that stoically bearing a defect built character; correcting it was vanity. By the early twentieth century, the procedure had shifted into the reconstructive category. In the Victorian era, ugliness was fate; bearing it with dignity built *character.* The inferiority complex implies that a physical flaw, on the contrary, mars the more psychological notion of *personality* (Haiken 1997). Appearance becomes the "face" of personality, or as Pitanguy says, the "outer edge of the psyche." From this perspective, improving looks can be viewed not as a cowardly or selfish refusal to endure destiny, but rather as an understandable search for mental healing and social acceptance. The point is that plastic surgery cannot be understood only as a disciplinary practice: it rests on a generally "progressive" and certainly more ambitious vision of health as not merely the absence of disease but rather a more amorphous state encompassing psychological well-being. One consequence and cause of cosmetic surgery's legitimation is the opening of the body-self as a new frontier in the pursuit of happiness.

: : :

In the postwar years in Brazil, plastic surgery was transformed from a fringe specialty to part of mainstream medicine. Head of a private clinic with twenty-two beds and a staff of sixty, Dr. Alceu has performed 16,000 operations in a career spanning almost forty years. He described the evolution of the specialty: "At the end of the 1950s, aesthetic surgery was not considered very worthy of respect. In 1955 the first world plastic surgery conference was held in Stockholm. It was very large, international, and it had only one or two small works devoted to aesthetic surgery. I just came back from New York where they had 1,600 people at a congress just on aesthetic surgery. It was a brutal change." In Brazil, media stories about cosmetic surgery have not only praised its rising popularity as a sign of economic health, but also emphasized its psychotherapeutic benefits. *Veja* opined: "There is nothing wrong in wanting to lose localized fat through liposuction, to eliminate crow's feet with a facelift, or to augment the breasts a little with silicone. Improving the body and rejuvenating the face, it's known, helps to maintain high self-esteem, with consequences for personal and professional life" (*Veja* 2002).

Many Brazilians would already have had some experience with the notion of self-esteem through psychoanalysis and other forms of psychotherapy. As in Argentina, psychoanalysis has enjoyed extraordinary popularity among those who could afford it. Both orthodox Freudian analysis as well more esoteric sects have flourished—sometimes long after they became obsolete in their country of origin (Russo 2000). Though, again as in Argentina (Lakoff 2005), their star may finally be on the wane as they are supplanted by pharmaceutical treatments and the array of techniques known as *medicina estética*, aesthetic medicine. I was struck by how often middle-class and elite patients combined plastic surgery with other mind-body (and soul) healing techniques, from Reichian psychoanalysis to New Age and older syncretistic spiritual practices.

Unlike psychoanalysis, plástica is a form of "action," as one surgeon said, based on mastery of technique, not on a frustratingly vague "knowledge." Some surgeons, however, recognize a gray zone where the two treatments overlap, complicating the process of making accurate diagnoses. In fact, some clinics rely on psychologists to screen out unsuitable patients. Pitanguy's daughter, Gisele Pitanguy, works as a psychologist at his private clinic. At Santa Casa all patients must undergo a psychological exam before being approved for surgery. Early European psychoanalysts believed some neuroses could be treated with plastic surgery. In Brazil too, a consultation with a psychologist (or with an ObGyn) can sometimes lead to an appointment with a plastic surgeon. One day in Santa Casa, I met two nuns in the waiting rooms. One had traveled seven hours by bus from the state of Minas Gerais to have cosmetic surgery. She had been "fainting all the time," she said, so went to see a psychologist. "He said my face was ugly, that it had flaccid skin in the neck, in the face. And I got rid of this psychologist but the idea stayed in my head, so I asked the Mother Superior and she wrote to Pitanguy."

Given Pitanguy's collaboration with psychotherapists, it is perhaps not surprising that psychoanalytic notions of transference and projection should enter into his medical writings and clinical practice. For example, Gisele Pitanguy recounted a case in which a woman went to the clinic for a nose job. After several sessions of psychological evaluation, Gisele detected that the patient had "grave sexual problems, camouflaged by the complaint about her nose." The patient had in fact "projected" a sexual neurosis into a facial feature. In such a case the priority was a psychotherapist, not a surgeon (*O Globo* 2002). In psychoanalysis, transference and countertransference refer to intimate feelings that may develop in the course of therapy. In plastic surgery, a similar process may occur. Postoperative reactions include not just depersonalization and crises of regret, but also "exaggerated gratitude and sexual invitations to the surgeon" (Pitanguy 1992: 271).

While patients may experience transference, surgeons for their part must guard against delusions about the power of their craft. Plástica ads and patients often emphasize the "aesthetic sensitivity" of the surgeon. If the body is a work of art, then logically the surgeon is an artist, or "architect" as the samba song put it. Pitanguy, though, downplays such claims to art-istry. When I asked him about the creative dimensions of cosmetic surgery, he responded somewhat impatiently, "I cannot—like a Picasso—have three breasts or whatever. But inside our limitations we can do many things." In fact, Pitanguy has identified a new danger peculiar to the specialty: the "Pygmalion Complex," a mental state of "excessive self-confidence in which the surgeon-artist repeats the statuary's drama and falls headlong in love with his work . . . not conscious that his 'sculpture' is a human being under his care" (1976, 1992: 271).

Despite confidence in the efficacy of their cure, Pitanguy and a few other surgeons have reflected on the challenges to good practice raised by the "psychological dimensions of plastic surgery." Mental suffering produces a bad body-image, while perceived aesthetic defects cause psychological symptoms. How, then, does the clinician decide where to intervene in this vicious circle? And which therapeutic techniques are appropriate? The conundrum is reflected in Pitanguy's attempt to produce guidelines for making a differential diagnosis between psychotherapy and plástica:

> Sometimes, plastic surgery is the solution for psychological problems.
> Sometimes, plastic surgery unleashes psychological problems.
> Not all surgery resolves psychological problems.
> Not all psychological alterations contra-indicate surgery [i.e., even psy-chotic, paranoid, and neurotic patients may benefit from surgery].
> Sometimes, psychotherapy prepares a patient for a better post-operative result (Pitanguy 1992: 270).

With only these "sometimes" to guide him, the novice surgeon might feel hopelessly confused. How can it be known when plastic surgery will un-leash or solve psychological problems and, most importantly, when the patient must be dissuaded from surgery? While the therapeutic rationale claims an expansive healing mandate, it also implies a major difficulty in finding the "right" level of suffering. The "good patient" must be "mentally suffering" just enough to justify intervention, yet not suffering so much that her body-image is *too* distorted, which would jeopardize the plástica cure.[11]

The surgeons' interest in psychology stems not just from a concern with making accurate diagnoses, but also from a desire to protect them-selves from unsatisfied patients. The psychologist is trained to recognize patients with a psychopathological syndrome called *dismorfobia*, distorted body-image. Such patients believe their defects are responsible for "all their afflictions" (i.e., instead of only some), and thus can never be satisfied by surgery (Pitanguy 1992: 265). When one problem is corrected by surgery, they may simply "transfer" their emotional disturbance to another part of the body. Unable to experience mental healing no matter how good the technical results, such patients become a major nuisance to the surgeon. They also suggest a problem with making diagnoses: isn't it precisely the emotional disturbance that makes the patient sick enough to need healing? The therapeutic rationale thus leads to a kind of double bind. If the patient is healthy with an "objective" body-image, then plastic surgery cannot perform a cure and thus loses its healing function. Yet if the patient is too "emotionally invested," blaming her defect for all her problems, she becomes contraindicated (270).

Listening to surgeons discuss the challenges of making good diagnoses, I was reminded of the dilemma faced by the clinician prescribing the SSRI class of antidepressants, such as Prozac (Kramer 1994). The more severe side effects of earlier generations of drugs helped anchor prescribing decisions, as potential benefits always had to be weighed against risks to the patient. A new generation of pharmaceuticals with less dangerous side effects made it more difficult to prescribe antidepressants according to systematic principles. Peter Kramer (1994) coined the phrase "cosmetic psychopharmacology" to imply that psychotropic medications are being used as a means of lifestyle enhancement or personality adjustment, rather than mental healing. The dilemma of the psychiatrist reflects the confusion faced by plastic surgeons who also can feel "ungrounded" in making diagnoses in the absence of clear criteria for a *contraindication*. Without diagnostic principles that distinguish between the sick and healthy, it becomes harder to make the case for either cosmetic surgery or pharmaceuticals as a form of medical healing. The problem now is not that the patient is not sick, but that everyone is potentially a patient. The samba song "In the Universe of Beauty" refers to this dilemma, no doubt unwittingly, when it claims: "The self-esteem in *each* ego awakens."

Pitanguy's writings reveal a hesitation in the formulation of the therapeutic rationale, a moment of doubt about how to make "real indications." Moving from medical writings to clinical practice, however, many of these problems disappear: patients are rarely turned away for reasons other than physical health. What I have been calling a therapeutic rationale is not so much a codified dogma as a tacit moral ground of practice. Surgeons generally display a confident, pragmatic attitude. They are more concerned with satisfying patients on a case-by-case basis, winning the esteem of colleagues, or expanding their practice than with justifying diagnostic principles. Any doubts they have may be answered by the long lines at their clinics and sincere expressions of patient gratitude.

: : :

Cosmetic surgery reflects a larger psychological ethos that targets the psyche as a universal domain for improvement and healing. As this ethos expands from a small elite to a broader segment of society, it also disseminates a specific way of seeing—and managing—the self. But as it takes root in new regions and clinical contexts, it must adapt to local forms of social suffering and medical systems. In Brazil, medicine has had enormous importance as a social and political institution. It's true that medical education got off to a slow start in Brazil. For 300 years, Portugal banned its colony from founding institutions of higher learning—with the purpose of enhancing dependence on imperial rule (Schwarcz 1999: 238–39). But in the nineteenth and twentieth centuries, medicine became the "most institutionally advanced and professionalized" branch of science in Brazil (Stepan 1991: 41). Together with law, it played a key role in providing the technical and ideological support for the civilizing project. Medical institutions and doctors held extraordinary power in a nation without universities, and a medical education often functioned as the normal and "often only route to scientific knowledge" (47).

Under the sway of fashionable European racial science, elites concerned with issues such as sexual decadence and racial degeneration promoted "mental" and "social" hygiene among an unruly population (Meade 1996, Stepan 1991: 46–54). The Bahian anthropologist Nina Rodrigues relied on skull measurements to medically "treat" criminals and the mentally ill (Schwarcz 1999: 256–65). And the state attempted to eugenically regulate the family and female health in order to promote the health of the nation, for example by sterilizing women with "perversity syndrome" (Caulfield 2000; Stepan 1991: 113).

But medical and psychological knowledge coexisted, and sometimes conflicted, with popular healing practices—many based in "barbaric" cults with African roots. With their loud drums and "fetish" worship, such threats to public order were repressed by politicians and police (Ortiz 2000: 130; Sevcenko 2000: 86). Conversely, some public health campaigns were resisted with surprising violence: for example, a vaccination program in early twentieth-century Rio de Janeiro resulted in large scale rioting (Meade

1996). In other contexts, a medical framework subtly mingled with folk idioms of suffering. Clinicians could diagnose the "madness of hunger" as *nervos*, "nerves," and treat it with vitamins and sleeping pills. Hunger — a profoundly social problem — was redefined in medical and psychological terms (Scheper-Hughes 1992).

Of course, medicine scored some spectacular victories in public health, and indeed Brazil has in recent decades made an epidemiological transition to the "diseases of civilization": diabetes, Alzheimer's, depression, and the like. In the postwar period, a national network of hospitals made biomedicine a normal presence — and sometimes a rare good invested with the mystique of the modern — in the lives of many of the urban and rural poor (Mello and Novais 1998).[12] The end of the dictatorship in 1985 brought ambitious new efforts to democratize healthcare. Citizens began to use "medicine and technology to enhance their claims for social equity and human/biological rights" (Biehl 2005). Although the national health insurance scheme was previously tied to labor rights (available only to some workers), Brazil's 1988 Constitution included a new "universal right to healthcare" (ibid.).

This new right represents in many ways a rupture from the social use of medicine during earlier periods of state-led modernization. Yet some of the older conflicts involved in the use of medical sciences to solve a broad range of social and political problems persist in the contemporary therapeutic landscape. The newly democratic state deepened the split between public and private sectors. From 1989 to 1993, per capita federal spending dropped from US$83 to US$37 (Biehl 2005: 47). Public hospitals — generally places where my middle-class informants would never set foot — suffer from infrastructure problems, salary freezes for doctors and nurses, a lack of medical materials, and long lines. Brazil now has for the most part a health system divided into a public and private sector with different standards of care. Faveret and Oliveira (1990, in Biehl 1999: 55) describe this situation as an "excluding universalism" in which the elite and the middle class exclude themselves from the constitutional right to publicly provided healthcare.

Within this ailing public health system, some plastic surgery patients were quite strident in asserting their "rights." As Vera, a woman in her forties who came alone to a public hospital for abdominal surgery, put it: "We ourselves have to take care of ourselves. I said to myself, 'I deserve this, it's my time now.' If it's something bothering me, I have to do it; I have the total right to do it." Despite new constitutional rights, interactions between surgeon and patient sometimes echoed older kinds of hierarchical and patronage relationships. Many doctors in public hospitals are friendly, even intimate, with patients; patients, for their part, are sometimes impressed by the doctors' generosity and ability to "understand" them. Other surgeons spoke of "the people," the "popular classes," "the poor," or "the needy" in tones that ranged from desires for solidarity to amused indulgence to outright contempt.

During the "surgical plan," patients disrobe in front of a room filled with residents and medical visitors while bodily flaws and the merits of particular techniques are debated. This exposure for the purposes of scientific discussion is offset by the gift of beauty extended by the doctor. In other cases, "the people" become obstinate reminders of Brazil's backwardness and political failings.

"They fell after I gave birth," Taís, a patient in Santa Casa, explains as she unbuttons her blouse in a tiny consultation room.

"How old were you?"

"Thirteen for the first."

Dr. Roberto turns to look at me but doesn't say anything. (After she leaves the room, he shakes his head. "The girls here are really *adiantadas* [precocious].")

As he gently lifts her right breast, pushing it to the side, Taís explains, "They are really spread out, ugly. I want silicone to lift them up a bit, to make them like they used to be."

Dr. Roberto sighs, though I can't tell if he is resigned or exasperated. "If you put in a prosthesis you'll still have a fallen breast, just a bigger fallen one. The correct operation is a *levantamento* [a lift]. Then we can put in a prosthesis as well."

"But Doctor, please, I only want one operation," Taís adds.

"Just the lift, then," he scribbles on her file. "What does your husband think?"

"He supports me," Taís says.

"Of course, he wants a *gatinha* [a little cat]." As she gets dressed, he asks about her work.

"*Vendedora* [vendor], but unemployed," she says. The entire consultation has taken less than ten minutes. As he shows her out, he says to me in English, "Lula has said he will give us 100,000 jobs, more like 100,000 jobless."

Dr. Roberto has restrained himself, waiting until Taís has left the room before commenting on her early pregnancy. Doctors in maternity wards of public hospitals are sometimes more direct, addressing young birthing mothers with "heavily ironic and disapproving comments" such as "Ah, it was good when you made it, now you feel pain" (McCallum and Reis 2005: 340). When Dr Roberto heard that this patient, who had unrealistic understandings of plástica, was unemployed, he couldn't resist a wry remark in English (thus excluding her from the conversation). He certainly doesn't blame Taís for her "desires"—after all, she only aims to please her husband, who wants a gatinha—but the juxtaposition of the desire for silicone, her "precocious" sexuality, and her evidently humble social position perhaps suddenly came to symbolize for the doctor the failures of Brazil and more specifically of "Lula" (da Silva, Brazil's leftist president).

Other surgeons were more openly dismayed, or even disgusted, by the patient population they attended. The chief surgeon at the public Hospital dos Servidores do Estado explained that during the dictatorship, it "was the reference in Latin America, with twenty two operating rooms, 800 doctors, 135,000 square meters [1.45 million square feet], escalators in the outpatient wards." But in 1980s and 1990s, the hospital declined as budgets shrank. Initially intended for civil servants, it began attending what he called "the general people," povo geral, and "all the people," povo tudo mundo: "Before it was for people [gente], more elite, more fine, who didn't break windows, who didn't spit on the floor and throw paper. It was middle class. Not now—now everyone on the street comes, and we need more cleaning because the people really mess it up [povo estraga muito]."

"There aren't any middle-class people in the hospital?"

"They have withdrawn into the private sector. Only a few come: those who like the doctors."

Democratic ambitions to improve healthcare have met with other contradictions in an era of market-reform. João Biehl (2007) discusses, for example, how Brazil's AIDS program guaranteed universal access to anti-retroviral medications while concealing a "hidden epidemic": a group of poor and marginal patients excluded from epidemiological data and who become "visible" only when they die. The "activist state" also acted like a "triage state," producing a "social death." In the field of mental health, activists inspired by Jacques Lacan and the European antipsychiatry movement succeeded in closing down some psychiatric institutions, which had incarcerated political dissidents (Biehl 2005). This democratic logic also coexisted with economic rationalization, resulting in the replacement of costly and labor-intensive hospital care with cheaper pharmaceutical management, with sometimes disastrous results (ibid.). Brazil's pharmaceutical markets were restructured, almost doubling to US$10 billion during a five-year period in the 1990s (Biehl 2005; Fritsch 1999). Deregulation and new marketing practices led to a number of problems, such as "prescriptions" given by untrained pharmacists, knock-off drugs, and experimental regimes of self-medication in Brazil and other regions of Latin America (Fritsch 1999, Lakoff 2005).

: : :

On offer in both a consumer market and a public health system, plástica is an experimental form of therapy growing during a time of rapid change in the political and market relationships underlying healing and suffering. While it partly echoes the expanded democratic aims of postdictatorship Brazil, it also reproduces some of the earlier contradictions underlying the medical management of diverse forms of suffering. As we've seen, in some ways cosmetic surgery is the heir to psychoanalysis, assuming the task of treating another kind of suffering that falls outside narrower biomedical definitions of illness. Many Brazilian plastic surgeons profess a particular sensitivity to the subtlety of mind-body interactions. Indeed, they avoid the Cartesian "dualism" that medical anthropologists and others have argued underlies an ethnocentric, sexist, and ultimately dangerous notion of health (Bordo 1993). And while psychoanalysis has often encountered difficulties in healing working class patients, plástica claims to be a more encompassing form of healing.

Ana Regina is one of three psychologists who work at Santa Casa, performing a psychological "screening" of all cosmetic surgery patients. She says, "My work here is not to prevent people from doing surgery; it's to support them while they do it. It's very rare I say they can't do estética." For one, she and some surgeons out of a genuine sense of empathy find it hard to refuse patients. Some patients were at the point of tears or else seething with anger when the professor balked at approving their surgery. Ana Regina adds, "And for the poor therapy is often not an option." Even if psychotherapy were more widely available, patients might still opt for plástica. Psychological worldviews—and treatments—have often been thought to be less prevalent among the working class in Brazil (Duarte 1986). Among her wealthier clientele, "who have access to other lives, cinema, theatre, consumption of everything," there is more willingness and ability to experiment with diets, exercise, and nonsurgical cosmetic techniques. The poor, she says, "prefer surgery." The idea that psychotherapy is not an appropriate or effective treatment for the working class goes back to the foundations of psychoanalysis. The "talking cure" offered to men suffering from shell shock was significantly limited to officers; the older "therapy" of electric shock treatment continued to be used on the common soldier (Gask 2004: 14). This class dynamic is ironically echoed here: psychotherapy becomes a luxury for the cultured, while plástica is offered as part of a basic right to health.

Pitanguy's writings reveal some hesitations in finding the "right" kind of neurosis for the cosmetic surgery cure. But when we look at clinical practice, different problems emerge. As one historian puts it, medicine is a "practice detached from what people say about it" (Clavreul 1983: 29 in Schwarcz 1999: 245). Medical writings in many specialties have often spectacularly failed to convey the unstable mixture of science and improvised technique that characterizes practice. And so, drawing on fieldwork in hospitals where I shadowed residents in their daily routine   and observed operations, consultations, and lectures — I now explore the *application* of the therapeutic rationale in clinical conditions.

: : : : : :   **HOSPITAL SCHOOL**

If I tried to conjure a mental image of a Brazilian plastic surgeon I might picture someone like Dr. Marcelo. He is maybe fifty, with a thick moustache and manicured hands. Dressed in a cream linen jacket and tie, he has a blandly masculine manner without being particularly good-looking. He is the kind of doctor who is excellent at putting his patients at ease, and has a flourishing private practice in the South Zone. He receives me in a consultation room that resembles a successful psychoanalyst's office more than the spare, fluorescent-lit rooms of public hospitals. Lying next to an issue of *Vogue* on his coffee table I notice a copy of *Plástica & Beleza* magazine (figure 5), its glossy cover featuring a silicone-enhanced actress in a white bikini. I ask him what he thinks of the publication.

"They kept calling the clinic everyday, and so I agreed to a couple of articles." He sighs and then adds, "But I don't think it's a good idea to advertise, so that's the last one for me." We get into his car and drive to Hospital Lagoa, a large public hospital where he directs the plastic surgery ward. His driver waves to a security guard and takes us straight to the clinic entrance. I ask Dr. Marcelo what he thinks about estética in public hospitals.

5. *Plástica & Beleza*: "The magazine that will change you."

"Theoretically, all surgeries are *reparadora*. A kid with 'donkey ears' doesn't want to go to school. He has an altered self-esteem, and surgery is not optional. It's the same with a woman with a fallen breast and a husband who doesn't want to have sex with her. Or who brushes her teeth and looks at the bags under her eyes and feels old—they're all reparadora."

Nevertheless, he is more conservative than some of his colleagues in authorizing surgery in the public sector. "Take, for example, a flat-chested woman who won't screw with her clothes off," Dr. Marcelo adds. "She *is* indicated for a breast implant. But not here." Her surgery is necessary for her self-esteem, yet not necessary enough to justify the use of public resources. "You see the residents get confused sometimes and don't know what is cosmetic and what isn't. A young resident promised this girl, the daughter of a hospital janitor, silicone here. But I couldn't allow it. If you attend her, you have to attend the families of 200 workers—because they all want surgery."

Here a resident, joins in: "Yes, especially the breast."

The conversation is interrupted while a woman serves us hot cheese bread and coffee. "Except her," Dr. Marcelo adds, "She is already so beautiful."

"But doctor I do want plástica," the snack vendor says, putting her hand to her chest.

"I don't believe it!" he says.

"*Quero silicone*" (I want silicone), she replies laughing. As we leave the ward, Dr. Marcelo says, "There has been a brutal increase in the demand for estética. This is a problem. Patients think everything is possible. They have this philosophy of the masses: the beautiful live, and the ugly die."

"So is there no estética in the hospital?" I ask as we return to the first ward.

"No, I do allow some. Today, for example, is breast competition, a once monthly kind of raffle." We enter an examination room, where a group of seven women are standing in front of the residents, a couple of senior surgeons, and some medical visitors. He explains these neediest cases were selected from around forty candidates. The job of the residents is to choose three "winners," who will each receive a free operation.

"How do you decide?" I ask.

"Age, breast size, occupation. There is a preference for the oldest— or else a young girl with very large breasts. The wait is maybe five or six months." Dr. Marcelo walks up to one woman, and addresses the room of doctors. "See, they're not *gigantesco* but the effect is pendulous . . . so this is a preferential case."

Later a resident explains to me that the hospital performs some other cosmetic surgeries as well. He tells me that sus, the state health system, reimburses the hospital for each procedure according to a "book of codes." "The problem is that it doesn't include aesthetic operations." I ask him then how they are able to do cosmetic surgery. "For estética we just put down another code. For example, under the category 'benign breast neoplasma of conjunctive tissue and other soft tissue'—well the surgeon can put down anything that isn't bone." In fact, sus *does* authorize free liposuction—officially classified as "cosmetic"—for HIV patients taking antiretroviral medications. These pharmaceuticals cause distinct patterns of fat distribution, which do not necessarily cause pain or functional problems, but can create "emotional and psychiatric disturbances" (*O Dia* 2004).

Dr. Marcelo limited the number of cosmetic procedures performed in part because he was concerned about the "cooperation" of the surgical team in public hospitals. If the anesthesiologist doesn't agree with the medical indication for a cosmetic procedure, he may resent having to do work he sees as outside his job description (especially given very low salaries in the public sector). But other public hospitals have creatively sought out ways to increase the number of estética procedures. Dr. José Humberto, chief surgeon at Hospital dos Servidores do Estado, seems distracted when we meet. I ask him if he agrees with Dr. Claudio that cosmetic surgery is a "necessity." "Look, no one would put in a prosthesis when there's no need. There are women with a really fallen psychological factor. After having four children, the breasts are so shriveled and ugly, *defeituosa*—they have a physical defect. And so psychology gives the indication and the hospital gives the surgery." Though he defends a psychological indication for cosmetic surgery, he also draws on his technical expertise to comfortably discuss the "ugliness" of the maternal body. Like almost all surgeons, he does not comment on the fact that so many of these defective bodies are female.

I ask him then what was the ultimate rationale for providing estética within a federally funded hospital. But he has a simpler answer than Pitanguy and Dr. Claudio: "Scientific training. The residents need to practice." Dr. José Humberto abruptly excuses himself from the interview, turning me over to a first-year resident who takes me up to the operating rooms, where I observe him perform his first "correction of the Negroid nose." The resident tells me that though cosmetic procedures officially should account for no more than 15 to 20 percent of all plastic surgery in the ward, the number can be much higher, more than half the total.

::: 

Brazil's plastic surgery residency programs, with their unique opportunities for training in cosmetic procedures, attract applicants from around the world, particularly Latin America and Europe. At Santa Casa, for example, I met residents from Italy, Switzerland, India, Mexico, Peru, and Columbia. In the United States, plastic surgeons generally must acquire experience in cosmetic procedures through a lengthy apprenticeship in a private practice, whereas in Brazil residents perform cosmetic surgeries beginning in their first year. One resident described the sequence of procedures he learned: "During the first year we do one 'donkey ears,' one eyelid surgery, and one breast. Second year, one each of nose, face, breast, abdomen, lipo, and one prosthesis. By the third year, we are doing everything." One European resident at Santa Casa told me had performed ninety-six surgeries during his third year of residency, of which 90 percent were cosmetic. "There is nowhere else in the world," he said, "where I could have gotten that kind of experience in so short a time."

The presence of estética in the public sector is perhaps an open secret. Though many Brazilians seem unaware of the residency programs' existence, newspaper articles have described them, and knowledge of opportunities for surgery spreads by patient word of mouth. In any event, surgeons certainly do not hide the fact that public hospitals offer a "place to have experience" in estética. Such experience is extremely valuable, particularly in Brazil as surgeons in the public sector are poorly paid. Many doctors say they are drawn to the specialty simply because it offers a "more just compensation," as Dr. Márcio put it.[13]

The ample opportunities for training in cosmetic surgery, surgeons say, have contributed to Brazil's reputation for excellence in the field. "It's like a restaurant," one senior surgeon explained. "The faster the turnover, the better the food." It was, in fact, the need to provide "scientific training" to new generations of surgeons that swayed the federal system to authorize estética in public hospitals. Of course, residents "practice" what they are learning in any medical specialty. Does the provision of cosmetic procedures in public hospitals simply create what one surgeon called "a game where everyone wins—the resident gets experience; the patient free surgeries"?

Dr. Rubens was the only surgeon who requested not to be identified. A member of the Society of Ex-Students of Professor Pitanguy, he was part of

Rio's first postgraduate plastic surgery class of 1959. I went to see him at his private clinic, housed in a pleasant tree-lined street. He told me about a lecture he'd heard at a medical congress. "[A surgeon] showed a post-op photo of a woman whose face was crisscrossed with scars and was applauded for having the courage to show his mistakes. And it was like 'Look what could happen to any one of you.' But I knew what his training was. I knew he didn't have the background in estética."

"But why couldn't he get the training?" I asked.

"Until the 1970s," he explained, "most public hospitals only did reconstructive operations. But surgeons in the public hospitals wanted to do it as well. In those days, though, almost all estética was taught in Pitanguy's school, and these other surgeons had not studied with him. How were they going to learn?"

In Portuguese there's an expression, *pra Inglês ver*, "for the English to see," which means an official, whitewashed view (originally to deceive British warships interfering with the trans-Atlantic slave trade) (Fry 1982). As Dr. Rubens spoke, it seemed as if he were revealing a more complex reality than the "English version" I had previously been shown. "They learned by practicing," he continued. "They opened the doors of the public hospitals to estética because they didn't know the techniques. They brought a surgeon in from Argentina to demonstrate a facelift. But you know I assisted facelifts for five years before I started doing them? How are you going to learn from [assisting] one?"

: : :

Plastic surgery is associated with a number of risks and complications. Liposuction can cause intestinal lesions or pulmonary edema. Tissue around breast implants may harden. Facelifts can result in necrosis of skin and infections. And coma and death are always a risk in procedures requiring anesthesia. At public hospitals, despite often aging equipment and infrastructure, surgeons claim that the rate of complications is low. As Dr. José Humberto told me, "Over the past three years, doing about 1,200 plastic surgery operations per year, there has been only one complication. Five percent of patients complain. Of these, half choose to reoperate. Look, there are risks, but at least in hospitals there is a life support system—most private clinics don't have these." And in fact, most of the deaths due to cosmetic surgery result from liposuction performed outside a hospital, leading one magazine to warn its readers against playing "Russian Roulette" with plástica (*Corpo à Corpo* 1998). Higher risks in the private sector may be due to aggressive cost cutting in a highly competitive market (*O Globo* 2001).[14] One successful surgeon, Dr. Lívia, said that clinics could only offer such remarkably low prices by cutting corners, "for example, by reusing a silicone implant, sterilized of course."[15]

The growth of plástica has also been accompanied by a rise in malpractice cases, insurance fraud, and media stories of horrific complications (Gonçalves 2001).[16] In 1996 30 percent of medical complaints were filed against plastic surgeons (*Veja* 1996b). According to the Federal Council of Medicine, in 2001 plastic surgery became the medical specialty with the most malpractice suits (*Veja* 2002). There is no legal mechanism to prevent doctors who are not certified as plastic surgeons from performing cosmetic procedures. Of the 130 doctors who applied for membership in the Brazilian Society of Plastic Surgery in 2000, only half passed (ibid.). I was told by a surgeon that in Brazil's vast, underpopulated interior, "specialization is a luxury."

Brazil provides a "good working environment," surgeons say, compared to the United States or Europe. One resident remarked, "Patients here do not feel they have the right to pursue a malpractice suit." He linked this to a cultural trait: "The Latin patient is friendly, more open, more sentimental. This is better for us because even if the patient is not satisfied, she is less likely to sue." He admitted this relationship can lead to problems: "They don't tell patients about all the complications, because they're afraid of scaring them off. They are less concerned about lawsuits because of this Latin relationship." In the United States, patients must sign a form saying they understand the risks of surgery—a formality often dispensed with in Brazil. In public hospitals, which often have very short consultations, some patients were uninformed about the possibility of complications or were even unaware that operations would leave a scar. When complications do occur, surgeons sometimes blame the patient's "response to surgery." Or else, patients simply blame themselves. One woman said, "Plástica is a lottery. Because of the first operation I had to do others, and others and others. They cut the nerves. It was an elaborate and sad road. . . . I was one of the rare ones who failed with plástica."

While the rate of complications in public hospitals may be low, a surprising number of patients I meet are seeking a *retoque*, a touch-up.[17] In 2001, 10 percent of plástica procedures aimed to correct errors created by previous cosmetic operations (*Folha Online* 2001). In fact, due to the subjective nature of body-image, it's not always clear whether a resident botched the job, or the patient is simply disappointed with the results. Aside from the quality of the surgery, Dr. Rubens raised another question: Are scarce public healthcare funds being diverted from other purposes? Most graduates of residency programs in public hospitals—who often receive stipends from the government—go on to open private practices. Public and private sectors are thus linked in a feedback loop. Public hospitals train residents, who then open lucrative private clinics. These experienced surgeons attract wealthier patients, including sometimes celebrities, who enhance their reputation. "Famous plásticas," as they're called, fuel demand in the public healthcare system. Whenever Pitanguy appears on television, Santa Casa receives phone inquiries from around the country.

: : :

What happens when a "First World," luxurious, or frivolous medical good (depending on one's point of view) is appropriated by a "needy population"? Straddling boundaries between public and private sectors, plástica incorporates global innovations but also produces local ones out of unique opportunities for practice. Yet patients too adopt an experimental attitude as they seek out a medical good in conditions of scarcity. Some surgeons complain about patients who misunderstand the true uses of plastic surgery, but these "bad patients" also expose problems with the therapeutic rationale.

I meet Mariza in a waiting room at Santa Casa. She is thin, with wavy brown hair and dressed in a loose blue blouse and pants—a uniform. She tells me she works as an elevator operator in a nearby office building. She arrived at the hospital at 4:30 this morning to beat the lines. A planned tummy tuck had been postponed when doctors discovered she had a myeloma. I ask her why she is back in the hospital then. "Oh, after all that waiting, I didn't want to lose my place in line. I decided to do a lifting so as not to lose this opportunity." Cosmetic surgery is ostensibly a cure for suffering associated with a *particular* area of the body. Mariza, however, does not only want to remove an aesthetic "defect"; she is attracted to what she sees as a rare "opportunity" to consume a highly desirable medical good. She says her husband thinks the idea is *besteira*, foolishness. "But my sister gives me support. It's because she wants it too, but she's afraid. Her friend did it at a cheap private clinic and came out with Japanese eyes." Mariza pulls the skin on her cheeks, laughing mischievously. "So now my sister's waiting . . . to see how mine comes out!" She laughs again, "*Sou a cobaia*" (I'm the guinea pig).

Whereas in more elite circles, patients seem to feel that discussing complications is in bad taste, in public hospitals patients often possess a remarkable sang-froid at the prospect of surgery. Not only do they describe procedures in graphic detail, but they also openly relish the black humor they see in stories of plástica that *deu errado*, "went wrong."

"She found the clinic on the Internet, and after the surgery her nipple fell off her body. She had to do a tattoo of a nipple."

"Instead of getting a "pear waist" [the narrow waist and wide hips that are the ideal], she got a pear breast." (The group laughs.)

Apparently amused by the unholy mixture of animal and human, one patient announces that a nurse had "died after having liquid silicone injected into her buttocks with a veterinary needle."

Dona Ecila finds a captive audience with the story of a friend who had a tummy tuck "for a very reasonable price" at a clinic in a poor suburb. "And?" her companion asked.

"She looked gorgeous," Dona Ecila says. Then she lowers her voice, "with her clothes on, nê?"

"What happened?"

"Her bellybutton came out in the wrong place. But she was happy. I wouldn't be, though. Your skin—you might not know if it is in the same place as before. But your bellybutton, you know."

Another woman compares plástica to having an abortion (which is illegal in Brazil): "Pay R$2,000 and you get one 'well done'; pay 300 and you get, well . . . what you pay for."

I came to think of these stories as a kind of "medical grotesque." As in the description by Mikhail Bakhtin (1994) of humor in premodern festivals there is a focus on the same "low" parts of the body: the nose, belly, lips and teeth, buttocks, breasts, and genitals. As a source of shame or disgust the body can humorously subvert "lofty" and "official" discourses: not only clerical ones, as Bakhtin shows, but also the medical, psychological, and consumer ones of the beauty industry.

Cosmetic surgery has always been to some extent an *experimental* practice, developed on the fringes of mainstream medicine by brilliant innovators and not a few quacks. From paraffin injections at the beginning of the twentieth century to Gore-Tex nose implants at its close, the safe techniques and materials of one era appear, with historical hindsight, to have been dangerous experiments. The experimental attitude among early beauty doctors to an extent survives, both among some surgeons in teaching hospitals, and among patients faced with a wide range of cosmetic medical, pseudomedical, and home treatments. For example, liquid silicone is an industrial oil injected with wide-gauge veterinary needles. Shunned (now) by medicine, it is applied mainly by male *travestis* (male transvestites) who inject up to twelve liters of the substance to give themselves the wide hips and ample thighs and buttocks admired in Brazil (Kulick 1998, Denizart 1998). But many women have used it as well, to fill in wrinkles, or enhance the feminine forms prized by travestis (some patients at public hospitals come to have hardened lumps of silicone surgically removed).

Compared to the spa-like, sometimes luxurious ambience of private clinics, public hospitals tend to have more boisterous environments. Patients turn waiting rooms into clearinghouses of information on the labyrinthine world of estética. Rumors circulate about which hospitals are offering which operations. Results of health exams or (often too-brief) consultations are meticulously deciphered. Preferences for implant sizes, residents, or operations, are collectively discussed. Determined to fix earlier surgeries or acquire new operations, patients negotiate hospital bureaucracy with enthusiasm and sometimes cunning, while often accepting "mistakes" with a fatalistic resignation. Sometimes pent-up frustrations and desires for surgery can lead to more drastic actions.[18] Some patients burst into tears when an operation is refused, increasing pressure on surgeons to perform a procedure they might otherwise deem unnecessary—a move that recalls the "scandals" created by some expectant mothers in public hospitals to force an Ob-Gyn to perform a Caesarean delivery (Béhague 2002). Most patients certainly do not seek out pain. Nevertheless, some seem to have a particular kind of aggression toward the body. A resident at a public hospital told me of a case of a candidate for a breast reduction burning her breasts (so that her case would pass from the estética to reparadora category).

Patients sometimes perform a kind of *aesthetic triage* on themselves, ranking defects by their severity to create a mental list of which operations are most "necessary." Their interactions at the clinic can alter—or expand—this list. Some simply choose the operation that has the shortest waiting time at the moment they arrive. Rachel wanted to have breast implants, but then settled for a nose job because the wait was too long. In order to give residents equal exposure to different surgical techniques, the hospital limits the number of breast surgeries offered. Raquel said she was "happy" with the results of her nose job, though it is not clear that she would have had the operation if she had been able to have breast implants (which she intends to have eventually anyway). In this case, the pedagogical needs of the hospital interfered with the therapeutic rationale.

Early on in fieldwork, I learn to ask right away if this is the "first plás-tica." Even those who have yet to have their first operation sometimes plan a series of surgeries: "Logically, after I do the breasts, I will do the belly, do a lipo. All that bothers me I will do, because you begin to like yourself more." When I ask what they want to have done at the hospital, one re-sponse I get is simply "Todas as plásticas" (All the plásticas). The medical specialty presents the "scalpel slave"—the patient addicted to surgery—as an anomaly, a contraindicated patient. Yet in fact, clinical interactions ini-tiate patients into a technomedical culture, which alters their body-image, anxieties, desires. In some cases, this means an "elaborate and sad road" of complications. In others, the patient is merely dissatisfied aesthetically, and compulsively comes back for endless "touch-ups," "little things," "little pulls" (*retoques, coisinhas, puxadinhas*). More commonly, the patient does ex-perience the sought-after boost to self-esteem, and is "superhappy," "more of a woman." Even here, though, when it would appear the patient's desire has been realized, the very success of the cure can lead to repeat treatments in quest of ever improved health.

Aesthetic defects are notoriously subjective. Kathy Davis (1995) shows how the inability to objectively define them led to the cancellation of an ex-periment that made cosmetic surgery available in the Dutch health system. "The big secret of plastic surgery," according to a plástica guide published by a Brazilian surgeon, "is that the indication is made not according to medical necessity but to the desire of the patient." In fact, I was often un-able to guess which procedure a patient wanted, an experience that Davis had as well while observing consultations. Even experienced surgeons, ex-perts in "beauty," are surprised by patient's "desires." In one consultation, a woman says she wants to "do" the breasts.

"Larger right?" the doctor asks. The patient is surprised.

"*Nossa senhora*; they are already too large." Then she adds respectfully, "For me."

The defect only becomes "operable" when the patient herself sees it, and *feels* it enough, to desire change. Despite the miraculous powers surgeons are said to possess, they are merely humble servants to the patient's tor-tured or at least bothered ego. Or at least they are in principle. While doing fieldwork, I realize that surgeons of course have their own aesthetic prefer-ences. Sometimes the surgeon is actually *less* critical than the patient.

"They're pretty," the surgeon says looking at her breasts after a candidate for silicone implants removes her T-shirt. The surgeon judges implants un-necessary because the woman's body is harmonious. Often, however, the surgeon's eye is more critical than the patient's. Carla tells me, "What bothered me most was this bone," repeatedly touching her nose as we speak. "But the doctor said my nose fell to the right. Funny I had never noticed this before but now I can see he is right."

Patients do not alter their plans for surgery under coercion, but neither can surgeons simply "follow the desire" of the patient because such desires are shaped through interactions with professionals. When the private and lonely struggle of "self-care" becomes too much to bear, the suffering is brought to an expert. Part of the cure perhaps comes from the surgeon's ability to understand the problem. The patient comes not just for an open ear, but also for judgment: "No you don't have to look like that. You're too young to have such flaccid breasts." The therapeutic process of plástica, then, is neither simply an objective evaluation of defects, nor a passive listening to the "complaint"; rather, it is a *negotiation* between the surgeon's expertise and the patient's anxieties and desires.

In his work on AIDS in Brazil, João Biehl (with D. Coutinho and A. L. Outeiro; 2001) analyzes how medical technologies affect sexual subjectivities. The government AIDS program rapidly increased the number of HIV testing centers, which attracted low-risk individuals who repeatedly had themselves tested in order to close the "open window" of risk (due to HIV-1 seroconversion lag). Such a situation creates new forms of sexual anxiety and morality, which return "to social reality as technoneurosis" (ibid.: 119). Plástica similarly shows the capacity of medical technologies to become fetishized as they are absorbed by patients in conditions of scarcity. On the other hand, this specialty operates largely outside the state concerns of monitoring and regulating populations. Rather than constitute life as a political object, it turns the body into an object of individual desire. Unlike psychoanalysis and the human sciences, it is not oriented toward knowing the truth of sexuality; nor does it depend on confessional techniques ("The plastic surgeon knows nothing, but changes everything"). This is, rather, a special form of medical healing in which the role of the diagnostician is played by the patient's own "desire."

The right to cosmetic surgery was never directly authorized by SUS, the state healthcare system. But through ingenious redefinitions of health, the assertion of "scientific" needs, and perhaps bureaucratic oversight, surgeons are able to perform cosmetic procedures in public hospitals. Although cosmetic surgery remains fundamentally "demand-driven," this demand—much of it rooted in desires and forms of suffering that take shape well beyond medical institutions—is also *useful* to surgeons. With their high turnover, ample opportunities for practice, and sometimes less-than-ideal operating conditions, public hospitals have enabled surgeons to develop what could be called a Brazilian "style" that is inventive and experimental.

As Dr. Adriano puts it, "I think in America, they have such good equipment that when surgery is not exactly as they planned, they get totally crazy. Here we work in messier conditions. Sometimes we don't have the proper equipment, and we have so many people to operate on. So we have to develop other, more flexible techniques. In the end, it's good for innovation." He seems to be echoing a central theme in Brazilian identity that underlies diverse social forms, from the *jogo de cintura*, "waist game" (making do in difficult circumstances) to the "beautiful game" of soccer. "Messiness"—a standard trope of Third World backwardness—is turned on its head, to become creativity and resourcefulness, tinged with just a touch of mischief.

While this surgeon may be boasting, Brazil's residency programs are in fact well regarded internationally. A British visiting surgeon at Santa Casa marveled that two operations were performed simultaneously in the same operating room, without appearing to have "an adverse effect on infection rates, which were well below two percent." He was even more impressed with surgical skills: "I was humbled by the beautiful results obtained with basic instruments in the hands of truly experienced surgeons trained in a master-apprentice relationship" (Lloyd 2005: 4). However justifiable the pride Brazilians take in the renown of their plastic surgeons, these teaching hospitals do raise questions about the social conditions that make "innovation" possible. The nationalist celebration of surgery hides how class inequalities and transnational relationships shape the development of scientific expertise. Brazil's public hospitals subsidize not just a booming private sector of cosmetic surgery; they also influence the growth of cosmetic surgery in other nations as foreign surgery residents spread the techniques and "philosophies" of Brazilian surgeons. And the rise in numbers of young surgeons with expertise in cosmetic surgery is driving down prices, making Brazil a prime destination for medical tourism. Vacationers traveling to Rio for a facelift may little suspect that the snack vendor who serves them a hot dog on the beach provided their surgeon with the scientific training that enabled him to open a private practice.

The next time I go to Santa Casa, it's a Friday, which is the day of the "surgical plan," a pedagogical discussion of technique led by a senior surgeon. Patients are called one by one into the lecture room and asked to expose the relevant part of the body. Residents sit at tiny school desks under a ceiling fan that ineffectually stirs the humid air. They take turns leading the examination under the watchful eye of Dr. Afonso, a man with a thick, gray beard addressed as *professor* by the residents. I find it hard to follow all the technical discussion, and as the morning drags on, I become sleepy in the stifling heat. Then, after a seemingly endless stream of routine estéticas, the group encounters a more difficult case.

Ludmila is a seventeen-year-old seeking a breast reduction and lift. Unlike most patients who try to demonstrate their bravery through a friendly, cooperative manner, Ludmila has a sullen expression and refuses to make eye contact with Dr. Afonso. Her shoulders are tense, her arms folded over her chest. Dr. Afonso tells her to lift up her shirt, but pauses to ask a woman standing at the back of the room if she is her mother. (Minors can't be examined at the hospital without the presence of a guardian.) I turn around to see a small woman with short hair, her color, like her daughter's, one that would fit into the all-expansive category of *moreno*, brown.

"Why?" she asks, but without waiting for an answer, pulls up her T-shirt. Sensing her discomfort, Dr. Afonso does not, as he usually would, pinch her breasts on the sides to simulate the effect of the lifting.

"How many kilos are you going to lose?" he asks. She mutters something. The mother seems embarrassed and tries to explain.

"Doctor, it's really hard. She has back pain." She pauses, then adds helpfully, "Her *auto-estima* [self-esteem] is low."

"ok get dressed." He takes Ludmila's hand and holds it firmly under his arm, a gesture he often performs with patients who are nervous.

"With obese and overweight patients—" He turns to look at Ludmila, and adds reassuringly, "And you're overweight, not obese. With these patients we can operate. But if they lose another ten kilos they lose it in the whole body, and the breasts become flaccid again. The ideal is to wait until you're the weight you want."

At this point she bursts out, "Wait? I've been waiting on line for three years."

"Well, we could operate now and then if you lose more weight, you'll come back for a touch-up. So what do we do?"

"I want the operation now."

Dr. Afonso signs her file, then polls the room after Ludmila leaves, asking for a show of hands from those who agree with him. The group is split in half. Some residents argue that a bad attitude disqualifies her from surgery. Others doubt her breasts really are large enough to cause discomfort. Becoming visibly impatient, the professor cuts the discussion short.

"I was fat, I am fat, I will always be like this. I've done everything. And her? She is not pretty, she has low self-esteem, and she's poor. And you think she'll lose weight? The reason we operate is not because of her back. She's hunching forward not because her breasts are too heavy but because she's ashamed. Her principal illness is poverty."

In public hospitals such incidents are rare. Dr. Afonso's outburst was perhaps a spontaneous expression of the frustration that some doctors and psychologists experience. Even if they are daily thanked for performing their miraculous cures, some surgeons wonder if they are not putting their powerful techniques to inappropriate uses. Indeed perhaps it is the very gratitude, whether considered to be normal or pathologically exaggerated, that leads some surgeons to quietly speculate: Are the povo really suitable candidates for cosmetic surgery? That day the diagnostic circle widened, as it were, from the exclusively psychological focus of the therapeutic rationale, to encompass another source of suffering.

Trying to understand the causes of Ludmila's illness, the different diagnoses she was given (back pain, low self-esteem, and poverty), and how cosmetic surgery became the preferred treatment, I trace connections between the suffering individual body and the body politic. I take as a point of departure an insight of Mary Douglas (1970) that the body is a microcosm of society. Politics is corporeally inscribed and inhabited, while bodily suffering acts as a metaphor for larger social ills. Plástica locates suffering in an ego that is diagnosed and treated in separation from the larger political and social field. Yet during fieldwork I found that appearance anxieties linked to the larger world of competitive labor and sexual markets, as well as to consumer aspirations, also enter into the clinic. I approach aesthetic defects then not only as products of a lack of harmony between the patient and "her own image," as Pitanguy (1985) argues, but as "symptoms" of a larger social disorder. So while surgeons believe the aesthetic defect is located in the patient's psyche, and imply that they are treating a psychosomatic disorder, the aesthetic defect is also *sociosomatic* (Kleinman and Becker 1998: 292): produced by connections between mind, body, and society.

I also take loose inspiration here from a body of work which, like plástica itself, one might say grew up in the ruins of psychoanalysis: theories that analyze "desire" as a social field in capitalism (e.g., Deleuze and Guattari 1983; Lyotard 1993). I start from the premise that the desiring psyche is a political and economic entity and that political economy is thoroughly invested with consumer and sexual desire. This approach will be useful for tracking how the notions of *self-esteem* and *rights* can surface in diverse social spheres. Used by doctors, NGOs, beauty corporations, and everyday consumers, these notions become interwoven with various institutions and naturalized as cultural common sense. Rather than focus on "unmasking" medical and beauty rhetoric, I instead read it against changes in the material and symbolic structures that define labor and consumption in Brazil. In earlier sections, I situated cosmetic surgery within a larger medical and psychological landscape. Here I switch focus, analyzing the therapeutic techniques of beauty in relation to the market identifications of consumer capitalism. The "right to beauty," I argue, can shed light on larger changes in notions of rights, as well as the significance of appearance in this era of market reform. I focus here on the period beginning with Brazil's democratization in 1985. During an era of privatization, deep market stratification, and growing social aspirations, beauty culture becomes an arena of self-governance.

: : :

While the expanding beauty industry made the innovative leap of defining beauty as a right, it did so in a time when "rights"—and the notion of citizenship on which they're based—have changed. When President Cardoso was inaugurated in 1995, he announced "the end of the Vargas era." His comment referred not to the demise of the populist dictator in 1954, but rather the end of a *paradigm*, which Elisa Reis (2000) characterizes as statist, nationalist, and Developmentalist. The Vargas regimes (1930–45) initiated a period of state-directed industrialization known as import substitution that aimed to replace foreign with domestic goods. Brazil did experience high GDP growth during much of this period, especially during the "miracle years" of 1968 to 1973 (Fishlow 2000: 5). Despite political turmoil, the period from the 1950s to the oil shock of 1973 was a period of optimism. As two Brazilian scholars remembered it: "Many imagined that we were witnessing the birth of a new civilization in the tropics, which combined the material conquests of capitalism with the persistence of the character traits that distinguished us as a people: cordiality, creativity, tolerance" (Mello and Novais 1998: 560).

Yet the historical trajectory toward a consumer society has been highly controversial in many Latin American nations because it sometimes involved political repression and pronounced market stratification (Mello and Novais 1998, Rebhun 1999, Reis 2000). For example, Brazil's military dictatorship (1964–85) justified its subversion of democracy by making a tacit pact to provide expanded access to consumer goods for the middle-class, while establishing a tax system that was detrimental to lower social strata (O'Dougherty 2002, Filet-Abreu de Souza 1980). Moreover, the state invested heavily in the southeast, provoking massive internal migration. But migrants and their children often found it hard to enter the formal economy and receive the social rights a signed work card confers. Many—Ester's mother and Dona Firmina, for instance—became maids or worked in the informal economy, settling in the favelas that have multiplied in cities such as Rio, São Paulo, Recife, and even the utopian capital.

There is, of course, disagreement about the legacies of "modernization" in Brazil, but many agreed that by the 1980s Brazil and other Latin American nations had entered a new historical era, often referred to as "neoliberal." *Neoliberalismo* had a positive meaning in Brazil when it first entered into public debate in the 1989 elections. Presidential candidate Collor de Mello equated the term with the end of the big government corruption of the past and made expanded access to consumer items a political issue (Karam 2007). Dubbed "Indiana Collor" by the first Bush White House (clearly recalling the action hero, not the archaeology professor), Collor de Mello in a sense *embodied* neoliberalism as a new political style (García Canclini 2001: 118). Photographed jet skiing or embracing a fashion model, he projected an image of efficiency, youth, and even masculine vigor (O'Dougherty 2002: 149).[19] He was impeached for corruption, and *neoliberal* would eventually come to have primarily negative meanings in most of Latin America. But the privatizations, open markets, and accords with the IMF and World Bank have been maintained by the later regimes of presidents Fernando Henrique Cardoso (1994–2002) and Luiz Inácio "Lula" da Silva (2003–) (Karam 2007: 7).

The term *neoliberal* can be problematic. Applying it indiscriminately may flatten regional differences. Its use may also implicitly project a contrast with a former golden age with more vibrant social relationships. The nation-state, of course, remains a powerful actor. Even a neoliberal one can take an active role in recognizing new groups of citizens with rights (Biehl 2005). The black movement, for example, has welcomed new affirmative action policies—while others have interpreted such identity politics as yet another aspect of neoliberalization. In any event, *neoliberal* remains a crucial local category of critique, present anywhere from university conferences to favela graffiti. I retain the term to refer to the historical period beginning in the mid-1980s, and focus not on macroeconomic policies but on the expansion of a market logic into new realms of social and biological experience. The broad question I'm interested in here is what kinds of social relations are emerging as the state shrinks, confidence in nationalist modernization wanes, and collective fantasy life pulses with the images of global consumer culture? Although this is admittedly inchoate terrain, I argue that such a broad approach is necessary to move beyond the psychological interpretation of the aesthetic defect and understand its links to broader changes in cultural citizenship.

: : :

Gisele tells me to meet her at Bar oo, a *moderna* place with frosted glass tables and young waitresses instead of the middle-aged men with mustaches who wait tables at more traditional restaurants. Now thirty, she looks back on her career as a moderately successful TV actress and model: "I remember when I was sixteen I was doing an audition for an ad, and I didn't fill out the bra. And the make-up artist said, 'Put in silicone! Put in silicone!' And that's when I went looking for a plastic surgeon." Though she's suffered many complications, Gisele says, the implants "totally changed my life." "I was happy. And I began to work more. I could do jobs I couldn't before. Like lingerie ads." The commodification of appearance—to put it somewhat clunkily—in the field of advertising is obvious. But plástica can be linked to work aspirations and anxieties across the socioeconomic spectrum.

In the waiting rooms of public hospitals and the cheaper private clinics, I meet patients who are either students or who work in a broad range of occupations, especially service work: receptionists, maids, cooks, hotel staff, vendors, telemarketers, events promoters, waitresses, secretaries. Aline—a twenty-four-year-old breast implant candidate—is a regular reader of magazines such as *Plástica & Beleza*. After seeing an ad for "plástica on the installment plan," she went with a friend to a cheap private clinic close to her home in Rio's North Zone. "I chose it because it was the cheapest. You could parcel the bill up to eleven times. I went for a consultation, and they gave me a price." At R$3,000, however, Aline thought the surgery would still have been a large "sacrifice." Then she decided to try Santa Casa.

I meet her while she is waiting in line for her psychological evaluation. Like most patients she adopts a matter-of-fact tone discussing her surgery: "When I go to the store and I can't use certain clothes, I feel outside the market. It's something for my work because they really demand a good appearance. I pass through a selection for each job I get, and the better I am . . . I'll have a return on that." Aline does product promotions, such as handing out cups of Gatorade at bars near Rio's South Zone beaches. The job pays well, she says, at least fifty reais a day, but work is irregular and there are no benefits. She's been doing it for five years, hoping to save enough money for a cheap, private college where she will study marketing.

"Lots of girls apply to the company, and we're selected by the body and appearance to do the events and promotions."

"Does this bother you?" I ask.

"I want to improve myself. After the breasts, I'll do a lipo on the saddle-bags and 'little tires.' I'll be able to wear uniforms that I couldn't before."

"Will you earn more money?"

"I think so . . . ; no one's going to hire someone who will ruin [queimar] the image of the product. They contract the best they can. And in any case, it will boost my self-esteem."

During a period of slow growth in the 1990s, the beauty sector has surprisingly thrived (O Estado de São Paulo 1997). A study showed that 44 percent of women in São Paulo spend more than a fifth of their salaries on "beauty," with the most poor in this group spending proportionally more (Dweck 1999). In 2007, Brazil had the world's third-largest cosmetics and personal hygiene market, valued at US$10.6 billion (Brazzil Mag 2008). Despite an overall rise in unemployment, employment in beauty professions doubled from 1985 to 1995. In fact, the only area of the beauty industry that declined in the 1990s was the barbershop, a traditional place of masculine sociability, as men began to frequent unisex beauty salons (Dweck 1999).

The growth of the beauty industry reflects not simply a "competitive work environment," as one economist argues (Dweck 1999), but also the changing significance of appearance and labor. Populist regimes had linked citizenship to industrial labor (implicitly male). The enormous state enterprises were engines of Brazil's modernization, while the factory worker—

an idealized symbol of Brazil's future—gained new social rights denied to other Brazilians. The privatization of the state companies beginning in the 1990s not only reduced the number of public employees, but also signaled a departure from an earlier mode of citizenship (Novelli and Galvão 2004). Many jobs in heavy industry, which had since the Vargas era offered expanded citizenship to the poor through a signed work card, have disappeared, while real wages fell (Sansone 2003).[20] The growth of the service sector and informal economy was also related to the larger presence of women in labor markets (Georges 2003; Goldenberg 2000). Moreover, there has been a relative shift away from labor and toward consumption and leisure as arenas for defining identity, especially for youth. In the state of Bahia, Lívio Sansone (2003: 34) found that older generations identified each other by trade (e.g. "Maria the laundry woman") while their children found such work shameful. One such area of consumption and leisure of special importance to this generation is "beauty": "For girls the main alternative [to formal employment] is a conspicuous use of the body, charm, and beauty (or knowledge of how to create beauty), either by working as seamstresses . . . or hairdressers (beauty parlors are springing up like mushrooms everywhere in Brazil) or by 'catching a man'—one who shows his affection by giving her presents" (ibid.: 36).

For those who work in the service sector, traits such as appearance, age, color, and sexual allure can "add value" to the service—or become hiring criteria (Fry 2005: 267–69). Across all occupations men and women who are more attractive than average enjoy a higher income, while the economic penalty for the below average is even higher (Hamermesh and Biddle 1994). In service interactions, the worker becomes, in a sense, part of the product that is being offered to the customer. These conditions present fertile ground for anxieties about appearance.

As I chat informally with patients about their operations, a wide range of problems and aspirations enters into the conversation. Aline—who said she felt "outside the market"—and Gisele embrace plástica as a way to boost income. Others worry about job security, or else hope to break into a new market. This is particularly true for those who work—or aspire to work—in occupations where appearance is a professional asset: from restaurant hostess to *mulatas pra exportação*, women who work in traveling samba shows. Some credit plans for plástica are specifically marketed to low paid service workers and domestic servants. Master Health, which finances 2,600 surgeries a year divided in up to eighteen small payments, "targets a clientele made up of secretaries, office assistants, and maids" (*Istoé* 2000, *Época* 2000).

Even in occupations where appearance may seem to count for little, anxieties can be "projected" into a perceived aesthetic defect. Zé, one of few male estética patients, had a nose job at Santa Casa. The surgeon said there was a "good result," but Zé wanted an additional operation. At this point he was referred to the hospital's psychologist, who discovered that he blamed an "ugly, wide nose" for being turned down for a job as a city bus change collector. The psychologist did not mention his color at first, but when I asked she said he was *negro*, black.[21]

As Zé's case suggests, work anxieties also reflect Brazil's color hierarchies. Color continues to act as a bar in some job categories, especially for women (Caldwell 2007, Lovell 1999). The *boa aparência* (good appearance) stipulated in some job announcements is a euphemism for "white or comparative lightness." In Rio, the term replaced statements of an overt preference for whiter workers in the 1940s and '50s (Caldwell 2007: 66). While recent liberal laws on racial discrimination prohibit such advertisements, appearance can be disciplined in informal ways in hiring practices. As Luiza said: "Employers want a 'good appearance.' I think I have a good appearance. But to participate in a training course, or job competition, you have to be *branquina* [whitish]." Color is a provisional classification in Brazil, subject to adjustment—hence the saying "Money lightens." By the same logic, subtle cosmetic changes may nudge a job hunter a little closer to a good appearance.

Ana Regina, a psychologist working at Santa Casa, believes plástica can have a therapeutic effect, but questions whether it's the right "therapy" for the poor. After the steely confidence of most surgeons, it is a relief to hear some ambivalence. One problem, she says, is that patients approach plástica as a means to "solve other problems": "The most poor want to enter the work market and think that estética will help . . . ; they think it will open doors for them. Or they are just afraid of getting old, of losing a job. Because she is a receptionist in a hotel and she imagines everyone is looking at her and saying she's ugly. They say, 'I lost my job because they think I'm old.'"

: : :

The growth of beauty industries reflects not just new labor markets, but also perhaps a more subtle shift in notions of rights and *cultural citizen-*

*ship*, a term that includes the broader beliefs and practices surrounding the sense of belonging to a collectivity (Flores and Benmayor 1997). One of the great paradoxes of political democracy is that many Brazilians feel less secure than they did during the dictatorship (Holston 2008: 271). Gang and police violence linked to the drug trade became a permanent part of urban life. In 1992, a particularly lethal year in São Paulo, military police killed 1,301 civilians (compared to 27 in New York in the same year) (358). Those who could afford to retreated from public space, living in fortified enclaves and relying on privatized security. Brazilian cities represented to the world some of "the most shocking landscapes of adjacent wealth and poverty" (Caldeira 2000: 254–55).[22] The World Bank ranked Brazil—the last country in the Western hemisphere to abolish slavery—first in the world in income disparity in 1996 (O'Dougherty 2002: 66).[23]

During a period of rising violence and insecurity in cities, many consumers increased their purchasing power and gained more access to credit (in Brazil many small, everyday purchases can be made in parceled payments) (O'Dougherty 2002). The ideology of credit is implicitly a utopian one: it transcends the social distinctions created by property by extending the availability of commodities to all. Credit also integrates consumers into a commodity-based social order through a combination of "social mythology and brutal economic pressure" (Baudrillard 2005: 176).[24] In Brazil, consumption became a central but also unstable basis of middle-class identity as inflation eroded wages and bred a proliferation of consumer tactics. In these circumstances, a consumer lifestyle takes on a particular political meaning.

In the United States, plastic surgery became in the postwar period essentially a middle-class phenomenon, one more aspect of the "good life." The American "middle class" is almost a mythic category, in which most can try to stake a claim to membership (DeMott 1990). In Brazil, on the other hand, the middle class is often viewed as a minority group with a precarious identity (though middle class *consumption* is often projected by media as the national norm).[25] (A closer parallel to the American notion of "middle class" might be the term *moreno*, brown, an encompassing color term and keystone in the "myth of racial democracy.") Ideologically, it is an achieved status, rather than a default position.[26] Though *Globo*'s vision dominates airwaves, many are excluded from the "lifestyles" it portrays. For example, a favela resident could tease her sister with the term "*Patriçinha* without money": that is, a status-conscious, "preppy" shopper who "buys into" the cultural meaning of brands without being able to afford them. This situation is one in which middle-class consumption is symbolically central in the public sphere, but often an elusive goal.

During a period when many felt there was a shedding of the social fabric, democracy also opened up a political space for new forms of "insurgent citizenship" and identity-based rights (Holston 2008). The human rights movement turned its attention to the criminal justice system—though often with mixed results, as it was denounced for promoting "privileges for bandits" (Caldeira 2000). Women's groups successfully took "feminism into the state" (Alvarez 1990). One of the most vibrant forms of social activism grew out of grass-roots struggles to legitimize urban peripheries that had been built by migrant workers (Holston 2008). These efforts gave birth to new notions of "rights-to-the-city" that would transform political discourse in Brazil. As Holston (2008: 255) says, "Today, everyone talks about rights."

Such changes in citizenship combined with massive market inequalities and delegitimation of judicial institutions created a new political climate, one where notions of rights can move from official contexts and resurface in surprising new ones: from everyday civilities to medical aesthetics, consumer culture, and gang talk. Since the 1990s drug cartels known as *comandos* have had a major presence in public life, attacking police stations, government buildings, buses, and local businesses. Combining anticapitalist idealism and brutal methods of torture, they consider themselves to be officially "at war" with the state. But their public pronouncements strangely echo the new rights talk common in NGOs and state institutions. In 2003, for example, a statement from the Comando Vermelho wonders whether there is a "crime more heinous than killing a nation with hunger and misery," and concludes, "ENOUGH, we only want our rights" (in Holston 2008: 301, 308). Police leaders explicitly mock the notion of human rights. Comandos respond by appropriating the still politically alive concept of rights to show the brutality and incompetence of the state. In both cases, rights show a remarkably plastic nature, acquiring a new political valence in different contexts.

The comando leaders ape the revolutionary language of leftist militants, perhaps due to a former policy of incarcerating political prisoners together with common criminals. Yet consumer culture is perhaps an equally important source of identity for the youth recruited into gangs. One effect of Brazil's neoliberal turn has been a change in the political significance of consumption. Markets opened to foreign commodities (and the subcultures linked to them). During this period, the categories of citizen and consumer became blurred. As faith in the "state as a powerful actor" declines, identities take shape within communities of consumers (García Canclini 2001: 45). When Vargas addressed the "workers of Brazil" by radio, he was expressing a particular vision of the body politic. Labor was reimagined as the essence of working-class citizenship, not the source of stigma it still retained after centuries of slavery.[27] In contrast contemporary media publics are more often interpellated as consumers by national and global markets (Ortiz 2000). Collective memory "vertically" linking generations through notions of nation, region, or blood is partly replaced by relationships between citizens "horizontally" connected in the every-changing Now of consumer culture. A pair of *Gangue* jeans, a rainbow flag, a Nokia, a tattoo— such brands and symbols cross older social and ideological divisions. They are perhaps a kind of "white noise" interfering with the clarities of class consciousness and primordial identifications. Some of this identity work transpires in spiritual and ethnic domains, but much of it belongs to an aesthetic and erotic sphere that values idealized femininity and masculinity, sensual bodily expression, and the shock of the new.

In this "universe of beauty," class identities can be reshuffled. As Brazil is inserted into the global economy as an important market, younger generations become better informed about the world. Access to cosmopolitan global culture, traditionally concentrated in the elite, has broadened (Parker 1999). Compared to older generations, poorer youth mix more with the middle class, frequent the same areas of the city as them, and share interests in a resurgent global black culture (Sansone 2003). On the other hand, there is a chasm between the possibilities offered by a diversified mass media and the means to realize them. The decline of communitarian identities has the potential to undermine collective political action. On the other hand, this shift reflects not only depoliticization, but also perhaps the loss of ideologies that legitimated authoritarian regimes and patriarchal moralities. In any event, appearance, style, and sexuality are central to many forms of identification flourishing in this historical period.

While beauty culture collapses some social differences by creating images of sexual desirability that hold wide appeal, it also differentiates consumers by their market position. As JD, an aspiring rapper, put it, "My dream is to use music to bring down barriers, win in life, make a revolution. Go to a *shopping* and buy something for my son without discrimination, have an imported car. Because I can't, because I'm black. I want to drive around in that big car and people say, 'Look there's that big black with the big car!' That's my dream. Rights for all." When citizenship is defined through consumption, rights can be resignified as the ability to acquire prestige items, while the antidote to social exclusion is imagined as market participation.

Talk of rights can thus signify other changes in the meaning of citizenship. A maid speaks of a right to beauty, a mother of a right to a Caesarean, and an unemployed favela resident of the right to a big car; a comando leader declares at a congressional hearing, "I am a person who fights for his rights . . . ; where is the state?" (Holston 2008: 307). These are not just degradations of rights, but also responses—parodic, angry, hopeful—to political transformations. They speak to the delegitimation of older political ideologies as well as to the centrality of a new expansive notion of health essential to the good life. And when an ad for a plástica financing plan promises the realization of a "consumer dream," in just 120 minutes with liposuction, it is tapping into the hopes and desires of a dream world of mass consumption.

Like some other rights, the right to beauty reflects larger tensions between the universalist aspirations of democratic political discourse and the marketization of new spheres of social life. But if plástica is offered as a "right," it is often embraced by patients as a *gift*. A consumer service that was once a luxury becomes invested with the mystique of modern medicine and the glamour of a luxury consumer service. Beauty practices can then offer a means to compete when anxieties surrounding new markets of work and sex mingle with fantasies of social mobility and glamour.

In this light we can perhaps see the emergence of self-esteem and rights as *therapeutic technologies*. They reflect not just the beauty industry's marketing hype, but also a mode of self-governance adaptable to diverse ends such as social activism, economic competitiveness, psychological healing, and sexual realization. Patient-consumers who work in informal and service economies, who live in privatized urban zones with limited access to municipal services, nevertheless find they can tap into social resources in the form of pap smears, Caesareans, tubal ligations, HIV tests, pharmaceuticals, and aesthetic medicine—offered for free or through various forms of subsidy (Béhague 2002; Biehl 2007; Caetano and Potter 2004; Gregg 2003). Surgeons often ask, does the surgery (i.e., aesthetic improvement) compensate the scar? Yet there is another compensation at work. The right to beauty compensates for other rights that have not been realized. And plástica compensates for the other interventions, the Caesareans and hysterectomies, that "take their toll" on the body. This partly explains the eagerness, even cunning, with which patients approach plástica, to finally get what is theirs. If they have not fully realized their citizenship, they can still remake themselves as "aesthetic citizens" as they experimentally use medical technology to negotiate markets of work and sex and pursue an often elusive notion of health.

: : : : : :   AESTHETIC HEALTH

During fieldwork I was sometimes struck by the sheer ingenuity (my father would say chutzpah) of the plastic surgeons' reasoning. They invoke the "progressive" notion of health defined by the World Health Organization, implying cosmetic surgery is part of a larger effort to treat the psychological and social determinants of disease. Like psychoanalysts, they suggest their methods of healing escape the narrow dualism of orthodox biomedicine. They even embrace an "anthropological" relativism (Pitanguy 1992: 264). Renouncing (officially) the role of a Paris or Pygmalion, a judge or sculptor of female beauty, the plastic surgeon is instead a "confidant" and healer of mental affliction.

In the glossy pages of *Plástica & Beleza*, in the aesthetic and economic negotiations of clinical practice, and in the social fantasies surrounding plástica, we have seen how this vision runs into contradictions. Although it's true that diverse societies have sought to perfect or improve the human body, I have argued that aesthetic defects have a particular significance for capitalist subjects in their dual nature as workers and consumers. In deregulating, globalizing economies, and in various sexual "markets," appearance is a form of *value*. In these conditions a diverse range of complaints can become "symptomatized" as aesthetic defects. Plástica enables the aged, the abandoned, the unemployed, the nonwhite, the unloved, to *name* their condition an aesthetic defect and objectify it in their bodies. The ugly, those who deviate from the average, have often been punished with some kind of social exclusion. There now seems to be an almost inverse process of reclassifying the socially excluded as "aesthetically suffering." Health has often been seen as beautiful; here beauty becomes healthy.

Beauty industries, however, also minister to the dreams of the consumer. With its powerful clinical and consumer visualization of the body, plástica taps into the aspirations of people on the margins of the market economy. A social imaginary of medicine as a modern good incites demand, as women in different market positions internalize the visions of mental and sexual well-being underlying enhancement technologies. Brazilian plastic surgery then is ironically coming full circle from its origins in the late nineteenth century, when the specialty rejected the experiments of "beauty doctors" in a bid to become legitimate medicine. The expansion of plastic surgery's scope has been made possible in part by technical improvements. But Brazilian surgeons go further, questioning the moral distinction between "vanity" and "necessity." As Dr. Claudio argues, "There is a great difficulty in knowing what is cosmetic and what is reconstructive." An implication of this reasoning is that once aesthetic problems are diagnosed as defects, they become not body-image problems *felt* by the patient but simply body flaws *seen* by the surgeon. Sagging breasts and "Negroid noses" become analogous to the congenital defects and injuries that reconstructive surgery treats. Plástica not only corrects flaws and heals psyches. It also produces them as surgically treatable.

Beauty industries target individuals with needs at the ostensibly universal stratum of female health. Yet market dynamics shape the social use of medical technologies. The popularization of plástica rests on contradictions between public and private sectors in Brazil's reforming healthcare system—reforms themselves shaped by the global movement of capital and ideas. The public sector subsidizes the development of scientific expertise, which then becomes a valuable commodity in the growing global market for "elective" surgeries. Such expertise, though, also powerfully affects its own therapeutic object: the patient's psyche. The doctor, a figure who historically possessed extraordinary social prestige, is here invested with new powers to understand and heal the suffering of the people. Patients do not passively accept his charity, but also assert rights to health, and learn to speak in the psychotherapeutic idiom of the beauty industry. In this experimental and didactic process, patients absorb clinical knowledge, thereby changing the nature of their suffering—and their hopes for recovery. Brazil's histories of the body and medicine then are not simply erased as a global medical practice takes root here; they also endure in the *availability* of the body to social commentary, medical experimentation, and technological intervention. Following a distinction made by Georges Canguilhem (1989), these conditions morally authorize medicine to *heal* rather than only to technically *cure* a particular kind of suffering.

: : :

Does plastic surgery then "medicalize" new spheres of human experience? Anthropology and other fields have critiqued the process whereby diverse values and practices are brought into the purview of medical technology and expertise. Biomedicine, together with a psychiatry aspiring to science, have created a range of new disorders: from histrionic personality to rejection sensitivity. Technology, experts, and drugs in many parts of the world play a role in women's experiences of sexuality and pregnancy (Martin 1987). And the "sick role" has become a means of resisting work regimes and participating in the redistributive politics of the welfare state. Drawing on notions of biopolitics and biopower (Foucault 1973, 1978, 1980), many studies have argued that medicine, psychology, and the human sciences act as normalizing institutions in modernity. In earlier periods, Foucault points out, "medicine related more to health than normality" (Foucault 1973: 35). Beginning in the eighteenth century, however, medicine increasingly defined a polarity between the normal and the pathological.

Plástica up to a point participates in this normalizing function of medicine. When the surgeon makes a "real indication," the patient's subjective perception acquires the objectivity of a physical defect. Yet plastic surgery does not just pathologize the body. For one, rather than monitor boundaries between normal and pathological, the surgeon must "follow desires." Although the physician is a trusted advisor and confidant, the diagnosis must be made by the patient herself. Plastic surgery works with a broader, "positive" notion of health, "not simply the absence of illness." In some ways, this vision of healing breaks with dominant medical models of health that prevailed for much of the modern period.

In fact, the medical profession initially viewed plastic surgery with suspicion because it seemed to threaten the efforts of other disciplines to understand and measure the human, such as criminology, anthropometrics, and phrenology. Gilman (1999: 27) argues that a "great social fear" in nineteenth-century Europe was that the "criminal, especially the Jew or black as criminal, would alter his appearance through the agency of the aesthetic surgeon and vanish into the crowd." Plastic surgery represented a dangerous power to change the "true" marks of racial degeneration and social deviance. Yet as the specialty gained legitimacy, this power to make the deviant "vanish into the crowd" became a humane capacity to treat individual unhappiness. Pitanguy (1976: 121) cites studies from the mid-twentieth century that correlate facial deformities with crime, but then argues that plastic surgery can help in the rehabilitation of criminals. More recently, Texan prisons have provided free cosmetic surgery to inmates to make the convict "feel better about himself." Raising "the level of self-esteem" reduces the risk of recidivism (Balsamo 1999: 181n). As a practice that either disguises or heals the criminal, plastic surgery disrupts, rather than defines, boundaries between normal and pathological. One slogan of the plastic surgeon then might be, reversing Freud's words: "anatomy is *not* destiny."

As medical power and paradigms expand, they absorb new demands. With its high prices, patient-dependent diagnoses, and sexy ads, plástica straddles consumer and medical worlds. Surgeons do not only "export" medical techniques and language into new spheres of experience; they also bring beauty into the clinic. Drawing on psychotherapeutic notions of health, biomedicine generates new regimes of self-management. Conversely, private regimes of self-management contribute to the rise of novel forms of biomedicine, such as plástica. The notion of biopower implies that modern medicine acts effectively as a form of politics by other means. But in some contexts, a disarticulation of medicine from state governance is also occurring. Plástica, thus, is a hybrid practice in which medical technology becomes infused with the desires of consumer society. Along with the medicalization of the body, there is what we might call a "demedicalization" of medicine.

Notions of medicalization or biopower can thus overstate the power of medicine. They can imply a hegemonic process of control, or overemphasize the role of states. Although these concepts do not inherently imply a loss of human freedom, many Foucauldian approaches stress the function of biomedicine as a form of discipline and social control. Foucault himself later distanced himself from the view that biopower was unambiguously pernicious (Rabinow and Rose 2006: 200). Yet in moving away from the social control argument, and towards an analysis of "technologies of the self," he was led to the ancients (1986). Perhaps Foucault didn't believe his contemporary world included any examples worthy of study. In any event, plástica and other enhancement technologies are examples of medical practices that do not often conform to the agendas of state biopolitics. For one, demand for plástica is growing during a period when there has been perhaps a general decline in collectivities as a statist and Developmentalist paradigm of governance loses steam (Reis 2000). State health budgets are shrinking, healthcare is decentralizing, and the private sector is growing. The state is not deliberately aiming to "aesthetically improve" the population. Plastic surgeons do not conduct epidemiological studies. And there are no support groups (or not yet) for the sufferers of "aesthetic defects." As opposed to "collective subjectifications" (Rabinow and Rose 2006), plástica is an example of an intensely "private mode of subjectivation," a means of seeing and working on the body as self. It reflects a new problematization of health, as an epidemiological and racial biopolitics is partially replaced by a psychological and aesthetic form of therapy. Ludmila's "illness" may have been poverty; nonetheless she experienced her suffering as a deficit in self-esteem that could be surgically corrected.

: : :

The Brazilian media celebrated the nation as "champion" of plastic surgery. To some observers, this was no doubt an ironic barometer of progress. Meanwhile, in the eyes of the world, Brazil is beginning to represent another kind of future. Anthony Giddens, for example, claimed that "if Europe fails, what awaits it is Brazilianisation": a future of fortresslike enclaves and the reign of youth violence (in García Canclini 2000: 38), a failed state and a failed modernity. But Brazil's culture of beauty challenges both the techno-optimism of surgeons as well as depictions of the nation as an infernal "past" to which Europe might return if it's unlucky. Brazil's history of matter-of-fact acceptance of racial mixing; its relaxed hedonism, free from the ghosts of a puritan past; its cannibalistic swallowing of the foreign without much hand-wringing about imitation and authenticity—this ethos indicates if not a model, then an attitude toward the dilemmas of globalization that other nations may, willy-nilly, be forced to consider. Brazil's leadership in "banalizing" plastic surgery also suggests that the transnational movement of images and technology is not always dominated by the West. Brazil may be not a country "always of the future," but one that is, in some ways, already there.

Critiques of enhancement technologies have tended to assume they originate in richer, Western nations, from which they may then migrate to other regions. Certainly an aesthetic logic does not seem immediately compatible with the public health agendas of developing nations. Yet the experimental ethos of Brazil's aesthetic medicine shows that peripheral regions can also be at the vanguard of medical innovation, as patients and surgeons adapt a global medical practice to local conditions, creating new philosophies of health as well as new opportunities for scientific training. The ethical questions raised by enhancement technologies concern not only the "posthuman"—the surpassing of a universal human biology—but also how sexual and class dynamics invest medical practices with a compelling therapeutic logic.

Perhaps what is more difficult to explain is not what is wrong with plastic surgery, but rather why demand is rising in many parts of the world, from Latin America to East Asia and the Middle East. One answer I think lies in the shared notion of "health" underlying plastic surgery and other innovative therapeutic technologies. Although Brazilian plastic surgeons may be pioneers, they do not simply pervert proper medical practice due to lax regulation in the "Third World," nor take advantage of some cultural propensity to vanity. Nor is plástica only a symptom of a larger denial of the reality of aging and death in narcissistic cultures (though it may also be that) (Lasch 1979). Rather, it is *productive* of new notions of health that clearly resonate with patients and define a new terrain for work on the self. I propose we call this particular vision of well-being, and the associated techniques and knowledge for attaining it, *aesthetic health.*

I use the term to refer to a qualitative notion of well-being that merges aesthetic, psychological, and sexual concerns, and often blurs distinctions between healing and enhancement. As opposed to what we might call a "digital" notion of health, which is either on or off, aesthetic health is "ana-logical" in that continuous improvement becomes desirable and possible.[28] I refer not just to cosmetic work on the body, but a form of therapeutics where quality of life and mental and erotic experience become proper do-mains of health subject to regulation throughout the life course. Here, we are on the border with psychoanalysis once again: mind and body are con-nected in a therapeutic feedback loop in need of continual calibration or maintenance work.

The notion of aesthetic health is quite explicit in a practice such as plas-tic surgery, but there are other examples in which aesthetics and health are entwined in subtle ways. In many emerging disorders such as male andro-pause, social phobias, and female sexual dysfunction, there is an implicit notion of well-being that is defined qualitatively. As we will see, one factor (among many) for high rates of "nonclinical" Caesarean deliveries is the "sexual-aesthetic motives" of patients (i.e., to preserve vaginal anatomy) (Carranza 1994). Among the side effects of antiretroviral drugs are dis-tinct patterns of fat deposits, which in themselves pose no major health risk but may be judged unattractive. These changes to the body can be-come incorporated into complex and tacit codes for recognizing HIV posi-tive men or "serosorting." The "aesthetic stigma" resulting from side effects can affect sexual behavior or decisions to begin a lifelong regimen of drugs, and thus become implicated in HIV treatment and epidemiology (Strong 2008). Other pharmaceuticals aim to improve a qualitative notion of well-being, from Ritalin used as "neuroenhancement" to SSRIS that subtly alter personality to sex hormones that boost sexual pleasure and performance (Kramer 1994). Prescribed to treat a recognized disorder, or else used off-label, many of these drugs are combined in experimental regimens by communities of users. A notion of aesthetic health is thus implicit in a broad range of body practices with a logic of self-optimization.

Pitanguy's vision of health is "aesthetic" too in that it seems to aim at a rather superficial realization of rights. Yet while for some observers plástica might represent a brazen example of medicine transforming social suffering into a mental problem, its expansive notion of well-being reflects the changing importance of health for modern selves. As the healing powers of modern medicine grow, it is perhaps inevitable that Enlightenment ideals of self-development and technological domination of nature will eventually apply to health as well. The democratization of aesthetic concerns in modernity also shapes a secular vision of well-being (Taylor 1989). Consider, for example, the Romantic notion that one's life can be turned into a work of art. This idea is reflected in the pursuit of health as a qualitative state, or in a view of the human body as malleable and perfectible material. Alternative health practices, such as Traditional Chinese Medicine and yoga—also popular in Brazil—emphasize inner experience and reflect the idea of an "art of health" (Schneirov and Geczik 1998). Such a merging of healing and aesthetic concerns is most evident in medical technologies that manage sexuality and reproduction. As the very phrase "aesthetic medicine" suggests, cosmetic aims become integrated within medical practices.

I have attempted here to situate plástica in relation to a medical, economic, and psychic landscape of late capitalism. Class identifications get redefined and reshuffled in the culture of beauty. New hopes and entitlements coexist with the starkest forms of market stratification, while medical practices are implicated in diverse fetishisms of the body and modern technology. In the next parts, I try to deepen this portrait, pursuing the same themes into the troubling and more intimate domains of racial aesthetics, family life, and sexuality.

# PART TWO

*Beautiful People*

The aesthetics of race is an uncomfortable topic. In part this is because many virulent forms of scientific racism have had a curious emphasis on beauty. In fact, the "scientific" typology of race, with its evolutionary lines of "degeneration," originated in the opinion of an eighteenth-century German naturalist that the inhabitants of the Caucasus region were "the most beautiful race of man" (Gould 1981). Perhaps, too, the social sciences find it difficult to approach something as chimerical and subjective as human beauty. When the aesthetics of phenotypic differences *are* discussed, it is often argued that color hierarchies simply reproduce social hierarchies. The beautiful are the socially dominant. The ugly are the socially excluded. Although this is undoubtedly true up to a point, such arguments in a sense make beauty an empty category, a domain of domination. Attractiveness cannot be reduced to a racial position. It is also a dimension of the self, and often a form of capital that actors *use* while moving through naturalized systems of privilege. This perspective will help us to grasp the specificity of the Brazilian case.

Pierre Bourdieu (1977) brilliantly showed that the capacity of social theory to expose the denuded machinery of power is ironically limited by the very distanced and abstracted understanding of lived experience that makes critique possible in the first place. The category of race in Brazil is a good instance of this paradox. Some researchers have found, to their dismay, that simply the attempt to discuss race (*raça*) is viewed as racist by interviewees. In many contexts, Brazilians may not think in terms of race at all, but rather colors or types, *tipos*. While race is an amalgamating concept suitable for official contexts such as statistical analysis, tipos is an atomizing one often used in everyday life. The poet Antônio Cícero (1995) puts this well in his oxymoronic concept of a race comprised of a single member: the idea here being that mixing between Portuguese, Africans, Indians, and later immigrants, produced a kaleidoscopic range of phenotypic variation that resists categorization. Whether this view is false consciousness or represents a different cultural organization of difference is a vexed question. In any event, the relational, contingent, and strategic nature of color identifications is crucial in Brazil. For this reason, I find it hard to exclude what may seem like an anomalous case, someone like Preta Gil.

I am peering at a video monitor, sitting next to Veronica, associate producer of a reality TV segment on Globo. Veronica is logging the video time code of Preta's rehearsal for her dance performance to be recorded in São Paulo on Sunday. We hear a voice through the monitor speakers: "*Meu silicone explodiu*" (my silicone exploded), Preta jokes after a particularly rigorous move. In a spiral notebook, Veronica scribbles down entry points of the "scene" along with a brief tag line. This is the kind of joke that might go into the montage of outtakes and bloopers. The show's concept was invented by a Dutch company and sold to Globo: a group of celebrities train in a different style of partner dance, which they then perform live on the popular variety show *Domingão do Faustão*. In Reality TV style, each week a panel of judges eliminates one couple. This week the dance style is Forró, a northeastern style that sounds something like a polka on speed with heavy African percussion. Preta's father Gil, a Baiano (from the northeastern state of Bahia), has recorded some of the most popular Forró hits in Brazil.

"Do you think Preta will make it into the next round," I ask Veronica. She nods her head.

"Because she is popular with the judges?"

"Because she's dancing well," she says.

"Who has already been eliminated?" I ask Veronica. "There was a *gostosinha* [a little sexy one], and someone from *Big Brother* [the Brazilian version of the reality show]."

After the rehearsal we head in a golf cart (as in Hollywood's studios, used to traverse long distances between studios) to Globo's canteen. There are endless *beijinhos* interrupted by only snatches of conversation. Guilherme, a blond romantic lead in a popular new novela, improbably chats with me in Russian-accented English, which he is imitating from cable TV, while a former supermodel breathlessly describes a party at Buzios resort that she missed. Preta nods at a table of portly middle-aged men—screenwriters I surmise—surveying the scene over cups of espresso. We veer off to an empty table and set down our trays of cheese bread and sodas. As we dig in, Guilherme reaches into Preta's pocketbook, pulls out a tiny edition of the New Testament, and begins a dramatic reading. Guilherme interprets the moral of the passage as something to the effect of "inner beauty triumphs." I look around the room, which seems to positively radiate beauty of another kind, but no one seems to perceive any irony in the lesson. We leave the studio and get into a yellow cab. The driver, a whitish man in his twenties who turns out to belong to Preta's church, reaches over his shoulder to offer his hand.

"This is Nando, my *faz tudo* [do all]," Preta says. "It's for security; it's more discreet. I decided to buy a taxi instead of a regular car because there's less chance of being carjacked. And then Nando can drive it at night to make extra money. It works out for everyone, right Nando?" I see him nodding his head in the driver's mirror. As we head out in the rush-hour traffic to a shopping mall, I ask her about her very unusual name, which means simply the color "black."

"The idea was my Dad's. He went to register my name as Preta, but the official wouldn't let him. He said I had to have a Catholic name too, and so he put down Preta Maria on my birth certificate."

"What did the other kids think?" I ask.

"I always knew my name was special because in school kids teased me. When I was six I wanted to change my name to Priscila. But later I realized the importance of my name, all its symbolism, and I got more attached to it . . . ; I formed a lot of my personality on my name." As Preta keeps talking, this story of coming to racial consciousness becomes more complicated. She was teased as a child because *preta* can have pejorative connotations. As she got older, however, some people rejected her name simply because "she didn't look preta." (Preta's mother is of European descent and has straight, blond hair.)

"As soon as people see me, for them I am *mulata*, or *misturada* [mixed]. I have straight hair. A kid once said to me, 'You shouldn't be called Preta; you should be called *Marrom* [brown].' And she was right, marrom is a color that has more to do with me."

"But I *am* negra [black, refers to people], I am preta [black, refers to people or the color of a thing], and I call myself Preta. But I hear this often, 'You are not preta.' And I say, 'Of course I am preta. My father is preto. My grandparents are pretos. My great-grandparents are pretos. I am negra, because I am of the black race. I have it in my blood. Just look at my nose!'"

This certainty about her racial identity came to Preta later in life—despite her name and her father's exploration of North American "black music" in the 1970s. As a child, Preta adds, she often felt confused:

Caetano [Veloso[1]] gave me the nickname Filipina, always called me Filipina, Filipina. And I went searching to see how the women of the Philippines looked, and I saw they really have this dark skin underneath the eye. I saw that I also have the Indian in me. Once when I was a kid, we passed on a bus ride through a region with lots of Indian villages—in that time there were many more than today. When we got off and I saw them, I had a hysterical attack. I was crying and crying, and my parents couldn't understand. 'What is it?' they said. I said, 'You came to leave me here! They are my parents, you aren't my parents!' I thought they were returning me to my tribe.

: : :

Preta's story of shifting racial identification illustrates aspects of Brazil's cultural common sense of color—as well as new challenges to it. The voluminous literature on race in Brazil often mentions a "folk taxonomy of appearance" (Hasenbalg and Silva 1999; Telles 2004). Rather than grouping people into races defined by ancestry, the so-called rainbow of color terms describes subtle variations in appearance along a continuum. It contrasts with the American "one drop of blood rule" that divides people into blacks and whites, with people of mixed ancestry placed in the group with lower socioeconomic status. The Brazilian system tends to work in the opposite direction: people of *some* African ancestry may be described with a range of terms including *white*.

This cultural system of perception partly explains why Preta's friends were puzzled by her name. With brown skin and straight hair, Preta could be described by numerous terms in everyday speech: *misturada* (mixed), *morena* (brown), *mulata*, and so forth. In fact, as some of her friends implied, the one term that ironically seemed wrong was *preta*, as this would be reserved for someone of "unmixed" African ancestry. This cultural logic becomes more explicit when we recall that Preta's father—a man almost universally known in Brazil—would normally be described as *negro*, black. Given the fact that she is Gil's daughter, why then this reluctance to see her as preta? But this is precisely the point: phenotype, in the traditional color taxonomy, counts for more than origin. If she *looks* marrom, mulata, or morena (brown), then she *is*—regardless of ancestry, or her first name for that matter.

There is, though, another reason for her friends' reaction. *Preta* can have pejorative connotations in Portuguese. It is often "softened" by putting it in the diminutive form, *pretinha*. In some contexts it can sound harsh, which is presumably why her father chose the name: to affirm black pride and draw attention to the racist implications of this taxonomy. His efforts, along with those of a generation of black activists, have begun to bear fruit. Black social movements have rejected "color terms" and embraced a bipolar system. In their view, morena, and worse, mulata, are terms that show racial alienation. The term *negro*, on the other hand, affirms racial pride. (This solution, however, does not deal with the question of racial identification for the vast numbers of Brazilians of some indigenous ancestry—a point that is often missed in the contemporary debate.) This particular politics of appearance enables "conversions" to a black identity. Doing fieldwork in favelas, I heard several stories of people who were born *morena* (brown) or even *branca* (white), and later "discovered" and affirmed a black identity by doing activist or community work. Often the conversion was accompanied by learning about Afro-Brazilian history, exposure to popular culture of the Black Atlantic, and significantly, beauty work that affirms self-esteem.

Despite these efforts by the black movement, the older, folk taxonomy of color persists. Preta's friend said, "You are not preta, because you don't look preta" (the logic of phenotype). Preta responded, "I am negra, because I have black blood" (the logic of ancestry). Preta was raised in an artistic milieu where a black identity might seem to be a matter of course. Yet even there she had to negotiate between a hierarchy that aesthetically prizes brownness over blackness and social movements affirming black pride. This is clearly not just a linguistic issue: the debate over color terms is occurring during a period of radical experiments with affirmative action.

Preta spoke of her personal negotiation between appearance and identity, but she is also one of a small but growing number of black media "personalities" that are changing the social significance of color. To understand these changes, I first discuss the place of mixture in a longer history of nation building. Female beauty is not only a theme in Carnaval marketing or fantasies of sexual life "beneath the equator." It has served, as well, as a key symbol in the ongoing political and cultural reimagination of racial mixture (*mestiçagem*) as crucial to modern Brazilian identity.

:::::: **MAGNIFICENT MISCEGENATION**

In recent years, there has been a growing interest in racial mixture in many parts of the world. *Creolization* and *métissage* have become metaphors for talking about globalization or challenging the racial classifications of identity politics. Eurasian and other mixed-race models, for instance, provide fashion with the shock of the new. But in Brazil racial mixture, mestiçagem, is neither chic nor marginal; rather, it is a dominant theme in twentieth-century politics and culture. (I use *mestiçagem* to refer to a cultural paradigm that represents the nation as racially mixed and which deemphasizes clear racial boundaries between groups.) Now, as Brazil experiments with multicultural policies—perhaps signaling an end to mestiçagem—it seems like an auspicious moment to reflect on the significance of this form of race relations.

What I am interested in here is not only the status of mestiçagem as an ideology, but also what is remarkable about this paradigm when compared both to the racial thought in Brazil it displaced and to multiculturalism, another ideology that has become ascendant in the West. With its openly erotic and aesthetic flavor, and contradictory mix of egalitarian and hierarchical color judgments, mestiçagem may seem puzzling to the multiculturalist, who might conclude it is simply evidence of pervasive racial alienation. Yet whatever judgment one ultimately makes about Brazil's cultural common sense of color, I argue that it is necessary first to understand this belief system in its own terms. In doing so, we can also see how local meanings of race and beauty shape the global medical and commercial beauty industry as it takes root in a developing nation.

Although the recent resurgence of genetic research on race has for some observers threatened a revival of eugenics in the twenty-first century, for the moment at least, the biological sciences hold that phenotypic variations occur on a continuum, thus making it hard to meaningfully define "races" or subspecies in humans (unlike in some other animal species). If race is a social construction, then all the more so is mixed race. This point should not, though, lead us to deny the obvious: the phenotypic range of Brazilians reflects a high number of unions over the past five centuries between peoples who had previously been living in Africa, Europe, and the Americas. The historical fact of mixing does not, however, mean that mestiçagem is not also a *myth*, a central ideology and symbol in Brazilian aspirations for modernity.[2]

Before discussing the intellectual origins of this modern myth, I point out that it appears in many realms of Brazilian social life. Schoolbooks, for example, tell of the formation of the Brazilian people through the mixture of the "three sad races" (Haberly 1983): Portuguese, Africans, and Indians—or rather, they did until a few years ago, when school curricula began adopting a "multiculturalist" discourse emphasizing discrete boundaries between races (Ribeiro 2006). Mário de Andrade's great modernist novel, *Macunaíma*, narrates the adventures of an antihero who is born black to an Indian mother in the forest, then later magically morphs to white as he travels to São Paulo. Three races mingle too in the culinary symbolism of the national dish, feijoada: black (beans), white (rice), and red (oranges)

(Fry 1982). Family genealogies often proudly emphasize Indian, African, or European ancestry, however distant. Though she identifies now as negra, Preta speaks of a phase in her life when she was convinced she was Indian. Mestiçagem is not just a metaphor or ideology; it has played a central role in defining Brazilian national and family identities. But this was not always the case. To appreciate the novelty of Brazil's affirmation of mestiçagem, it is useful to recall the climate of racial thinking that preceded its arrival on the intellectual scene in the 1930s.

As the new sciences of man, including anthropology, took root in Brazil in the end of the nineteenth century, the elite had to confront "evidence" that racial mixing endangered the moral and physical health of the population (Stepan 1991, Fry 2000). The influence of such ideas obviously presented a problem to nationalist aspirations to turn Brazil into a modern republic. In response, Brazilians developed the ideology of *embranquecimento*, or "whitening": a hope that European immigrants would gradually lighten the population and enable Brazil to join the ranks of modern nations (Skidmore 1974). While it still reflected assumptions of white superiority, the whitening ideal was meant to challenge the "racial pessimism" of European science. It would soon be replaced, however, by a more radical reevaluation of racial thought in the 1930s, effected in part by the work of a scholar from Pernambuco State, Gilberto Freyre.

Freyre saw a different and more immediate solution to the problem of racial mixing: drawing on the authority of another new science, a nascent cultural anthropology, he simply declared it wasn't a problem at all. Freyre claimed that as a master's student at Columbia University he acquired from his mentor, Franz Boas, new ideas to combat the "Aryanizing theses" back home (Vianna 1999). In fact, Hermano Vianna (1999) shows that nationalist sentiment and admiration of Afro-Brazilian culture had *already* led Freyre to a conviction that racial inequalities had social determinants; the encounter with Boas helped give these ideas the stamp of science. The thesis that Freyre wrote contained in embryonic form the work that would appear over a decade later in 1933 as *Casa-grande e senzala* (The Masters and the Slaves), the first volume of a monumental study of "lusotropical civilization."[3] Ostensibly a historical account of life on Brazil's sugar plantations, it is also a carefully constructed attack on racial science that stresses the environmental causes of poor health. The work also can be read as an origin myth of the Brazilian people in its search for their meaningful (but not pure!) roots in the colonial past. (The fact that it also includes scientific and scientistic theory as well does not make it any less mythic—perhaps the creation of modern myths, from Marx to Freud, depends on just such a mixture of new science and literary finesse.) Freyre provocatively reverses the scientific discourse on "miscegenation" as he defends what he calls the "most ample miscegenation that has occurred in human history" (1986: 55).[4]

One doesn't have to read between the lines to see the eroticism in Freyre's reinvention of the Brazilian body politic. An oft-quoted passage, for example, has a tone of nostalgic recollection: "The female slave who rocked us to sleep. Who suckled us. Who fed us, mashing our food with her own hands . . . and the mulatto girl . . . who initiated us into physical love and, to the creaking of a canvas cot, gave us our first complete sensation of being a man" (1956: 278). Freyre draws on an eclectic collection of sources for this portrait of "sexual intoxication" in the colony: inquisition documents which, in their fastidious cataloguing of sin, read as a kind of Catholic Kama Sutra; the sexology of Havelock Ellis; Brazilian modernist painting and erotic poetry; and presumably his own proclivities and experiences. Freyre clearly seems to be enjoying himself as he reverses received wisdom. He claims that African and Indian men had inhibited sex drives (why else would they need drums and other inducements to indulge in orgiastic festivities?). The Portuguese, on the other hand, emerge as priapic cosmopolitans—to whom Indian, African, and mulata women are irresistibly drawn (as if to convince any skeptics, he adds that the Portuguese possessed larger sex organs than those of the colonized men). The "sexual excess" of Brazil as a theme in explorations of national character has been well noted (Bocayuva 2001; Parker 1991). What I want to highlight here is how this eroticism was often joined with a vision of the *aesthetics* of mestiçagem. Sexuality—especially across racial lines—becomes a key symbol for the formation of a new, mixed population with positive traits, such as cordiality and physical beauty.

Eugenics notoriously linked race not just to health and intellect but also to beauty (Gould 1981). According to the racial typologies of Carl Heinrich Stratz, a fin de siècle German anthropologist, only "Nordic women could be truly beautiful, because they alone did not arouse mundane sexual interest" (Hau 2003: 83). Freyre no doubt would have been amused by the philosophical assumption that underlies this claim. Stratz was perhaps working with a Kantian notion of beauty as disinterested contemplation. Freyre, who borrowed Friedrich Nietzsche's ideas of Apollonian and Dionysian cultural oscillations, also subscribed to the philosopher's "reversal" of Kantian aesthetics. It is not the separation of the erotic and aesthetic, Freyre believes, but their mingling in the human body that represents the truest form of beauty.

The image of Brazil as a *mestiço* society doomed by luxury and misery was still current in the 1920s, in books such as *Portrait of Brazil* (1944) by Paulo Prado. Overindulgence—provoked by nude Indians and mulata seductresses—led to tropical lassitude and physical exhaustion. Attacking this image of a population suffering from postcoital *tristeza*, Freyre paints a "sex-positive" portrait of the country that has persisted to this day in Brazilianist writing (Goldstein 2003). For support of then unconventional views, he points to modernist painters who, along with Freyre himself, reinvigorated the cultural and intellectual scene in the 1920s. Freyre (1986: 63) celebrates sensual portraits of phenotypic variation as a "maliciously innocent" attack on Europe's "Apollonian canon." For these modernist scholars, artists, and musicians, the path to modernity required an affirmation of the indisputable fact of racial mixture and cultural syncretism (Vianna 1999). Freyre's celebration of female beauty as a natural product of miscegenation was then part of a nation-building project that transformed mestiçagem into a potent symbol of Brazilian identity.

This discourse is a gendered one that remakes female beauty—once the property of the colonial patriarch—into a kind of national patrimony: "Magnificently miscegenated Brazil would easily gain first place in an international competition of the racial, inter-racial, and meta-racial colors of women's appearances" (Freyre 1986: 63). I return to the question of how such views are reflected in contemporary beauty practices and critiqued by black activists. But what is striking about Freyre's work is that at a time when Europeans were describing (with great seriousness) the racial purity of blond Aryan conquerors, Freyre was celebrating (with quite a bit of playfulness) the erotics and aesthetics of *impurity*.

Although the defense of nonwhite beauty has become familiar in the United States since the "black is beautiful" movement, Freyre's views are actually quite different from multiculturalist affirmations of non-Anglo ethnicities and races. Embracing the beauty of brownness should not stimulate racial pride but rather help to *transcend* racial consciousness as such. Morenidade distinguishes Brazil from North America and Europe, but also *unmarks* distinctions internal to Brazilian society: "Fashions need to honor a Brazilian mentality that is not just democratically interracial but *meta-racial*: that is, I insist, the Brazilian's overcoming of the consciousness of racial origins considered in their purity . . . by a type that is . . . cultural anthropologically Brazilian, nationally Brazilian. And darkly *moreno* [brown]. Meta-racially moreno (1986: 116)." This passage links two concepts central to Freyre's thought: *meta-racial* and *moreno*. *Meta-racial* is a neologism that describes a kind of blissful ignorance of racial origins "considered in their purity." Not surprisingly, the clunky *meta-racial* never made it into everyday vocabulary but *moreno* is one of the most common color terms used in informal speech.

Moreno refers to a range of appearances, from a European brunette to a person with African and/or indigenous phenotypic traits. The term leaves open—one might say deliberately—the question of racial origin. The term *moreno* illustrates the relational quality and egalitarian aspirations of Brazil's classifications of appearance (see Telles 2004 and Collins 2007 for discussion of the literature on racial and color terminology). Appearance can be defined contextually: responses to questions about color, for example, are affected by the color of the questioner (Sansone 2003). The census gives respondents a choice of five "color" terms. But in everyday speech, over 130 terms have been identified, with *moreno* and its variations (*moreno claro, moreno escuro, moreninho*, etc.) the most common (Levine and Crocitti 1999). In everyday life, terms like *moreno* can symbolize belonging to a mixed family or even a national population seen as mestiço (and often beautiful as well) (Baran 2007: 390; Burdick 1998). For Freyre, the concepts of meta-racial and moreno are linked: they both refer to a process of miscegenation that, by blending races, diminishes racial consciousness as such. On the other hand, as if by compensation, mixing augments national pride.

A common proverb, "money lightens," suggests that social mobility changes the perception of color. Color, however, is susceptible both to the *social* and to the *physical* environment. In the early twentieth century, Freyre spent his youth giving Latin lessons to his schoolmates (and dallying with a mulata maid), not taking sun on the beach. He interpreted the nation's later embrace of suntanning as a reversal of a centuries-long rejection of the tropical climate and new identification with brownness. Not surprisingly, he was a fan of the bikini as a badge of pride in brown beauty. Women of all social classes, "daughters of the sun," "Are embracing suntanning as an almost religiously aesthetic rite, which both overcomes the importance formerly attributed to social origins, and reveals . . . the positive aspects, in contrast to the supposedly negative ones, of a triumphant Brazilian miscegenation" (1986: 39). Displayed seminude, bronzed in various hues of brown, the body is partially stripped of its social markers. The sun itself then becomes for Freyre "browning and Brazilianizing," as it creates "ecological morenos."

His views on the importance of morenidade were in some ways prescient. The beaches along Brazil's coast, where the great majority of the
population is concentrated, attract 55 million visitors a year (Farias 2002:
263). Beach-going has generated its own specific habitus. The hedonistic
pleasures of health and display of the erotic body coexist with tiny nuances
of class and subculture. In Rio de Janeiro, beaches are divided into num-
bered "points," each one drawing a different crowd: from *surfistas* to *playboys* to *jurássicos* (middle-aged people). Within this differentiated world,
skin color—given or acquired—is sometimes seen as a democratic leveler.

In an ethnographic study of beach life, Patrícia Farias (2002) argues that
the term "bronzed" (*bronzeado*) occupies the top position in a hierarchy of
skin tones. It contrasts favorably both with "black" and "white" or "red as
shrimp" ("the punishment of whites who try to become brown"). The capacity to become brown marks Brazilianness, health, and beauty. It also has
democratic meanings. As a doorman who works in a wealthy condo puts it:
"I do what the people in my building do. For them the beach is just theirs,
but the beach is for all. When they see my color, all toasty brown like theirs,
I look like one of them. . . . Who sees me there can't even imagine my life"
(ibid.: 280). Another of Farias's informants argues that "the sexy Brazilian
blond is not [really] a blond. . . . The sexy Brazilian blond [*loura gostosa*] is
a black [*negona*] with white hair" (279). The blond is not "really white" because she is actually a negona, part of the racially mixed people. The notion
of the "black blond" echoes the belief held by Freyre (and some plastic surgeons) that "even whites" in Brazil are mixed, thus affirming hybridity as
an encompassing ideal.

Freyre opposed the dream of a future white Brazil with a paean to brownness. His praise of "miscegenated beauty," however, echoes eugenic discourse: "Whoever wants to understand the current Brazilian population
must understand the effects of both miscegenation and mansion-shanties
reciprocity. The great part of the Brazilian people is miscegenated, as if
miscegenation were accomplished through anthropologically eugenic and
aesthetic experiments. Experiments that avoided Africanoid exaggerations
as well as Caucasoid deficiencies in the protuberances of the body" (1986:
61). Freyre is claiming here that social conditions on the slave plantation
essentially created an experiment in accelerated sexual selection. As to
the "protuberances," he makes clear elsewhere in the text he is referring
to the *bunda*, a word of African derivation for "bottom." Freyre is clearly
replicating the colonial gaze on the female body, even if the old trope of
sexual decadence has here been given a positive spin. Despite his embrace

of the nascent culture concept, his thinking could be described as a kind of "inverted eugenics," where it is hybridity rather than racial purity that is beautiful.

The eroticization of race became a central dimension of the colonial enterprise in many regions. But the situation in Brazil—which gained independence in the early nineteenth century—is different. Here the objectifying gaze is internal, pressed into the service of a nation-building project, directed "defensively" against advocates of racial purity, segregation, and "Apollonian" whiteness. Freyre's celebration of mestiçagem, though, functions as a kind of compensatory nationalism. It establishes a national identity that offsets negative comparison to Europe or the United States made according to a liberal yardstick (Fry 2005). In the myth of mestiçagem, one might almost say that race is transcended by beauty and eros. Preserving but also inverting eugenic thought, mixing creates a corporeal type that blurs racial identities and forges a national one. Yet "triumphant miscegenation" reflects the persistence of eugenic thinking as well as informal color hierarchies that stigmatize blackness. Brown is beautiful partly because it avoids "Africanoid exaggerations." It is almost as if mestiçagem dissolves the category of race, only to reinscribe it on the "miscegenated body" (a tension that is repeated as we will see in plastic surgery).

Freyre's intellectual legacy has been fiercely debated. Critics charge that his work fostered a "myth of racial democracy" that masks racial discrimination (Hanchard 1999). In recent years, those who have objected to affirmative action, for example, have been labeled neo-Freyrians (Fry 2005). In the past few decades empirical studies have shown that darker Brazilians are excluded from a range of social institutions (Telles 2004). Moreover, Freyre's vision of history was not only nostalgic, but frankly revisionist in its treatment of slavery.[5] Although racism is more readily acknowledged today, the image of Brazil as a *país misto*—a mixed country, characterized by racial conviviality—is still popular, often affirmed in national media and everyday talk (Baran 2007). A not untypical example is the song "Etnia" (1996), by the Pernambucan group Chico Science & Nação Zumbi:

> We are all together a miscegenation [*miscigenação*]
> And we can't flee our ethnicity
> Indians, whites, blacks, and mestiços.

It's true that some activists have argued that mestiçagem should be jettisoned to allow for political mobilization around the issue of racism.[6] But before moving to a discussion of new black identities, I analyze how this cultural logic of race and aesthetics is reflected in contemporary cosmetic practices. How can beautiful morenidade encompass the nation yet coexist with color hierarchies privileging whiteness, especially "white" facial features and hair?

::::::    **THE NATIONAL PASSION**

We have seen how Freyre critiqued the racial pessimism of his peers to make "magnificent" miscegenation a key emblem of modern identity. The national enjoyment of female beauty, then, is part of a larger inversion of formerly negative symbols. These symbols continue to be ambivalent as they hint at both an unrealized potential to be modern and an alternative tropical modernity. Not only mestiçagem, but also female beauty is a kind of "populist myth." As one liposuction patient put it: "Our country is a country of pretty people. This miscegenation here gives us a different tone I think." Transcending race, class, and region, and embraced by men and women, it is *popular* in both senses of the term—"of the common people," and thoroughly enmeshed in sophisticated culture industries. Freyre's use of the nascent culture concept was shadowed by eugenic thought. Similarly, contemporary surgery reflects the persistence of eugenic ideas of racial improvement, as well as celebrations of the beauty of miscegenation. Beauty cultures thus reflect a particular kind of fetishism produced by the encounter of an older color logic with the intensive visualization and fragmentation of the female body in medical and consumer worlds.

Michael Hanchard (1999: 78) has argued that "Afro-Brazilian cultural practices" are paradoxically "residual and dominant"—in other words, they are influential in many spheres of civil society at the same time as darker Brazilians remain socially excluded. As an example of an "Africanism" that pervades everyday life, he cites a particular corporeal aesthetic of the female body that "emphasizes distinctly African considerations of physical attractiveness—large hips and buttocks, and a narrow waist, with little attention to breast size—as opposed to more Western standards of feminine beauty, which . . . favor small hips, a narrow waist, large breasts, and thin thighs."

Such a corporeal ideal is celebrated in different social realms. It explains, among other things, a distaste for "thin thighs" and narrow hips. In a short story by Monteiro Lobato, thin-hipped women are the victims of a scoundrel who gambles, correctly, that if he marries them they will die in childbirth, bequeathing to him their pensions (Queiroz and Otta 2000). It is true that in recent years, a few highly publicized deaths of fashion models from anorexia have raised the prospect that thinness, as in other parts of the world, is partly displacing a "traditional" corporeal aesthetic. Yet I also often heard evocations of such traditional ideals by women and men across social classes. Some female adepts of Brazil's *academias* (gyms) not only aim to lose weight; they engage in body sculpting that augments curves. Denise, a woman who lives at the top of Santa Marta favela, lamented that she was unable to afford to go to a gym, but then laughed, "Just going up the stairs, that's enough to *engrossar as pernas*, thicken the legs." Hanchard's claim that aesthetic ideals belong to a distinct erotic tradition is also perhaps reflected in the large range of slang terms, some of African origin, used to describe the "bottom": *rabo, traseiro, popô, rabicó, bumbum, tralalá, bagageiro, balaio, banjo, bomba, bubu,* and so on. Such "traditions," though, are inseparable from the intensive fetishization of female body parts in commercial mass media and medical culture. As Priscila, a favela resident and community activist, put it:

> The attraction is the bunda. The ideal is the *popozuda*. *Popô* is bunda; *popozuda* is *bunduda*. Even women think so—you look at a guy, even a nice guy, and then when he turns around, flat, like a table, he loses points. Carla Perez is an imbecile, but she has an enormous gyrating [*rebolanda*] bunda. You go to a *funk* dance, and there is a bunch of women *rebolando* their bundas.[7] [The band] É O Tchan, their music is junk, the words even worse, but they have a marvelous blond and a morena gyrating their bundas. So the Brazilian has a lot of business with the bunda.

As Priscila's comments suggest, the "bunda" is a frequent medium of commodity exchange. Photographs of the nude female body have become a ubiquitous feature of the cultural landscape in Brazil, to the point where a humor magazine, titled *Bundas*, featured a large, unerotic close-up of a naked posterior. The commercialism and sheer tedium of the televised culture of beauty has led to some critiques. A popular rapper, Gabriel o Pensador, mocks the "national preference" in a song called "Nádegas a declarar" (Buttocks / Nothing to Declare):

> But still you sign up for any Miss Bumbum contest [. . .]
> A-ahá! [the photos] will come out in magazines and the people
> will say you're an artist
> Because now the bunda is culture, it's sport

It's even philosophy, almost a religion
And if you're lucky, it could be your passport to fame
Or to bed, it could be your bread winner.

Like Seu Jorge's samba song about *siliconadas*, the lyrics seem to critique the commodification of sexuality as well as fantasies of using the erotic body as a means of social ascent ("passport to fame").

Hanchard's description of a corporeal ideal would ring true enough to many Brazilians, though they might be puzzled by his location of such an aesthetic in Africa, or even in "Afro-Brazilian culture"—a term that has been used only recently in Brazil. Rather, corporeal ideals are seen as part of a distinctively *national* tradition, itself rooted in a "biotype" more prevalent among the Brazilian population. A blue jeans company, for example, announced it was forced to modify its jeans sizes after an "anthropometric" study revealed that Brazilian women have shorter legs and wider hips than North American women (Queiroz and Otta 2000: 49). Calling the bunda an "acclaimed national product," the TV news show *Globo Repórter* (1999) told the story of a patient who "traded her bumbum, on the thin side, which God gave her, for another that a plastic surgeon molded according to the national preference." Plástica marketing explicitly invokes this notion of a national preference, or what Freyre (1984) calls the "national passion." Introduced to Brazil in 1986, the silicone buttocks implant has been promoted as a means to "conquer a typically Brazilian bumbum" (*O Dia* 1999) (figure 6).[8] Echoing Freyre's racial aesthetics, Dr. Raul Gonzalez (2007) claims that "it is indisputable that the feminine bumbum is a national preference reflecting the diversity of ethnicities that compose the Brazilian population. There was a mixture of the exuberant forms of the bumbum of the black race with the slender body of the Aryan." He offers a diversity of techniques for different "indications." Gymnastics "lifts" the bunda, Bioplastia "highlights gluteal projection," and *lipoescultura* "augments the volume of the buttocks."[9] While media coverage minimizes risks,[10] one surgeon warned potential patients: "It's a treatment insufficiently tested . . . which exists only in Brazil" (*Istoé Gente* 2001b).

It is difficult to say whether patients are swayed by this kind of marketing, but patients too invoke the notion of a Brazilian biotype. Regina explained her decision to have a breast reduction: "Because small breasts make a better combination with the Brazilian's structure. Look, she already has a large bunda and thick thighs. We're different, for example, from Americans, who have large breasts. If we had large breasts, it would be too

# sim
# não

**Dr. Luiz Carlos Martins**

O prof. Dr. Luiz Carlos Martins
é diretor do Centro de Estudos
de Cirurgia Estética de São Paulo.

Tels.:(11)3034-0808/3032-5161
/ 3814-9000

Entrevista com Jô Soares sobre prótese glútea

dera o marketing agressivo visando minimizar o ato cirúrgico de uma plástica estética, fazendo-a simples demais para o leigo, o que é um grande erro que deve ser severamente combatido. "A relação médico-paciente, na vigência de uma cirurgia estética, torna-se um ato de cumplicidade responsável. Ao contrário de um paciente que, por exemplo, sofre um acidente e necessita de atenção médica urgente, independente de onde ou de quem o atenda, a modificação estética pretendida pressupõe uma análise conjunta dos desejos do paciente e da possibilidade do cirurgião em atendê-los. Uma falha nessa análise conduz à inevitável frustração tanto do paciente quanto do cirurgião."

Toda cirurgia implica em riscos que devem ser claramente expostos e discutidos com o paciente. "Da compreensão da complexidade maior ou menor da intervenção proposta o paciente terá elementos para decidir se deve operar-se no Albert Einstein, por exemplo, ou numa clínica devidamente equipada".

Segundo o Prof. Martins, a relação médico-paciente em uma cirurgia estética é fundamental. ●

"O Luiz, além de competente, é carinhoso e humano com seus pacientes, que acabam, como eu, por tornar-se seus amigos." (Leila Cordeiro)

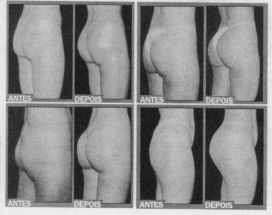

Plástica & Beleza 91

6. Dr. Luiz Carlos Martins promotes the gluteal prosthesis on the talk show *Jô Soares.*

much." Flávia received medical plástica in a private clinic, but had previously had liquid silicone injected into her buttocks by an "aesthetician." Now banned by the Brazilian government due to health risks, this procedure was commonly performed in the 1980s. While cosmetic surgery is modern, prestigious, and even glamorous, liquid silicone is looked upon as a "plástica of the people"—cheap, dangerous, and a little vulgar. When I ask her why she had the procedure, she says it was in order to "better fit the Brazilian *padrão* [pattern]."

While buttocks implants make up a small portion of all cosmetic surgeries, a cultural logic of beauty is visible in other types of surgery that "contour" the body. In Brazil, liposuction and breast surgery are particularly popular procedures, together accounting for 76 percent of all cosmetic surgeries in 2004 (compared to only 38 percent in the United States) (ASPS 2006, SBCP 2005). Liposuction is hailed as a revolution in cosmetic surgery because it creates subtle "body contouring" effects that leave minimal scars (Pitanguy 1993: 18). One variant removes fat from one part of the body and injects it in another to accentuate curves—a procedure called *lipoescultura*, "fat sculpting."

The popularity of breast reductions and lifts reflects a national aesthetic that traditionally idealized smaller breasts and saw larger breasts as unfeminine or even "ugly" (*Veja* 1992). Such a corporeal aesthetic partly explains how a fashion for breast implants could threaten "tradition." Notably, the American Society of Plastic Surgery classifies breast reduction as "reconstructive," while in Brazil it is considered cosmetic. Many published "before and after" pictures of breast reductions portray minor modifications that would probably not be seen as "cosmetic improvements" in North America (figure 7). Of course, some breast reductions have "functional" justifications (e.g., alleviation of back pain). Yet many of these surgeries make slight reductions that nonetheless leave prominent scars—generally in an inverted "T" shape in the lower half of the breast. In order for this "unaesthetic" scarring to be acceptable to patient and surgeon, the benefit of a minor reduction must be judged high. Many surgical operations thus inscribe a culturally specific ideal on the body.

There is rarely an explicit racial dimension to breast aesthetics, but plastic surgeons do openly mention "miscegenation" in discussing beauty. They claim that "pure whites" age more rapidly than people of some African descent, while the latter have a tendency to gain weight more easily (both "defects" that can be offset by surgery). "Different patient demographics" require small alterations in surgical technique. Mixed patients have a greater

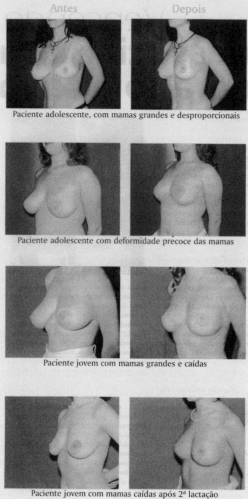

7. Plastic surgery ad: "Adolescent patient with precocious breast deformity" (second image from the top). Patients are shown before (left column) and after (right column) breast surgery.

tendency to form keloid scars, requiring new cost-benefit calculations. The unaesthetic effect of a prominent keloid scar may not be justified by the aesthetic benefits of minor alterations. But the problem in Brazil, surgeons say, is that it is not always clear which patients have African ancestry: "I had one patient, a beautiful woman with blond hair, green eyes, light skin. She had abdominoplasty and ended up with thick keloid scars. The population here is so mixed up. I had no idea her father was black. . . . When she came back in the summer to correct the scar, she was tanned and then I saw how dark she was." The resident could have avoided this error if he had followed a technique pioneered in Brazil: a tiny incision made between the breasts before the operation to test for scarring. Another surgeon even claimed to trace the propensity to form keloid scars to particular ethnic groups in Africa. In doing so, he echoed a long colonial discourse in Brazil about the supposed inferiority of slaves from "Bantu" regions (e.g., Angola) in relation to the "Yoruba."

Plastic surgeons often praise the aesthetics of mixture, but they also distinguish between different *kinds* of mixture. A senior surgeon explained: "The miscegenation of the white with the black resulted in a very attractive product: the *mulato*. The Indian no. He has an ugly body which is the northeastern type, that is, short legs, thin and flat, large torso. The *mulata* [note the switch in gender] no, she has a bumbum, a breast and a waist, like the white principally of the Iberian Peninsula." His comments echo themes in Freyre's works. The African and European mixture is seen as more "attractive" than the indigenous and European mixture (often simply ignored by Freyre). The remark about the Indian's "ugly body" reflects intense prejudice against northeastern migrants in cities such as São Paulo and Rio. The surgeon's comparison of the mulata with the Iberian also recalls Freyre's reversal of "Aryan theories." The older scientific racism held that the Portuguese were divided into a blond, conquering race in the north and a brown, subjugated race in the south. Freyre argues instead that the Iberians were a mixed people due to centuries of Moorish rule (1986: 61). For him, mixture is a norm that includes whites, or at least Iberian ones. A resident similarly contrasted the mixed Carioca not with "whites" per se, but with southern Brazilians of Polish or German descent, implying that many ostensibly white Brazilians are really mixed, due to Iberian or African ancestry. As Freyre puts it, "Every Brazilian, even the most light, with blond hair, holds in his soul, and when not in his soul in his body, the shadow or the physical mark, of the indigenous or the black" (1933: 307). In these discussions there is still a link between beauty and race, though it is often only implicit (or as Freyre would have it, "transcended"). This slippage between racialized biology and a populist beauty myth allows "mixture"—whether in the body or soul, whether of the Iberian or mulata variety—to serve as an encompassing ideal, a "model for all."

I have so far been discussing *bodily* beauty ideals and cosmetic practices. Yet a different cultural logic applies to hair and facial features, suggesting almost a schizophrenic split between body and visage. Having grown up in New York, a city with many of its racial and ethnic enclaves still intact in the 1980s, I was often surprised by the lack of racial tension and segregation in many neighborhoods of Rio. On the other hand, one has only to watch a few minutes of Brazilian television to perceive that the nation's institutions are dominated by the white or rather *whitish* (as one can say in Brazil). Flipping channels from a novela to news coverage of a street scene, there is a striking visual juxtaposition of two different demographics. It's true that in recent years, some black actors and models have begun appearing in prime-time dramas and TV ads as ordinary consumers. Still, the old proverb has not lost its force: *quanto mais branco melhor* (the whiter the better) (Schwarcz 1998: 205), in work markets and the "marriage market" as well (Twine 1998: 105). But significantly, the proverb does *not* simply say, "better to be white" but rather "the whiter the better," implying a notion of relative whiteness.

What is "relative whiteness"? Whiteness, like brownness and blackness, is not a natural category. To underline the cultural specificity of this semiotics of color, consider the situation throughout much of South and East Asia. There paleness is social capital, and not surprisingly much beauty work focuses on lightening skin tone through cosmetics and dyes. In Brazil, facial features and hair mark whiteness at least as much as, if not more than, skin color. Winddance Twine (1998: 90) cites an informant claiming that "the hierarchy's like this: hair, nose, and mouth, these are the three major things—and skin color afterward." Goldstein (2003: 121) analyzes how "purely African characteristics with no mixture of white characteristics are considered ugly" for residents in a Rio favela. Brazil's particular notion of whiteness—in which skin color sometimes only plays a minor role—stems from the fact that the hybrid body and the golden brown "ecological moreno" are idealized and eroticized. One implication of the relative lack of emphasis on skin color as a racial trait, however, is that other markers become more important: facial features and hair.

As we have seen, the ideology of morenidade is one of racial exclusion as well as inclusion. While the moreno color term may blur distinctions between "white" and various kinds of racial mixture, it often does not extend to the "un-mixed." The split between face and body may also reproduce racialized sexual stereotypes. If the face is identified more with the person, it is also logically an indicator of social status. Associated more strongly with sensuality, the body is figured as black, mixed, or often simply, as *nationally* Brazilian. Such a hierarchy also implies that "lightening" beauty work will focus on the face. With hair, the cultural rule seems to be "the straighter (and often the blonder) the better." The preference for long, straight hair even extends to whites with slightly wavy or curly hair, who also often straighten hair, reflecting perhaps a cultural anxiety in a context where "real whiteness" is a fantasy, "never fully achieved, never certain" (Segato 1998: 147).

Some women view hairstyling as an explicit means of lightening. Luisa said that "after putting in hair implants I went from being preta to mulata." She did not change her skin tone or make any other cosmetic change. Simply by acquiring long, straight hair, she implied, she would pass into an eroticized and aestheticized rather than simply lighter category. In these circumstances, it is also not coincidental that the black movement has focused on hair as a privileged site of racial identification. A "black" hairstyle becomes a primary symbol—but also—*vehicle* of transformation.[11] Before I return below to the topic of hair, I first discuss cosmetic surgery on the face: a form of beauty work that points to disturbing contradictions underlying Brazil's self-image as a land of beautiful mixture.

:::::: **NANCI'S RHINOPLASTY**

I meet Nanci, a fifty-eight-year-old patient, at the public hospital Servidores do Estado the day she is to have a nose job. Simply dressed in jeans and a white t-shirt, she briefly tells me about her former job as a cook. She says she is divorced, then shyly mentions a new "companion." She is surprised when I ask her why she wants to have an operation, as if it were obvious. "It's ugly, very flat. I want to refine it, turn it up." Three residents conduct a brief exam, squeezing her nose and lifting it up gently. While they lead her to an operating room, another resident gives me a tour of the ward. The enormous hallways have a cold institutional feel. In one room, nurses and residents joke pleasantly with a young liposuction patient as she wakes up from anesthesia. A resident picks up a five-gallon jar filled with fat that has been removed from her body, but it slips from his hands, spilling the yellow, granular liquid on his coat. "Porra!," he swears under his breath, spraying some disinfectant on the stain, without bothering with a few puddles left on the tile floor. The patient, still groggy, hasn't noticed anyway.

Nanci arrives in an adjoining room. The anesthesiologist, Dr. Aluísio, is a foul-tempered man in his fifties with a handlebar mustache. He begins his work in silence. After twenty minutes, when his patient is presumably unconscious, he curses under his breath. "The whore who gave birth, what kind of indication is this? It's a black woman with a Negroid nose. And? Fuck, it's Friday afternoon."

Dr. Aluísio is in a bad mood because he'd have the afternoon off if he hadn't been called in for an operation "without an indication." Sensing a good audience among the residents, he recalls another case. "An eighty-year-old woman who wanted to have her little breasts raised. What difference would it make? They would fall again the next week." The residents start to laugh, while one begins to measure her nostrils with a calipers. The others debate whether there is an "indication." "There isn't much indication," Dr. Márcio says, "It's a very Negroid nose, it's her type."

His colleague replies, "Her nose is very ugly. There's not much we can do; not even Pitanguy could make that a pretty nose. It's not going to be a well-defined nose. But we can do something, and it bothers her a lot so I think there's an indication."

A third agrees, "It's difficult to make it pretty, but it's not difficult to do."

I ask whether the operation will be supervised by a more senior surgeon. They say that by the third year they often perform routine operations alone, though a professor may show up later. By now the resident has "opened" the nose and is making incisions at the base of her ears. He removes a tiny piece of cartilage with a tweezers and inserts it in the point of the nose, "to give it more structure."

A fourth resident is filling out a medical form. I lean over his shoulder to see what he is writing. In a box marked "Pre-operative diagnosis," he scrawls, "Negroid nose." Seeing these words written on the official medical form is chillingly clinical. The diagnosis implies that the "racial trait" itself is the illness, or condition, to be treated in an otherwise healthy patient.

Nanci's operation is simply called by plastic surgeons "correction of the Negroid nose." It is performed in both the public and private sector and is advertised in magazines such as *Plástica & Beleza* (figure 8). One ad titled "beauty without limits" recommended the procedure to "all those who have a flat nose and want to correct it," noting that "the satisfaction of the patient

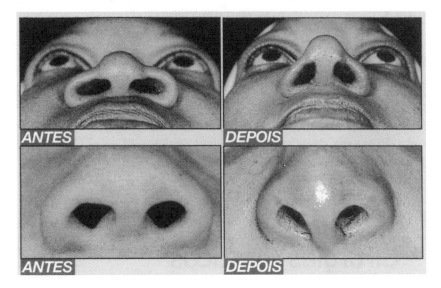

ANTES

DEPOIS

ANTES

DEPOIS

8. Advertisement for a plastic surgery procedure called "correction of the Negroid nose."

is very great" (*Plástica & Beleza* 2000: 110). How does this surgery reflect larger racial relations in a land of "racial democracy"? Eugenia Kaw (1993) has argued that in the United States demand for cosmetic surgery on racial traits—such as eyelid surgery performed on Asian Americans—is fueled by stigma experienced by racial minorities in a white-dominated society.[12] This analysis seems plausible to me, but when applied to countries where the racial minorities are majorities, it raises new questions. Perhaps such surgeries reflect a neocolonial position in the global economy. But East Asian countries, where eyelid surgery is on the rise, cannot simply be seen as subordinate to the West. In a rich, ethnically homogenous country such as Japan, it is not clear whether such procedures reflect an attempt to look "white" (L. Miller 2006). And in Brazil, how does one classify a "racial minority"? The 6 percent of *pretos* in the census? The 39 percent of *pardos* (browns)? The 42 percent of *morenos*? (*Folha de São Paulo* 1995) While such cosmetic procedures likely reflect white dominance, they also imply that color, beauty, and power intersect in historically specific ways.

Most plastic surgeons believe that "changing race," even if desired by a patient, would not be a proper use of plastic surgery: "It is very common among Oriental patients to not want the eye of an Oriental. Or because the nose is very flat, and they want the Caucasian nose. And so our mulato sometimes does not want such a flat nose; the *criolo* wants a nose a little more white. If it's possible, we do it; it's legitimate. Doesn't like the wide nose, doesn't like that it's flat here? Okay, there's no problem. But if the patient says, 'I want to be a *branca* [white woman]'—you can't make a white, it doesn't work." Surgeons often point to Michael Jackson as an illustration of the misapplication of plastic surgery. While surgeons can't "make a white," they can, they claim, make a facial feature "a little more white." During fieldwork I was surprised that the "correction of the Negroid nose" was not a taboo topic. Some surgeons, such as Dr. Marcelo, mentioned miscegenation in a rather matter-of-fact tone: "The black Brazilian is more miscegenated, mixed, than the black American. And so he is more inclined to improve the nose, diminish the wings, lift the tip. In the United States no. The black wants to maintain his own characteristics so he doesn't do much nasal surgery there." The bipolar logic of race locates racial identity in the interior through the concept of ancestry or "blood." It thus allows the possibility of "passing"—or hiding "real" race. But in a fluid and environmental color system, modifying facial features will not necessarily be seen as a deceptive attempt to change race if the "mixed" patient does not identify with a racial group in the first place. The consequence, according to Dr. Marcelo, is that Brazilians are more willing to have operations that "correct" racial features. Or perhaps more accurately: such surgeries are chosen precisely because they do *not* correct racial features, but simply "beautify."

It is true that some candidates for such procedures do not, in fact, identify as negro or preto. Vilmar, a forty-year-old rhinoplasty patient, works as a security guard at Bangu, one of Rio's most notorious prisons. During her examination—in front of thirty-five residents at the hospital—the professor described her surgical indication simply as "Negroid nose." But with light tea-colored skin and wavy hair, Vilmar does not identify as black.

"I have one black grandparent, one Italian," she told me.

"And the others?"

"Don't know. But my nose took after [*puxou*] the black one. Everyone else in the family has a thin nose, but I have one like hers, this nose of a little pig."

Though Vilmar clearly was bothered by her nose, she did not seem ashamed of the operation. She does not identify as preta or negra, indicating that perhaps she is rejecting identification with a subordinate social group. In fact, even if she desired to be perceived as black, she would face stiff resistance from her social circle, not just out of prejudice, but because to do so would contradict the evidence of the senses. It's true that if she came into contact with the black movement, she might be "converted" to a black identity based on her ancestry, though this is unlikely given her age and low level of education. The point is that Vilmar cannot plausibly be seen as trying to "pass" as white, despite the indication for her surgery: she is *already* white or morena. On the other hand, she is clearly rejecting a nose that she identifies with her black grandparent, reflecting a larger color hierarchy. A plastic surgeon acknowledged this point when he said the patient "doesn't want a nose with a foot in Africa, but with a foot in Europe, nê?"

Beauty is harmony and regularity. Approximating norms of proportion, beauty paradoxically also transcends them, becoming anything but normal. Beauty is radiant—it literally draws the eye to it—while normality is inconspicuous. Mestiçagem in Freyre's thought is beautiful in part because it creates harmony; it avoids "exaggerations," creating a synthesis that is greater than the sum of its parts. Similarly, patients and surgeons often see mixture as aesthetically desirable. But mixture is not always successful. Though it may flatten out the extremes of "pure races," it can also create areas of disharmony that need "correction." As Farid Hakme, the former president of the Brazilian Society of Plastic Surgery, puts it: "Due to the mix and match of different races . . . the nose sometimes doesn't match the mouth or the buttocks don't match the legs" (in Gilman 1999: 225). His view echoes earlier concern among the Brazilian elite about racial mixing, though now the problem is not physical and moral degeneracy, but aesthetic defects.

In Brazil family members sometimes have permutations of skin color, facial features, and hair that allow color to be socially ascribed in different ways. Family inheritance becomes an aesthetic lottery with winners and losers: those who come out with "bad hair" or too dark skin. Vilmar's attempt to correct such an unwanted feature suggests that harmonious brown beauty is at risk of disaggregating into an assortment of parts, some valued (or fetishized), some stigmatized. Such views call to mind a distinct and intimate style of racism in Brazil that has a logic of internal contamination, as contrasted with a United States logic of boundary policing. As Rita Segato (1998:147) puts it: "Racism in Brazil is a purge that starts from the inside of the white being, a fear (and a certainty) of being contaminated somewhere. It has to do with intimacy and relatedness, not with ethnic distance and fear of aliens."

Some beauty practices may be motivated by desires to "purge" traces of nonwhite ancestry. They also point to a long tradition of seeing "whitening"—whether enacted through marriage, state policies promoting European immigration, or cosmetic practices—as a viable means of collective or individual improvement (Andrews 1991; Skidmore 1974). Although Freyre fought against the whitening ideal by affirming the cultural and aesthetic benefits of mixture, his vision of "magnificent miscegenation" has not entirely countered the earlier ideology of *embranquecimento*. Concerns about racial mixture, however, have now been transformed from a project of social hygiene into a private practice aiming at happiness and self-improvement.

: : :

My aim here has not been to show that mestiçagem is simply a false ideology that covers up real racism. Rather, mestiçagem and multiculturalism are distinct ways of envisioning human differences and similarities that are subtly manifested in contemporary beauty practices. A comparison with multiculturalist aesthetics may help clarify the nationalist aspects of mestiçagem. In recent years, North Americans have begun to view appearance through a multicultural lens, at least officially, through which each race and ethnicity possesses its own distinct beauty. Despite overall growth of plastic surgery, there has been a backlash against correction of ethnic traits, for example, the Jewish nose job, once "routine" in the 1960s (Haiken 1997). As a *Self* magazine article put it in 1992: "New thinking on cosmetic surgery: keep your ethnic identity" (Gilman 1999).

All this may seem—to the multiculturalist—progressive. This trend, though, also reflects a cultural common sense about race that emphasizes the naturalness of racial boundaries defined by ancestry. In Brazil, on the other hand, there has been a tendency to believe that racial mixing creates one distinct (and aesthetically superior) national ideal of beauty. This contrast is too schematic: multiculturalism coexists with color hierarchies, while in Brazil, a black movement rejects color terms. Yet to view beauty practices *only* as alienation runs the risk of assuming "pure" racial categories are natural while ignoring how beauty is also a social domain of national identification and popular aspirations.

The growth of the beauty industry in the developing world seems to be a particularly disturbing aspect of homogenization as it inscribes Western aesthetics on non-Western bodies. In Brazil, however, plastic surgery takes a localized form as it is used to emulate the sensual ideal of "magnificent miscegenation," correct unharmonious mixtures, or lighten appearance defined by a folk taxonomy of phenotypes. The international medical specialty is thus not simply overriding—but also inciting—a national cultural logic of beauty.

Beauty practices also reflect a particular history of racial domination.

Roberto DaMatta (1991: 153) argues that the body is a privileged area of "ideological (or symbolic) elaboration" due to Brazil's history of race relations. Like the United States, Brazil in the nineteenth century was a multiracial society with an agrarian economy based on slave labor. In both countries abolition was imposed by legal decree on a society that had for over three centuries been based on white dominance. Yet, each country organized racial inequalities in different ways in the postabolition period. In the United States, Jim Crow laws *legally* re-created the old power relations. In other words, faced with the same "problem" of sudden legal equality, Americans turned to the impersonal, formal sphere of law to shore up the old social hierarchy. Brazilians, on the other hand, reestablished the old social hierarchy in an extralegal realm: a subtle code of social prestige based on bodily appearance and personal hygiene ("bathing, cleanliness, fashions in clothes and footwear"). DaMatta (1991) points out that Freyre refers to the period after abolition as a time of "drastic egalitarianism," in which the Brazilian became "almost a Hindu, so scrupulous was he about cleanliness with respect to his underpants, shirts, and stockings" (shoes too took on enormous cultural significance as slaves were prohibited from wearing them). Appearance became an especially important index of social position because origin—unlike in the United States—could not.

The intimate nature of hierarchy partly explains why Brazilian racial prejudice, DaMatta argues, has "a strong esthetic (and moral) component but never a legal one" (1991: 154). I found that Brazilians often place importance on intimate measurements of racism, rather than criteria used in official contexts (e.g., statistics on institutional discrimination). Some friends were particularly shocked to discover that the United States once had laws stipulating different drinking fountains or cemeteries for blacks and whites. Refusing a social kiss in a patronage relationship—a rejection of intimacy—can be seen as a particularly hurtful instance of prejudice. And conversely, interracial sexual relationships—"erotic democracy"—become the sign of racial democracy (Goldstein 2003). The Racist can be defined as the one who doesn't "love" the other. In this context, the intimate realm of hygiene and beauty becomes particularly important in defining indicators of social inclusion. As suggested by the efforts of darker Brazilians to launch careers as actors or models, beauty can grant a social visibility that is an antidote to a particular understanding of racism where to be ignored is worse than to be hated.

The search for a distinctive national identity fed the reversal of racial pessimism and an embrace of mixture. At the same time, the dominance of the "relatively light" was maintained through an informal color hierarchy defined in the face, the part of the body most identified with the social persona. This separation between facial and bodily aesthetics particularly affects women, for whom appearance is more often a form of "value" both in patriarchal erotic traditions and in markets of work and sexual relationships (Caldwell 2007). This split also mirrors another division between spheres of popular culture: a whiter world of telenovelas, fashion, and advertising and a more mixed world of music, religion, dance, and sports. Both splits reflect a persisting conflict in struggles to define a modern Brazil. Does the country represent an alternative modernity, a "luso-tropical civilization" with a unique mestiço identity? Or is it a modernizing country, emulating sometimes elusive European and North American economic institutions? I now discuss how the relationship between these two competing visions of Brazilian modernity has taken a new turn with the emergence of black identities in state policies, social movements, and beauty industries.

: : : : : :   **MY *BLACK* IS MY BRAND**

> "All the colors flow together,
> dying the sky, the sun
> the earth, the epidermis
> the consumer, the citizen, the elector.
> The beauty of this diversity [. . .]
> How to define it
> The better to capture it?"
> —"Abrindo caminhos" (article in Brazilian marketing journal)

Extroverted and charismatic, Jéssica says she is proud of her "suburban identity" (*suburban* connotes the poor periphery). She works as an on-camera presenter for the in-house TV program of Petrobras, the national petroleum company, and also runs an NGO that offers cultural excursions for disadvantaged youth. To make ends meet, she sells cosmetics to beauty parlors. Jéssica would be described as black in the United States racial taxonomy, but she might fit into any number of popular color categories in Brazil, such as *morena* or *mulata*. Jéssica wears her hair in a way that is quite rare in Brazil—a large round mass of very tight curls. She calls it simply "my *black power*." Ever since she was a child, she had straightened her hair—until she "discovered she was *negra* at age twenty-five." She explains: "A professor was talking about the history of blacks and I realized I only knew the part about slavery. When I learned about Malcolm X and Nelson [Mandela], when I saw that Machado de Assis [a Brazilian novelist] was black, I began to embrace my race." Though she receives teasing comments, such as "do you need some money to buy hair straightener?" she says she would never change her hair: "My *black* is my characteristic; it's become my brand."

In activist circles, other women had similar narratives of racial pride that stressed the transformative effects of adopting a black hairstyle: dreadlocks, *tranças* (braids), or a *black power* (an "afro"). In Brazil, such styles are often seen as a more or less radical break from normative femininity. (For men, there is much less social compulsion to straighten hair.) The dual adoption of a negra identity and black style can thus be a highly emotional experience. Often, social activists stressed the importance of self-esteem in this beauty and identity work. As one woman from a black cultural organization put it, "We don't follow anyone. We really work on our minds so that we can just do what we want. We think we are beautiful as we are, and we want to stay as we are. Our *auto-estima* is really worked on [*super trabalhada*], and we're working on it even more. We want to save the auto-estima of other women too." The identity as negra becomes an important tool in collective struggle as well as in individual efforts to raise self-esteem.

From a North American perspective, these might seem to be fairly straightforward accounts of coming to racial consciousness in a white-dominated society. But consider Lise's account. Like Jéssica, she also runs an NGO in the Baixada Fluminense region in Rio de Janeiro, "a vast area hedged by enormous favelas, where there are no *shoppings*, no libraries, no culture only drug trafficking." She says, "I don't have black parents. I was born white, and so I was created by the black movement." I ask her what she means. "Black is that person with hard hair and totally dark skin. It says I'm white on my birth certificate, can you believe it? But I consider myself negra." With light brown skin and long, wavy hair, Lise would likely be described as white in both official and informal contexts. Her identification as negra thus not only affirms a subordinate identity but also *creates* one that flies in the face of Brazil's traditional color taxonomy.

Such adoptions of a black identity are happening during a time of rapid change in state racial policies. Debate about racial discrimination had been suppressed by both the Left and Right. But the postdictatorship state abruptly reversed its (lack of) racial policy beginning in the mid-1990s, when President Cardoso's regime officially admitted that Brazil is "racist."

Governments introduced controversial quotas reserving up to 40 percent of university admission slots for *negros* (blacks) (Htun 2004). A debate erupted in the public sphere over whether such policies represented a betrayal of the Constitution, Brazil's tradition of interracial sociality, and the masses of the nonblack poor (Fry 2005). Although affirmative action was controversial in the United States, the Brazilian laws had to reckon with another problem: how to define the category of person targeted. In the last census 6 percent of Brazilians identified as *preto* (black), and so such policies are counting on a number of "conversions" from other color terms to fulfill the quotas.[13]

The economic and political stakes of "blackness" rose considerably while ethnic identities in general became more socially visible.[14] Here was one of those moments in history when social processes seem to unfold before the observer's eyes. Yet the new focus on race in media and state policy does not only represent the goal of achieving equal access for minorities. It also reflects conflicts over market-based cultural and political identifications emerging in a neoliberal period. Some have decried new "aestheticized" racial identities for undermining collective social movements, and reflecting a North American multicultural vision of difference that is narcissistic and commodified. Others insist that aesthetic self-affirmation is necessary to overcome internalized racism. Seen in a larger framework, the beauty industry provides a glimpse into how Brazilians are recasting racial identity during a time of rapid change, as a nationalist paradigm of racial mixture encounters—and confronts—transnational representations of racial difference.

For the moment, activists such as Jéssica and Lise remain a minority. Many women prefer the terms *morena, mulata,* or the like, not only because they carry aesthetic and social capital, but because they seem more accurate descriptions of their phenotype. The black movement in Brazil thus faces particular challenges. It must pressure a state with a history of denying racism to adopt racial politics. It must alter the cultural perception of appearance. Moreover, it must confront not only color hierarchies favoring relative lightness, but also a celebration of brownness that has nationalist, erotic, and aesthetic dimensions. These circumstances have created some odd bedfellows. A generally leftist social movement found itself allied with a "neoliberal" state promoting multicultural policies. More odd still perhaps are the convergences between grass-roots activists and the marketing strategies of multinational corporations. These various actors, in different ways and sometimes unwittingly, are beginning to visualize and address consumers in a "black market." This social fact simply did not exist twenty years ago. Why does it today?

: : :

Carlinhos pulls up in front of a tiny house in the São Paulo periphery and honks his horn lightly. Milena—short, lithe, and looking much younger than her fifty years—skips out the door and gets in the Peugeot, reaching forward to squeeze my hand. Milena has long played the role of a character in the "court" that receives the Carnaval samba school parades. Carlinhos, a filmmaker friend, has shot footage of the parades over the past few years for an experimental film. After hearing about my research, he decided that Milena would make the perfect guide to an expedition to *Cosmoétnica*, hyped (by itself) as the "biggest event of black beauty in Latin America."

For the next six hours, Milena maintains a steady flow of manic enthusiasm, sexual innuendo, and *palavrões* (swear words). Her speech, modulated from throaty whispers to low pitched shouts, is filled with the words *racha*, *buceta*, *viadaso*, and other references to homosexuals and female genitalia. Immediately I feel I am in the presence of a free spirit. She is also drawn to foreign words, throwing in the odd Spanish verb now and then, relishing the names of neighborhoods such as "Nova York" and "Brooklin." She pronounces my name in its more exotic English rather than Portuguese form, which she occasionally mutters from the back seat as we drive along the endlessly winding and merging highways of São Paulo.

Held in a hall the size of an airplane hangar, the event, I realize, is an industrial trade expo bringing together a smattering of small entrepreneurs and multinationals venturing into the new terrain of ethnic marketing. There are black dolls, a black beauty fashion show, even a video-dating service. Dominating the event are cosmetics and hair products displayed in sleek Plexiglas pavilions decorated with posters of black models. I ask an entrepreneur why she started her line of hydrating creams. "Necessity," she replies. She rubs a fragrant, greasy lotion onto the back of my hand, then explains that creams for white skin don't penetrate well "dense black skin." Other brands emphasize color schemes—silver, copper, gold, and blue—specially made to flatter darker complexions. The products are aimed at what the bilingual press kit calls a "new market niche of 36 million black and mulato beauty product consumers in Brazil." This segment—almost half of the total beauty market—"practically did not exist five years ago," the press release breathlessly claims.

At this point I have one of those rare moments in fieldwork when the maddeningly abstract notion of "social change" seems momentarily to come into focus. Suddenly, a market niche of 36 million black and mulato consumers emerges out of . . . what? Some news stories have heralded the "consolidation of a black middle class" after the stabilization of the currency in the mid-1990s. Yet sociological studies have found that there is limited social mobility for nonwhites. The income of nonwhites remains about half that of whites, a difference that remained stable from 1995 to 2001 (Gacitúa-Marió and Woolock 2008: 16). But if the sudden emergence of the market niche cannot be explained purely by upward mobility, then how can it?

I look up from my notebook to see that Milena has come to introduce me to a Nigerian selling West African art. Many Afro-Brazilian Orixás, or deities, are of Yoruban origin; hence the dealer is hoping to find interested buyers among Brazilian practitioners. Next to figurines carved in wood, he is also selling the "Afro Card." Resembling a credit card with an image of an African mask, it offers discounts on gyms, pharmacies, and beauty parlors. The glossy plastic suggests to me another hypothesis that perhaps can answer the question raised by the press release. Was the emergence of a black market due to a shift in perception and visualization of the consumer, a process in which marketers, corporations, consumers, and activists were playing active roles?[15]

The idea of targeting products at an ethnicity or race is a new one in Brazil (Fry 2002). While such research identifies consumer microniches defined by subtle variations in lifestyle, income, age, and so on, it did not—until recently—include color as a demographic variable. In a reflective editorial published in 2001, the Brazilian Society of Market Research chided itself for "a lack of awareness" that led to this omission and began to urge the discipline to collect data on color. "If the researcher will sometimes risk facing an interviewee offended by having been asked his color, how many opportunities and problems are made to disappear by the absence of this question?" ("Abrindo caminhos" 2001: 13) But as we will see, marketing does not only make "problems disappear"; it also can make *visible* new categories of people (Hacking 2006).

Still somewhat cautious, the organization decided to first conduct an exploratory poll asking consumers what they thought of including the question "What is your color?" in market research. Curiously, it found that over a third of respondents reacted negatively, viewing the question itself as "racist, strange, irrelevant, or awkward." The lower the education level, and the darker the skin tone, the more negative the reaction ("Abrindo caminhos" 2001: 13). This result reflects the notion, still common, that the word *raça* is itself racist, as suggested by the phrase "um sujeito da raça" (a person of race) (Schwarcz 1998: 178). Despite this less-than-encouraging signal, and the lack of information about this terra incognita, a number of corporations were confident that a black-consumer market was out there and began launching products aimed at the new niche. Specialized stores with names such as Preta-Pretinha sold purses, beachwear, and a doll named Susi Olodum (after a Yoruba deity). Other entrepreneurs marketed African-style clothing items (these haven't sold well) and the more popular t-shirts with expressions such as "100% negro." Most products, though, were in the beauty and personal hygiene sector: not just make-up and hair products, but black sun lotion, bath soap, and even band-aids to blend in with darker skin tone.

Occasionally, a company would err. One ad for Rexona Deodorant depicted a dashing couple in a sailboat with the copy "Double the passion, double the protection."[16] It is hard to imagine the Rexona ad being launched in the United States, with its doubly offensive stereotypes of excess sex and sweat. The ad was pulled after some consumers complained, but the fact that it appeared at all suggests that corporations and ad agencies are still finding their feet in the new territory of ethnic marketing. Although a few consumers wondered whether these kinds of products weren't "racist," most seemed to welcome them and the new visibility of black consumers. As one black activist put it: "We used to complain that we had nothing that suited us, lipstick, blush, even clothes—there was just that rice powder, which made you look like a circus clown."

Many of the first products were launched by the large multinationals, which had already discovered a lucrative market in the United States. Domestic cosmetics companies quickly followed suite. O Boticário, for example, attributed 30 percent of its 1998 sales to its make-up lines "Naomi," designed for black skin and "Camile," "for mulatas" (*Veja* 1998). The hype in national media and marketing trade journals grew. A 1999 market of "36 million black and mulato consumers" had by 2006 more than doubled to "75 million *afrodescendentes*." Dumping the older category "black and mulato," the media now often used a new term, *afrodescendente*, suggesting perhaps an ancestry-based racial logic. In any event, the afrodescendente consumer was now imagined as belonging to a larger "black market of the Americas" estimated by the World Bank to have an annual income of us$800 billion—50 percent larger than Brazil's entire GDP. While blackness had historically been "dissolved" in the nationalist myth of mestiça-gem, it is here reconstituted as a feature of an international market that cuts across national boundaries.

: : :

Does the black-consumer market simply reflect the long-overdue recognition that some extra money can be made by defining yet another niche in the endless differentiation of markets in consumer capitalism? In fact, the new emphasis on race in marketing stems in part from the belated "discovery" that the submiddle-class consumer is willing to buy a much larger range of goods on credit than previously imagined. Once thought too poor, and perhaps not "modern" enough to be the target of ad campaigns, such consumers are less likely to default on financing plans for cheap consumer items than the middle class, according to one ad agency. And so corporations are perhaps simply recognizing that poorer Brazilians—on average, darker—are "good consumers."

Such economic motives are certainly important proximate causes of the new visibility of the black-consumer market. But they don't explain why it is emerging only in recent years in Brazil, when ethnic products and marketing have existed in the United States for decades. In fact, beauty historically was one of the only sectors in the industrial economy open to African American entrepreneurs (Peiss 1998). Ethnic marketing does not just design new products and services for particular demographic groups. It must also create stylish and sexy *images* to distinguish the brand in a competitive marketplace, and with which the consumer can identify. This is a crucial issue as it suggests that the psychosocial process of racial identification is intertwined with the economic and cultural forces that shape media production. With this point in mind, let us shift perspectives now and try to "see color" from the point of view of advertisers working to reach consumers within the constraints of a changing cultural logic of race and corporate business plans.

Consider the apparently trivial example of bath soap. In Brazil it was considered a landmark when the first soap for *pele negra e morena* arrived on the market (figure 9). Lise pointed out, "It would have been impossible to market soap to *negros* in the 1970s. It would have been seen as racist. Soap for us—why would we need it? Are we different people?" Now, thirty years later, soap "for black skin" can be hailed as a sign of acceptance of black beauty (though one brand promotes its product as being for "black *and* mo-

*Ligue o Chuveiro.*
*Cubra-se de Espuma.*
*Transforme-se*
*em Pérola Negra.*

Lux Skincare
Uniformidade da Pele
Morena e Negra.
*Sua pele por inteiro.*

LUX
SKINCARE

9. "Turn yourself into a black pearl. . . . Lux skincare,
uniformity of brown and black skin."

rena skin," suggesting that some corporations are still cautious about exclusively targeting black consumers). Why? For one, promoting the products with black models and actresses was itself somewhat novel and made "black beauty" more visible in mainstream media. To be "invited" to model in ads can often be seen as a kind of honor in Brazil. And so the celebrity Taís de Araújo could complain, after her success as the lead in a novela: "If it had been any white actress, she would have done all the commercials of Brazil. And I did only two or three at most." Taís stressed that this was not only about "earning my little money," but that she should "serve as a reference, for the public to be able to consume and identify with what they consume."

Significantly, the ad was for a *luxury* soap called Lux. For decades darker women in the media were portrayed as domestics, and the only kind of soap they were shown using was laundry or dish soap, not luxury soap for their own skin. In other words, blackness has not always been seen as compatible with Globo's populace moving toward "modernity, glamour, and a comfortable, materially enriched, upwardly mobile lifestyle." For this reason, the ad had a symbolic significance, marking a new visibility of the ordinary black consumer in advertising and TV dramas (Fry 2002).[17] But recall again that black Brazilians have not experienced upward mobility on a large scale, and so we must look beyond strictly commercial motives and ask what larger social processes are producing this change.

In post-Fordist capitalism, profits often depend more on the emotions and styles associated with the brand, rather than on productive capacity. The human body has perhaps a special capacity to create an affective response in the consumer. The hypermasculine or hyperfeminine celebrity in particular can become a valued "face" of the brand. This market environment has created needs for new kinds of professionals who specialize in understanding the nuanced messages appearances convey—creative directors, photographers, casting agents, brand managers, and so on. Like earlier specialists, such as phrenologists and physical anthropologists, they are experts in reading the human form. Their business depends on being able to know—or convince the client they know—all the subtle connotations of "types." Although ethnographers can ask anyone to interpret a given ritual, they would generally consider their analysis incomplete if they did not consult a ritual specialist. It thus seemed logical to me to consult the certified experts in media meaning.

Advertisers readily acknowledge that ultimately all creativity is subjected brutally to the bottom line. As Luiz, a creative director, put it, "Ads are not a vanguard art, though we have to know the vanguard. Nothing is done without demand. There is no area of risk. Ads are simple. You have to say what the client wants in a form the consumer wants to hear." But Luiz here I suspect is being too modest, as finding out this form is anything but simple, which is why corporations spend so much money on external ad agencies. When Luiz says he must put the client's message in a "form the consumer wants to hear," he means it must be delivered by an appropriate spokesperson, the actor or model. How are they selected, and why after decades of exclusion, are some darker faces now appearing in ads?

Often, the ad agency or photographer suggests a model to the client, who will then have final say. In general, the more popular the product, the better the chance of having a darker model accepted. Note that *popular* is a keyword for advertisers, which usually connotes poorer. Another creative director said, "In an ad for a cell recharge card, which is for a more popular public, we put in a negro." Since the product was a *prepaid* card, which cost as little as fifteen reais, it could thus be considered "popular" (in favelas and other areas where land lines are hard to come by, residents rely heavily on cell phones).[18] He added, "Then I tried to put in a black couple for a laptop ad, aimed at class A [the highest income segment], but the client didn't accept this. We ended up with a white couple." He told me the client used a phrase I often heard: "This face doesn't combine with our brand."

The principle here is *identification*: a consumer must be able to see herself in the model representing the product or brand. In some cases, identification can create an implicit requirement of whiteness. When one creative director chose a black child model to portray an angel for yet another mobile phone ad, the client responded, "I've never seen a black angel," and the model was replaced with a redhead. In this case, the client feared the consumer would not identify a nonwhite model with a cultural icon, thereby diluting the "brand message." Although such fears are perhaps "rational" if the product is aimed at the relatively whiter, upper-income strata, this doesn't explain why—given the size of the nonwhite population—there should be such a *general* scarcity of darker models.

In fact, along with "identification" there is another logic, what we might call "aspiration": the idea that lighter models stimulate consumer desires. This is particularly relevant in Brazil, where color is relational and fluid and as the saying goes, "money lightens." If the purpose of consuming is to be upwardly mobile, then it makes sense that consumer aspirations will reflect color aspirations. But more recently advertisers seem to acknowledge that aspiration can conflict with identification: nonwhite consumers may identify better, not surprisingly, with nonwhite models. Nádia, a creative director at another agency, and an account executive, Olívia, told me about an ad campaign they did for Coke.

N: It was for a banner to put in bars, and we used a black woman, gorgeous.

A: Did you do market research to choose her?

N: No, I just briefed the photographer, "I want someone like this, like this, like this."

A: And what were the "like this's"?

N: I thought all of sudden it would be cool to put in a negra, a super pretty negra with a gigantic *blackpower* [hairstyle]. Because [the ad's for] a popular place . . . a little bar, a true *boteco*. And it's a soda with a really accessible price.

A: But isn't it just Coke?

N: [surprised at my ignorance] There are sixteen types of packaging, all with different prices. This was only fifty centavos. You return it. It's popular.

O: [explaining patiently] The higher class doesn't buy that kind, they buy those two-liter bottles at the supermarket.

A: Did you say to the photographer you wanted to use a black woman?

N: No, I said "a woman who has more the color of Brazil." Could be mulata, could be negra, could be *escura* [dark].

N: I wanted an *identificação* for someone who is walking in the street all the time.

O: Those who walk in the street are more povão, nê?

N: Only more popular people would stop in one of these types of bars.

O: You, for example, wouldn't go to one of these places. Who goes is your maid.

A: And when Coke saw the model you chose, what did they say?

O: They thought she was marvelous.

This exchange shows that even a single beverage is highly segmented, with different types of packaging aimed at different demographic groups. The reason the client "accepted" a black model for this particular banner was that it was destined for botecos, tiny bars where only more "popular" consumers would buy Coke. Given the popular, and hence relatively darker target niche, the principle of identification in a sense "allowed" the choice of a black model.

When I first began fieldwork at ad agencies, I tended to use the language that I commonly heard in activist circles and in the national media, asking questions—in retrospect, foolishly—about the "representation of race." Soon I realized that the term *race* has a whiff of social science and state policy to it that does not always sit well in a commercial world more interested in hunting down the latest trends. Corporations do not only consider whether they want a black or a white face. Rather, particular combinations of facial features, hair, and skin color can convey tiny differences about a brand.

Another cell phone company used nonwhite models for a campaign, but specifically wanted dreadlocks and tranças—new, trendy black hairstyles that signify youthful irreverence. In another case, a giant in the global cosmetics markets launched an inexpensive shampoo line with fruit extracts aimed at hair damaged by chemical perms, though it didn't exclusively target black consumers. With this briefing, the ad agency thought it "natural" to have a black model. But after the photo shoot, the client requested the image be altered to make it "within the branding" described as "young and light, *leve*" (lightweight, not light colored). I asked if a specific change had been requested.

"They said, 'Alleviate the African traits in the post[-production].'"

"And what were the traits?"

The creative director paused, then said, "Well, obviously, nose, lips, hair. But also the forehead. Once we showed the client a video test of a girl we'd selected for a callback. And they said, '*Nossa Senhora*, what an enormous forehead.' She was refused for the forehead. I don't know why, but you often see it in black women. It's caused by chemically treated hair I think." The digital "alleviation of African traits" here echoes the discourse of mestiçagem that aims to avoid "Africanoid exaggerations."

Noemi is the most successful of a group of aspiring models and actors represented by a Rio agency. She is discussing with her colleagues how perceptions of color affect casting opportunities. The agency's initial mandate was to represent "black" models and actors, but each of them describes how they are slotted into the nuanced distinctions of Brazil's rainbow of color terms. A man who identifies as "negro" says there are only certain roles for him. Ironically, he is cast more by foreign companies from Angola and the United States who are looking for "pure blacks." (Agencies cast and shoot ads in Brazil because the population resembles demographics in the United States, but production costs are lower.) Another woman says she is often cast as a "mulata," for example in Carnaval-themed ads. Noemi says, "But I am morena. I am all mixed—white, Indian, black. I have light skin, whitish features, straight hair. I can go in several directions." In Brazil's flexible taxonomy of color terms, she can fit several types, giving her more casting opportunities. Despite this advantage, Noemi later reveals that she is scheduled to have a nose job, at Globo's request (Globo's press department denied the charge). "I have a potato tip. I'll have it thinned [*afinado*]. And also he'll increase the projection."

The old color hierarchies have certainly not disappeared. In a highly competitive market, they are as important as ever. But they coexist now with a new semiotics of color. We might see this as another kind of "narcissism of minor differences" (Freud 1961: 58–63), here applied not to national identities but to corporate and consumer ones. Tiny adjustments—made through plastic surgery, cosmetics, clothing, digital alteration, and the like—shift appearance from one category to another. In the not-so-distant past a non-white actress was often cast as a maid or a slave in a period drama. Now with straight hair, she can be a bank customer; with braids signify exotic chic; with photoshopping be a shampoo model; with blackpower hair be a dancer in a hip-hop clip. This is not to say that all is possible. She can still be refused for a role in a margarine commercial "because she doesn't combine with the brand," as one model complained. And she may say to herself, "Don't dark people eat margarine?" and go on to the next audition. Or she may straighten her hair to look lighter and then find herself refused for a role as a dancer in a drama about a samba school for "not being black enough." Or she may go further, risking a nose job, as Noemi did, in order to boost her chance of landing the most coveted job for an actress in Brazil: a novela heroine.

: : : : : :   **ROLE MODELS**

The taste for novelas may be hard to acquire for some foreigners. Yet these dramas—more than their cousins, the "soaps"—are truly a popular art form, shown at prime time, adored by the nation, and exported around the world from Moldova to Indonesia. If one feature of late capitalism is a difficulty drawing the line between art and advertising, this is particularly true in novelas. As the name *soap opera* suggests, these dramas were originally sponsored by personal hygiene companies such as Colgate-Palmolive (Hamburger 1998). In addition to heavy advertising, brands are directly incorporated into scenes, a practice known as *merchandising*. Given porous boundaries between culture and commerce, it is not surprising that the new visibility of the black-consumer market should be paralleled by the emergence of black actors, models, and TV hosts. Just as much as the slick multinational ad campaigns, these personalities interpellate their fans as black subjects within Globo's universe of glamour and modernity.

Zezé Motta was one of the first black actresses in Brazil to achieve national recognition. She is in her fifties when I meet her on the set of a Globo novela, where she is playing a lead role as a domestic slave in a period drama. She has a grueling recording schedule, as up to twenty scenes from various episodes might be recorded in a single day, but she agrees to talk during her breaks. She begins by pointing out the irony of discussing, while dressed in costume as a house slave, new opportunities for black actors in Brazil. Daughter of a seamstress and a musician, she was raised in Pavão-zinho favela, a rocky outcropping overlooking Ipanema beach. She jokes that she has been a "girl from Ipanema for thirty years." Though she never thought TV was a possibility, at sixteen she won a scholarship to a theater school.

At this point in her life, she says, "I was in a phase of whitening. I was the only black in the theater course I was doing. My little friends used to say, your nose is flat; your bunda is large; your hair is *ruim*, bad. And so I straightened my hair and thought of doing plastic surgery on my nose." Then she adds, joking, "I even thought of doing plástica on my bumbum — scarcely did I know then that my bumbum would be such a success later!" At this everyone in the room (two actors and a Globo publicist) laughs. Soon after graduating, though, Zezé had an experience that would profoundly change her — what I later came to think of as a "conversion narrative," a story about racial affirmation. Significantly, it happened in New York City.

> As my parents were black, we were ugly. I considered myself ugly. And then I went to the U.S. to do a play called *Arena Sings Zumbi* [about a rebel slave]. We performed in Harlem and in those days I used a Chanel wig. Imagine — right in the middle of "black is beautiful" — I do a play called *Arena sings Zumbi* with a Chanel wig! They said to us, You are portraying the life of Zumbi, and you have an alienated person with Chanel hair. I almost died of shame. But I stopped using my straightening product and went on stage with a blackpower. That was in 1969.

The event was a turning point in her career. After returning to Rio she heard of an audition for the part of Xica da Silva in a feature-length film. Set in the early eighteenth century, the film dramatizes a folk legend about the story of a mulata slave who became the mistress of a rich diamond merchant. When I asked Zezé why she got the part, she said she still had short hair. "I looked androgynous, like a transvestite. Cacá [Diegues, the director] was looking for something different. I wasn't within the standard of beauty like the others, who were models and dancers, because there were so few black actresses." The film was an international art house hit, but even after this success Zezé had trouble finding parts. She was offered a minor role as a maid, which she mustered up the courage to refuse. Soon after she took a part as a "mulata, the type everyone wants to screw." The film belonged to a genre of Brazilian cinema known as Pornochanchada. Such "sexploitation" pictures became the bread and butter of the film industry during the military dictatorship because "they didn't speak of what was really happening in the country."

In both *Xica da Silva* and the "erotic film," Zezé portrayed a seductress.

Both films played on the heady mix of race, sex, and power that pervade Brazilian popular culture. The role of Xica was clearly more dramatically challenging, though the film was controversial for the black movement as it seemed to reinforce the sexualized stereotype of the mulata. In this light it is significant that Diegues cast Zezé, who does not embody what she called the "Brazilian *padrão* [standard]" of mulata beauty. In fact, the film portrays Xica less as a traditional beauty, and more as a woman possessing almost occult sexual powers, which make her lovers scream. (To this day Zezé is often asked by fans—who in Brazil are notoriously uninterested in the line separating fact and fiction—what Xica's "secret was.") Zezé was attracted to the role because "Xica was not resigned to the condition of slavery but used seduction to achieve everything she wants." Both film and TV versions dramatize the erotics of racial domination, a theme that apparently resonated with many viewers. After being adapted a second time in a novela, Xica da Silva has become a household name. Her story also exemplifies a social fantasy in contemporary culture: the "treasure chest coup" or seducing an older, richer man as an escape from poverty (Goldstein 2003).

A sizeable portion of novelas are period dramas, a fact that in itself creates opportunities for black actors. As one actor wryly put it, "When there's a slave, it becomes very hard for them to avoid casting a black." But the novela set in a contemporary period remained an almost all-white world (with the exception of criminals, maids, and a few other "types" played by nonwhites). And so the 1980s marked a new turning point for Zezé—and perhaps for black actors—when she was cast as a middle-class, landscape architect with a white boyfriend in the novela *Corpo a corpo* (Body to Body).

Novelas are a principle forum of public debate in Brazil through daily engagement with a mass audience (Hamburger 1998). With an interracial couple, the novela's creators saw an opportunity to address racism as a theme. In one episode, a white man says to Zezé's character: "I don't want my son to marry you, because I don't want grandchildren to be little blacks *beiçudos* [having large mouths]." Zezé said she was shocked by reactions of the public to her character: "One man said, 'I don't believe that Marcos Paulo [the actor playing her boyfriend] needed so much money that he would submit to the humiliation of kissing that ugly black woman.' Marquinhos at the time was one of the biggest sex symbols in Brazil and he would arrive home to find furious messages from his fans, aggressive ones. It was crazy." Zezé was worried such negative responses could even affect her work with Globo, which guards its dominance of the media market with meticulous research. One strategy is to sound out viewers' opinions of a particular character in order to increase—or sometimes diminish—its role in a drama.

In the two decades since the novela's groundbreaking portrayal of an "ordinary" black protagonist, a new generation of black actors is facing quite different attitudes. Around the time I talked to Zezé in 2006, I also met Taís de Araújo, who was acting in a leading role in *Cobras & lagartos* (Snakes & Lizards), a contemporary "eight o'clock novela" (novelas are often simply referred to by the time they are shown; eight is the prime slot, often filled by dramas with more social realism).[19] Taís's character, Ellen, is a "social Alpinist," defined by her "craziness to consume." She is not a villainess, but an ordinary lower-middle-class person. Taís's character Ellen has two lovers, one white, one black. Unlike the reaction to Zezé's romance, the public "accepted" both couples.

Like Zezé, Taís grew up in Rio de Janeiro near the beach but in a quite different area, called Barra da Tijuca. Barra is almost an archetypical example of a new suburban world in Brazil, home to the *emergentes*, "emergers" into a middle-class consumer lifestyle. Built along the beaches far south from the city center, it is a growing residential area of condos, highways, and massive malls. The only black student in the private school she attended, Taís said she had few role models growing up. "My teachers saw I walked with my head down. And they began to really work my self-esteem, giving me the state flag to carry, which is an honor normally for the most intelligent students. And I wasn't one." Taís is less active in the black movement than Zezé, but also strongly identifies as negra. This talk about "working self-esteem" echoes the language used by many black activists (and of course the beauty industry). Yet while her teachers worried about her low self-esteem, Taís had her mind on other things. Early in high school she began asking her parents to take her to acting auditions. They humored her—"only so I couldn't say later they had ruined my life"—but never imagined they would see their daughter on TV.

As Brazil's perhaps most well-known black actress, Taís is conscious of "carrying a burden": "I am a role model for the youth of Brazil. Parents come up to me and say my daughter is like you. I think this is cool—people identifying themselves. Even when I was growing up, there was no one on TV I could admire and say, I'm like that person, because no such person existed." Faced with this responsibility, Taís has tried to change the depiction of racial issues in novelas in which she starred. For example, she objected to racial epithets her character, Ellen, encounters.[20] But Taís was even more disturbed by the author's portrayal of Ellen's own racial identification. The synopsis described her with the words "She doesn't like being black; she denies it." Taís told the novela's author (who is white) that she thought he had misread the character he himself had created. In Taís's view, "Ellen wants to consume. She has blond hair; she sees Jennifer Lopez has blond hair, Beyoncé has blond hair, and she wants to be so powerful that she can have the diamonds and houses these women have. It's not that she doesn't want to be black; it's that she doesn't want to be poor."

The author's "mistake" was perhaps understandable, since in Brazil moving up the social scale can be seen as a form of whitening. The author thus perhaps interpreted Ellen's intense desire for higher status as a repudiation of blackness. But Taís saw it differently. If Ellen dyes her hair blond, it's not because she "doesn't want to be black." Ellen's goal is power: whitening would just be an unintended effect of social mobility. I was reminded of the conversations about plástica patients having "correction of the Negroid nose," not to "change race" but to beautify. Both cases suggest the persisting tension over the question of whether social class or race is the more important barrier to social mobility for the poor. After Taís told her objections to the writer and director, they were able together to change the portrayal of Ellen as "denying" being black.

The experiences of Zezé and Taís suggest there has been a shift in representations of race in the past twenty years, from the early 1980s to the early 2000s. While Zezé's ordinary character was rejected by a large portion of the public, Taís's characters have generally been "accepted."[21] Like a few other black models and actresses of her generation, Taís has become a glamorous icon in popular culture. Is it also significant that Taís has light skin, "fine features" (as a viewer put it), and, at the moment, long, straight blond hair—that is, she falls within traditional Brazilian aesthetic ideals. Taís identifies as negra, as do both her parents. The public also perhaps sees her as negra too (partly in "contrast" to the mostly very light faces in the media). But had she lived in poorer, less cosmopolitan milieus, she might easily have been described with other terms, such as *mulata*, or the racially ambiguous *morena*. The point of course is not whether Taís is or is not black, as the term is a social label. There is nothing surprising in the fact that a lighter-skinned beauty should become a principle incarnation of "black modernity and glamour." It does suggest, however, that a fluid system of color terms "crystallizes" into an origin-based, bipolar system within a market-based beauty culture. It is perhaps not accidental that the rise of a multicultural emphasis on racial diversity is emerging simultaneously with the "aestheticization of race"—that is, a growing importance of black style and beauty for racial identifications.

###### : : : : : :   THE ECONOMY OF APPEARANCES

Brazil imported more slaves than any other country in the Americas, and in some regions during the colonial period blacks and mulatos vastly outnumbered the European population. Brazil has been seen as the largest center of African culture in the Americas. It is ironic, then, that recently many transnational flows of black culture are moving *into*, not out of, Brazil. Popular music from the Black Atlantic, principally Caribbean reggae, and North American soul, R&B, and hip-hop have a particular significance in Brazil, where they are referred to with the English term, *black music* (figure 10). In part, the term stresses the foreign origin of these pop forms. It suggests as well that there is no equivalent concept in Brazilian Portuguese. Many Brazilian genres with African roots—Samba, Pagode, Jongo, Axé, Forró, the musical rhythms of Capoeira and Candomblé—are not traditionally considered black music, but rather have been absorbed into national culture.[22]

Peter Fry (1982, 2000) has argued that one important legacy of mestiçagem is that Afro-Brazilian syncretisms—such as samba and culinary traditions—became transracial symbols of a mixed national identity, rather than expressions of a minority group. In other words, these practices were nationalized, and hence could not serve as a source of black identity. For this reason perhaps, there is no notion of a "black" linguistic or body expression in popular culture. Of course speech in Brazil, as elsewhere, is a rich semiotic code that marks class, region, gender, generation, and so on—in fact almost any social position *except* race. In contrast, the United States has not only Black English, with a distinct syntax described by linguists, but even perhaps a folk notion that the grain of the voice is racially marked. Conversely, the black body in Brazil is generally not "marked" as having a characteristic style of movement or speech. In this situation, foreign black culture can serve as a resource for the affirmation of a black identity by providing distinct—and, of course, cool—models of style and aesthetics.

Consider these comments from Tiago, a twenty-four-year-old, black male fashion model.[23]

10. "Black Music," special edition of *Raça* magazine.

I used to dream all the time of being a basketball player, to study abroad, to go to a high school in the USA . . . I never went out without a basketball T-shirt, shorts, or sneakers. I was obsessed. I identified with the black players. My older brother when he was 14 or 15 played but I didn't like it at first. Then I started hanging out with those guys who were into that culture, and I started to want to do it. I would watch videos of games. The guys shaved their heads and put a knife in and I went to the barber and asked him to make me look like that. At 15 I drove my parents crazy. I used those clothes and felt American. I saw those good-looking guys and thought I could look like one of them. Jordan, Grant Hill, Karl Malone. I walked around bald all the time, because of them.

This story of aesthetic self-affirmation is remarkable coming from a successful fashion model; that is, a man who is tall, athletic, good looking, and well paid (though not as well as female models). Yet it was only through an identification with black American athletes and style that Tiago managed to find himself attractive and accept his appearance. His story is significant because it points to the lack of models of black style and success in a social world where prestige and recognition are often defined in consumer culture. Being visible in the media is not only a route out of poverty, but can be a way to social acceptance as black. The flow of African diasporic culture to Brazil is thus filling a cultural vacuum, providing the symbols of a black "modernity and glamour" that Globo has for decades denied to nonwhites.

Black pop culture is also entering into Brazilian grass-roots activism and mass media, reflecting a new affirmation of black aesthetics. NGOs such as Afro Dai, for example, offer citizenship lessons in conjunction with techniques of black beauty to disadvantaged teenagers in order to "raise self-esteem." Run by a former militant from the Communist Party and black movement, the NGO has a leader who says that "aesthetic work is the most effective political strategy that she has yet found" (Fry 2005: 266). Community groups such as the Lens of Dreams in City of God favela offer fashion-modeling courses to teens and younger kids. New media aiming at a black public have a strong focus on aesthetics. By the end of the 1990s there were at least eight such magazines with titles such as *Negro 100%*, *Raizes* (Roots), *Black People*, and *Raça*. The new publications made a strong link between "fashion, beauty products, and a discourse of rescuing the self-esteem of the black Brazilian" (Filho Dias 2000: 4, figure 11). In the inaugural issue of *Raça* the editor announces: "*Auto-estima*, that's the word. We try to do it on every page. The reader will open the magazine and say, 'this is building my self-esteem'" (see Fry 2005: 267). Founded by a former fashion model, the monthly covers aspects of concern to black readers, but the bulk of the stories focus on "black beauty" or black celebrities—with an average of about twenty stories on fashion per issue (Filho Dias 2000). In a context where consumer desires are being incited while formal avenues of mobility remain limited, racial visibility in mass media can become a crucial index of social inclusion.

Creative directors see themselves as more culturally hip ("We have to know the vanguard") than their corporate clients. It is often the ad agency or photographer who pushes for a nonwhite model, which the client may or may not accept as "within the branding." So I was surprised to learn that ad agencies, in turn, were following the lead of another actor—the eminently unhip state, which has played a central role in changing the representation of color in Brazilian media.

Even after privatizations beginning in the 1990s, Brazil still has dozens

BRASIL

novembro/dezembro

Mês da
Consciência
Negra
Sim, temos o que
comemorar!
Integração social,
leis contra a
discriminação,
queda do
preconceito...

ROSA
lilás e
laranja:
as novas
cores da
maquiagem
de verão

Cabelos
soltos
e naturais
Novíssimas
técnicas
de alisamento
deixam seus
fios lindos

MODA PRAIA
Biquínis e
maiôs para
você arrasar
nesta estação

MÚSICA
25 anos sem
Candeia, nosso
Zumbi da
era moderna

Preta Gil
Gordinha, sexy e
abusada, ela
dá receitas
de auto-estima
Gilberto Gil Moreira:
o ministro que fez
a ONU dançar!

SÍMBOLO

11. "Preta Gil: plump, sexy, and outspoken, she gives recipes
for self-esteem."

of state companies, which are major sources of employment. The bigger
companies, such as Banco do Brasil and Petrobras, are major clients of ad
agencies. In the past few years, a number of *diretrizes* (guidelines) have been
issued by the Ministry of Communications, demanding the "equal participation of browns, blacks, whites, and indigenous peoples" in all ad campaigns produced for the federal government (SGPR 2006). For example,
a Petrobras ad for a "more advanced gasoline" portrays a group of men
working at a gas pump. The darkest of the group speaks several languages,
leading a worker to comment, "This guy is really intelligent." Although the
explicit aim of the ad is to associate the intelligence of the polyglot and the
particular brand of gas, the ad also subtly challenges the cultural common
sense of color. As a creative director told me, "It was funnier because you
expect him [the darker worker] to be a person of less culture."

Why is the state launching such ads? For one, state companies have a policy of holding colorblind entrance exams, and their workforce is more racially diverse than that of comparably large private companies. Petrobras, for example, chose to have a black presenter, Jéssica, for its internal television variety show. In part the state is simply trying to accurately "represent diversity"—to use the multicultural idiom now gaining currency. Yet there is more going on here. Such companies are not only selling gasoline and bank accounts; they are also selling themselves as state enterprises. As such, the "representation of diversity" is itself a marketing technique, making the multihued face of the people the "brand" of the state. The product is both the commodity or service, and diversity itself.

Cynically, one could say this is progressive policy that comes at almost no cost. After all, requiring the employment of nonwhite actors costs little to implement (compared to, say, investing in primary education). On the other hand, the policy is no doubt coming from a change in racial thought among the elite. There have long been black social movements in Brazil that worked with notions of racial solidarity, such as the Black Brazilian Front (FNB). Since Getúlio Vargas shut it down in 1937, rightist regimes have often suppressed racial organization. The Left in turn emphasized class formations until very recently (Andrews 1991; Hanchard 1994). In the post-dictatorship era, from the mid-1980s on, however, new black movements have scored unprecedented victories with a newly democratic state.[24] So ironically even the pared-down, privatizing state is a principle actor—not only in the legal sphere but also in consumer culture.

The black-consumer market then is not an isolated phenomenon, nor mere marketing hype. It is a part of a larger paradigm shift that is underway, though it is too soon to say if it signals the "end of mestiçagem" (Vianna 1999). For the moment, in fact, the idealization of hybridity remains popular in everyday life, and color terms such as *moreno* are even growing in popularity (Sansone 2003; *Folha de São Paulo* 1995). Many Brazilians still reject racial identities as such, preferring to see themselves as part of Freyre's meta-race. On the other hand, the black movement, numerically small, has succeeded in putting race and identity politics on the national agenda. And representations of race in national media are undeniably changing, if slowly, as Brazilians become accustomed to seeing black consumers of "luxury" bath soap, mobile phones, and credit cards; as black models and actors gain more visibility; as racial diversity becomes a new goal of state and private corporations. How can we evaluate the implications of such shifts in the "color of Brazil" for inequality and the social organization of difference?

: : :

As mestiçagem became a key symbol in the nationalist search for a distinctive Brazilian identity, it took on the status of a kind of social contract—accept a mixed identity and you belong to a democratic povão. But such belonging comes at the price of mitigating the ability to denounce racial inequality. This recognition has in part motivated the black movement to reject such a social contract and to ask for a new one, drafted along multi-culturalist lines. The state and parts of the private sector have complied, rewriting the textbooks of the public schools, promoting racial diversity in the media, and implementing racial quotas. These policies are remarkable in that they mix ambitious redistributive social justice with an attempt to shift the cultural perception of race; they do not only favor a discriminated group but also, together with other social forces, make it visible.

The new emergence of black identities has in turn sparked controversy. Multicultural policies have been forcefully criticized as symptomatic of a neoliberal turn that is undermining Brazil's national identity and "sociological intelligence" (Fry 2000). Bourdieu and Loïc Wacquant (1999) even claim that the American *doxa* of multiculturalism is a form of cultural imperialism. Others have maintained that identity politics is necessary to overcome internalized racism and jolt Brazil out of complacency (Hanchard 1994).[25] Rita Segato (1998: 141) argues that American multiculturalism reduces black alterity to market-based styles and fashions which link "particular ethnically marked merchandise to a population of ethnically marked consumers. This canned ethnicity so characteristic of the United States does not . . . constitute a real alternative to total integration and the thorough eradication of marks of difference."[26] While genuine difference cannot be found in market identities, she sees more hope in Afro-Brazilian religious practices: "Enclaves [that] guarantee the non-peripheral alterity that is receding in the United States" (1998: 143).[27] Compared with these impressive spiritual traditions, market-based black identities may indeed seem "inauthentic." Furthermore, the evident narcissism of the culture of beauty may make it an unsuitable domain for political mobilization. Yet, the culture of beauty seems to have remarkable hardiness in a neoliberal climate, and may ultimately prove highly effective in disseminating black identities.

Take, for example, the beauty parlor. As Susan Ossman (2002) points out, this institution has been a central place of sociability in modernity, though it has received relatively little attention compared to coffeehouses, long recognized as playing a crucial role in the rise of a modern public sphere (and after all, in Brazil one often has a coffee with a haircut). Although the NGO Afro Dai is exceptional in how explicitly it links care of the body and citizenship, thousands of other salons offer places for long hours of informal talk (black styles such as tranças are particularly time-consuming to maintain). Beauty work may seem mundane, but its repetitive rhythms and discipline make it a powerful tool for "working self-esteem." Beauty salons are also a stable source of employment and often do well in urban zones where other businesses do not. Perhaps most importantly, aestheticized racial identities may in the end act as a kind of compromise between the two paradigms of multiculturalism and mestiçagem. The notion that a racial identity *should* consist solely in the superficial, *should* be "reduced" to phenotypic difference alone, is after all more compatible with Brazil's tradition of aspiring to "transcend" racial origins.[28]

Of course, black beauty itself faces many obstacles as a vehicle for overcoming internalized racism: the prestige of relative whiteness creates incentives to "lighten" through cosmetic use, marriage, or color terms. But together with other political developments that are creating real rewards for and recognition of black identities, the international prestige of black culture, and the glamour of black marketing, it seems entirely possible that Brazil will fundamentally alter its "principles of racial vision and division" (Bourdieu and Wacquant 1999). I feel now that I am facing the wall of the great modern dilemma about ideology. Beauty certainly is ideology, but it is not (only) false. I do not know which kinds of racial identifications will best aid in the struggle for social equality. But an anthropological analysis can perhaps contribute by raising awareness that both mestiçagem and multiculturalism are equally unnatural yet naturalized paradigms of race, that each have historically coexisted with racism, and that each allow—and deny—distinct forms of human relatedness and cultural creativity.

The case of Brazil also illustrates the significance of the aesthetic dimension of modern subjectivities. In the wake of scientific racism, national pride affirmed the ethical, erotic, and aesthetic dimensions of hybridity, and denied the racial exclusion that has always coexisted with mestiçagem. The whitening ideal never went away; instead, it mingled informally with mestiçagem in a powerful color hierarchy that made appearance a central marker of social status. Given this history, it is perhaps not surprising that the current opposition to mestiçagem, and to white dominance, should be framed in the same aesthetic idiom, that is, as an affirmation of black beauty and of the black consumer. As citizenship and consumption become blurred, it seems logical that marginal groups will seek social inclusion in a consumer culture that aestheticizes everyday life.

# PART THREE

# Engineering the Erotic

From the beginning of the Enlightenment project, beauty and motherhood have been question marks over women's freedom. Reform of women's fashions was a central goal for the earliest feminist visionaries who knew that long before the slogan, the body is a battleground. Modern motherhood presented perhaps an even greater challenge to the extension of natural rights to women. Healthy populations depended on hygienic and responsible mothers, who became national resources as well as wards of the state. In 1847 one hygienist, for example, addressed the Brazilian mother in these terms: "O Mothers, before nature and society, you can transmit with your noble milk excellent virtues and give to society strong men capable of supporting all work!" (Costa 1979: 77). The liberal rationale of natural rights encountered biopolitics.

The contemporary management of motherhood and sexuality represents a rupture from the earlier interest in race hygiene, matrimonial eugenics, and the juridical regulation of family "honor." Oriented toward individual happiness and health, the beauty industry's rhetoric is one of progress, choice, and freedom wrested from biological destiny. Yet, earlier tensions persist between women's "nature"—as a reproductive and sexual being—and the realization of ideals of equality and autonomy. While female reproduction is no longer subject to state concerns about improving a degenerate population, it has been infused with an aesthetic rationale: "preserving" the prepartum body and vaginal anatomy. And the earlier "splitting" of female sexuality between motherhood and sexuality in moral, medical, and legal discourses is echoed by patients' embrace of "aesthetic medicine" to negotiate conflicts between the maternal and erotic body.

Many societies have associated women with the domain of "nature" (and men with "culture") (Ortner 1974). In the West, women's social identity was often defined in the private domain of the family, through the familial roles of daughter, wife, and mother. In the past few decades in the industrialized world, however, a number of trends point to a fundamental change in the structures of familial and sexual relationships (Castells 1997; Giddens 1993). The severance of sex and reproduction through medical contraception is still a relatively recent social fact. No less important is the decline in the ideological support for the social control of female sexuality: the complex of related concepts such as virtue, honor, virginity, and so on. As the domain of female nature is partially freed from older forms of moral and political regulation, it is redefined within psychotherapeutic, consumer, and medical cultures.

This massive "unveiling" of sex can open the door to its marketization and biologization. Brazil has become a notorious destination for "sex tourism" (including the sexual abuse of children). Women assert new sexual rights in an uncertain landscape of sexual-affective relationships where male promiscuity is often "naturalized." The class aspirations I described earlier also mingle subtly with sexual aspirations and dreams of personal self-transformation. Contact with clinics can itself initiate a "biologization" of sexual experience, as desire and desirability are defined in "objective" medical terms (hormones, measurable anatomical defects, skin elasticity, and so forth) and subjected to technical improvement. Beauty work can in these circumstances become a practice of self-management that aims to maintain or enhance a form of value defined in biological and market terms.

I began this book asking why plastic surgery was growing in a developing country, one known, furthermore, for its embrace of sensuality and bodily pleasure. I have sought answers to this question by analyzing medical practices, market relationships, and national and racial ideologies of beauty. In this final part of the book, I aim to bring together the different threads of the book by addressing the missing piece of the puzzle: gender and sexuality. I focus on the often paradoxical relationships between sexual and reproductive rights and duties, between freedom and objectification, as female nature is transformed in the beauty cultures of consumer capitalism.

: : :

Before beginning fieldwork, I have the chance to live in Brazil for a year on a predissertation fellowship, taking anthropology courses at the National Museum. During this time I start *namorando* (dating) Joana, who is studying theater at the university. A year later, when I am well into fieldwork, I discover that Joana's mother, Cecília, has had *plástica*. Neither has hidden the fact from me. But I am reminded that the anthropological ideal of ethnography that I have taken for granted—total immersion in a social world—is at best a difficult concept to explain to others, perhaps especially those most close to us. Though Joana knows the topic of my fieldwork, it doesn't occur to her that I would be interested in something as mundane and natural to her as her mother's liposuction operations.

As Joana and I spend more time together, I gradually get incorporated into her household (like most unmarried women in Rio, she lives with her family). To Joana's brother Pedro, I am merely a *namoradinho*, a "little bit" her boyfriend. But Joana's younger sister begins calling me *cunhado*, brother-in-law. I am reminded of the letters I receive from a fellow student doing fieldwork in Papua New Guinea filled with references to his "mother" and "brothers." Although in my thesis I have called Cecília an "informant," ignoring the context of our relationship, I now find it anthropologically fitting that I met her through one of the fictive-kin relations that fieldworkers have often found to be the only means of assimilation into a different society.

This is a world that is certainly not matriarchal, but almost all female (Cecília is separated from her husband, Miguel, who supports her—Pedro, her son, is seldom at home). Many evenings we sit in the den, tuned into a *novela*, continually snacking on microwaved leftovers from *almoço*, grilled cheese, and cans of Skol beer. The conversation lazily meanders from the action on the screen to the action in the *bairro*, which often rivals the spiciest dished out by Globo. Often Jussane, from the upstairs apartment, or a cousin will drop in, and after a few drinks the audience will begin to drown out the passionate voices of the *artistas*. Once Cecília—curious as to why I should spend so much time in this feminine realm—asks me if I am not bored, and Joana replies, half-joking, "Don't worry about him, anthropology is the science of gossip."

I see much less of Miguel, Joana's father, who lives in a bachelor flat. The daughters are solicitous and affectionate, calling him *papai* and kissing him frequently, while Pedro addresses him formally as *o senhor*. Miguel arrived penniless in Rio in his twenties, and worked his way up from truck driver to owner of a small interior renovation company. He never "had time for college," but sent his three children to private high schools to give them a shot at entering the highly competitive public universities. He employs over a dozen workers, and his income supports a considerable number of people—his wife and children, his *namorada* (girlfriend), a couple of maids, a cook when the kids were younger, and two ne'er-do-well brothers who lean on him for loans to provide their families with the rites of passage into middle-class life. Miguel also has a number of *padrinho* (godfather) relationships with domestic workers, and distant, poorer kin. Weighed down by these responsibilities, he has spells of insomnia and even panic attacks. Conquering a deep suspicion of doctors and drugs, he now takes prescription anxiolytics. But as a young man he was "Bohemian." Rejecting his peers' explorations of a global counterculture, he hung out at the bars in Lapa—a run-down area that was home to some of the greatest samba composers of the 1930s. His was a kind of nationalist Bohemianism that blended samba and soccer enthusiasm with a touch of *malandragem*, street smarts and suave roguery.

It was in this phase of his life, soon after winning the city's billiards championship, that he met his future wife. Though her father has mostly African and Indian ancestry, Cecília's reddish hair and honey-colored complexion leave no doubt that she is simply *branca* (white). Cecília grew up in the poorest suburbs of Rio. Her parents, Léia and Josefe, were migrants who fled poverty in the interior of Ceará. With only a couple years of schooling, Léia escaped a tyrannical mother by moving to Rio. At fifteen, she gave birth to Cecília. Josefe learned enough English to pass the entrance exam for the Coast Guard, thereby escaping a life of menial labor. The couple managed to send their only daughter to college, where she studied psychology (a relic from those days is the Portuguese edition of the collected works of Freud, displayed in pristine hardback in the living room). Soon after graduating, Cecília married Miguel and became a *dona da casa*. It is hard to imagine a couple less temperamentally matched. Miguel is compulsive, intense, with an acidic sense of humor, happiest when absorbed in a Bingo game, where he plays four cards simultaneously. Cecília is the life of the party—relaxed, dreamy, given to sunbathing during the day and French and Italian cinema at night.

On weekends Joana and I go to the social club where Cecília meets her friends, women in their fifties who are mostly divorced or separated. Either chain smokers or heavy drinkers, they are a formidable bunch, with deeply tan skin and voices that seem both booming and husky. A member of the group will occasionally wander out of the restaurant into the brutal Rio sun, rejoining the table a few minutes later in a bikini dripping with pool water. The conversation is studded with words such as *safado* (bastard) and *galinha* ("chicken"), a man who picks here and there but won't stay committed.

Cecília is quite open discussing her marriage and separation. She seems to bear no ill will toward her husband, who is now dating a younger woman. But Léia took the breakup less in stride. A tiny, fair-skinned woman, she is a fierce tempered *figura* (character) mostly ignored by everyone except Joana. Given a drink, she ritually sniffs the glass, turns up her nose, and says, "cheiro de ovo," egg smell. Once a follower of an Afro-Brazilian sect, Léia converted to a Pentecostal church and now enthusiastically denounces such devil worship. She is also disturbed by the loose morals everywhere in evidence on television. After a pop singer appears on a talk show, she asks Joana to write a letter to the host: "Tell him that if she were a good singer, she wouldn't need to show her *xereca* [vagina] on television." To me she says several times, "If you've come to *namorar* my granddaughter [by which she means "court to marry"], then you're already family. Otherwise, don't wear out my sofa." She is most critical of her daughter, whom she blames for the separation with Miguel. A somewhat typical exchange, reconstructed with Joana's help, went something like this. Léia would say: "I made you dresses, I lightened your hair, I taught you to do your nails, to iron and bleach your clothes, but it didn't make a difference. You've *largada* (let yourself go)."

"*Cala a boca* [shut your mouth]," Cecília would respond. "I was with little kids, and I didn't have time to take care of myself. And we didn't have a maid then. I didn't give a shit what my husband thought—I smelled like his children. If he didn't like me when he came home, it's his problem."

Léia, though, didn't see it that way. "After having children, you cut your hair too short. You began to use loose clothes, brutal, masculine clothes. Your husband came home and saw a relaxed woman, with each bit of clothing a different color. And what happened? He got himself another one without children."

Though only fifteen years apart in age, Cecília and Léia are separated by large cultural gaps. Cecília usually dismissed these types of comments, and said, using a *moderno* idiom, "My marriage ended because we had grown apart." It was at this time, when she was in her late thirties, that she decided to have plástica—abdominal surgery and liposuction on the thighs and stomach (followed by an additional liposuction operation some years later). She explained how the operations were designed to "correct" the effects of her three Caesarean births: "I did it on my belly, which had a very flaccid part due to the *cesáreas*. . . . And it bothered me a lot, because when I put on a bikini there was that little piece of skin hanging above the bikini, and so I decided to fix it. And the doctor made a cut a little bigger than the Caesarean scars, and took out that piece of meat that was really flaccid, without life, and then he sewed it up, and did the liposuction." While it feels odd—and often inaccurate—to use the blunt language of class to discuss the lives of those we know well, Cecília might be described as inhabiting a world where the middle class and the *povão* blend together. She spends much of her time around two illiterate women—her mother and maid—and through charity work at a nursery, many others from the "popular classes." In Portuguese she might be called *emergente*, emerging, *into* middle class, and *away from* a more popular background.[1] This social passage is marked symbolically and materially by acquisition of key commodities and rites of passage.[2] In Brazil, a lavish debutant party for fifteen-year-old girls is common—or else the more moderno alternative chosen for Joana's coming-of-age ritual, a trip to Disneyland. Over the past three decades, a new addition has made it to the list, plástica, which, as *Veja* puts it, "has become integral to middle-class aspirations" (*Veja* 2002).

Cecília may have chosen to have plástica because it has become part of a normal, middle-class lifestyle. Yet her operations were also part of another social passage—through the female life cycle. When she was pregnant with her third child, she had already begun to think about having plástica. She wanted to combine the birth, which like the others would be a Caesarean, with a tubal ligation and a cosmetic correction of abdominal "flaccidity." After her gynecologist told her, however, that he couldn't "fix her belly" during the birth since he was already "tying the tubes," she decided to postpone the plástica. A few years later she had combined liposuction and abdominal surgery to "repair" the Caesareans and reduce "localized fat" she had gained during her pregnancies.

Cecília associated plástica with other surgeries as a form of managing her reproductive body. Performed together with her last C-section, the tubal ligation reflected a decision to definitively end her reproductive life. Abdominal surgery removed the "unaesthetic" effect of the Caesarean deliveries, but the liposuction also corrected what she saw as the unwanted bodily changes due to pregnancy itself. Her plastic surgery was also linked to sexuality: she discussed the procedures in the context of her marriage, and the ending of the reproductive phase of her life.

Cecília's experience is somewhat typical, at least for an urban, middle-class woman in her fifties. She is not compulsively interested in surgery and not particularly *vaidosa*, vain. Before having surgery, she sought the advice of a family acquaintance, a doctor and husband of a friend, a "sensible person, who would never recommend a plastic surgery unless it was necessary." She also did not deliberate much about the decision. Her operations seemed a natural response—one of course made possible by modern medicine—to a physical defect caused by the event of pregnancy. What I explore next is what social forces have made plastic surgery a "normal" part of female reproduction and what, in turn, this practice can tell us about larger tensions between motherhood and sexuality.

ESTER

PLASTIC SURGERY WARD, SANTA CASA HOSPITAL

SANTA CASA WAITING ROOM

MISS BRASIL CONTEST 2001

JULIANA BORGES, MISS SILICONADA

DONA FIRMINA

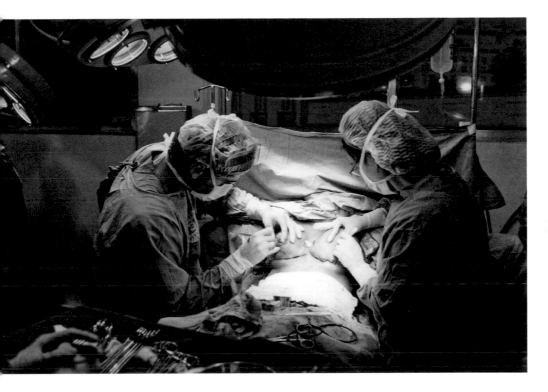

BREAST REDUCTION SURGERY

GRAZIELE AND LUANDA

MODELS, CITY OF GOD FAVELA

LENS OF DREAMS STUDENTS

Scholarly critiques of cosmetic surgery often assume that the practice essentially disfigures the body, or at least makes unnatural-looking changes: faces stretched in a mask, caricatures of the pert nose, balloonlike breasts. Complications, as well as aesthetic disappointment, are always possible. Nevertheless, to understand the appeal of this practice, it must be acknowledged that—setting aside any ostensible psychotherapeutic benefits—plástica often meets and exceeds the aesthetic expectations of patients, that is, makes them look younger and sexier to their social milieu and themselves. Patients often enthusiastically show off results, which are praised and envied by friends.

A related point is that it is hard to understand the rapid growth of plástica without acknowledging that patients actively seek it out. The image of the surgeon's scalpel or gaze "colonizing" (Morgan 1991) the female body implies that patients are passive, even gullible. The line between agency and cultural coercion is tricky to draw, and patients certainly do not make completely "free choices" (see Davis 1995). In fact, the rhetoric of choice is a marketing tactic. But patients have diverse attitudes and motivations. Some harbor doubts all the way to the operating room. Others act with conviction, never question the assurances of surgeons, proselytize to friends or family, and act—not in line with male pressure—but against the wishes of husbands, boyfriends, fathers, or sons.

Yet, it would be difficult to underestimate the gendered aspect of plastic surgery. It is true that the male percentage of the total number of estética patients grew from 5 percent in 1994 to almost 30 percent six years later (*Época* 2000). Nevertheless, in 2004, 69 percent of operations were performed on women in Brazil (SBCP 2005). This percentage is probably higher in public hospitals where male cosmetic patients, aside from a few cases of "donkey ears" and enlarged breasts, are particularly rare. Walking into a plastic surgery ward, I had the impression of entering a distinctly feminine realm, and those patients who have not yet learned or reject the therapeutic language of the specialty often describe their operations as simply "uma coisa de mulher" (a woman's thing).[3]

Not only are a majority of patients women, but plástica is intertwined with major milestones in the female life course: puberty, pregnancy, breastfeeding, and menopause. Plástica can mark key rites of passage: initiation into adulthood, marriage, and divorce. At fifteen Teresa received a nose job as her coming-out present (another substitution for the traditional debutante party). Menstruation becomes the ground zero for plástica: the minimum age for surgery is calculated from the time of the patient's first period. After menopause, a facelift boosts the self-esteem. Body contouring can be combined with sterilization, "after the factory has been shut down." These events divide the experience of female nature into various "before and afters" that are managed with aesthetic medicine.[4]

The transformative events by far the most often mentioned in connection with plástica are pregnancy and breast-feeding. Cecília blamed pregnancy for a weight gain while a Cesarean delivery created "dead tissue" that needed to be removed. Rosa said her pregnancy and breast-feeding led her to seek a breast lift.

> I was young when I had a kid, nineteen. My breasts were small and they grew too much. They ended up falling and were full of stretch marks. . . . My surgeon cut them out—he even took out the nipple, he put in a prosthesis, and he made another breast in me. And it was *so* well done, even the gynecologist when he palpated it, only when he saw the little scar did he say, "You did a plastic surgery; I don't believe it!" I was very satisfied with the first plástica, because this is the second, nê?

Rosa and Cecília began to think seriously about plástica only after giving birth. In some cases, though, women already plan future cosmetic surgery *before* having children. As a woman in her early twenties put it, "I want to put in silicone. But first I want to have kids. I'll wait; after the law of gravity acts, and everything falls, then I'll do it."

Other patients similarly blamed pregnancy and breast-feeding for thickened waists, Caesarean scars and stretch marks, and localized fat. Body parts could be described as *acabado* (finished); *caído* (fallen); *murcha* (shriveled); or compared to a *maracujá da gaveta*, a passion fruit left in the refrigerator drawer, dried out and wrinkled. Patients and surgeons see plástica as a powerful technique that corrects such defects. As a popular lay manual puts it, "During pregnancy the breasts grow, and then eventually become smaller, losing their projection. This is one of the routine motivations of patients in search of a plástica" (Ribeiro and Aboudib 1997: 125).[5] Breast lifts and reductions create a breast that is "higher, firmer, and smaller; totally different than that sluggish and dispersed breast" (69). Breast surgeries are the most common type of cosmetic procedure in Brazil, but abdominal operations are a close second (not counting liposuction, as it can be performed on many areas of the body) (SBCP 2005). Finally, some patients have recourse to *plástica na intimidade*, or "vaginal tightening." Both patients and surgeons then view several (but not all) operations as a kind of "postpartum correction," even if they followed the patient's last pregnancy by three decades or more.

Plástica, though, is only one tool in a larger array of practices that manage female reproductive, sexual, and psychic health. Called *medicina estética* (aesthetic medicine), or *estética feminina* (feminine aesthetics), this experimental field combines several specialties, including Ob-Gyn, dermatology, geriatrics, nutrition, psychotherapy, and plastic surgery, as well as pseudomedical cosmetic services.[6] What is most remarkable about medicina estética is its ability to forge links between diverse medical and nonmedical specialties and effectively merge notions of health and beauty.

Michelle said her gynecologist had "frightened" her: "He is accustomed to seeing me thin, *magrinha*, and he said I was a cow. Because my breasts were flaccid, because of the pregnancy and maybe not using a bra made it worse." Such direct criticism is rare. More commonly a medical specialist—a general practitioner, gynecologist, or even psychotherapist—might make a friendly suggestion or informal referral. Lídia said she had asked her gynecologist "about her belly" after giving birth: "He said that my belly would never go away with exercise, that I could only get rid of it with plastic surgery, and that's when I began to think about it." She then went to see a plastic surgeon: "He said, 'You are really young . . . no way. You have to have a surgery. If your husband can't pay for your breast [surgery], I'll do it for free, because it's absurd, a young woman of your age having to look like that.'"

Such comments recall a tradition of seeing the body as a highly social surface and fair target for public scrutiny, as well as a history of "intimacy" between doctor and patient. They reflect not only "aesthetic expertise," but also perhaps a certain amount of misogyny in the medical gaze. Such critical attitudes—often adopted by patients too—do not necessarily indicate a disciplinary attitude. The same patients who enthusiastically embrace plastic surgery often take evident pleasure in displaying the body on the beach, even in its "flawed" state, or express a confident sense of embodiment through sport, dance, or body-centered spiritual practices. This discrepancy suggests that plastic surgery does just fuel bodily alienation, but also disseminates a "productive" notion of female health.

Plástica is linked to other specialties not just through referrals but in a "discursive field"—if that term can adequately refer to the lavishly illustrated materials of marketing and news media. For example, a *Veja* article on estética feminina lists smaller liposuction needles that minimize bleeding and "more modern" texturized breast implant materials next to improved procedures for diagnosing breast cancer. One article on medicina estética defined the "essential points" in the field: "The treatment of physical, constitutional and aesthetic alterations . . . and unaesthetic sequelae of illness and trauma. The postponement of aging . . . and the reeducation of the individual to make him [sic] realize the possibility of preserving his biological patrimony through the development of mental, physical, and nutritional hygiene programs."

The tone of such marketing and medical publications—evoking notions of progress, hygiene, and development—almost recalls the modernizing ideology present in many Brazilian institutions. Fields such as medicina estética are emerging in other parts of the world as well, but they take a localized form as they adapt to Brazil's medical and gender systems. In Brazil, the management of female reproduction and sexuality has mirrored the hopes and anxieties of the modernization project. In the early decades of the twentieth century, the state promoted the "hygienic family" as a cornerstone of a civilized nation. Matrimonial eugenics and the juridical regulation of female virginity reflected elite concerns about the moral and physical health of the mixed people (Stepan 1991). But over the past forty years, the medicalization of reproduction in Brazil must also be understood from the perspective of "demand" as reproductive healthcare emerged as a modern good.

In the 1970s, the Brazilian state retreated from a pronatalist position (snubbing the Catholic church) and made cheap medical forms of contraception widely available within the public health system. The expansion of healthcare thus helped to institutionalize and secularize reproductive practice. State involvement in the area of family planning perhaps reduced the "psychological costs" of fertility control for Catholics (Martine 1996). Doctors, sexologists and psychologists promoted a rational, scientific understanding of sex (Parker 1991: 87). The dual processes of modernization and the medicalization of reproduction contributed to a spectacular decline in Brazil's fertility rate, from 6 children per woman in 1960 to below 2.5 in the mid-1990s (Martine 1996). By comparison, Britain experienced a comparable drop over a longer period, from the mid-1870s to 1930 (Pfeffer 1993: 5). The point is that the movement of sex *away* from a religious and folk idiom and *into* a medical and consumer one has been relatively fast and recent in Brazil (though certainly not "complete"). This transformation helped create a medical culture particularly receptive to aesthetic medicine.

It is perhaps not coincidental that Brazil has some of the world's highest per capita rates of cosmetic surgery as well as C-sections and tubal ligations. The national sterilization rate for women in union in 1996 was 37 percent, accounting for half of all contraceptive use in Brazil (Caetano and Potter 2004). Interesting in this connection is that the rate of surgical *male* contraception, that is, vasectomy, is much lower in Brazil, less than 1 percent in 1986, compared to almost 13 percent in the United States in 1988—another indication of how the notion of "choice" may mask gender ideologies that make women more likely to have "elective" female surgeries (Carranza 1994: table 4, Potter 1999: table 1).[7] C-sections accounted for 36 percent of all deliveries in the 1990s, but can reach 70 percent or more in some hospitals (Hopkins 2000). According to the WHO, rates above 15 percent indicate the operation is being used for non-clinical reasons (Béhague 2002: 473). A "culture" of Caesareans and sterilizations began with the expansion of the public health system in the 1970s and, like plástica, has rapidly spread across social classes.

High rates of surgical intervention in female reproduction point to the presence of a market logic and class aspirations in medical practices. The healthcare system has built-in financial incentives to perform C-sections.[8] Economic pressures can also lead to the abuse of sterilization. A parliamentary commission in 1992 found that some employers were demanding "sterilization certificates" from female job seekers (Carranza 1994). Caetano and Potter (2004), though, argue that coercion is a minor factor in the spread of sterilization; they focus instead on "demand." Sterilization can become a valuable medical good—and even be traded for votes in regions with clientelistic politics (Scheper-Hughes 1992: 337). Sterilizations also feed C-section rates as the two procedures are piggybacked in the public health system (plástica is similarly linked to other operations to reduce costs). The dual sterilization and Caesarean procedure can provide both free contraception to the mother and benefits to the clinic (Potter 1999). A study found that 75 percent of sterilizations occurred during the course of a C-section (Martine 1996: 54). But some women also see Caesareans as desirable in themselves: modern, convenient, pain-free, and even safer. As the director of a São Paulo clinic puts it, "We have evolved. I think the Caesarean is an improvement, and nobody can halt progress" (Downie 2000).

The logic of distinction behind Caesareans can be traced back to the 1920s, when large numbers of women for the first time left home to give birth in clinics. As medicine gained in prestige and technological sophistication, the middle classes lost their prejudice against hospitalization (Besse 1996: 21). Demand for medical care seen as "progress" is magnified by a healthcare system with deep inequities. The fact that wealthier women have higher rates of C-sections reinforces a notion of technological intervention as a "medical good." Conversely, poorer women see denial of a C-section as a form of negligence or even medical incompetence. They may respond by using informal tactics—including "making a scandal" (screaming and tears)—to force an Ob-Gyn to perform the procedure (Béhague 2002). Even slight inequalities can create a "market for unnecessary interventions among women who feel marginalized from access to medical technology" (Béhague et al. 2002). Béhague makes this argument in reference to "elective" Caesareans, but a similar dynamic shapes desires for elective cosmetic surgery in a context of scarcity.

Caesareans and tubal ligations are, of course, different procedures than cosmetic surgery. All surgery carries health risks, but estética (by definition) has no physical health benefit. C-sections, though, can be lifesaving, and tubal ligations expand contraceptive choice. All three procedures, however, are linked in a management regime of reproduction and sexuality. Caesareans and tubal ligations familiarize women with surgical interventions (and resultant scarring). Like plástica, Caesareans may themselves be chosen for "sexual-aesthetic" motives. Scheper-Hughes (1992: 338) reports that sterilization was combined with cosmetic surgeries such as "vaginal-tightening," which "became fashionable among middle-class women wanting to maintain their husbands' sexual interest." And Maria Carranza (1994: 113–14) points to a "popular belief" (shared by some Ob-Gyns) that a C-section is "capable of preserving the vaginal and perineal anatomy of the woman, while a vaginal birth would produce distensions making sexual relations more difficult." The naturalization of medical procedures as tools of reproductive and sexual freedom can mask the inequalities underlying medicine. Abortion, for example, which remains illegal in Brazil, played a key, though "hidden," role in the decline of Brazil's fertility rate (Martine 1996). But only wealthier women have access to them in clinical conditions.

High rates of Caesareans and sterilizations and a more general medicalization of reproduction fuel demand for plástica by making elective surgery a normal part of female health. Former experience with surgery can make it seem easier to undergo more. As Cecília said, "I liked it. The hospital was good, hygienic, it was simple, superficial, only seven days." There is thus a kind of self-perpetuating logic of surgery whereby an initial intervention sets in motion a chain of operations. Cecília said that her abdominal surgery was not "*really* plastic surgery; it was a repair of the three Caesareans, mainly the first two, which were on top of each other—this isn't good." Due to the close spacing between her first two pregnancies, she was not able to wait the recommended three years between C-sections to allow her body to fully recover. On the other hand, she could neither have a natural birth after having had a Caesarean only a year earlier "because this ran the risk of tearing things inside." The first Caesarean birth was thus linked in varying degrees of "necessity" to six subsequent operations: two more Caesarean births, the last one combined with tubal ligation; abdominal surgery to correct flaccidity resulting from the Caesareans; and two liposuction operations.

: : :

Aesthetic medicine aims at a notion of health where sexual happiness can and should coexist with control over reproduction. Yet it also reflects—and perhaps exacerbates—a split consciousness in which the roles of mother and sexual being are separate and potentially in conflict. It's not that most patients reject motherhood or breast-feeding. Some, in fact, see plástica as a tool that helps them to enjoy being mothers without suffering aesthetically or sexually. Tatiana asked, "Is there anything more healthy than to breast-feed your own child? No. To those mothers who look in the mirror every day and say, 'Oh my God, do you see what breast-feeding did to my chest?' I would say: 'Go and fix it with plástica.'" Tatiana even suggests that plástica enhances the "libido": "I've already seen many women doing plastic surgery after having a child, and then . . . become pregnant again. Right after operating. Feeling so beautiful, marvelous, the libido rises in the head, and she gets pregnant!"

This argument is perhaps a defense of plástica against the charge that surgery implicitly rejects motherhood. Tatiana turns the tables: plástica is a technological auxiliary that resolves a potential conflict between sexuality and maternity. Maria José speaks even more explicitly of a duality in gender roles (her comments are taken from an interview in Ribeiro and Aboudib 1997). Before having her first plástica, she hesitated, wondering "To what extent it wasn't an excess of vanity" (ibid.: 152). Was it right to intern herself when so many people are suffering from injuries and illness? Then she realized her doubts were based in a moral sanction against altering the body: "The guilt of interfering with that sacred thing, the body. But women interfere with it in any case, with Caesareans, hysterectomies, many times, mastectomy. But when it comes time to do a plastic surgery, which is good for the self, they themselves hesitate. . . . They have difficulty making an effort for the healthy and the beautiful. The human being insists on carrying around innumerable kinds of guilt." Having suffered through earlier surgeries, she sees plástica as a reward.

> My life is divided into before and after [the operation]. As I said, it was after the operation that I touched the tip of an iceberg—sexuality. [Why?] Because a woman of my age has a very complicated and confused sexual development. . . . We have a culture that limits us. We end up adapting ourselves to these limitations. Marriage, children come, time passes, and we feel old, ugly. It's in the superficial, in the skin, that we perceive this. We end up letting our bodies suffer a whole range of aggressions and then when we wake up, we ask why? In truth, it's because women have difficulty living out their own sexuality. As if after becoming a mother, the role of woman becomes secondary. (ibid.: 155)

Paradoxically, Maria José argues that the "aggression" of technological intervention should make women seek out *more*, not less, elective surgery. The larger question she raises is: If modern medicine has already routinized intervention in the female body—often with negative aesthetic, sexual, and psychological effects—why not have plástica, which has positive ones?

While some patients embrace plástica as a modern solution that enables them to enjoy the roles of "woman" and "mother," their words also suggest a rejection of the "postpartum body." Dani, an IT specialist, had a breast reduction for her sixteenth birthday present. Now turning thirty, she is contemplating a liposuction and more surgery after having children, which she hoped to do in her mid-thirties. "After having kids, I'll have to do a *recauchutagem* [refurbishing, normally of a car]. After shutting down the factory, nê?" Comparing her body first to a car that needs to be outfitted and then to a factory that will be closed down is meant to be amusing. It's funny because obviously the body is not a factory, and the kind of body Dani desires—curvy, clean, soft—provides a humorous contrast with industrial dirt and angular lines. It's also funny because to speak lightly of motherhood perhaps seems profane. Other women compared having plástica to buying apartments or cars, objects which have value but which must be "maintained." These comparisons suggest that the body marked by motherhood becomes alien, an object external to the self. Patients often insisted, however, that they were not trying to change their identity, but *restore* it: the marks of aging and childbirth make it hard for them to recognize themselves. Plástica can then become "good for the self" while surgical correction of such marks reinforces the perception of them as defects external to the self.

The remarks of these patients reminded me of an argument by Iris Marion Young (1990: 196) that a "patriarchal logic defines an exclusive border between motherhood and sexuality." Drawing on psychoanalytic theory, she argues that for heterosexual men, the repression of sexual desire for the mother diminishes desire for a sexual partner who is acting in a maternal role. Conversely, she argues, women are led to deny either a maternal or sexual role: "The virgin or the whore, the pure or the impure, the nurturer or the seducer is either asexual mother or sexualized beauty, but one precludes the other" (196–97). This "logic" might be particularly pronounced in Latin societies. Luiz Tarlei de Aragão (1983:142) states that many of the Brazilian men he interviewed "obsessively worked to transform the category of wife into mother," or else simply married a "mãe-zinha" ("little mother"). The consequence for female sexuality, he adds, is that "women who flee the model of modesty, fidelity, and resignation represented in the maternal metaphor are more or less soon identified with the ideological amalgam covering the category of prostitute" (139).⁹ Aragão claims that women who are not mothers risk being seen as whores, but he doesn't spell out a converse proposition, which is that women identified too strongly with a maternal role may cease to be sexual beings. This risk is perhaps greater as sexual desirability as a norm expands to cover new demographic groups of women for longer parts of the life cycle—from the early teens to middle age and beyond.

The infamous "virgin/whore complex" is perhaps in decline in many Latin and Mediterranean societies, as medical and consumer cultures disseminate a view of female sexuality as a domain of health and happiness (Goldstein 2003). Yet, a marked split between sexual and maternal roles evident in patients' words suggests the persistence of at least some aspects of this dichotomy. While older moral notions persist in contemporary beauty culture, they appear in a new, sometimes "aestheticized" form. As a tool to correct the postpartum body or enhance erotic allure, plastic surgery is also performed on the genitals. *Plástica & Beleza* and news media have extensively reported on a rise in "intimate plásticas."¹⁰ The field refers to a range of operations: from injections of fat into "flaccid labia" to liposuction on a "voluminous mons venus" to "corrections of vaginal widening," "a problem most often presented by women who have opted for normal [vaginal] birth" (Clínica Vitalitá website 2006b). Note the word *opt* here implies

plástica

"Algumas mulheres são capazes de fugir de uma grande paixão, se tiverem vergonha do seu órgão genital"

12. Intimate plástica: "Some women are capable of fleeing from a great passion if they are ashamed of their genital organ."

that a vaginal birth is a "choice," but one that might create a sexual or aesthetic problem needing later correction.

Intimate plástica is marketed as a form of "progress" that allows the overcoming of psychological complexes (figure 12). The website of Clínica Vitalitá advises clients that "aesthetic aspects" of the genitals are "increasingly important for self-esteem." And a surgeon invited to the national talk show *Jô Soares* speaks about "the end of taboos" (*Plástica & Beleza* 2006a). One magazine story recounts how a patient went to see a plastic surgeon after watching this TV program, then underwent correction of hypertrophied labia. "Since I was a girl, I always thought my vagina ugly," she said, "which left me with complexes and depression. . . . Now, I am another woman, more vain, more happy, more secure. I look at my vagina every day with a mirror. And it is beautiful!" (ibid.).

There is a certain irony to "intimate plástica" if we consider Freud's (1953 [1905]: 156–57) observation that genitals, unlike the rest of the human form, are fundamentally ugly, though exciting. The perception of beauty stems from a sublimation of erotic interest. The ugly or "animal" appearance of the genitals breaks the spell of sublimated eros cast by the beauty of the nude female body, and thus stimulates a desire for intercourse. This perspective is probably not shared by most patients, but it does at least point to the strangeness of the idea of aesthetically pleasing genitals. The growth of intimate plástica shows that aesthetic stigma can apply even to an area of the body not usually on display. It also suggests the role of pornography in making images of "beautiful genitals" culturally visible.

Intimate plástica aims not just to correct "deformities," but also to enhance sexual experience, including female pleasure. One advertisement claims that "vaginal widening" following normal birth "reduces vaginal orgasm." It offers both a surgical procedure to correct such problems and a nonsurgical "sexual therapy" for "anorgasmic women": "An apparatus that fits in the palm of the hand, and placed over the clitoris, augments blood circulation in the region and vaginal sensitivity, facilitating orgasm" (Clínica Vitalitá website 2006a). (The American College of Obstetricians and Gynecologists, concerned with the popularity of such procedures in the United States, stated that "vaginal rejuvenation" and "G-spot amplification" are not "medically indicated" and that there is "no scientific evidence regarding their benefits" [ACOG 2007].) While it is unclear how such procedures affect sexual experience, their mode of justification expresses a cultural logic of sexual happiness as bedrock of the healthy self.

Despite the emphasis on freedom and pleasure, some parallels exist with the earlier eugenic and hygienic regulation of the female body. Female virginity had been a key site of social control—and resistance—in earlier stages of Brazil's civilizing journey. Reasoning that a healthy family meant a healthy nation, medical and legal authorities tried to protect family "honor." "Marriage at the police station" referred to the forced union between the perpetrator and victim of the crime of "defloration." In order to establish whether a woman had actually been deflowered, authorities performed hymenal exams. Like contemporary plastic surgeons, these forensic experts developed their techniques in relation to European norms, but also staked out areas of Brazilian superiority due to greater experience. Afrânio Peixoto, for example, claimed that from 1907 to 1915, he had personally observed 2,701 hymens (Caulfield 2000: 17). The novelty of such experience is suggested by the fact that many Brazilian doctors had traditionally refrained from vaginal examinations if they thought the patient was a virgin (Peard 1999: 228). While this medicojuridical system reflected patriarchal notions of female sexuality, it could also be appropriated by youth challenging parental authority: young lovers conspired to use the "crime" to force parents to accept their marriage. Ironically, the very attempt to regulate virginity led to new debates over Brazil's civilizing process. After medical examiners discovered the "complacent hymen" that does not rupture easily, some authorities began to doubt whether the state of virginity could be established by physical evidence at all, and debated whether such uses of medicine were a sign of "progress," or rather a vestige of a "backwards" tradition (Caulfield 2000).

Defloration is no longer a legal concept, though as late as the 1960s surgeons experimented with "hymenal reconstructions" to combat the prejudice encountered by women whose hymens were damaged through disease or accident (Caulfield and Esteves 1993: 70n). Contemporary genital surgery does not heal suffering caused by the social stigma of "lost virginity," but rather aims to augment self-esteem. Instead of the opposition of virgin and prostitute, there is an opposition between the "nulliparous" body (the body that hasn't given birth) and the body "deformed" by motherhood. Rather than a site for the moral control of family honor, female genitals become an object for the psychotherapeutic management of individual health and hygiene. A moral notion of virginity has been replaced by what might be termed "aesthetic virginity." Although sometimes oriented toward women's sexual pleasure, this notion perhaps reflects the presence of older fetishizations of the female body in health practices. Consumer capitalism has a remarkable ability to commodify lost traditions and values, presenting them to the market anew in aestheticized form: as historical theme parks, retro design, and so forth (Ivy 1995). Perhaps this capacity can extend also to the female body, as the "lost" value of virginity is offered in an aesthetic form to the happy consumer.

Understanding the desires aroused by the glamorous medical good of plastic surgery raises difficult questions about changes in modern sexual experience. The separation between motherhood and sexuality, which Young (1990) relates to psychological dynamics in patriarchy, is also inflected by cultural and class differences. In the next sections I analyze the elaboration of femininity within the intimate realm of family, class, and sexual relationships. This area of life is often fraught with ambivalence—a point that is obvious enough but often missing in accounts that view sexuality as a domain of normalization. How are dichotomies between sexual and maternal roles shaped by Brazil's often intimate hierarchical relationships? How do class and sexual aspirations mingle in beauty culture?

I am having lunch with Gláucia and Pilar one day when the conversation veers from talk about race and aging to the vanity of *empregadas*, maids. Both women come from cosmopolitan milieus. Gláucia, the ex-wife of a diplomat, is as comfortable discussing plastic surgery as Lacanian psychoanalysis (she is a veteran of both types of therapy). In her early fifties, she has two adult children and a *namorado*. Pilar is the daughter of friends of Gláucia (who are also divorced), another diplomat and an acclaimed poet. After a childhood split between Washington, D.C., and Brasília, Pilar became a self-taught painter. Her last exhibition—still lifes inspired by indigenous feather work—was a critical success, but she still earns some cash as an occasional "tour guide" for notables visiting Rio. In this world, far removed from material necessity, commodities have little prestige value in themselves, and the vulgar ostentation of the socialite *perua* (turkey) is the target of fun. When Gláucia hears of my research topic she invites me to lunch at her apartment, a condo with a view of lush vegetation that contrasts with austere, imported furniture. Over a long (if rather light) meal, conversation moves from the fine arts to female beauty, from Europe to Rio, and from the life of the *patroa*, mistress, to that of the empregada.

Gláucia decided to have her first plastic surgery after her then husband commented that her breasts resembled those of a model appearing in a copy of *Playboy* he was browsing. "*Meu Deus* [My God]," she said, "a breast of that size? Let's be done with it. I wanted a reduction, but not that little breast, you know the breast of a thirteen-year-old—"

Pilar interrupts, "Because you know back then, what was pretty was that little bit of breast . . ."

"To me it looked like a fried egg. A round circle with a big nipple in the middle. That was the first time I tried out plástica, and it turned out very well."

Ironically, the desire for plastic surgery was here provoked not by a desire to emulate a model, but rather by a wish to differentiate herself from a commodity-image. Despite the new fashion for silicone implants, breast reductions and lifts are among the most commonly performed procedures. After lunch, we move to the sofa as Gláucia's maid, Nilma, serves us tiny porcelain cups of *cafezinho*. Pilar passes around a bottle of liquid aspartame and a plate of biscuits. Gláucia comments that the European woman is "beautiful until the age of thirty or thirty-five, then she begins to get really ugly." She then begins a discourse on the "vanity of the Brazilian woman" but abruptly interrupts herself: "Logically I am referring to the better classes — Nilma, poor thing, at forty-two she is doing herself in, the way she works; at sixty she will be just a fragment of herself, nê? But you know even the lower-class woman, she is really vain. Have you seen my empregada; did you see her going out *inteirona* ['really perfect'] hair done up, all — "

Pilar interrupts, "A person can be without one centavo, but always with nails done, whatever the class, if they're not beggars — "

Gláucia interjects, "My maid does her nails. And her hair . . . she is all *produzida* [produced]!"

"Fátima, my mother's maid," Pilar says, "is black, and every time she goes to her little house in Resende she comes back all done up, those little braids, nails done, always. Class doesn't matter; it's a vanity of the Brasileira." As they continue talking, the tone ranges from pity to a kind of awe at the sheer pluck necessary for social inferiors to have a "proper vanity," to be — and stay — beautiful in difficult conditions.

Pilar and Gláucia were discussing nonmedical beauty practices, but some maids have also had plastic surgery. Eduardo, didn't quite feel comfortable performing breast implants on his private cook, Ester, referring her instead to Santa Casa. Other surgeons have themselves operated on their own domestic help. While I was interviewing Dr. Adriano, one of Rio's elite surgeons, his empregada came in to serve us coffee and cake. He proudly showed off the results, explaining, "She used to work for my grandmother, and then when she came to work for me I did her face [lift]."[11]

Other surgeons seem more bemused by the "vanity of maids" and other poor patients they encounter in public hospitals or cheap clinics. Dr. Ribeiro argued that "plastic surgery in Europe is not a popular surgery, it's an elitist surgery, right? Here no, here even maids do plástica on the breasts, the belly . . ."

A young surgeon, Afonso, then interrupted his mentor, "Five, six years economizing, they put money away in the savings account in order to give it to themselves as a present. And it's the breast, nê? Breast and abdomen. They struggle their whole lives to have it. They don't want a car; they don't want a vcr; they want a breast [plástica]. And always a reduction."

: : :

How can we understand this "vanity of maids" in a nation where domestic service is an ubiquitous feature of everyday life? It's necessary first to gloss the meaning of both terms, *vaidade*, vanity, and *empregada*, maid. In some regions of the West, a judgment of vanity is often applied to male minorities (who wear "ostentatious" clothes, cologne, etc.) or feminized men. In Brazil, I slowly realized that *vaidade* exists in a different moral field. At first I avoided the word, assuming it would be insulting. In everyday speech, though, *vaidosa* often has a neutral meaning of "self-care" (for women, not men) that aims to preserve or enhance femininity, and perhaps even health. In fact, to express a negative judgment of someone else, people resort to the phrase "an excess of vanity," as vanity in itself is not necessarily excessive.

One surgeon argued that vanity impels us "to take care of ourselves, take baths, perfume ourselves, wear clean clothes. If we didn't have vanity, we would walk around just like animals. Vanity propels society, civilization." This may be a rather cynical promotion of cosmetic surgery, but vanity does often have positive meanings in everyday life. One patient said, "I consider myself vain, but I would like to be more vain. To take better care of myself." Or as Rosa, a patient in a public hospital, put it, "To be vain is to feel good, feel that you are pretty, everything in place, a pretty body, nê? Always *cheirosa* [fragrant]." Many women stressed being cheirosa as an essential dimension of femininity, and in general viewed a well-groomed and well-cared-for body as a basis of attractiveness, with comparatively less attention to facial features. Conversely, a woman could be critiqued for not having *enough* vanity—that is, not realizing her own worth, as well as neglecting an almost hygienic duty of self-care.

The relative acceptance of vanity implies a greater acceptance of beauty work, as part of the category of hygiene, grooming, or self-care. Some patients see fat and loose skin as abject material, both self and not-self, and implicitly dirty. After having a facelift, one patient remarked, "I felt cleaner, as if I had shaved." Another woman compared a plástica procedure with a session at a beauty parlor. (It is perhaps not coincidental that both medical interventions, and more intensive kinds of nonmedical beauty work, have become normalized. For example, the full body wax is a cosmetic procedure that is becoming globalized under the name of the "Brazilian.") "Normal" grooming practices, however defined—from bathing to removal of hair, warts, or tumors—are often a basic social duty. In fact, neglect of them can signal a state of physical or mental *ill* health. If plástica is seen as a species of hygienic self-care, its cosmetic rationale becomes more compatible with health, as well as morally necessary. One consequence of this blurring of hygiene and beauty is the minimization of the risks of surgery. Such a cultural elaboration of femininity is also helping to make elective surgery a normal part of reproductive health.

Seen in this light, remarks about the vanity of the maid are not necessarily insulting. The notion of vanity links mistress and maid within the more or less natural category of woman, or at least the Brasileira. But the vanity of the maid—exercised within difficult conditions—also evokes the enormous social gulf between her and social superiors. The surgeons and mistresses perhaps felt something like bathos confronted with a patient of such low social status struggling to do what is "normal" for women of their own milieu. At the same time, as humor often does, their amused tone points perhaps to some deeper social tensions. Taking these elite remarks about maids as a cue, I turn now to analyze a distinct body culture where intimacy and familiarity coexist with hierarchy.

Hierarchical relationships in Brazil, as we saw in part 1, are often suffused with familiarity that can mask and "soften" class distinctions. Such hierarchy is notably *inclusive*, a notion conveyed by the proverb "a place for everyone and everyone in their place" (Holston 2008, DaMatta 1991). It finds expression in diverse social forms: from miniature living quarters for domestic servants to patronage relationships. Social interactions can reflect an easy familiarity with the bodies of others. I often heard direct comments about appearance, a verbal proximity that mirrors physical closeness. Friends or acquaintances exchange kisses, rub the shoulder or arm, keeping lengthy eye contact (another form of touching). This physical intimacy is often accompanied by verbal intimacy in discussing bodies. Roberto DaMatta (1986: 83) has argued Brazil has a corporeal culture rooted in colonial society, where the slave's body was property subject to intense scrutiny: "From there, certainly, this enormous capacity to know . . . details of the other's body, to permit so much observation . . . and with this, all the importance we give . . . to the appearance of bodies, something which has shocked Europeans and North Americans, appalled by our observations of fat, of full faces, height, size of feet and hands, etc."

Contemporary medical practices reflect such a tradition of bodily intimacy. Some patients, as we saw in part 1, spoke of an "intimate" relationship with the doctor in which he becomes "your friend." Plastic surgeons too were not only remarkably frank in discussing "defects," but also felt comfortable operating on social intimates and kin. Dr. Ox performed liposuction and breast surgery on his wife, and gave his mother and sister an identical "chin dimple" (a strange-looking hole in the center of the chin).

He proudly explained to me that this was a new technique he had "invented for his family." Another surgeon performed a cosmetic breast reduction on his niece when she was in high school, though this was perhaps a case of "too much intimacy." After he botched the job, his patient went for a correction to another surgeon, leading to a delicate situation in the family. More commonly, surgeons operate on their friends and wives' friends; on family members of colleagues and friends; and on work subordinates such as nurses, receptionists, and hospital functionaries.

Such bodily intimacy can also characterize hierarchal relationships, whether between doctor and patient, mistress and maid, or elites and "the people." While there is more privacy in private clinics, in public hospitals patients are asked to disrobe in front of a lecture room while surgeons discuss bodily flaws and the merits of particular techniques. Familiarity can temporarily dissolve social boundaries, but it can also coexist with ambivalent emotions. Dr. Paulo worried about an undignified vulgarization of his craft. He complained of a seventy-five-year-old patient, "short and fat," who asked if a facelift would make her look like a photo of a beautiful eighteen-year-old girl in a wedding dress. Exasperated, he said: "If I operate on a woman who is old and ugly, she is going to continue old and ugly, but with her skin stretched. 'How many years am I going to rejuvenate, doctor?' they ask me. And I say, 'I'm not going to operate on your heart, operate on your liver. I'm not going to operate on anything—I'm going to stretch the skin of your face!'" Some surgeons, in contrast, are heartened by demand among the people, seeing it as a healthy sign of "democratization." Of Pitanguy's many rewards, including recognition from the international community, he was significantly most moved by the samba parade. His reaction suggests that it is sometimes the people who grant legitimacy to elite healing projects (Lehmann 1996).

It has often been pointed out that various forms of "master-slave" relationships create a mutual dependence. The point is perhaps particularly relevant for understanding the intimate relationships involved in domestic work, a realm where masters and servants are brought into daily proximity. We have already seen that the notion of vanity has a special cultural and moral significance in Brazil. So too does the category of "maid." It refers often not simply to an occupational category, but to an almost archetypical female identity. It is a social position ambivalently "inherited" from mothers, aunts, and grandmothers, for some linked hazily to a family history of slavery (many residents of Rio's favelas are descendants of slaves, who settled there in the decades after abolition). Historically, domestic work often served as the only viable port of entry into labor markets for new migrants (Goldstein 2003). Perhaps a legacy of the older plantation economy, menial labor of all kinds is stigmatized and especially so domestic service (Owensby 1999: 16). For women such as Ester and Firmina, "working for a family"—a euphemism for the often stigmatized word *empregada*—is a dreaded last resort.

The prevalence of domestic work is a highly charged political question, though one that often remains invisible within the daily cordial, and sometimes intimate, relationships between masters and servants (Goldstein 2003). Modernization policies increased the numbers of female domestic workers during the period of rapid industrial growth from the 1940s to the 1970s. A decline in real wages prompted working-class women to seek employment as domestics. In 1970, half of all women working in urban areas were in paid domestic service (Filet-Abreu de Souza 1980: 40–41). Upper-income brackets were able to essentially "privatize" the labor of the surplus population in occupations such as chauffeurs, housekeepers, cooks, and the like (Mello and Novais 1998). In Rio's urban peripheries I found that many families have at least one relative with some experience in paid domestic work. According to the 2000 Brazilian census, there were 5 million maids in the country (Goldenberg 2000: 109, 113).

Domestic service reflects the intimate forms racial domination has often taken in Brazil. "Intimacy" between slaves—and their free descendants—and masters figures prominently in nationalist (often revisionist) accounts of Brazilian syncretism, represented by the image of the mulata nanny who both nursed the sons of the patriarch and sexually initiated them (Freyre 1956: 278). The expression to have "one foot in the kitchen" is used by elites (e.g., by ex-president Cardoso) to refer to distant African ancestry (Goldstein 2003). It also implies that a black ancestor was the one doing the domestic labor. Color hierarchies are even reflected in distinctions in domestic labor markets: lighter women are more likely to be employed as nannies, and some employment agencies have either refused women with "bad hair," or listed as job criteria traits such as "good teeth"—recalling DaMatta's evocation of a tradition of bodily scrutiny extending back to the colonial plantation (Caldwell 2007).

The subordination involved in paid domestic work is not just about class and color; it is also subtly linked to sexual relationships. The division of labor in domestic work creates a symbolic split in the category of "woman," Maria Clara Mariani and Ilana Strozenberg (1976:12) argue. Marriage becomes a relationship between a man and two women: "The empregada and

the wife, the maid being 'the other face of the wife.'" The maid then is identified with a defeminized role, the laboring side of the category "woman."
Of course, maids often marry and have children of their own. But domestic service can involve the forfeiture of a public work identity, and the in-
dignities of attending to the private needs of others (Goldstein 2003).[12]
Class domination can coexist with remarkable intimacy between maids
and family members, leading sometimes to an uncomfortable blurring of
household roles. Gilles Deleuze and Felix Guattari (1983: 353) suggest that
the presence of the maid within the bourgeois household provokes "an ex-
emplary hesitation in Freudian thought." They argue that erotic tensions
between family members and domestic servants make clear that the field
of "desire" is a larger social one traversed by class divisions, not confined
to the Oedipal drama. In Brazil, the maid was once "archetypically" the
sexual initiator for the sons of the household, "to the pride of the father
and the understanding of the mother: after all, it was the nature of masculinity" (Mello and Novais 1998: 612). Sexual relations between domestics and family members are not unheard of today. One patient spoke of a
scandal that had occurred in the household when she was a teenager: "My
mother saw my brother getting a blowjob from the maid once—she was so
dirty, ai—but she didn't fire her." Such "scenes"—while disturbing—are
sometimes seen as an inevitable result of male desire: "He is a sex machine,
maids, everyone, he knows women." Maids and mistresses too can become
emotionally intimate as they share with each other details of life events:
births, marriages, separations, and female health issues. Or they discuss
the problems of dating as single middle-aged women—or of mothers worried about teenager daughters. Intimate relationships can sometimes become an unsettling (to patroas) form of mimicry. Maids may wear clothing
and make-up in the style of their mistresses, or match their exact pitch
of voice when answering the phone (Filet-Abreu de Souza 1980: 53). Employers mentioned fears that maids would steal or try on their clothes or
underwear. Such mimetic relationships can stem from the maid's refusal
to identify with her own low-status work, or from her intimate role as pro-
vider of food and childcare. Domestic work is thus a key site where class and
femininity intersect in the Brazilian social imagination.

: : :

With these remarks in mind, we can now return to the "vanity of maids."
For some surgeons and mistresses, the desires for plastic surgery among

maids represent an ironic commentary on female nature. But the image of such a low-status woman wasting precious resources on the same forms of self-care practiced by those in their own milieu perhaps raised the prospect for these elites of *too much intimacy*, of an inappropriate imitation. On the other hand, for servants beauty work can reflect a wish to repudiate the specific forms of subordination involved in domestic work. Demand for plastic surgery—as a symbol of modern femininity—is perhaps stimulated in a context where cross-class mimesis occurs between social strata living in intimate contact.

Plastic surgery, however, is not only a status good; it is also linked to reproductive and sexual health. Recall that the surgeons said the operations women in public hospitals most desire are specifically on the abdomen and breasts. Why do maids and other low-income women specifically desire these interventions? Usually their aim is to lift and sometimes reduce the breasts, not enlarge them, and to flatten the stomach. Rosa was currently out of work when I met her in Santa Casa, but hoped to find a service job. At thirty-six, she said she was "of a certain age," and thought it a good time to correct defects she blamed on childbirth. "I detest large breasts, I think they're horrible. I was talking about this the other day in a bar, and even men don't like big breasts; they are something more to do with an artista. *Deus me livre* [God help me], to walk around with a thing of that size! I like a small breast, it's *bonitinha* [cute], inside a bikini, inside anything. Lots of people I know, friends of my daughters, are taking them out."

Rosa rejects media "fashion"—large breasts are identified as strange, "a celebrity thing," not for regular people—and prefers instead the bonitinha breast. Hanchard claims such an aesthetic ideal is a legacy of Afro-Brazilian culture. Perhaps, but it is also possible that it derives from a tradition of fetishizing the adolescent body, the "nulliparous" body as sociobiologists put it, which has not yet given birth. Recall again how patients often relate their operations to pregnancy, childbirth, and breast-feeding. Their beauty work is elaborated not just in relation to a cultural ideal, but to their own reproductive history, as they attempt to "restore" their body to an earlier state. As Flávia said, "I only want to take out the flaccidity, so a prosthesis is not necessary. He [Pitanguy] said that he will only take out the skin, with his own technique, and he will suspend it. It will *become the way it was*." The preference for the bonitinha breast suggests again conflicts between maternal and sexual roles as plastic surgery is embraced as a means to make the breast "become the way it was" before childbirth.

Such conflicts echo the class split in the category of woman into wife and maid. These rifts in femininity suggest how class and sexuality are inter-twined in the work of beauty, mothering, and domestic labor. The point can perhaps be clarified with an historical example. Long before the rise of mod-ern medicine, European women feared that motherhood could threaten sexual relationships. Popular beliefs dating to the Middle Ages held that breast-feeding could deform breasts, and made sexual intercourse during breast-feeding taboo, since sperm would spoil milk. Some women who did breast-feed feared abstinence would lead to adultery on the part of their husbands. These sexual and aesthetic concerns contributed to the practice of wet-nursing. Medical and clerical authorities attacked the practice, see-ing inappropriate carnal desires to preserve the erotic breast and prevent motherhood from interrupting sexual activity (Yalom 1997, Badinter 1980: 70). Wet nursing was also intricately linked not just to sexual identities, but later to upheavals of class structure. At first only common among aris-tocrats in Medieval and Renaissance Europe, the practice eventually spread to lower social strata as a prestige service in eighteenth-century France (Badinter 1980). In Brazil, moreover, wet nurses historically were often slaves or darker women; class and race thus complexly mingled in divisions between roles for women. In the latter half of the nineteenth century, wet nursing aroused fears of dangerous "promiscuous mixing" with the people (Caulfield 2000: 56; Rebhun 1999: 105).

The embrace of plastic surgery, like the earlier fashion of employing wet nurses, points to class tensions underlying sexual and reproductive experience in modernity. Both practices aim to maintain the aesthetic and erotic form of the maternal breast. But unlike wet nursing, plástica mar-kets itself as a technology that "allows" the mother to breast-feed her own infant, making it possible to assume the duties and pleasures of natural motherhood without showing the marks of it. In both cases the ability to manage conflicts between sexual and maternal roles is a positive feature of a modern, middle-class or elite identity. In these circumstances, "aesthetic health" can seem to promise not just sexual desirability, but also social mo-bility.[13]

In recent decades, attitudes toward breast-feeding have changed. Inter-national campaigns targeted the use of baby formula in the developing world as a threat to infant health (Yalom 1997). A middle-class movement in Brazil, as elsewhere, rejects technologized obstetric practice and valo-rizes breast-feeding. Yet older tensions between social position and repro-ductive labor, between maternity and sexuality, continue to shape breast-feeding. Some poorer women reject breast-feeding due to the prestige of fortified infant powder available in slick packaging, a commodity with prestige value (Scheper-Hughes 1992). In other cases, women decline to breast-feed out of a fear of "deforming" the erotic body. Flávia said she chose *not* to breast-feed her daughter out of fear her breasts would "fall." More commonly, women schedule surgeries around their reproductive lives to make sure that breast-feeding will not *estraga*, "ruin," the operation. Some patients see plastic surgery as a solution to the dilemma caused by conflicting desires for breast-feeding and "beauty."

Whatever universal basis there is for "vanity," I have tried to shed light on its historical forms. Vanity can reflect the aspiration to distance oneself from both the mundane domain of female nature as well as the class domain of domestic labor. Rather than just representing an ironic mimicry of elite women, the "vanity of maids" suggests that class and sexual aspirations are entangled in modern elaborations of femininity. Desires for liberation from an imagined "biological destiny" can mingle with desires to escape the "social destiny" of a subordinate class position. Such uses of medicine may occasionally discomfort elites, but they do not necessarily threaten the status quo. While beauty work is not "resistance," it may be useful to view it as a "tactic," in de Certeau's (2002) terms: a maneuver performed by the weak on terrain defined by the strong. Such a tactic is a response to a social contradiction: motherhood is socially valorized and essential to femininity, whereas the body visibly marked by motherhood is stigmatized. Patients embrace *plástica* as a solution to this conflict; in doing so, they expose the contradictory demands of normative femininity.

:  :  :  :  :  :    **LENS OF DREAMS**

While many societies have some notion of a superhuman being, perhaps only in the modern period do these beings represent *imitable* masculine and feminine ideals. However much we know we are not like celebrities, they remain a presence in the murky realm where childlike desires for the transcendence of mundane routine mingle with anxieties about attaining recognition and love. From this perspective, we can begin to understand the dream of transforming oneself from consumer of the image into an image, of making the magical passage from the fan to the star.

This dream is a characteristically modern one in that it testifies to the capacity of images of female beauty and glamour to stimulate projects of self-transformation. It also breaks with older gender roles confining women to a private realm. To be sure such "dreams" are often lost with adulthood, but this fantasy play is important for understanding the psychosocial process of developing a sexual persona. The role of celebrities is particularly crucial for understanding how beauty cultures target the fragile masculine and feminine ego. Celebrities project idealized forms of sexual allure that are, as much as commodities themselves, essential to understanding consumer desire. More capable of mobilizing libidinal drives than ordinary commodities, they are in a sense supercommodities (Rojek 2001: 189). As they appear to instantaneously fulfill wishes, these beings seem to inhabit a dreamlike "universe of beauty" removed from utilitarian concerns. Their biographies—often known to fans in intimate detail—can also signify a "magical" crossing of life barriers, especially in circumstances when formal routes of social mobility are blocked.

Here I focus on the dream of becoming a particular kind of celebrity— the fashion model—as a *social fantasy*. I use the term to include both the playful realm of nonrational desire as well as the political and economic structures that shape them, both the pleasures of private dreaming as well as the public realm that imbues dreams with shared meaning. There is perhaps a human need for emotional connection, love, and recognition. But what historical forces underlie the dream of being seen by those one can't see, the fantasy to be the object of others' fantasies, the desire to be desired by those one doesn't desire?

I met Amélia through an anthropologist who made a documentary about Afro-Brazilian religion. Amélia makes a brief appearance in the documentary, shot in the favela where she lives. But she dreams of appearing in the media another way. It's the first evening of the formal Carnaval parade competitions. We're in an old neighborhood in downtown Rio, a center of the "Carnaval Off," the alternative shows to the main parades in the Sambodromo. The heat from the day seems trapped by the concrete and augmented by the crush of bodies. An open-air concert draws a large crowd that overflows into the cobblestone streets that flank the quarter. There are few costumes here. Drunks lounge or sleep on the dirty grass next to children. Cachaça, consumed in cocktails with condensed milk, slowly begins to animate the streets as the night wears on. This is a "bohemian" area, where black intellectuals, communists, and *malandros* (suave con men) meet, and students from the Catholic University slum it on Saturdays.

Amélia is medium height, muscular, with tightly curled hair and light brown skin. She had dreamed of modeling as a child, but never thought it would be possible for, as she puts it, "someone like me"—until a friend told her of a course given to girls in "needy communities." (The word *favela* has become politically charged and some residents prefer instead the term *comunidade*.) There are now several such courses in urban peripheries that provide professional training to work in the fashion and beauty sector. Amélia says, "The course taught me lots of things . . . how to talk, how to walk, how to behave in certain locations, make-up, hygiene. And logically: nails. Models always have to have their nails done, their eyebrows done, plucked. Because suddenly a job could appear, and you have to be ready for any emergency."

We drink a warm beer then wander to the fringes of the crowd, passing fire throwers and stray dogs. Street vendors do a brisk business selling tough corn rolled in margarine or fried dough injected with *doce de leite*. Frozen in a spotlight, three men stand on the old trolley tracks high above the plaza. The drums start up, and they explode in a frenzied samba, joints popping, bones bending, feet cutting circles in the stone. We sit on a patch of ground, and Amélia discusses her work in a tone that seems determined and yet almost hopeless.

She says she has only done a few jobs, a couple of runway shows in a *shopping* and a clothing catalogue. To "pay the bills," she works as a receptionist in a doctor's office. "I advised the boss right away that I was a model and might need time off, to do a photo shoot." Meanwhile she works extra hours, saving money for the next step, a *book* (portfolio). "With the photos, if God helps me, my teacher can present me to some clients. Because there's no way without the photos. How could he sell my image? But it's expensive. The best are R$1,000." I ask her why she chose this profession. "I don't want to be Naomi [Campbell], but I want to do some good jobs so that people see me and say 'Ah, Amélia did that!' I want to be recognized."

Her profession requires special attention to her body. She "lives on diets," skipping lunch except when she has to work a twelve-hour shift. "I eat chicken breast with salad, very little soda." Then she adds, "If I had the money, I'd do a liposuction. Put my belly in place. I am horrified by my stomach." As with many other women, she discusses plastic surgery in relation to other "female surgeries": "After I had an ovarian surgery, I got a slack belly. . . . And in my profession you can't have a belly. So that's my dream—but it costs something like R$2,000." She pauses then says, "Now, a flat nose and thick lips, that doesn't matter to me. In fact these days thick lips are becoming fashionable. I see patients at the doctor's coming in to augment their lips. I don't need those artificial measures, but the belly . . ."

The father of Brazilian "soul"—an "old schooler" now rediscovered by a current generation of rappers—is on stage now. Amélia says she prefers hip-hop, not the Americans, but a Paulista (from São Paulo) group, or else Whitney Huston. I ask her if she is going to parade during Carnaval. She tells me Carnaval used to be important when her favela had its own samba school. Along with her aunts, Amélia was a *passista*, a dancer who leads a wing of a parade. This year she wasn't sure what she would do. "The *fantasias* [costumes], some of them cost more than R$400. There are people who spend the whole year putting together that money; sometimes they need dentures but they prefer to be toothless and parade." I am reminded of a comment by a plastic surgeon: "It's absurd that women who earn one minimum salary want aesthetic surgery. It's not a luxury. But you have to have clothes, put kids in school. The people don't have food, but they buy *fantasias* for Carnaval, and people without conditions want plastic surgery."

I ask Amélia if she too thinks Carnaval is a waste. "Carnaval is a business," she says. "We used to do it out of love. Now the Carnaval queens are only actresses. Some of them can't even samba!" Amélia later makes a more general critique of selling oneself (*se vendendo*). "Brazil sold itself to your country," she tells me. "The IMF, the World Bank; now they own Brazil. Our money goes to pay the interest." Samba schools have sold out, losing their roots in the community, just as Brazil itself has sold out to the United States. Money here replaces "love." Cultural loss and economic dependency mingle in the notion of se vendendo, symbolized both by Carnaval parades and IMF loans. Perhaps her efforts to make her own image into a valuable commodity are linked to her perception of larger processes of "selling oneself."

The samba schools' betrayal lay not only in their understandable desire for the media attention a celebrity confers. They also closed down one of the only spaces, Amélia says, for *beleza negra*, black beauty. Her feeling of exclusion was also illustrated by an experience she had in a shop in Ipanema. "I went in and no one asked me anything. [Rio's shops are usually overstaffed with solicitous sales people.] After circling around and around, they must have thought I was going to rob something. So I finally said, 'I want that lipstick there.' 'Oh, we're out of it.' But I stayed a half hour wandering around the store, *as if I wasn't there*." The invisibility of the negra in the media is paralleled by her own experiences of invisibility: as a low-paid worker living in a favela, as an aspiring model unable to break past color barriers, and as a consumer, both ignored in the store, and without, as you say in Brazil, sufficient *poder aquisitivo*, acquisitive power. The dream of modeling, to appear, is perhaps a definitive negation of a particular kind of social invisibility.

: : :

I use the term *model* broadly here, to include not just the tiny number of women who work—and the much larger number aspiring to work—in the fashion industry, but also the range of occupations where some kind of public visibility is achieved almost entirely through attractiveness, from the porn industry to local beauty contests to the TV "personality." Visual media in the form of Hollywood films had already played a crucial role in defining the image of the "modern woman" in Brazil in the 1920s and 1930s. Outfitted in outrageous garb, this notorious figure gained a new public visibility in a society that had long insisted on the seclusion of the "honest" woman. Inspired by film and fashion images, she discarded the corsets and parasols of her mother, cut her hair short, applied lipstick and rouge (a "painted woman" had formerly been a prostitute), and even appeared on the beach in a costume that revealed her thighs (Besse 1996: 28). Some fashions were limited to the wealthy, of course. But in the first half of the twentieth century, cinema became a major leisure activity for many social strata, as Hollywood stars became "heroes and symbols of modern life" for Brazilians (Besse 1996: 22; Meneguello 1996).

With the expansion of TV beginning in the 1970s, there has been an *indigenization* of mass-mediated glamour and sex appeal. Although Hollywood stars are still household names, TV has replaced cinema as a truly popular medium, and Brazilian artistas are national sex symbols. The figures of the model and the TV *apresentadora*, presenter, have perhaps displaced the movie actress as the ideal incarnation of femininity. *Veja* (1999b) claims that "nine out of ten Brazilian girls want to be a model." This must surely be an exaggeration, but the dream of modeling and more generally of "entering TV" is widespread across regions and social classes, judging by the turnout at talent searches run by modeling agencies and TV shows. Favela residents have founded NGOs such as the Lente de Sonhos, the Lens of Dreams, based in Rio favela City of God (Pereira 2008). In addition to runway and make-up classes, girls and boys from the age of eight can also get lessons in "citizenship, social etiquette, table manners, and all that is necessary for a career as professional model." The founder points out that even those who don't posses the necessary physical assets for success will be able to "raise their self-esteem and valorize themselves" (Netto 2003).

The supermodel Gisele Bündchen is currently the world's best-known female Brazilian celebrity. But the career of Xuxa was probably more important for imprinting a mass-mediated ideal of femininity on an entire generation of children and teenagers. Xuxa's career was launched as a model when, at seventeen, she began to namorar the soccer star Pele during Carnaval.[14] A blond southerner, she incarnated a "sex kitten" persona and posed nude for magazines (Simpson 1993). She also appeared in a film where she is depicted having a sexual encounter with a boy aged "ten to twelve." Despite being an unlikely figure to host a children's show, her program the *Xou da Xuxa*, which has been broadcast on Globo since 1986, was an extraordinary success that redefined Brazilian television.

This "cabaret for children" is a hybrid of disco, talk show, and personality cult of Xuxa. The star arrives on and leaves the set on a spaceship adorned with a giant plastic red lips, while the audience screams, "*Volta! Volta!*" (Return! Return!). To a soundtrack of booming pop, a chaotic flow of games, dance, and endless kissing unfolds in an amusement-park-like setting. The Xou is often explicitly about "beauty," blending dress-up games and grooming tips for viewers with a focus on Xuxa's body. National media began to speak of the Xuxa "empire" as the brand expanded to Spanish-speaking markets. In a nation with no shortage of musical talent, Xuxa became the first Latin American to make the Forbes list of the world's wealthiest entertainers (Simpson 1993: 150).

Her success, though, also provoked concern in the media about the sexualization of childhood within a highly commercial environment. Boys on the program try to peek up her miniskirt, kiss her on the mouth, or comment on nude photos of her; while Xuxa brags of the erotic interest she excites in the fathers of the children. Xuxa is assisted by the *paquitas*. Ranging in age from thirteen to eighteen, these *ninfetas electrônicas* (electronic nymphets) are more immediate role models for viewers. The first career move of one paquita after quitting the Xou was to pose nude in *Playboy* (Simpson 1993: 147). Like Xuxa herself, the paquitas become absorbed into teen and child culture through MTV spots, CDS, live performances, and movie appearances. *Veja* warned of a "wave of juvenile eroticism in the country" even as it featured a photo spread of Xuxa's younger rival, Angélica, in seductive scenarios (ibid.: 146).

Strangely enough, Xuxa's managers initially worried not that she wouldn't have the skills to host a children's show, but rather that kids would actually hurt her image. The solution was to portray Xuxa herself as a kind of child. Rather than a surrogate mother, she is a magnificent "Queen of the *baixinhos*," the shorties. Although the show represented this move as a pedagogical innovation (kids like to be addressed as equals), Amelia Simpson (1993) argues it also was designed to protect Xuxa's sexual appeal—the chief value of her brand—from any potential contamination resulting from her identification with a maternal role. After Xuxa had a child of her own, media reported that she "submitted to a liposuction and turboed her breasts. Happy with the results, she posed for sensual and exuberant photos" (*Plástica & Beleza* 2001). Such stories represent plástica as a necessary tool for a highly successful woman to manage the postpartum body; they also suggest that an older tension between motherhood and sexuality is reproduced in Globo's world of modernity and glamour.

Apresentadoras such as Xuxa are a Brazilian or perhaps Latin American figure quite different from traditional notions of the journalist or talk show host. Most of them are models or dancers who initially achieve fame through their corporeal "perfection" or ties to male celebrities. Though they may do journalistic-style interviews, the actual subject of the shows is, in a sense, the beauty of their hostesses, and their bodies more specifically—often known to their audiences through nude photo essays. These celebrities also represent a radical reduction of sexual charisma to the naked body. The most prevalent type of staging shows them alone, on the fashion runway, reclining on giant outdoor billboards, dancing *samba no pé* (without a partner), reining like lone monarchs over the fantasy domain of their *show*. Seemingly ageless during her more than twenty years on TV, surrounded by her teenage helpers (themselves replaced as they age), Xuxa presides over a realm of plastic beauty where sexual and commodity fetishism are thoroughly entangled.

Consumers in some instances place their bodies in a direct mimetic relationship with these sexual icons. The point was oddly enough made by a president of the Brazilian Society of Plastic Surgeons, who said, "The fact that actresses and the famous speak publicly of their prostheses stimulates the imagination and desire of women who also want to augment their breasts" (*Istoé Gente* 1999). Gisele said she found a picture from the magazine *Good Form* that had a body that she "idealized." She then cut out an image of her own face, glued it onto the photo from the magazine, and put it on the door of her refrigerator. "I look everyday at that image programmed for what I want to become. An ideal for me, to realize myself as a woman." Gisele is one of few women who have actually made a living from modeling. But modeling can be viewed not just as one occupation among many. As a major emblem of beauty, it also has a particular capacity to shape ideals of femininity.

If a celebrity is famous for being famous, then the model is in a sense the purest illustration of a kind of fame that is not dependent on inner qualities of the person. More so than for the actress or singer, for the model beauty outshines the notion of talent or personality as a job requirement. The model also illustrates the significance of physical attractiveness for attaining fame and wealth. The fact that models are becoming "role models" for many young people also points to the importance of the body in defining gender ideals. The model can be compared to the figure of the maid, as a contrasting alternative, but no less archetypical, definition of femininity. In Brazil, the maid, as we saw, represents a "lopsided" fulfillment of a gender role where domestic labor can exist in tension with the role of mother, sexual being, and publicly recognized worker. Often excluded from more socially valued aspects of gender norms, the maid can represent a defeminized femininity. The fashion model is thus at one level a negation of the maid, a different "model" of a feminine role—mobile, rather than housebound, public rather than private. From this perspective, perhaps we can begin to understand the apparent irony of young domestic workers and their children dreaming of becoming fashion models.

: : :

I'm standing at the foot of the favela that steeply rises into a forest-covered rock face above. I'm waiting for JD, a rapper in his mid-twenties, to escort me to the home of the family whose lives I'm documenting in an ethnographic video. I met JD, who writes political lyrics about police violence, through one of the numerous NGOs active in Rio's favelas. I have recently discovered that in so doing I have unwittingly taken sides in a major issue dividing the community: the role of drug traffickers in distributing favors and social services to residents. This NGO is run by a "militant," a resident who mixes Marxist thought with the new lingo of citizenship (his politicization occurred after he was incarcerated together with political prisoners: "Being in jail opened my mind"). Some residents disapprove of the fact that his NGO accepts funds from the drug trade.

JD and I begin walking up the central road, merging into a stream of commuters pacing themselves for the long climb. After several minutes we branch into a tiny alleyway that will take us to the family's home near the top of the hill. We pass by a group of boys, all with dyed blond crew cuts. JD says they are called *crilouros* (black blonds). "One soccer player did it, and all the kids are copying the style." We enter a "rural area," as he says, where chicks hobble over packed dirt. In one clearing, kids make a bonfire. Farther away, more precarious shanties made with scraps of metal and wood lie next to a garbage dump. "That's where the newest arrivals live, the northeasterners," JD says.

Iraci's house is an older two-story home made from exposed brick that she inherited from her parents. "*Oi de casa*," we say, announcing our presence, as we make our way up the narrow staircase. Iraci looks dressed up, and explains that she has just come back from a memorial service for a fourteen-year-old who "was found by the police with drugs." Iraci's daughter says, "Really, if someone is dying and asks help from the police, they will want the person to die soon, will spit in his face and step on him." Her friend Dúina adds, "I prefer to stay by the side of the bandit because I know when I need something, he will open his hand. And what will the police do?"

Iraci, who is thirty-nine, worked most of her life as an empregada in the Zona Sul, a short bus ride from the base of the favela. She is descended from the first migrants who settled the steep slopes, an area thought not fit for human habitation though it affords magnificent views. Iraci lives with her mother, two teenage daughters, Lana (fifteen) and Jacinta (nineteen), and a young son. Both daughters' "dream" is to be a model (though they say they have lost the phone number of the "agent"). We move to the roof to get some air, and as the sun begins to set the group begins a discussion of how to *cuidar do corpo*, take care of the body. We are joined by Paula, a neighbor in her mid-twenties.

Iraci says, "I never liked this thing of being thin. My *bunda* [bottom] only appears when I'm fat. Then it gets pretty. They start saying 'Good to see.' And the dogs come around . . . ; but when I'm thin no one looks at my face. You only see bones. When I'm thin no one sees me. When I'm fat I *appear*. I can put on jeans that 'call' my little bottom; I can fill them out."

"What do you eat Iraci?" Paula asks.

"Everything, if there is *angu, quiabo* . . ."

Jacinta shakes her head. "I'm on a diet. No soda, no beans."

Lana says, "The exercise in the favela is going up and down day and night." She points to the steep path leading to the top of the rockface.

"If I could," Paula adds, "I'd do a *plástica*, a lipo for sure. Get a slender waist, but leave the hips black [*preto*], traditional and wide."

"I hate being thin," Lana says. "I want to be strong, with fatter legs." She adds with a wicked smile, "My exercise is *rodadinha*, turning. Dancing in bed. Which is the most important, nê? It's hard to see me sleeping, just playing around *messssmo* [realllly]!" she says, drawing out the last syllable for several seconds.

Paula seems a bit shocked and remarks, "They start young now."

Iraci's son, a shy boy, is almost swallowed up by his bright yellow soccer jersey. The only "man" of the house, he brings out a tray of glasses of Coke.

Dúina says, "*Tudo que e bonito é pra mostrar* [Everything pretty is for showing]. So I show my little body. While everything is on its feet. Because after it falls you can't."

Lana nods her head. "All the girls on the hill said that I am *fogenta* [hot], that I'd get a belly before them. But Sissa already got one; Fabiana; everyone already has a kid."

JD chuckles. "It's just like with birds, everyone at home in winter, all hidden. And then in summer, the bellies appear."

Dúina adds, "One friend said, 'I'm a virgin.' But when I went to see her she already had a belly. I gave at fourteen and I don't regret. I gave because it is really good. If it wasn't, I wouldn't have. Period." She briskly smacks her hands together and smiles defiantly.

Paula shakes her head, and says to JD, her peer, "So advanced. I lost myself after I was old. Values have changed today. No one marries."

Iraci just laughs at her daughter. "You think just about drowning the goose, watching the cobra eating the spider, girl. You have to be a realist. Cobras don't eat parakeets."

With bawdy humor these women affirm a sexual culture they identify with "the community." They speak of traditional foods such as angu "filling out the bottom" or of "traditional and wide" hips, and use slang to wittily comment on the relationships between eating, sex, and various animals. They also associate beauty not with the psychological notion of "self-esteem," but with sexual pleasure, which Dúina affirms "because it is good." While most models in Brazil are white, the girls' ideal is Naomi [Campbell], the African American model. In this conversation at least, beauty work and ideals do not simply reflect global fashion or color hierarchies. These expressions of sexual frankness are also shaped by images of the culture and sex industries. When JD asks Lana how she got the idea to be a model, she says, "Since I was little I watched TV." JD, whose own physical gesture and style mirrors hip-hop videos, gestures at the view from the roof of Iraci's house, a dense thicket of antennae.

"I like to see films and practice together," Dúina says.

"She means with a man," Lana says. JD asks which women they like on TV. Dúina is quick with a response: "The truth is they have to pull them out and put me in. I do everything, parade with this little 'guitar' [body] of mine."

"Yeah, but we're poor and we don't have this opportunity. But who knows one day?" Lana says. Then she speaks again of her dream of modeling, telling the story of how she met someone who gave her the number of a fashion school.

"*Cuidado* (Careful)," the group exclaims.

Dúina says, "I want to be a gynecologist of men."

JD laughs. "It's not a gynecologist; it's a urologist."

Undeterred, she responds, "You are abusing us in your speech. I have all the materials to do the exams in my house. We'll treat the men for sure."

Lana nods her head at this. "The dream of being something in the world is the last to die. I'll continue and maybe suddenly I'll succeed. Maybe I'll win the lottery and employ some men in my house. I don't want a woman empregada, only a male maid. To clean the house, to work." Paula and Iraci laugh at this.

Dúina adds, poker-faced, "He can also help to pass me the soap when I'm taking a bath." Now the whole group cracks up.

For those who will go out, preparations begin. Iraci takes a quick shower. She rubs a white cream in her hair, sharing the mirror with her daughter Jacinta, who admires herself in a pair of new jeans. The group drops off the youngest at the house of the neighbor and descends the narrow staircase, Dúina and Lana heading down to a *funk* dance, while Iraci climbs higher up the hill, to a tiny square at the edge of the rockface. A single fluorescent light hangs above a makeshift bar. Couples swing jerkily to the staccato laments of a *forró*. The men hunch up their shoulders, and draw the dancers into a tight embrace. Next to her crocheted blouse, and brilliant white skirt, Iraci's partner is barely visible in the dark shadows.

The joking in these conversations is perhaps a kind of fantasy play that reverses actual forms of domination (see Goldstein 2003 for a discussion of black humor in Rio's favelas). The daughter of an empregada dreams of having a male maid. The notion of the "gynecologist for men" is not only a joke, but reflects experiences in healthcare. On another occasion Iraci says, "Health in Brazil is zero. When it's a little white woman, the gynecologist calls her 'love.' When it's a black woman, it's '*deita, tira roupa*' [lie down, undress]" (a remark her friends find hilarious). The sexual independence these women assert is also shadowed by violence. Referring to her lover, Iraci says, "I haven't seen any errors yet. But I've already lived in the lap of terror. I don't care if he's a worker or not . . . but drugs count me out. Fifteen years of aggression, beatings, hospital."

The next time I see the family, Iraci tells me her daughter Lana is pregnant: "She was in a lot of pain, but everyone has pain and I thought it was hunger. I almost killed her. I don't want to be a grandma." Lana's friends throw a baby shower for her. She unwraps a few pieces of Tupperware, and then, seized by the giggles, the group smears a piece of red lipstick over her face and body. Lana says she still "dreams of modeling."

: : :

Media images of modeling and plastic surgery often emphasize a fairy-tale-like metamorphosis where "beauty" becomes the vehicle of a new, dream-like existence. Yet, despite the glamour and apparent autonomy of the model, the lines between the fashion, entertainment, and sex industries are often blurred. Ângela had first met Dr. Ox as a patient looking to have a botched breast surgery corrected. After the two were married, he also performed liposuction on her waist, flanks, thighs, and abdomen, as well as lip and calf augmentation. "It's possible to construct the woman of your dreams without her becoming artificial," he told one of the magazines that profiled them. But this story I found out was also about Ângela's "dreams" (figure 13).

I had already read in the media about this "real-life" Pygmalion story, but wanted to talk to the couple in person. I arrange to meet at Dr. Ox's private practice. They make a striking pair. Ox is middle-aged, short, balding. Ângela is around thirty, at least six feet in her heels, and has brilliant blond hair a few shades lighter than her homogenously tan skin. When I arrive she is flipping through a pile of magazines to show me. Ox describes the work he's done, then says, "It was necessary for her to attain the perfection necessary to rapidly rise in life."

Ângela portrays her life story as a struggle to realize her dreams against the opposition of men. As a kid, she had wanted to be a model. "But my dad thought all those women were easy. Once I was in a fashion show, and he came and grabbed me from the runway. *Nossa*, I almost died of shame. I was locked in my room three days." She gave up this "dream" in order to study nursing. Then, her first husband made her withdraw from the class "out of jealousy." At age twenty, she had a baby, and "only stayed home,

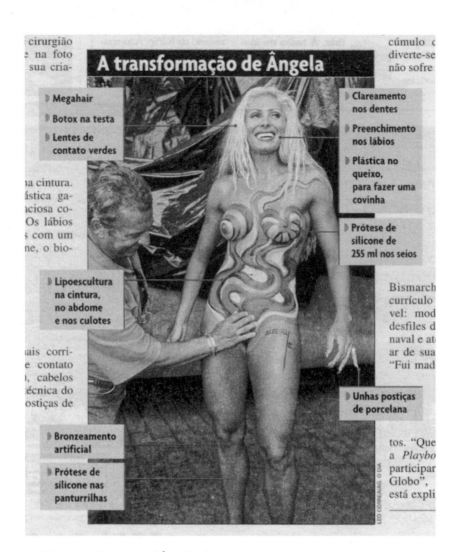

A transformação de Ângela

- Megahair
- Botox na testa
- Lentes de contato verdes
- Lipoescultura na cintura, no abdome e nos culotes
- Bronzeamento artificial
- Prótese de silicone nas panturrilhas

- Clareamento nos dentes
- Preenchimento nos lábios
- Plástica no queixo, para fazer uma covinha
- Prótese de silicone de 255 ml nos seios
- Unhas postiças de porcelana

13. "The transformation of Ângela: plastic surgeon operates on his own wife from head to calf."

taking care of my son and my husband." She left her husband and began training to be a surgical nurse. A second husband, though, made her drop out of the course because he didn't want her to "be in the middle of those doctors."

At this time, Ângela had breast implants at Santa Casa (she was referred by a lecturer in her nursing course). After she suffered various complications, she went with her then-husband to see Ox. At this point in the story, Ox interrupts. "The guy didn't have money to pay for the surgery. So he gave me the whole woman. He traded the woman—"

"Lies, lies," Ângela says.

"He solved the problem of the prosthesis and costs of the woman. He didn't have conditions to pay for the prosthesis, so he gave me the woman," Ox laughs.

"He didn't let me grow," Ângela says.

In her story, the house is a feminine zone where men try to keep her (first as a fifteen-year-old daughter, locked in her room, then as a wife and mother). The *casa* is also opposed to a space of realizing dreams, which is not just the "street," but specifically the *avenida*, the avenue where Carnaval samba schools parade and where Ângela's career as model was launched.[15] Only after the surgeries could she "appear"—both in the media and on the avenida, "for the nation to see." She adds proudly, "They called me the 'airplane made at home.'"

Ângela's story echoes the themes raised in the telenovela, *Sin tetas no hay paraíso*. Catalina trades sex with a plastic surgeon for breast enlargement surgery. Ângela instead marries the surgeon who gives her implants. Catalina seeks to become a prostitute and to have plastic surgery to achieve wealth and power. Ângela seeks to become a model and have plastic surgery to *appear*. Breast implants and *plástica* are vehicles of fame, but are also linked with economic and sexual exchanges. Whereas Ângela dreams of being a model, the fictional heroine Catalina sets out to be a *pre-pago* prostitute. These two occupations based on desirability can be seen as binary opposites. The model sells her image legitimately; the prostitute sells her body illegitimately. In fact, the lines between modeling and "sex work" are also blurred. A novela actress spoke of the "sofa audition"—the expectation that she must trade sex for TV roles. And modeling for Ângela means not the global world of haute couture, but Brazilian fitness magazines and "soft porn."

I did not know Ox and Ângela well enough to speak about the emotional tenor of their relationship (when I returned to Brazil I discovered that Ox had been murdered). Ângela said their relationship was a partnership that enabled her to realize her "dream"—one that had been opposed by jealous men. Ox, though, underlined their economic exchanges. Her former husband "traded the woman," he said, because he couldn't afford her (i.e., pay for her implants). Thus both stories in different ways suggest that dreams of autonomy, glamour, and fame are entangled with risks of self-commodification.[16]

In these conversations, women mention in different ways the notion of *aparecer*, appearing. Amélia dreams of appearing as a model in order to gain social recognition and a better living. For Iraci, visibility is equated with presence in the flesh. This embodiment is a negation of an invisibility equated with death and absence ("only bones"). But carnality is cautiously and jokingly asserted because Iraci associates sexual relationships with violence. Iraci's daughters and Dúina echo the affirmation of fleeting pleasures, but their fantasies also reflect the commodified images of the sex, beauty, and entertainment industries. Ângela's dream is in part an escape from the control exercised by "jealous" men. Yet her use of plastic surgery suggests her lingering dependence on men who "trade" her and on a medical technology necessary for her to "appear." Ângela said she was "trapped"; Iraci spoke of being thin and invisible; Amélia recalled not being "seen" in a store. Appearing can be seen as a forceful reversal of an invisibility often felt acutely in the body itself.

The model also represents the dream of superseding racial exclusion. Lana, Jacinta, and Amélia don't dream of being white, or lighter; they dream of being black, glamorous, admired, and desired. They sometimes critique the whiter and "foreign" thin ideal presented in the media. And their heroine is, significantly, a foreigner: Naomi Campbell. Perhaps only a black American has the stature to compete with the whiter Brazilian artistas.

The dream of modeling also suggests the relative scarcity of other viable routes of social mobility. Ester dreamed of obtaining a public university education, but said she had no chance without having attended a private high school. In a society where patronage relationships are prevalent, meritocratic achievement is undermined by behind-the-scenes maneuvers and obscure forces. Authority appears to be a built-in feature of the social world. When transparent or formal routes of advance are unavailable, those who do succeed seem to do so "magically," a situation that mirrors the rise of the celebrity. In beauty marketing, total transformation often has a fantasy aspect.

Becoming a supermodel is perhaps no more statistically probable than a soccer player making Brazil's World Cup team. This dream may seem like a distraction from more pressing needs. Yet however irrational it may seem, it is born from an accurate perception of the role of physicality and sexual charisma in the nation's social imagination. Born in the murky borderland between the mainstream star system and the sex industry, it reflects the capacity of cosmetic, photographic, and marketing technologies to define the psychosocial meaning and value of sexual desirability. For some women, modeling might also seem to triumphantly reject the elusive goal of reciprocity and recognition in sex and love. As the glamorous and rich version of the woman who "sells herself," the model might represent the ultimate incarnation of narcissism: consumed but not touched (in her work), admired by millions who are kept at a distance by the cold medium of electronic images.

:: :: : :    I LOVE MYSELF

The scale of carnage in modern warfare created the experimental conditions that enabled plastic surgeons to perfect techniques of facial reconstructive surgery. Skills gained practicing on thousands of soldiers who were severely burned and mutilated made it possible to contemplate elective surgery on the face (Gilman 1999). Oddly enough, experimentation in a military context also contributed to one of the most popular and controversial cosmetic procedures on the female body: breast augmentation. Invented by the Dow Corning Corporation, liquid silicone was first used during the Second World War (e.g., as an engine lubricant). The product soon found medical applications. After failing to achieve reliable results with goat's milk and paraffin, liquid silicone was used to enlarge the breasts of Japanese prostitutes during the war (Haiken 1997: 246). (Breast augmentation later became associated with pornography and commercial stripping before becoming legitimated as a mainstream practice [Kuczynski 2006].) The experimental context of war suggests tensions in the justification of cosmetic surgery. On the one hand, war contributed to the rise of a therapeutic rationale for cosmetic surgery as the public witnessed the ability of surgeons to aid the veteran's return to civilian life. On the other hand, the breast augmentations of sex workers have a different rationale. Such procedures seem oriented not toward psychic health and "normality," but rather the enhancement of an asset.

The point was made, for example, by a U.S. tax court judge, who accepted the argument of an exotic dancer from Indiana that her breast implants were a tax-deductible expense because, in her words, "the size of your breasts was in direct proportion to the size of your salary" (Kuczynski 2006: 249). Of course, breast augmentation in some cases may also aim at normality, or to remove the "defect" of smaller breasts (a defect that becomes "operable" only in some contexts, such as the sexual and economic exchanges that occur around military bases). There is, though, a tension between a therapeutic logic that seeks normality and health, and an erotic rationale that instead aims to enhance sexual allure and a competitive edge.

In this section, I analyze how beauty cultures redefine female sexuality and aging as a domain of self-management within consumer, therapeutic, and medical cultures. Some mothers reach for the tools of aesthetic medicine to augment freedom. Other women find themselves, as consumers and sexual subjects, facing new kinds of market competition. An expansive notion of "health" targets larger groups of female consumers during longer periods of the life cycle. Patients say they do plástica because they love themselves, not to please others. Yet their words often show ambivalence, provoking questions about the landscape of love, sex, and family in which they search for happiness and health. What are the local inflections given to the sexual freedom promised to the modern woman by medical and consumer culture? How do cosmetic techniques reflect changing notions of female nature, as women of different generations work on a body defined as a biological domain of desire, aging, and reproduction?

: : :

Sueli lives in one of the massive condominiums of Copacabana on the border between the female and male prostitute territories. Her friend Janaína is visiting for a few weeks. Though not far from the magnificent art deco Copacabana Palace, the area now attracts backpackers and thieves. In my now fading American common sense of color, Sueli is "Latina," Janaína, "black." The color difference between them could in more elegant neighborhoods mark the pair as boss and maid. Here in "popular" Copacabana, it is not unusual to see friends like these spanning the color spectrum. Inside a cramped flat, I accept a cafezinho thick with sugar. Janaína—now in her mid-thirties—begins reflecting on her years spent working as a "mulata" in the traveling samba show "Oba, Oba."[17] I ask her and Sueli why they decided to have liposuction.

Sueli says, "I've been doing therapy for two years, and I'm still not better. Then I tried working on the body and that diminished [my suffering] more than fifty [psycho]therapies would." Janaína says she'd once seen a famous therapist ("Switzerland is a marvelous country, but you fall into depression"). After three sessions she realized that she "became the psychologist. He couldn't understand his own mind." Janaína is one of a minority of patients I meet during fieldwork who either do not accept or simply scoff at the therapeutic rationale. She adds, "Look, I'm going to do this surgery not because I'm bad in the head, but because I'm bad in the body."

"But then why have the surgery if you already feel okay?" I ask.

"Because I looked at myself in the mirror and I saw that I was a pig [*porcaria*]. It doesn't do to look at myself and say, 'Hum, I'm sexy [*gostosa*]' if my eyes fight with my thoughts. I was fat and full of cellulite. This isn't good." She mentions that she had already done *lipoescultura* to "sculpt" her body: "It delineates your forms. I didn't have a waist. It makes a waist. It makes a visual in your bottom."

The few scholarly accounts of plastic surgery that focus on understanding the motivation of patients tend to stress their desire to simply look "normal." Sander Gilman (1999), for example, develops an interpretation of plastic surgery as a means of enabling stigmatized people—originally syphilitics and racial others—to "pass" as normal. Kathy Davis (1995) also adopts a perspective sympathetic to the Dutch cosmetic surgery patients she interviewed. In defending them against the charge of being "cultural dupes," she similarly argues that they "do not have cosmetic surgery because they wanted to be more beautiful . . . but to become ordinary, normal, or just like everyone else."

One problem, however, with the notion of plastic surgery as a normalizing institution is that it minimizes the competitive, aspirational, and sexual dimensions of beauty practices. In Brazil, some patients do aim to correct traits they believe make them fall outside norms. But as plástica has been "popularized" more patients—at younger ages—use aesthetic medicine to make often minor adjustments to enhance sexual allure. "Contouring" the body is not confined to the more specialized worlds of celebrities and the sex industry. Some minor breast reductions and lifts and buttocks implants aim at a national erotic *ideal*. Perhaps the most popular method of body contouring, liposuction, was invented in 1978 by a French doctor based on technology used in suction abortions (another link between Ob-Gyn and plastic surgery). One popular variation called lipoescultura ("fat-sculpting") removes fat from one part of the body and injects it in another (figure 14).

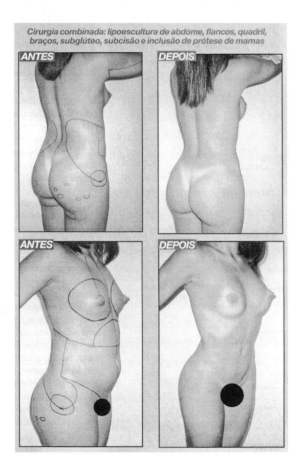

Cirurgia combinada: lipoescultura de abdome, flancos, quadril, braços, subglúteo, subcisão e inclusão de prótese de mamas

ANTES DEPOIS
ANTES DEPOIS

14. "Lipoescultura on the abdomen, thighs, hips, arms, and gluteals, and insertion of breast prostheses."

Once controversial, liposuction eventually became part of the "arsenal of every plastic surgeon" (*Veja* 2001b). Such body-contouring procedures are often used by young women and teenagers who do not feel any need to "correct" the effects of aging. Dr. Lívia—a surgeon in her early thirties—said, "I get these young women who have marvelous waists and breasts. . . . You look at the patient and say, 'Look, if I had your body, I wouldn't do surgery, because you have a body more beautiful than mine, and so I can't indicate anything for you to do.' But they still want to have surgery to become even more perfect."[18] The promise of the redundant "more perfect" forms is attracting younger women. The average age of the patient dropped steeply from fifty-five in 1980 to thirty-five in 2000 (*Veja* 2001a). Although the trend in part stems from a shift toward "preventative" cosmetic surgery, the younger patient profile also reflects the use of plástica to "engineer the erotic" (Denizart 1998).[19]

The goal becomes not a one-time passage into normality but an active and competitive pursuit of the elusive notion of a "more perfect" body. The focus on detail, perfection, and technique suggests that we are near the "hot center of a competitive system where small differences matter a lot" (Douglas and Isherwood 1979: 145). Some younger patients seemed to have a competitive ethos that was fueled by the game of competition itself, rather than being oriented toward attainment of a desired object. René Girard (1966) argues that desire is fueled by rivalry between two subjects rather than by a particular object. His concept of mimetic desire points to the imitative and competitive dimensions of beauty practices that are missing from accounts of normalization and medicalization. Such a model of desire also helps explain the addictive quality of beauty work, as desires are fed by a competitive process of beautifying itself.

The rise of such erotic body-sculpting practices is occurring during a time of change in two social domains that shape female sexuality: the family and aging. Anthropologists are—or once were—specialists in kinship. Although they have consistently shown the family to be culturally variable, they have also made clear that patriarchy underlies diverse kinship systems. Oddly, they have had relatively little to say about the weakening of the patriarchal family, a form of power that historically has governed nearly all societies. Manuel Castells (1997) argues that in the industrialized world there has been a persistent decline over the past four decades in the "family based on patriarchal domination that has been the rule for millennia" (139). He argues that the undoing of the patriarchal family "summarizes and concentrates" a larger dismantling of patriarchy, since the family is a primary realm for reproducing psychological and social structures of domination. A number of related trends point to an increase in economic, reproductive, and sexual autonomy for large groups of women in many regions, including Brazil.[20] For example, there are widespread shifts toward delayed coupling and toward cohabitation instead of marriage, and a rise in separation, divorce, single households, and households with women as wage earners (ibid.: 134–61).

Changes to the family are perhaps particularly significant in Brazil, where male family members enjoyed extraordinary powers in earlier periods of the nation's history. This form of patriarchy is the literal "power of the father": a historical system of "generational as well as gender relations, in which children and women are subordinated to the male head of family, who controls the wealth of the family, the sexuality of its women, and the labor power of all its members" (Besse 1996: 207n). This quasi-feudal system was archetypically located on the largely independent slave plantations that were the focus of Freyre's portrait of Brazilian society.[21] Beginning in the nineteenth century, the unlimited power of the *pater familiae*, with its occasional but spectacular displays of cruelty, was displaced by a new paternalistic state managing sex and reproduction. In the words of statesman Ruy Barbosa, "The Fatherland is the family enlarged" (Caulfield and Esteves 1993: 49).[22] The state effectively limited and "guided" the authority of husbands and fathers over wives and daughters through matrimonial eugenics and the regulation of female labor (Besse 1996: 5, Stepan 1991: 124–27).

In the postwar period and especially since the 1970s, a number of social forces weakened the formal structures of the patriarchal family. The (last) military dictatorship liberalized family law, most notably legalizing divorce in 1972. Ironically, this was a swipe at the Catholic Church, sections of which had opposed military rule. It was not until 1985 that a measure recognized the married woman as equally the "head of the couple" (Alves and Barsted 1987: 180).[23] In the transition to democracy, feminist movements successfully pressured the state to make women's rights a human rights issue, resulting in a "major paradigmatic shift" (J. Pitanguy 2002: 809). Brazil became the first country in the world to offer "women's police stations" for battered women (Santos 2005). In 2001, the Brazilian Congress guaranteed equal rights for women and eliminated an infamous 1916 Civil Code statute requiring a bride be "intact." On the other hand, cases of domestic and sexual violence are difficult to prosecute despite a landmark 1991 decision that struck down the "defense of honor" as a justification for wife killing (Goldstein 2003: 271). Liberal laws premised on sexual equality coexist in practice with persisting expectations that women behave "honestly."[24] Daughters of single mothers are sexually exploited by their mothers' boyfriends in urban peripheries (Goldstein 2003). While the economic activity rate of Brazilian women more than doubled from 1970 to 1990 (Castells 1997: 134–61), much job creation occurs in low-paid service and domestic work (Goldenberg 2000: 109–13; Georges 2003).

The family is a multifaceted political, sexual, and psychological institution. Along with legal changes, there were also more difficult to characterize changes in gender roles as consumer culture became a more important domain of identification. In older forms of the patriarchal and hierarchical family, Figueira (1996) argues, kin were defined relationally, according to their positions and functions within the family. The reciprocal duties and rights of mothers, daughters, fathers, and wives played a larger role in gender identities. With new family relationships arising in consumer capitalism, family members recognize more differences defined by personal idiosyncrasies and desires oriented toward youth or consumer subcultures. Parents and children are not only differentiated relationally, by age and gender; they also identify as consumers with similar rights to pleasure and freedom. Age differences are sometimes minimized as the mother's consumer and sexual rights are also extended to the daughter.

Families are a crucial domain for the construction of body-image. Physical appearance is often seen as an inheritance. Older generations also provide maps of the aging and maternal body, and models of femininity that are rejected or embraced. Female family members often placed their bodies—aging, mothering or "dating"—in a striking comparative context. Although Flávia is proud of how her mom looks at age forty-four, her mother's aging is also a sign of her own inevitable decline. Flávia says, "Aging is horrible"; "I try not to even think of how I'll be at fifty." She falls silent suddenly, perhaps remembering that her mother is almost that age. Bete then says, as if to reassure her, "I haven't done the face yet. I did the breasts and she saw them and liked them. And so later she'll also see how good the face will come out." Flávia looks to her mother as an "inspiration": "I saw what she was and I see what she is now after the operations, and there's just no comparison." She also mentions her own daughter: "One day she is going to know that her grandmother did it and her mother did it, and she is going to want to do it too. She is five now, and I'm twenty-five—the same age difference I have with my mom. And when she is my age, I want people to make the same comparison they do now with my mom. I want to go out on the street one day and hear, 'I can't believe it—she must be your sister!'" Plastic surgery links the aging body across three generations, as Flávia witnesses her mother's beauty work and already imagines the future plastic surgeries of her daughter.

Flávia often places herself in relation to her mother. They both "need" similar "postpartum body contouring" which becomes, like motherhood itself, almost a female rite of passage. They are also both single mothers, namorando (dating) "in the market"—an experience that creates another bond between them. While they are differentiated by age and the mother-daughter relationship, they are also linked as sexual beings "managing" motherhood. Men are relatively absent from discussions of body-image, and both stress that plastic surgery must be "for yourself." But when Flávia does talk about boyfriends, she immediately mentions her mother. "I usually say to men, look at your mother-in-law to see what you're buying, taking home. Mom is a snapshot of me in the future."

Rather than defined relationally through different rights and duties, mother and daughter become "equal" sexual beings, though situated in different moments of the aging process. Age does not separate them as mother and daughter but links them in a biological process that requires management. This equality, though, also puts them in a comparative and even competitive relationship. As Flávia put it: "In the past, a forty-year-old woman felt old and ugly. And she was traded for a younger one. But not these days. A forty-year-old is in the market competing with a twenty-year-old because of the technology of plastic surgery. She can stretch [her skin], do a lift, put in silicone, do a lipo, and become as good as a twenty-year-old." A dream of liberation and progress coexists with intense anxiety. Her words almost seem intended to be a comfort to herself: unlike a mythic woman "in the past," plástica will help her not to feel "old and ugly." Yet now at age twenty-five, aging is precisely her greatest fear. While plástica may be imagined as a technology that rescues her from the biological destiny to which women of the past had to resign themselves, it also opens up the body as a field of work and competition for large parts of the life cycle. Interpellated as consumers, sexual beings, and mothers in need of aesthetic management, generational differences between women are collapsed. At the same time, the notion of youth as precious capital with a value "in the market" is reinforced.

: : :

Sexual relationships in many societies are organized around social roles defined by age and familial status. Mother, wife, virgin, grandmother, and other positions bring with them specific sexual rights, duties, and prohibitions. Flávia's notion that a forty-year-old is competing with a twenty-year-old reflects a new configuration of family structures and affects. The family had long been seen in Brazil as a zone of moral order centered in the house, *casa*. In this sense, "the families" were distinct from "the people," the barbaric and uncivilized masses (Borges 1992 in Peard 1999: 113). But as Elizabeth Kuznesof (2003: 242) puts it, Brazilians have never been "a marrying population." For example, de facto "polygamous" families (men with parallel households) were, and are, common in all social sectors (Kuznesof 1993). Still, the Catholic sacrament of marriage has remained a norm for the propertied classes, and an ideal—not always accessible—for many of the poor (Vainfas 1989). Since the legalization of divorce in 1972, there has been an increase in separations (Novaes 2004, *Veja* 1999a). Brazilian households headed by women de jure jumped from 14 percent in 1980 to 20 percent in 1989 (Castells 1997: 149). There has also been a shift in perceptions of what constitutes "normal" familial and sexual relationships. Popular media began to portray the "ambiguity of female desire" (Goldenberg n.d.: 22). One popular novela, *Laços da família* (Family Ties), which aired in 2000, depicts a wide range of relationships that did not conform to the ideal nuclear family: families with wives or daughters as the providers, for example, or marriages based on physical attraction, not childrearing (ibid.: 19). Television dramas known for greater social realism featured *separadas malhadas*, "separated women with toned muscles."

Changes in family structure reflect shifts in ideals of love, sex, and marriage. To describe the mingling of "modern" with older structures of feeling in northeastern Brazil, L. A. Rebhun (1999) uses the metaphor of a palimpsest, a parchment that has been erased and then rewritten, leaving a layered history of ideas. She argues that more traditional models of marriage referred to a notion of "companionate love" based in long-term daily living, traditional gender roles, and mutual economic dependence, rather than on inner emotional experience.[25] *Paixão*—strong sexual attraction—was often seen as incompatible with marriage. With modernization, new norms and ideals of love arose, which often uneasily coexist with older ones. The notion of companionate love was, in a sense, unified with passion, creating the novel amalgam of *amor-paixão* (love-passion), or what is referred to sometimes as *lóvi*. The English term connotes the novelty and oddness of a model that stresses emotional intimacy and voluntary, rather than dependent, partnership. Such *moderno* notions are not equally accepted by men and women or by different generations, provoking conflicts over family roles and styles of intimacy.

Flávia's notion of a "market" of sexual relationships points to new difficulties and opportunities in namorando, during longer parts of the life cycle. For some, the Catholic image of the white wedding—symbolizing "purity of the heart if not the body"—is a fantastic dream. Other women spoke of an "epidemic" of separations, divorces, and *traição*, cheating. Luisamar voiced a sentiment I heard often among the middle class and elite: "In the past man didn't separate. He had his lover, or lovers, but the family was sacred. This is changing, not only in cities, but in the interior. Everyone separating. I think it's absurd, a man living forty, fifty years with a woman, and then leaving her. It's a kind of cruelty. Forty years of marriage, and they marry a twenty-ear-old. I don't know if there are more women [than men]; the offering must be enormous." She paused for a moment, then added, "But a person can't stay with someone they don't like anymore . . . ; it's a knife with two sides."

In most social strata, male infidelity was naturalized. Though not always tolerated, it could be seen as part of men's nature as *cachorros*, "dogs." Male promiscuity is the flip side of female beauty in that both are mythologized in accounts of national identity. As one bar story had it, the "difference" between the United States and Brazil could all be dated to the moment of European discovery: "What happened? The Puritans brought their wives and created a democratic society. The Portuguese came alone and what did he do? He 'ate' [fucked] everyone [*Ele comeu tudo mundo, nê?*] Black, Indian, white, didn't matter." Valéria joked about men who trade "one woman of 40 for two of 20." The number of men aged forty to fifty-nine marrying women in their twenties doubled from 1978 to 1996 (*Veja* 2000b). (The number of women in the same age group marrying men in their twenties increased as well.) Such changes in family relationships were linked to beauty culture. Women described gyms as hubs of flirting, where men newly freed from the responsibilities of family life became galinhas, "chickens" who pick here and there at the offerings in the "market."

In an environment perceived as uncertain and changing, some women asserted their sexual autonomy. Rejecting the moderno notions of reciprocity and emotional intimacy, Lucinda referred to the notion that "amor da pica dai fica" (the love that lasts is love of the prick); that is, sexual attraction is the basis of enduring love. Others rejected the notion of cohabiting with men. Flávia said, "I don't want to live with a man; I want to live with my mom the rest of my life. I am happy, I love myself, and I'm independent; I fix all my problems. Every time I shared a house with a man, I had to resolve their problems, so I just picked up one more problem for myself, nê?"

Enhancing sexual allure can also be seen as a means to "arrange something good." Bete said, "We are more flirted with [*mais paquerada*] with a different body. I think that everything changes. And maybe we can succeed in arranging something good." I asked her if her life improved after her latest plástica operation.

"*Claro.* Men have more *tesão* [sexual desire], nê?" She looked at her daughter, with what seemed an almost guilty look, and laughed. "This isn't good Portuguese of course," she explained. "But men have more desire, more sexual appetite. It was a good change in this sense."

Married women, on the other hand, said that having plastic surgery could make their partners jealous. Márcia, married three times, joked that she had "done a plástica with each husband" but mentioned that her current husband opposed surgery: "I am completely against this plástica," he told her. "It's absurd, you have nothing in your face." Then she realized that her husband feared that she would attract more sexual attention from other men after having the operation. Other women seem to see plastic surgery as a means to mimic the male pattern of seeking younger lovers in middle age. Zília, a middle-class plástica veteran in her early sixties, said that she and her peers were *subindo o morro* (climbing up the hill), that is, to favelas.

"Why?" her friend asked.

"*La não tem brocha, não tem bicha, e não importa ficar com mulher velha*" (There is no impotence, there are no "fags," and they don't mind sleeping with old women).

This irreverent comment was no doubt a critique of her circle of male peers, who are here depicted as lacking virility compared to men "on the hill." Reversing the notion that youth is a kind of capital that women gradually lose, she implies that with her greater economic resources she can also have sex with younger and poorer men "who don't mind old women." There is nothing new in elite women finding sexual pleasure with social inferiors (Needell 1987). But for Zília, sexuality seems to be envisioned explicitly as a fungible asset that requires maintenance. Plastic surgery becomes a tool to negotiate markets where the sexual capital of age and beauty can be exchanged with various kinds of cultural and economic resources.

: : :

New sexual norms reflect changes in the social meaning of aging as it is defined as a process requiring self-management within consumer, medical, and therapeutic cultures. The lower as well as the upper limit to the "age of sex" is expanding, as the adolescent, the middle aged, and the elderly are interpellated as autonomous sexual beings. News and health stories, for example, have made "Sex after 40" a new topic of discussion. A *Veja* news article on the "arsenal of middle age" touted the benefits of a range of therapeutic, and sexual aids, for "him and her": from Viagra and antidepressants to aphrodisiacs that "combat frigidity" to aesthetic medicine. Such tools and techniques enable middle-age men and women to have a "much more active sexual life" than their parents and grandparents did. Readers could learn that the Ministry of Health found that "86 percent of Brazilians are sexually active between 41 and 55, a higher proportion than among youth from 16 to 25 (*Veja* 2000b). Medicine is also changing attitudes toward postmenopausal sex. The experience and "management" of menopause varies widely in different societies. In Japan, for example, despite the prevalence of biomedicine, menopause is much less "marked" as a biological or psychological event compared to in the United States (Lock 1993). In Brazil, the biomedical model of physiological atrophy is prevalent, at least among the middle class—or rather, *was*, until the discovery of hormonal replacement therapy, including testosterone, the "whipped cream of hormonal repositioning" for women (*Veja* 2000b). A gynecologist described a "degenerative process": "The skin aged, there was a loss of calcium in the bones, and a drying of the vagina. It was the end" (*Época* 1999a). This threat can be averted: "With medical intervention, women can now have sexual relations for as much time as they want."[26]

Once a "young country," over the past fifty years, Brazil has experienced a major demographic transition, with the percentage of elderly doubling as fertility rates declined in the 1960s and 1970s and life expectancy increased (Leibing 2005: 17). Brazilians physiologically aged, but the elderly also became socially visible as a new population. Government pastoral programs targeted a powerful political demographic, while aging was redefined as a process requiring active management in order to maintain a broad, qualitative notion of health. Gerontological experts began promoting exercise and cultural consumption as techniques for augmenting self-esteem. For this population too, health can also include appearance and beauty. A "Miss Third Age" beauty contest was launched in the 1990s, with the rationale of "augmenting the self-esteem" of the elderly. The 1996 winner was "judged by her plastic surgery, elegance, and empathy with the audience" (among the prizes was additional plastic surgery) (Leibing 2005).

The notion that the sexual body must be managed is extending to women at both ends of the lifecourse, from the elderly to that paradigmatically modern figure: *the teenager*. There is nothing new in the "precocious" (to their elders) sexuality of adolescents, and girls have married at very young ages throughout Brazilian history (Kuznesof 1993). The precocious sexuality of the "popular classes" was—and still is today—a theme in some elite expressions of contempt (including by doctors working in maternity wards and in plastic surgery clinics). What is more recent is the emergence of the female teenager as a central subject and object in Brazil's consumer culture. The Catholic ideal of pre-marital virginity has declined in many regions (Goldstein 2003: 310n), and teenage sexuality is emerging as a "normal" domain of pleasure and health within consumer, therapeutic, and medical cultures. According to *Veja*, in 2000 only 32 percent of youth "gave value" to female virginity at marriage and the average age of sexual "debutant" (fifteen for girls, seventeen for boys) declined from the 1980s to the 1990s. More teenagers had sex for the first time in their parent's home than in motels or cars, indicating greater parental permissiveness (*Veja* 2000a). The older norm of *namoro*, courtship, with or without a family chaperone, has been partially displaced by the practice of *ficar com*: to kiss one or more partners during the night. Relatively successful campaigns against STDS have brought sexuality within a domain of health (Parker 1999). On the other hand, older forms of patriarchal morality persist, and the notion of the *puta*, whore, figures strongly in a moral double standard for boys and girls. Ironically, while medical management of the erotic adolescent body was growing, many teenagers still had difficulty accessing reliable contraception. From 1993 to 1998, the birthrate increased 19 percent among girls 15–19 and 31 percent among girls aged 10–14 (Goldstein 2003: 246). Since the 1990s, rates of plástica among teens have also been growing: in 2004 21 percent of all cosmetic surgery patients were under the age of nineteen (SBCP 2005). Surgeons disagree about the exact moment in physiological development when it becomes "safe" to perform surgery. Dr. Froes argues simply that as long as the "the girl is organically ready for plastic surgery, there is no reason to wait. If you're offering a benefit to the patient, it should be done as soon as possible."

Medical and media technologies, as we have seen, often reproduce the fetishisms of the female body that characterized the sexual cultures of periods with more formal patriarchal control. Markets are also, however, leveling forces that can undermine traditional forms of authority. Family members become equals as consumers, separated by biological rather than social differences. And while beauty culture interpellates women more insistently than men, in some ways it also creates new similarities between male and female sexuality. Men are becoming bigger consumers of the medicocosmetic and psychotherapeutic enhancement of masculinity as they compete in sexual and labor markets (Bordo 1999). In Brazil, men are the fastest growing demographic group of cosmetic surgery patients, accounting for 30 percent of operations (figure 15). Common anxieties and aspirations center on losing weight, gaining muscle mass, reversing receding hair lines, and enhancing virility—much of this self-tinkering done through high-tech medicine and legal and illegal pharmaceuticals.

More than plastic surgery, weightlifting has become for many men the

15. The male beauty consumer: "How much does your *plástica* cost?"

preferred means to the ideal *sarado* (hard) body (Sabino 2000, 2002). In Brazil anabolic steroid abuse is widespread, which can lead to erectile dysfunction, a problem that can in turn be treated with pharmaceuticals—often available at the local pharmacy without a prescription. Homoerotic images of the male body (for example, the once-risqué ads for Calvin Klein underwear) have ironically become mainstream corporeal ideals for heterosexual men seeking women's sexual attention (Bordo 1999). The cultural ideal of masculinity may also be shifting toward a younger age or at least younger-looking body (*Veja* 2000c). Furthermore, the rise of female sexual and economic autonomy—and of separations and divorces—extends the logic of "sexual selection" to men. In new markets of work and sex, appearance becomes a more central arena of competition for men as well. There is still, though, a central asymmetry. As one woman dryly remarked, "A fat, ugly, old, bald man with money will never be alone."

: : :

While beauty cultures reflect an extension of market forces into new spheres of human experience, the implications of this process for human flourishing are not immediately apparent. Perhaps out of fear of committing essentialism, anthropologists often now shrink from substantively describing cultural differences. But different styles of bodily comportment and sexual play are evident to even causal observers. They can also enter the political realm: for example, a French prime minister publicly interpreted the lack of flirtatious eye contact in Britain as evidence of widespread homosexuality. When a middle-class patient, Gabriela, remarked, "When even a doorman 'sings to you' [flirts], it raises your spirits," she expressed a particular cultural common sense. Like the surgeons' discussion of maids, her comment reflects the intimacy of class relationships in Brazil. The doorman, *porteiro*, is a ubiquitous personage in the daily life of the middle class. Mostly migrants from the northeast, they are viewed by their Carioca employers as poor, slow, and even ugly. Gabriela's point, then, is that to be *cantada*, "sung to," is pleasant even when it comes from a man at the very bottom of the social hierarchy. As Goldstein (2003: 232) points out, "In Rio de Janeiro, public flirtation is an elaborate and beloved game, not scrutinized as an objectification of women's bodies." Sex is partially socially constructed but so too is sexism, and it is sometimes difficult to evaluate differences in sexual cultures according to liberal values of autonomy, freedom, and equality.[27]

For example, how does one find a universal moral compass with which to measure body "commodification"? Lesley Sharp (2000: 295) argues that the presence of bodily fragmentation and objectification is frequently a sign of body commodification. Conversely, "the very sense of self-as-body is frequently obscured by commodification" (ibid.: 290). Such critiques of commodification, however, raise the question of how to identify the non-commodified body. The ideal that authentic sexual relationships and "free" bodies must be protected from economic exchange is itself historically specific. In Brazil it competes with other notions of love as a reciprocal obligation rooted in economic interdependence (Rebhun 1999). Non-Western concepts of personhood often do not equate a body with a self: the body or even body parts can "belong" to social or cosmological relationships (Knauft 1989). As a student of Capoeira put it, bodies in Brazil are "often pre- or post-Cartesian," free from the dualism between body and mind that critics such as Susan Bordo (1993) have blamed for body alienation in North America. The body in Brazil exists in a political, legal, and moral field quite different from Anglo traditions, which tend to view the body as a domain requiring protection against state incursion (as well as from "contamination" from other races) (Caldeira 2000). The notion of a commodified body may thus implicitly depend on a contrasting opposite—the autonomous body whose "value" can be defined outside of the sphere of exchange—which is not universally held.

As an anthropologist and outsider, I have thus felt the need to balance critique of the structures producing the culture of beauty with a retrieval of local meanings and values. This is a perspective I find often missing in Foucauldian critiques of the medicalization and commodification of the body. In the enormously influential *History of Sexuality*, Foucault (1978) argues that the rise of a "scientia sexualis" created sexuality as a crucial arena of modern power and social control. His analysis provocatively challenges psychoanalytic—and popular—notions that modernity represents a progressive liberation of repressed desires. It also implies a judgment about the ethical implications of such a process for human freedom.

The problem is made worse as the analysis of "power" in Foucauldian scholarship often disavows any attempt to *evaluate* specific forms of domination. The advantage of the older, "sovereign" notion of power that Foucault critiqued is that one knew who or what had power over whom. The Foucauldian model of power, as has often been noted, is a metaphysical principle: everywhere and nowhere at once. This is precisely its appeal: it allows one to explain people's participation in their own noncoercive oppression without having to define oppression according to an anchoring value. But perhaps this "power" is simply a fancier name for the unsexy notion of socialization. It says that people act and think according to social norms of health, normality, beauty, and so on. To get from there to power, it's necessary to either show coercion operating, or to have a positive notion of freedom to determine that people have false values and are oppressed without their knowing it. Yet this is precisely what most scholars are unwilling to do. Ironically, Foucault who seems outraged by latent morality hidden in the ostensibly objective human sciences, in the end perhaps cannot escape the age-old role of the *moraliste*. This move finesses rather than solves the Marxist dilemma of false consciousness.

I make this point to suggest that beauty cultures are intertwined with a historical process that is also changing views about the role of sex in the "good life." For early liberal feminist thinkers "sex"—what we call gender—is something to forget: "When human beings are regarded as moral beings, sex, instead of being enthroned upon the summit, administering upon rights and responsibilities, sinks into insignificance and nothingness" (Sarah Grimke [1837] in Warner 2002: 41). Women attain equal rights in the public sphere on condition that sex differences are forgotten and become merely private. This liberal vision ran into contradictions. Ironically, as women increasingly *did* achieve legal rights, sex did not disappear; it was thrust into the open so to speak: the public roles and visibility of women made sexual difference even more important. From a contemporary perspective, this liberal ideal seems to suffer from a denial of the power of sex differences to affect public life. But problems with the liberal approach also reflect the changing social significance of sexual experience. For contemporary female subjectivities, sex is perhaps a more important "source of the self" (Taylor 1989) and a social resource, both "uses" of sex inhibited in earlier periods. In these conditions, it would perhaps be undesirable, or at least unlikely, for sex to "sink into insignificance and nothingness."

An advertising copywriter in a film declares, "I get paid to make women hate themselves." Media, however, did not create the self-esteem concept, which is now central in diverse spheres: not just cosmetics and plastic surgery ads, but also minority rights movements, self-help, and psychotherapy. So while the lowering (and raising) of self-esteem may be big business, this commercial significance is only possible due to larger changes that redefine the value of beauty, sex, and appearance for modern subjects. Foucault (1978) focused on the role of medicine and psychology in creating sexual pathologies such as homosexuality and hysteria. The application of his work to other regions and periods, though, can minimize important changes in female sexuality in the last few decades. Reading accounts of Foucauldian disciplinary institutions and "docile bodies," I have a feeling of cognitive dissonance living in a consumer culture with its diverse bodies oriented toward athletic mastery, self-expression, and the varieties of sexual and sensual experience.

The incitement of sexuality reflects dual forces: on the one hand, the domination of science, medicine, and psychology; on the other, the consumerist ethos of late capitalism. Colin Campbell (1987) has argued that the emergence of mass consumption depended on a capacity to engage in fantasies of future enjoyment and techniques for regulating private emotions. He links this ethos to early modern sources such as the culture of novel reading and the cult of sentiment. In later phases of capitalism, such an ethos has perhaps expanded to encompass a range of techniques explicitly focused on the manipulation and enhancement of hedonic experience: from pharmaceuticals and cocaine to ecstatic dance and "s&m lite." Foucault (1978: 58) laments that "our civilization has never produced an *ars erotica*," but this claim could be disputed, especially if we look at the consumer culture emerging in the period that followed his publications. While the New Age consumption of the Kama Sutra, for example, may seem inauthentic and market-tainted, it reflects a larger social shift toward a consumer-hedonism that experimentally deploys commodities, bodily practices, and medical technologies to control and enhance the immanent experience of pleasure.

Perhaps what is more difficult to explain is not what is *wrong* with plastic surgery, but what makes it compelling as demand increases in new regions and across a range of social strata. I have argued that plastic surgery is not an isolated technological fad; rather, it is enmeshed with other medical specialties managing the reproductive and sexual body across the life span. Inequalities in healthcare help create a market for the fetishized consumption of the high-tech services of medicina estética. And mass media and a populist beauty myth fuel fantasies of social mobility and self-transformation. While beauty cultures reflect dichotomies between sexual and maternal roles, they also unify the category of "woman" by targeting biological processes. The frontier between mind and body becomes a domain of work for patients and consumers in diverse market positions as they seek an expansive notion of well-being.

The physical and emotional suffering caused by beauty practices and images is real (historicizing notions such as "low self-esteem" does not make them less acutely felt). But viewing beauty practices only as an oppressive practice makes it difficult to understand why they are being taken up with enthusiasm by women in "emerging markets"—from Latin America to the Middle East to China. The female body and its aesthetic alteration can serve as a touchstone for fears and aspirations surrounding modernity in the developing world. Applying the patriarchal analytic lens to beauty practices across cultures must be balanced by attention to local economic pressures and aspirations for mobility. In some regions, beauty practices—including the more disturbing forms of body work—are actively embraced by some women and resisted by those defending socialist or religious ideologies. Brazil, on the other hand, is renowned for a bodily habitus embracing sensuality, grace, and warmth—hardly qualities associated with discipline. Perhaps plastic surgery there thrives not off alienation from the body but rather an ethos even better suited to the expansion of the beauty industry: compulsory love of the body. In the words of Flávia, "I will never be with an ugly man, fat, badly taken care of. Never in my life. I am a slave of beauty. I like myself; I love myself. I like to look in the mirror and say I love myself, I adore myself, I am pretty."

# Conclusion

Techniques of erotic body sculpting are not exactly new. Fashion has often been seen as a kind of symbolic class war. The lower imitate the upper (and often nowadays vice versa), fueling notoriously swift cycles of fashion. But fashion does not simply code status on the body. It also augments and hides, compresses and reshapes, teasing and directing the eye to areas of erotic interest—at least since Renaissance Europeans shed their loose-fitting tunics and robes (Lipovetsky 1994). Male corsets and shoulder pads emphasize shoulder-to-waist contrasts, while tights enhance a now somewhat curious sign of virility: the "well-turned calf." And the codpiece, obviously not simply a convenient waist wallet, "covers" a part of the body only to draw attention to it. In female fashion, despite a dizzying pace of shifting hemlines and necklines over the past 600 years, there has been at least one near constant: the use of undergarments to lift and project the breast (Kunzle 1981; Marwick 1988).

In the Medieval period, the breast referred almost exclusively to its "august Maternal function," and images of the nursing infant Jesus showed a small, mostly concealed breast in somber settings (Hollander 1993: 187–89). Anne Hollander dates the break from this tradition with a single painting: Jean Fouquet's *Madonna and Child* (c. 1450). The Virgin Mary now holds the infant at some distance from her, giving the viewer an unobstructed view of what is clearly the center of the painting: a large, white luminescent globe that seems to leap out of its confinement in a tight bodice. Since that period, the female breast has become a primary site in struggles to define female nature and sexuality. Fashion has molded and displayed the erotic breast, while clerics, philosophers, doctors, and others have emphasized the maternal breast—symbol at once of sanctity, comfort, and not least, the health of future generations, and hence the nation.

The rise of medical, sexual, and aesthetic enhancement represents a new chapter in struggles over the meaning of female nature in modernity. Many cosmetic procedures seem to echo the corset's effects, emphasizing contrasts between the waist and hips and projecting and lifting the breasts. But plástica is also different from clothing fashion in that it strikingly eschews the logic of dissimulation and provocation. Rather than mask defects as a "positive and innocent" measure (Sant'Anna 1995), it stresses instead objective measurements and scientific corrections of the body. Unlike commodities worn and used on the "outside," it seems to extend the fetishistic logic of fashion *into* the human body with its prosthetic materials and surgical penetrations of the organic world. Moreover, medical procedures cannot be displayed as prestige items in the way many other commodities can. Patients usually aim for natural results ("That Park Avenue look [too-taut skin] is totally out"). Scars and bandages are inevitable, not desired, signs of an operation (or at least usually; in some parts of the Middle East, the bandage signaling cosmetic rhinoplasty is a prestige marker). It's true that other commodities can also be seen as prosthetic enhancements of masculinity and femininity. Plastic surgery, however, directly targets reproduction and aging. Rather than compensate for flaws or hide them, it aims to alter the signals sent by the organism. This practice not only reflects the splitting of the category of "woman" along racial and market lines; it also unifies it within the notion of a female nature defined biologically. In a sense, it reduces the social body of fashion, speech, and movement to a naked biological state.

Giorgio Agamben (1998) draws on the Greek distinction between *zoë*, "bare life," and *bios*, "qualified life," which differs from pure biological existence by being lived within the public world of the city. His writing made me think of a similar distinction we might make between "qualified sex"—sex as constituted within symbolic and moral realms—and "bare sex"—defined biologically. The objectified and commodified sex of "medical pornography" might be seen as one such example of bare sex. Unlike fashion, this is not a domain of small, expressive differences, artful dissimulation, and masquerade. *Plástica & Beleza* portrays a different kind of beauty. Smooth and shiny with skin like armor, the body appears in its naked or near naked "truth." Sexual allure is defined purely objectively in the *medidas*, measurements, of the body. Decontextualized, without reciprocity, narrative, and often movement, the body is "bare" in the sense that it repudiates the ceremonial symbolism of seduction. It's true that vestiges remain in the occasional props of what are called "sensual photo essays": high heels or tidbits of biographical information. But these details in a sense are unnecessary. The real story of these photos is the body itself in a naked, animal-like state, fragmented into parts and radically divorced from the social person.

If we admit such a distinction between qualified and bare sex, however, it must be a relative one. Sex can never be known "in itself," as a biological fact separable from its symbolic elaboration. Yet, the view of sex as a social construction that has become nearly orthodox in the social sciences and humanities also has problems. For one it reduces sexual desires—and to use a word that has become unspeakable, *drives*—to inert matter, infinitely malleable by culture, institutions, and performances (Sedgwick and Frank 1995). But sex is also a force animated by the species life, which can arise even in situations of brutality or moments of affective intensity when cultural norms recede into insignificance. Desire or joy in sex can cross social boundaries, or else transport the self to a level of being that seems animal-like in its opposition to normal rules and experience. The taboos and rituals surrounding sex in many societies testifies not just to a functionalist need to organize potentially disruptive desires, but also to an awareness that the symbolic realm of culture is only imperfectly melded with biological existence.

One might object that the categories of *nature* and *culture* are themselves social constructions, perhaps even Western ones. And yet, as the ethnography of the Americas suggests, humans in diverse societies seem to be uncertain about how to define their relationship to other animals or to understand their own status as self-aware animals (Viveiros de Castro 1998, 2004). I mention this point to suggest that the symbolic work that transforms biological needs into cultural products is not always complete or seamless. Relationships between culture and nature are unstable and can change historically. I want to here analyze one such change—never complete or finished—toward a *biologization of sex* as the physiological organism is constituted as an object of technical manipulation.

Such a "return to nature" is paradoxical given the fact that the many forms of body modification practiced in diverse civilizations have generally worked "against nature." The point was made by Hegel (1920 [1835]: 42) who argues that body modification stems from a basic human impulse to dominate and leave a mark on nature, and thus has a rational basis: "He [mankind] will not permit it [his natural form] to remain as he finds it; he alters it deliberately. This is the rational ground of all ornament and decoration, though it may be as barbarous, tasteless, entirely disfiguring, nay, as injurious as the crushing of the feet of the Chinese ladies, or the slitting of ears and lips." What is barbarous to us may be beautiful to the barbarian (though Hegel [42] is quite confident that "among the really cultured alone" will a change of figure "issue in harmony with the dictates of mental elevation"). Although Hegel doesn't give much evidence for his claim, the later ethnographic record has shown that among the diverse rationales for body modification there is a common theme of transforming the "raw," childish, or animal-like state of nature into the "cooked," adult, and human state of culture (Lévi-Strauss 1983). Many adornments and modifications have either damaged the physiological organism or reflect indifference to the natural body. The infamous "bound" Chinese foot was also broken, enforcing a hobbled gait (Ping 2000). Caduveo Indians seemed to become more excited by the artworks they created on their faces than by their own naked bodies (Lévi-Strauss 1973: chap. 20).

It's true that within the West there has been a moral discourse attacking cosmetics as "artificiality" (often by equating it misogynistically with femininity) and advocating a return to the natural. St. Paul admonishes women to "adorn themselves with good deeds," "not with braided hair or gold or pearls" (Steele 1996:14). In nineteenth-century Brazil one term for a prostitute was a *painted woman*. Often, however, moral critiques of "artificiality" have been ineffective faced with the rise of modern fashion—broadly understood to include a fascination with novelty, adornment, and the "small arts" of seduction. In fact, the very call for the natural can easily become aestheticized and sexualized within the markets of consumer capitalism. The flapper, for example, rejected the artificial constraints of earlier fashions, yet her naturalness (itself highly adorned) became a fashionable style. And though fashions in the 1950s ostensibly symbolized a return to a more natural femininity centered on childbearing, new brassieres projected the breasts into an artificial, torpedo-shaped form that became an erotic fetish. Charles Baudelaire, an often prescient observer of modern erotic culture, critiques "philosophers" who "stupidly anathematize" cosmetics. Echoing Hegel's defense of body modification, he too sees a resemblance between civilized and savage: "In their naïf adoration of what is brilliant—many-colored feathers, iridescent fabrics, the incomparable majesty of artificial forms—the baby and the savage *bear witness to their disgust of the real*" (1995: 32). Modern fashions, as much as "savage" ones, have thus often illustrated a "horror of nature" (Lévi-Strauss 1973).

Contemporary medicocosmetic practices partly break with this logic of symbolic transformation as they make the aesthetic and erotic body into a natural object. By this I mean not the embrace of "the natural" as a style, but rather the creation of a notion of desirability defined around the naked organism. Many of the techniques of aesthetic medicine visualize and quantify a notion of attractiveness in relation to processes of aging and mothering understood as objective changes to tissue structure, skin elasticity, and so forth. They also encourage a self-administered biotechnical tinkering, or what João Biehl (with D. Coutinho and A. L. Outeiro) calls in reference to AIDS testing, an "auto-bio-administration" (2001: 112). Such forms of intervention thus create a *subjectivation*—a new domain of subjectivity—based in the biological organism. Patients often develop their own "folk biologies" as they speculate about the role of *hormônios*, *natureza*, or *menopausa* in sexuality and aging. Hormonal changes are seen to "deform" the body. Conversely, plástica makes the libido "rise to the head," boosting self-esteem. The self is imagined as a domain of biological activity that can be regulated or enhanced with medical techniques.

The biological stratum specifically targeted by plástica includes *secondary sexual characteristics*. This notion used in biology to refer to bodily traits that arose as a product of sexual selection, and which are developmentally produced by sex hormones, seems to have disappeared from the interpretive social sciences and humanities. In view of the bewildering varieties of human erotic experience, it is perhaps impossible to isolate a biological significance of such bodily traits for sexual desire. On the other hand, to argue that the sexual body is a tabula rasa on which cultures are free to write their codes any which way they choose also seems, to me at least, too radical a proposition. It is likely, for example, that the distinct hemispherical shape of the human female breast is the product of sexual selection (as it serves no apparent functional purpose; large fat deposits are not necessary for lactation and can even interfere with breast-feeding). As Angier (1999: 134–56) puts it, "The aesthetic breast is nonfunctional to the point of being counterfunctional." It's true that different societies prefer or fetishize larger or smaller breasts, or even seem to neglect this area of the body. But variation can also be exaggerated, and the upright, firm, protruding breast is seen in diverse societies as an erotically alluring sign of youth and beauty (Etcoff 2000).

Plastic surgery specifically targets the female breast and other signals of youth and reproductive history. It's true that some operations enlarge, while others reduce, the size of the breasts, suggesting once again the presence of culturally variable ideals. On the other hand, there are also similarities between enlargement and reduction procedures, both of which aim to project and lift the breast, and to remove flaccidity or sagging. The goal of both types of surgery can be to simply make the breast, as Flávia said, "as it was before" (childbirth). Other operations too are frequently used to remove the marks of childbearing and "contour" a youthful-looking body. Unlike the diverse forms of body modification that inscribe cultural ideals on the body, these techniques seem to target the aesthetic-erotic marks of biological processes. Much of what aesthetic medicine regards as beautiful resembles the aesthetic ideals that sociobiologists claim are the product of evolutionary processes: traits such as symmetry, uniform skin, flat abdomens, upright breasts, and hip-to-waist contrasts. They argue in particular that males have an inherited aesthetic preference for females with an *apparently* "nulliparous body" (never given birth) because such women are less likely to be already pregnant (and thus more likely to impregnated) (Etcoff 2000). Many (though not all) techniques of aesthetic medicine aim to create or enhance such signs. Facelifts and peels homogenize skin. Some nose jobs and breast operations enhance symmetry.[1] Liposculpture and other surgeries flatten bellies or redistribute fat to enhance waist to hip contrasts. And many procedures, as we have seen, specifically aim to create the youthful breasts, flat abdomens, and slender waists of the nulliparous body.

There are many problems with evolutionary approaches to human beauty and sexuality (Lancaster 2003). For one, these theories seem to reproduce traditional Western gender ideologies in which men "select" women for their attractiveness, and women select men on the basis of their "resources." Moreover, some beauty ideals, such as that represented by the fashion model, diverge from a supposedly near universal human preference for relative plumpness in the female figure. Sociobiologists respond by saying that thinness is only one trait among others that together indicate youth and the nulliparous body. They claim, as well, that most fashion models still have relatively large hip-to-waist contrasts (Etcoff 2000). In a sense, the extreme thinness of fashion itself resembles an evolutionary process biologists refer to as "runaway sexual selection." Exaggerated versions of sexually desirable traits confer reproductive advantage, even when they undermine overall fitness, a principle that explains how male peacocks could arrive at their patently useless and biologically "expensive" tails (G. Miller 2000: 55–57). Perhaps global fashion exhibits a parallel process of "*runway* sexual selection" whereby the exaggerated thinness of the model acquires value not in biological sexual competition, but in the economic competitions of global markets.

Culture is not simply an edifice built on top of a biological foundation; rather, we were already cultural beings during long periods of our evolutionary history (Geertz 1973: chap. 3). Aesthetic preferences based in evolution cannot be known "in themselves"; the natural is always already cultural. But perhaps this is too easy a conclusion, leading to the radical proposition that humans are entirely free in their sexual behavior from biological processes and constraints. The very popularity in diverse societies of techniques that shape the biological processes of "performance" and pleasure—from Viagra to sex hormone therapies to myriad illicit and alternative chemical boosters—suggests not just a drive to control nature, but also an awareness of a biological stratum to experience. The medicocosmetic alteration of female genitals or secondary sexual characteristics is mirrored by such tinkering with neurochemistry, reflecting a biologized self arising through technological enhancement.

Perhaps it would be more accurate to say that the social organization of biological needs and drives changes historically in ways that shape the significance of "nature" for social life. I have tried to show one such historical shift: as attractiveness becomes a form of capital "liberated" from other ideologies and institutions, the selections of markets begin to mimic evolutionary sexual (but not natural) selection. One implication of this change is that the subjects of beauty cultures work on biological processes of aging and mothering defined through medical techniques. Mary Midgley (1988) points out that the rise of Darwinian theory made the boundaries between humans and animals more emotionally and morally charged in the West. It is perhaps a great paradox of the Enlightenment project that the progressive conquest of nature has been accompanied by a biologization of the human body: its reduction to a bare life and bare sex defined within modern medicine, politics, and markets.

::: **FATAL ATTRACTION**

Human sex and reproduction have been partially unlinked through a technological invention: a historic event perhaps already presaged in the ancient evolutionary history of primates, who unlike many other animals, have "freed" sexual activity from the period of female estrus. It is now a cliché to speak of the "pill" as a revolution, a technology compared sometimes in its significance to nuclear fusion, even if many women still don't have access to reliable contraception. But the implications of this historic severance of reproduction and sex for family and sexual relationships have yet to become fully evident. Medical control over reproduction is also happening during a period when religious, political, and kinship ideologies that regulated sexual relationships are declining in some regions. For new sectors of society and periods of the life span, forms of "elective" and "recreational" sexuality are emerging, delinked both from marriage and from heterosexual normalization (Giddens 1993). One result is an "autonomy of sexual expression" based in the "increased distance between people's desire and their families" (Castells 1997: 236–37).[2] On the other hand, sexual allure becomes a fetishized object within medical practices and diverse kinds of markets. Beauty cultures reflect not just technological innovations but also larger tensions in the forms of sexual and economic exchange arising in consumer capitalism. I would like to end therefore by returning to the issue I began with: beauty as sign and symptom of the social conflicts of modernity.

Capitalist development is not just driven by technological innovation. More subtle changes to desire and affect accompany the penetration of market forces into new domains of experience. Often markets show a remarkable capacity to undermine traditional forms of social organization and metaphysical supports of authority. In Marx's metaphor, this is a process of "creative destruction" that allows the increasing circulation and exchange of capital (Berman 1982). Or in Deleuze's terms (1993: 236), wealth frees itself from social and moral restraints to become "pure and homogenous capital." The world economy represents a "universal cosmopolitan energy that overflows every restriction and bond" (1993: 236). Georg Simmel argues in a similar vein that money levels traditional distinctions: through generalized transactions, it draws attention to the "relativistic character of existence" (1990 [1907]: 512). In earlier stages of capitalism, such fungibility aided the rise of the bourgeoisie, enabling the conversion of economic resources into social position. In late capitalism, this process might be said to be extended to the body as it is exchanged in the markets of production and reproduction, work and sex.

As capitalist development undermines older forms of authority, including a paternalistic state and some patriarchal structures, it also paves the way for the expansion of beauty culture. Religious institutions, ideologies of male dominance, aristocratic mystique, and other absolute metaphysical supports of power are challenged by visible and fungible forms of capital:

beauty, sexuality, and of course, money. The weakening of moral restrictions on cosmetics, legal constraints on women's economic activity, and the social regulation of female sexuality "free" the body—but also insert it in the market. Aspirations rise with flows of cosmopolitan culture. This "creative destruction" not only commodifies the female body; it also generates new desires. Beauty, one might say, thrives in the cracks of a basic contradiction in modernity: the tremendous incitement of social aspirations coexisting with class stratification. Of course, markets are embedded still in older networks of power and privilege. Yet they remain "free" enough to enable the social fantasy of mobility and self-invention, and competitive enough to arouse the anxiety of redundancy, of being "traded" as Flávia said.

In beauty culture bodies (or even parts) have a value that either can be enhanced and maintained through expenditure, or else exchanged for other kinds of capital. Such fungibility of sexual allure and youth is perhaps even clearer in recent gay cultures. Older forms of homosexuality in Brazil were based on a distinction between *homen* ("man") and a stigmatized passive partner, *bicha* ("fag") (Fry 1982; Parker 1991). This historical distinction defined around the act of penetration has been partially displaced by a new identity of *gai* defined as a "sexual orientation" and linked to a global gay culture (Parker 1999). While antigay violence still exists in democratic Brazil, gay men and women have successfully won new rights. Intensely appearance and consumption centered, this global gay culture has also brought more open mixing between classes and between foreigners and Brazilians. The circuits linking areas such as the Castro of San Francisco and the Posto Nove of Rio de Janeiro (and many cities now have such areas) might seem elite, but in fact they draw together a variety of classes and sexual subjects from Brazil and abroad (ibid.: 55). In relatively open and free markets, youth and attractiveness become a form of value that can be exchanged for symbolic and material capital in a range of cross-class and transnational romances and sex-for-money encounters.

In these circumstances, beauty exhibits a certain tyranny. The gay beauty industry may be even more hegemonic than the female one. In Brazil, the term *barbie*, used to describe a gay man, evokes the manufactured, plastic qualities of physiques identically tanned, depilated, and "forged" in gyms. Yet while this culture may unfairly punish the unattractive and old, physical attractiveness, and implicitly, youth itself, become qualities that can "cancel" the class and color hierarchies that otherwise prevail. The normal symbolic and material markers of status (speech, fashion, education, and so on) can be partially suppressed in situations where sexual exchange is based primarily on physical qualities. Not everyone has equal access to such cosmopolitan milieus. But with a small amount of economizing, most of the poor can at least occasionally visit the bars and scenes of consumption frequented by wealthier Cariocas and tourists (Parker 1999). This is a situation of radical *fungibility* between different forms of economic, cultural, and also *sexual* capital—the last form generally neglected by Bourdieu (1984) in his masterful analyses of how conversions between symbolic and material forms of privilege naturalize class domination.

Like Clarissa, Graziele said she "loved beauty" and liked to read magazines, admiring the "beautiful artistas." Like Flávia, she also has injected liquid silicone in her buttocks. Like Renata, she dreams of "entering TV" as a dancer. Like Gabriela, she likes to receive praise from men: "When I pass in the street and guys say that I am beautiful, and *gostosa* [tasty] or sexy." But Graziele—a young *travesti*—has a quite different relationship to beauty and body modification than these women. She must take female hormones and liters of liquid silicone to acquire the feminine forms she admires, and then sells as a sex worker. Unlike modern and prestigious medical cosmetic surgery, these body-shaping practices are seen as vulgar and dangerous, and travestis are considered *marginais*, criminals, in Brazilian society (Kulick 1998; Denizart 1998).

The travesti often has a radically experimental ethos, subjecting her body to a series of dangerous and highly invasive procedures that transform her from a poor, inconspicuous, and stigmatized adolescent into *a gostosa*, "the sexy one." Though still not accepted in mainstream society, she now "calls attention," is admired and envied, and generally earns more money than she could otherwise. This new persona is achieved through a remarkable quantification, fragmentation, and commodification of the body, Don Kulick shows (1998). Liters of silicone, hormone dosages, or body-part dimensions are discussed in minute detail. They are also linked to increased earnings "on the street." The travesti seems to experience contradictory forms of autonomy and commodification as she turns her body into a valuable asset. Subjected to a sexual market, she paradoxically spends her earnings to keep a dependent "husband"—a man who "eats" her, thereby providing the ultimate proof of her femininity (Kulick 1998).[3]

Despite having myriad differences with gay men, women can experience similar tensions between sexual and economic exchange in beauty culture. Some women saw sexual relationships or marriage as a means to convert beauty, youth, or exotic difference into an improvement of one's "conditions." Fantasies and plans revolve around diverse figures: a *coroa* ("crown"), an elderly and wealthier man; a *gringo*; a trafficker; or simply a middle-class man. Or they could be directed at travel abroad, whether as a student, an entertainer, or an unskilled migrant. Donna Goldstein (2003) discusses how women in a Rio favela sometimes initiated sexual relationships to acquire material items immediately needed for household subsistence. The ability to seduce is also imagined as a possible route of social mobility in the social fantasy of the *golpe de baú*, the "treasure-chest coup." In these stories, sexual appeal is a crucial resource, a means of attaining a better life, in situations of scarcity.

The fetishism of technology and "progress," as I've argued, is often allied with a fetishism of the female body as the life force of sexuality is drawn into the inorganic realm of commodities. The body fragmented into parts reflects other kinds of fragmentation in the modern domain of femininity. Beauty culture splits the role of woman into mother and sexual being, and then offers techniques to work on self-esteem. The marks of motherhood become defects, separate from the self. Market stratification also fractures the role of woman between categories of maid, wife, and publicly recognized worker. Beauty work can be embraced as a means to transcend such "separations" through attaining feminine ideals defined in an idiom of health. In uncertain service economies, youth and sexuality become forms of capital exchanged in markets. Sexual allure can also be envisioned as a vehicle of fame, promising a radical transformation in life possibilities. Artistas who come from "humble" backgrounds demonstrate the lesson that physical assets can be converted into wealth and power. The career path of the aspiring artista, however, may also "teach" media viewers that professional success depends on sexual exchanges. Even a star as successful as Xuxa must continuously assert the line between her work as a model and prostitution. Ângela, Lana, and Amélia dreamed of "selling their image" partly to counter other forms of dependency and invisibility.

Beauty cultures reflect another gendered tension of modernity: elective sexuality and free choice in romantic love accompanies sexual competition. Attractiveness can be seen as an asset of the self but also a constraint on freedom as the consumer encounters the objectification of female bodies in the market. Baudrillard (1990: 25) makes a similar point: "As the feminine becomes a subject, it also returns as object, as generalized pornography." Modernity enables new possibilities of self-determination in the arena of love and sex as family control and patriarchal morality weaken. But the search for autonomy and freedom is jeopardized by the extension of a market logic to biological and sexual experience. So in a sense, beauty mirrors the ambiguous emancipatory power of capital itself: it challenges traditional hierarchies, yet exposes the "liberated" body to the new hazards of generalized exchange.

: : :

I was first drawn to this research by a plastic surgeon's provocative comment that the poor have the right to be beautiful. Trying to contextualize this comment through fieldwork, I came to see a "hidden" (to me at least) meaning of beauty. For some workers and consumers on the margins of the market economy, physical allure can be an asset that actually seems to disrupt the class hierarchies that pervade many other aspects of their lives. Though this belief also testifies to relative powerlessness, it cannot be simply dismissed as false consciousness. The point is recognized oddly enough in the rigorous analysis of the class body by Pierre Bourdieu (1984). He argues that class-based notions of taste and style literally shape the body by determining everything from eating habits to posture. But Bourdieu makes a glaring exception for physical beauty. Bodies "*should*," he writes, "be perceived as strictly corresponding to their 'owners'" position in the social hierarchy" (1984: 190, my italics). Yet, he argues, they do not. Why? His answer is that the "logic of social heredity" exhibits a kind of black humor in that it "sometimes endows those least endowed with the rarest bodily properties, such as beauty." This quality of beauty, he continues, is "sometimes fatally attractive, because it threatens the other hierarchies, and . . . denies the high and mighty the bodily attributes of their position, such as height or beauty" (190). These physical attributes are a kind of dangerous residue that does not fit within the class culture created by the socially dominant. Beauty then can be seen as a kind of "double negative": an unfair hierarchy that can disturb other unfair hierarchies.

Social sciences have tended to emphasize the structural forces constructing and policing social demarcations, neglecting the forces of attraction that also link humans as biosocial beings, and that make such divisions "necessary." In some moments at least, the veil of metaphysical authority or cultural common sense evaporates, revealing human beings as organisms with roughly similar needs and desires. One example of such a moment is when the beautiful person exerts a power, however rarely, against the entitlement of privilege. Although it's true that the masculinity and femininity of the lower classes can appear "vulgar" to elites (who in turn, perhaps more rarely, have disgusted lower social strata in their moral failings), such reactions also testify to the always present danger of seduction, the fact that physical attractions can, lightning-like, move through and across social obstructions. There is always the possibility that the attractive person will not return the love of the powerful and unattractive social superior, providing a moral lesson about the limits of privilege.

This social fact not only demonstrates to the punished ego the nonnegotiable limits to the realization of desires, but also makes plain to all observers the power possessed by the physically attractive person. She or he attracts the gaze of the world, redirecting the energies of social life, serving as a reminder of the limits of high birth, wealth, and even sometimes masculine and aristocratic prerogative. Such powers of course are quite limited by other more stable sources of authority, and point to the transient and often deceptive nature of power exercised. The beautiful but poor heroine in Victorian and Georgian marriage markets had quite a limited "window" in which to convert her capital into more durable sources of power and wealth. Yet, as other metaphysical and moral dimensions of normative femininity (a good family, virginity, virtue) decline in value, perhaps physical attractiveness may even increase in importance to subjects exercising agency in a social domain where elective sexuality is the norm or ideal for larger parts of the life cycle.

This is a "democratic" movement in that it undercuts the symbolic importance of material class markers. It also invests youth and sexual allure with greater value in societies where choice is made possible by the decline of regulatory institutions and moral and spiritual ideals of femininity. In these circumstances, class competition is partially replaced by sex and age competition. The symbolic class wars fought in the arena of material commodities or learned bodily culture are displaced partly by other contests in which the brute, bare criteria of youth and secondary sexual characteristics are forms of capital. Of course, attractiveness is only one of many factors that shape one's life path, but it is especially significant in the domains of love and sex. As attraction is "freed" from some forms of social control, beauty defined by biological markers and youth becomes a more significant social and emotional site of identity for new groups of people.

Health reflects many kinds of social inequalities, but biological decay is also a leveling or "equalizing" process in societies in which appearance is a principal form of capital. Nakedness dehumanizes in part because it removes the body of social signs. Plástica—in its emphasis on naked corporeal beauty over style, dress, jewelry and other material objects—thus seems to naturalize and biologize the body, reducing it to a presocial condition. In its naked state, the organism is less readable as a social body and more or less "democratically" susceptible to the aesthetic predations of time. The poor may "suffer as much as the rich faced with the aesthetic defect"; conversely, the social effects of attractiveness cross class and cultural boundaries. The cult of youth and health might also be democratic in that it partly redistributes social status from (generally wealthier) older to (generally poorer) younger generations. Plástica responds to, and incites, this view of beauty as an egalitarian form of social capital, one that depends less on birth, education, and connections to cultivate.

Beauty then may have a kind of democratic appeal, perhaps especially during a time when authoritarian structures are losing their legitimacy while opportunities for social mobility remain limited. In such a situation beauty can occupy a similar position in the social imaginary for girls that soccer does for boys. While boys living in poverty often dream of becoming professional athletes, many girls in poor communities have the equally impossible dream of becoming fashion models. In both fantasies, the invisibility of poverty is best negated by media visibility. When access to education is limited, the body—relative to the mind—becomes a more important basis for identity as well as a source of power. This theme often emerges in the dominant popular genre in Latin America, melodrama, in stories about "fatal attractions" that cross class lines. While the rich girl may have all the advantages, the poor girl's beauty (or more rarely the boy's masculine appeal) is so strong that it threatens social barriers. These stories seem to express a folk notion of justice that sees in beauty a magical capacity to reverse fortunes, as even the rich and powerful may be seduced by the poor or may dream of being beautiful themselves. Like the samba parade, beauty too can be seen as a popular form of hope, even if as another Carnaval song has it:

> The happiness of the poor is like
> The great illusion of Carnaval
> Working the whole year
> For a moment of rest
> To make the costume [. . .]
> And all ends on Tuesday
> Sadness has no end
> Happiness, yes.
> ("Felicidade." Lyrics by Vinícius de Moraes; music by Tom Jobim)

# Acknowledgments

I have accrued many debts writing this book, which has traveled with me through five moves to four continents. It is a pleasure to try to acknowledge them. First, I am grateful to those, too many to list here, who agreed to participate in the research, and often made Rio de Janeiro feel like a second home. Thank you for repaying my nosiness with thoughtful reflections and generous hospitality. Hermano Vianna has been a dear guide to Rio de Janeiro and Brazilian thought and popular culture. His friendship sustained me through many periods of doubt, and his humor and writing provoked me to examine many of my "Brazilianist" (and North American) habits of the mind. Mirian Goldenberg is both a friend and mentor. Our discussions—as we walked along the long boardwalks of the Zona Sul— were invaluable for doing fieldwork. Peter Fry's pioneering scholarship on race made me appreciate the difficulty of cross-cultural interpretations. Our anthropological conversations were delightful. I am grateful to Joana Collier do Rêgo Barro, both for her friendship and generous help in filmmaking. Shanti Avirgan, a fellow traveler in Brazilian anthropology, made the journey more fun. I am grateful to John Collins both for his wonderful scholarship and his conversations in the field. Thank you to Stéphan Malysse for early introductions to the field and to Brazil. I am forever grateful to Joana, who indulged me, tolerated my "Spockiness," and made Brazil work on me as much as vice versa—*fico seu orelhão*. In Ceará, I found a collaborator and kindred spirit in Simone Lima, whose enthusiasm for ethnography and film were infectious. Olívia von der Weid, Ludmila Fernandes de Freitas, and Gisele of IFSC provided invaluable research assistance. Lucas Bennet gave helpful advice on photography. I'm also grateful to many other friends in Rio de Janeiro for innumerable ways they helped me along the way: Patrícia de Oliveira, Sandra Kogut, Tom Levine, Jonathan Nossiter, Amber Levinson, Claudia Pereira, Daniela, Carmen, Sasha, Ilana, "Cabeça," Marilene, André.

This research began as a Ph.D. thesis, and I would like to thank Princeton University's Department of Anthropology for years of support. James Boon helped me to appreciate popular fashions, and to become more critical of academic ones. The wisdom and generosity of his thinking are inviting and inimitable. Abdallah Hammoudi's Socratic teaching helped me to see the masters in a new light. I am especially grateful to Vinçanne Adams for her mentoring and for generously agreeing to continue on my committee after moving to a new department. Carol Greenhouse was a welcome presence on my dissertation committee, and Isabel Nabokov, Rena Lederman, and Gananath Obeysekere were influential teachers. I'm grateful to Arnie Eisen, Bernard Faure, and Jean-Marie Apostolidès at Stanford University for getting me excited about social theory. I am particularly indebted to João Biehl, my Ph.D. thesis advisor, without whose guidance and support over many years I would not have been able to complete this project. His mentoring and readings of my work amounted to an initiation into medical anthropology and fieldwork, and enabled me to finally find a way to write about Brazil. His writing and research have been an inspiration.

For research support I thank Princeton University's Woodrow Wilson Society of Fellows, the Council on International Studies, a Mellon Field Methods Grant, and a Princeton University Dissertation Fellowship. I'm grateful to the Social Science Research Council for Pre-Dissertation and Dissertation Research Fellowships. A Woodrow Wilson Postdoctoral Fellowship, and the Center for Modern Studies at the University of California, Los Angeles, provided support for writing sections of this manuscript. A Macquarie University New Staff Research Grant funded fieldwork on media and racial identities. I thank Gilberto Velho for generously providing a research affiliation with the Department of Anthropology at the Museu Nacional in Rio de Janeiro. I'm grateful to have found scholarly company there, and in particular I thank Otávio Velho and Eduardo Viveiros de Castro for their seminars. At UCLA, I'm indebted to Vince Pecora and Kirstie McClure for their support in the writing process, and for creating a challenging and fun intellectual climate for their rookery—or was it an "ascension"?—of postdocs. Special thanks to Niko Besnier for his mentoring and encouragement to publish. I'm also deeply grateful to the two anonymous reviewers for Duke who extensively commented on this manuscript and challenged me to reach much further than I thought I could.

In the United States, Australia, and the Netherlands, I had many colleagues who became friends and made anthropology seem worth doing. Thomas Strong and Lisa Wynn were comrades from the beginning—my thinking about anthropology owes much to their support, kindness, and brilliance. Thank you both for generously commenting on many drafts of this manuscript. Kirsten Scheid, Susanna Trnka, and other members of the Princeton anthropology cyber forum gave many useful comments to chapter drafts and created a wonderful spirit of camaraderie across huge distances. Thanks especially to Sarah Pinto for in-depth comments and for suggesting the title of this book, and to Rachel Newcombe for giving feedback on the entire manuscript. I'm grateful to John MacDougall for his initiations into fieldwork and warm friendship. Julie Park's insights and sense of fun enriched long days of dissertation writing. I was lucky to find in Adriana Abdenur a friend and fellow fieldworker both in Rio and in Princeton. More thanks to close friends who accompanied me on the often difficult path into academics, and who shaped in many ways how I think and write: Tamara Griggs, Marwa and Omnia ElShakry, Emily Wittman, and Clara Han. Corvin Russell and Jed Friedman have been a part of everything I do, and your voices are in here too.

In Sydney and then in Amsterdam, Pál Nyíri made me rethink everything about anthropology (and a lot else)—his friendship and comments on the manuscript were invaluable. Thanks to the other members of the Macquarie writing workshop for feedback—Kirsten Bell, Kalpana Ram, and especially Chris Houston for detailed notes on the introduction. I was fortunate to land in Amsterdam down the hall from a wonderful thinker and writer with a shared love of Brazil, Mattijs van de Port. Josien de Klerk, Marie Lindegaard, Jarrett Zigon, Oscar Verkaaik, and Jojada Verrips gave many useful comments to chapter drafts. I'm grateful to Lotte Hoek for agreeing to be a paper respondent and helping me through difficult late stages of writing. Thanks to the participants in the *Medische Antropologie* symposium on beauty and health, and particularly to Sjaak van der Geest for helping me to rethink my ideas about health. At Duke University Press I'd like to thank Ken Wissoker for his early enthusiasm for the project, Sonya Manes and Mark Mastromarino for their helpful editing, and Mandy Earley for her work on the manuscript production. Many of my students contributed to my thinking by making me appreciate what is important—and what isn't—in anthropology. I'm grateful to my parents, Barney and Julie Love Edmonds, and my sister, Zöe Edmonds, for their love and support over the many years of research, and for feedback on this manuscript and photographs. My last debt is to Laura Murdoch, who in the last years of writing added generous doses of love, mystery, and fun to my life and made so much possible.

# Notes

## INTRODUCTION

1 Unless otherwise noted, all translations of Portuguese quotations from interviews and published material are my own.

2 Names are mostly pseudonyms. Exceptions are made for participants such as Ester who appear in a photograph and agreed to be identified by name, for celebrities discussing their public persona, and for surgeons who were interviewed in their capacity as chief surgeon of a plastic surgery ward in a public hospital. Fieldwork was conducted in Brazil during two extended periods in 1998–99 and 2000–1, as well as during shorter visits in 2003, 2006, and 2009.

3 Brazil subsequently slipped to second place in the rankings (after the United States), though according to *Veja*, it has higher per capita rates of cosmetic surgery than European countries. In 2004, 616,287 plastic surgery operations were performed in Brazil, of which 59 percent were cosmetic (SBCP 2005).

4 By "beauty" I mean several related things: *beauty industries* broadly understood (including plastic surgery, fashion, sexual allure as a central commodity in mass media, advertising, the star system, etc.), *beauty culture* (the historically variable traditions surrounding the aesthetics and erotics of the human form), *beauty work* (body practices aiming to improve appearance), and *physical attractiveness*.

5 This comment was made during a seminar held at the Museu Nacional in Rio de Janeiro.

6 Perhaps because many of these practices are so violent or harmful anthropologists seem to have felt a particular burden of interpretation. An image of a dangling lip plug threatens to resurrect the image of the savage laid to rest by sensitive ethnographic description.

7 The very plethora of commodities can also suggest a "feminine" extension of pleasure and material prosperity. Jean Baudrillard argues that, "Utopian continuity and availability can only be incarnated by the female sex. This is why in

this society everything—objects, goods, services, relations of all types—will be feminized, sexualized in a feminine fashion" (1990: 26).

8 See Foster Wallace (2005) for an analysis of the American pornography industry as a microcosm of the larger entertainment-oriented consumer society.

9 As Campbell (1987) points out, the "romantic ethic" of mass consumer culture was tightly linked to the rise of a new, often female, public: novel readers. Describing a new inner world of feminine wants and pleasures, the novel also represents the rise of a psychological worldview.


## PART ONE. THE SELF-ESTEEM IN EACH EGO AWAKENS

1 She is referring to the 1960s countercultural movement led by her father, Caetano Veloso, Gal Costa, and others. Inspired by the rallying cry of "cultural cannibalism," the group mixed British psychedelic rock with Afro-Brazilian traditions. Upsetting oppositions between "authentic" acoustic music and imitative rock, it cannily provoked critics of imperialism on the Left as well as the right-wing military regime. Several members of the group, including Gil, ended up in exile in Europe.

2 In Jonathan's screenplay, Pitanguy's character—to be played by Pitanguy—has a light seductive banter with his counterpart, a British plastic surgeon played by Charlotte Rampling.

3 Clinics keep meticulous photographic records of all patients for the purpose of research—or in the unlikely event of a malpractice suit. Some doctors also use "before and after" images in ads, a practice that Pitanguy condemns as it can create "unrealistic expectations."

4 Some patients similarly argued that operations classified as estética were in fact actually reparadora, because they "repaired the effects of time," or "restored" their previous appearance. A facelift patient said: "I don't consider my surgery to be estética; it's reparadora actually. It's going to repair the effects of time, what time has been destroying. The body is the same as a house: it loses value and has to be renovated."

5 Pedagogical techniques, hospital procedures, and patient demographics at Santa Casa (which receives a mixture of state and charity funding) are similar to those at public hospitals, and so I sometimes include the clinic in my discussion of public hospitals.

6 On the phone, he had advised me to take a taxi, as the month before a surgeon had been assaulted on his motorcycle as he left the hospital. Mangueira is informally run by a traficante, who declared that all hospital workers were under his personal protection. When word about the mugging got out, the surgeon's possessions were returned and his assailant killed.

7 Ironically, the notion of "dependency" itself is partly a native product. This

Marxist theory of core-periphery relations was developed in part by the leftist sociologist and later "neoliberal" president Fernando Enrique Cardoso.

8  With their emphasis on unilinear evolution and progress, these ideas seemed perfectly adapted to the related projects of "civilizing" (and healing) a barbaric population and reforming cities (Oliven 2000: 56).

9  This reevaluation of popular culture was not without conflict. So many samba songs romanticized the malandro, "rogue," that the propagandists for the Estado Novo began to urge composers to depict "well-behaved characters and ex-*malandros* converted into peaceful workers" (Severiano and Mello 1997: 196).

10  The monthly's success led Norberto to launch *Models*: "The magazine for whoever has always wanted to be a model." It has also spawned rivals, such as *Plástica & Você* (Plástica & You), and *Plástica & Corpo* (Plástica & Body). Norberto does not seem overly concerned. "I think we can still double our circulation, to 160,000, because we were the pioneer. I know the market is there; it's just a question of promoting it the right way—TV, radio, everything." Plans are underway, he adds, to furnish content to publishers from Portugal and Spain.

11  Pitanguy's (1976: 124) published case histories suggest the difficulty of applying these principles. One describes a patient with the complaint that everyone considers her "old and ugly." A psychiatric evaluation revealed that the patient suffered from an underlying "depressive phobic neurosis." Pitanguy deferred the facelift until benzodiazepines and psychotherapy had had a beneficial effect. In this case the "aesthetic defect" perceived by the patient—being "old and ugly"— was not an illness to be cured by plástica, but rather a symptom of *another* illness: "depressive phobic neurosis." This distinction raises a larger question: Is "feeling old and ugly" the illness itself or a *symptom* of another underlying illness?

12  As we shall see in part 3, high rates of nonclinical Caesarean deliveries and female sterilizations in public hospitals are partly fed by patients' desires to get access to what they see as a more modern form of healthcare available to wealthier women in the private sector.

13  A serious man in his mid-twenties from a working-class district, he told me, "Look, I chose to be a doctor because I knew I'd never be without a job. And I chose surgery because I like the work. But the problem is that salaries are absurd." In a public hospital, he said, a surgeon's fee for a hernia operation is only 150 reais. In the South Zone, a surgeon would receive not less than 1,500 reais to put in an implant, a similarly "simple" procedure. There is one problem, he added: "Attracting your first patients." His strategy was to target overseas Brazilians with low prices advertised on the Internet.

14  For example, a São Paulo clinic advertised a liposuction operation for only 600 reais, but with only local anesthesia, performed in the doctor's office. For 2,500 reais, the patient would receive general anesthesia and be interned in a hospital (*Corpo à Corpo* 1998).

15 Another factor contributing to a rise in medical error is the popularity of lipo-suction (*O Dia* 1999). Unlike a facelift or nose job, it is an operation that is "apparently easy," Dr. Pitanguy argued, and thus more likely to "fall into the hands of those without training" (*Veja* 2001b).

16 In one such case, followed closely by telenovela fans, a famous actress entered into a coma for four days during her third plástica operation. A news article alleged that her surgeon had once reported a facelift as "brain surgery" to the insurance company (*Veja* 1996a).

17 At Santa Casa, patients were given a choice between operating with a resident or paying R$1,000 more to have a professor. Many ask for the more experienced surgeon, implying there is lingering unease among some patients about undergoing cosmetic surgery with "students."

18 Public hospitals officially fulfill a mandate to provide a universal right to healthcare, but unofficially they are understood to be for "the common people" (though no attempt is made to determine financial eligibility). Occasionally, however, middle-class patients will "sneak into" a public plastic surgery ward, though they may be shocked by conditions there: One such patient said: "Not everyone has the courage to go to a public hospital, where you wait in endless lines in the heat, where you have people from the super low class."

19 Many believed that media conglomerate Globo helped engineer his victory, as well as President Cardoso's later reelection (Green 2000: 8).

20 The number of workers with a signed "work card" declined from 57 percent in 1990 to 45 percent in 1996 in metropolitan São Paulo—a significant indicator since only workers registered with the Ministry of Labor receive many social rights (Georges 2003).

21 Zé would officially be a "contraindicated" patient, a very rare occurrence. It was not the link between employment and the aesthetic defect per se that was a problem. (Gisele's belief that a breast implant would enhance her career prospects might be judged rational, since after all the request came from her agent.) Rather, the hospital clinicians judged that he had an *irrational* belief that the operation would resolve his problem (as a *nariz afinado*, thin nose, is not part of the job description for bus change collector).

22 In 1997, the top 10 percent concentrated 48 percent of the total income (Reis 2000: 9).

23 Brazil later lost its first-place ranking in this category.

24 During periods of hyperinflation, consumer indebtedness can also become a kind of political indebtedness. Carlos Menem, when running for reelection in Argentina, made this point: "If you don't want a return to inflation and higher taxes, which will make it impossible to pay off what you bought, you should vote for me again" (García Canclini 2001: 39).

25 Defining its size is a charged political question of course. A 1993 government

report, for example, stated that of a total population of 150 million, only 30 million citizens "participated in the market economy" (Levine 1997: 33).

26 Throughout Brazil's history as a Republic, the health and relative size of the middle class has frequently served as a barometer of national progress and modernity (Owensby 1999: 3–8).

27 Even today, it is possible to interpret the marked emphasis on manicures and other forms of bodily hygiene and grooming as a means of creating symbolic distance from the stigma of labor, including domestic labor.

28 I borrow the distinction between digital and analogical from a discussion of affect by Sedgwick and Frank (1995).

## PART TWO. BEAUTIFUL PEOPLE

1 Another prominent Bahian singer and songwriter of Gilberto Gil's generation.

2 I am indebted here to the insightful discussions by Peter Fry (2000) and Hermano Vianna (1999) about the role of the "myth of racial democracy" in nation building.

3 A more literal translation would be "The Mansion and the Shanties." The English translation was published in 1956.

4 The term *miscegenation* is itself rooted in the virulently racist fear of interracial mixing, which in the United States took the form of "antimiscegenation" laws. I retain the word here because it is used by Freyre and sometimes in contemporary media.

5 Several historians have since challenged Freyre's claims that the Brazilian treatment of slaves and women was in fact more "benevolent" than in other colonial societies (Russell-Wood 1982).

6 Others have maintained that mestiçagem—as a cultural paradigm governing racial relations—should be conceptually distinguished from the "myth of racial democracy" (Fry 2000, Vianna 1999). Racism can be acknowledged and fought, in this view, without adopting multicultural identity politics.

7 Like samba nearly a century earlier, *funk* is an urban genre born in the favelas of Rio de Janeiro (Vianna 1988). Once dismissed as violent and vulgar by the middle class, but now mainstream, funk is a prime example of popular culture's bunda fetishism.

8 Though the silicone implant is a recent invention, it was perhaps anticipated by the nineteenth-century custom of wearing *anquinhas* ("little bottoms"). Made of diverse materials such as whalebone, newspaper, or metal foil, the prosthesis was designed to "give the feminine posterior an even more luxuriant form" (Del Priore 2000: 58). Brazilian clothing stores still offer items such as padded underwear and brands of jeans with a special weave designed to mold the bunda.

9 Articles in *Plástica & Você* and *Plástica & Beleza* similarly promote the tech-

niques with headlines such as "Buttocks Implants: The Fever of the Millennium" and "Don't Miss Out!!! With Silicone Implants Make Your Bottom the Size You Want."

10 According to Dr. Raul, the surgery leaves an "invisible scar," and the implants carry "almost no risk of rupture or rejection."

11 Such "black styles" are still seen as somewhat exotic, and many women who identified as negra didn't feel that straightening their hair was either a form of lightening, or a sign of internal racism or self-rejection.

12 Biologically speaking, rhinoplasty does not correct a "racial feature," since the nose is not a "mark" of race. Unlike with some species of animals, human populations defined by geographical region have a broad range of phenotypic differences that do not vary "concordantly" with other genetic traits.

13 The census retains the "color" term *preto*, while debate about racial quotas has tended to use the term *negro*, preferred by many in the black movement.

14 For example, Brazilians of Syrian-Lebanese descent were once a marginal minority with a dubious reputation as "cunning" peddlers. But during the neoliberal turn, they have "ethnically projected themselves as export partners, ethical politicians, and diverse connoisseurs," gaining a new visibility in Brazil's consumer culture and globalizing economy (Karam 2007: 2).

15 I had to put the question aside for six years until I returned to do ethnographic research in 2006 on advertising agencies, black actors, grass-roots activists, and others.

16 There is perhaps less sensitivity to racial stereotyping in Brazil, relative to the United States. Caricatures of black features, which vanished years ago from the American mainstream press, are still seen in Brazilian newspapers.

17 See, too, Fry (2002) for an insightful discussion of new representations of black consumers in ads. While Fry focuses on reading ads as texts, I draw on ethnographic fieldwork to analyze production and consumption of media images.

18 Poorer users often lack cash to buy credit, however. Hence, a slang term for a cell phone that only takes incoming calls is a *pai-de-santo*, i.e., a priest in Candomblé who "receives" spirits.

19 She had also starred in two earlier novelas, including the role of Xica da Silva in the TV adaptation.

20 A rival of Ellen's puts a powder in her jacket and says, "I adore seeing her scratch herself like a monkey." After speaking with the director, the line was changed to "I adore seeing her scratch herself like a dog." "That was better," Taís said, "blacks being called monkeys—we've had enough."

21 The fact that opposition to Zezé's character focused on a liaison with a white Brazilian male icon may seem to indicate social attitudes toward interracial romance rather than black protagonists per se. But in Brazil, negative reactions to social mixing, including interracial sex, are often seen as a sign of racism (Goldstein 2003).

22 Even Candomblé—generally considered the most "African" of Brazil's panoply of faiths—has a problematic status as a source of black cultural pride. For example, there has been a recent rejection of syncretism, with some practitioners attempting to "re-Africanize" the religions by incorporating Yoruba in the liturgy (Jensen 1999). This shift suggests that in order to serve as a source of black pride, Afro-Brazilian practices must be purged of non-African elements. Equally, it shows the difficulty of success: the religions are losing converts to Pentecostal churches, which generally have no politics of identity, and despite high numbers of nonwhites, reject Afro-Brazilian practices on a cultural level as primitive and on a theological one as devil worship (Burdick 1998; Lehmann 1996).

23 This interview was conducted by Mirian Goldenberg, who kindly lent me the transcript.

24 The shift in racial policies began in the mid-1990s with President Cardoso's regime (Fry 2005; Htun 2004). For example, the Foreign Service introduced a program to increase the number of black diplomats. The Ministry of Education also introduced curricular changes based on a multicultural vision of the nation. For example, a school text of 1999 still preserved the language of mestiçagem, with its talk of a "cultural broth." The text underwent numerous editions in subsequent years, until finally adopting explicitly multicultural language (Ribeiro 2006).

25 Another line of critique argues that an "aestheticized" black identity weakens the ability of social movements to make political gains (Filho Dias 2000; Segato 1998; Sodré 1999). Muniz Sodré (1999: 254) finds that "the current media discourse about the negro is more aesthetic than political, doctrinaire, or ethical" (see Fry 2002: 17). The emphasis on beauty produces an "other" which is indistinct from the white of the dominant society. The market then acts as a homogenizing force, masked by the promotion of merely superficial differences.

26 Segato also criticizes North American scholar Michael Hanchard (1994) for ethnocentrically dismissing such traditions as "facts of the past" and critiquing the black movement's "culturalist" strategy. Instead, she points out, Afro-Brazilian religions are a "very important niche of culture preservation and creativity" which have "inscribed a monumental African codex containing the accumulated ethnic experience and strategies of African descendents as part of a nation" (1998: 143).

27 On the other hand, the notion of "black spirituality" may still seem exotic to many practitioners. Burdick (1998) points out that the success of Pentecostalism among darker Brazilians is due in part precisely to its lack of interest in racial politics and identities, combined with the real possibilities for them to find respect and power within church organizations.

28 Even within black social movements, there is sometimes an effort to be inclusive in ways that suggest a lingering fluid view of racial boundaries. An activist

who started an NGO called Black Evolution (in English) later decided to change the name to Melanina, since "everyone has *melanina*." Given existing rifts in some favelas between native-born Cariocas—many of them darker—and *nordestino* migrants—who generally don't identify as negro—a "culturalist" rather than "racial" emphasis is perhaps also chosen as a strategy to avoid local conflicts.

## PART THREE. ENGINEERING THE EROTIC

1 This has a less pejorative sound than *nouveau riche* in English, as the term emphasizes escape from the poverty of the masses into the "normality" of middle-class life.
2 One study even tried to specify, appliance by appliance, the ladder of purchases leading up to a middle-class identity (Dressler, Balieiro, and Santos 1998: 430).
3 The interaction between surgeon and patient is also gendered, as senior surgeons are typically male, though more women are now entering plastic surgery residency programs.
4 Dr. Farid Hakme sketched out a "typical timetable":

> Age 15 to 20: Breast reduction
> Age 20 to 25: Liposuction, even before marriage
> Age 25 to 35: Breast-lifting and liposuction, to correct the sags and bulges that can come with child-bearing. . . .
> Age 43 to 50: Facial surgery. (*Los Angeles Times* 1987)

5 The most common procedure for performing a reduction—the inverted "T" technique, so named for the scar it leaves—was invented by Pitanguy in the 1960s.
6 Though *medicina estética* does not refer exclusively to *female* health, I use it to indicate plástica's links to other medical specialties with a concern with aesthetics.
7 Another cultural factor perhaps is greater male anxiety about medical intervention. One man who was considering the operation ultimately decided against it, citing the Brazilian proverb: "It's not good to mess with the team that's winning."
8 A Brazilian law tried to remove the incentive in the 1980s, equalizing reimbursement for Caesarean and vaginal birth but was not completely successful, as C-sections take less time to perform (Carranza 1994).
9 One woman remarked that as a child she had been deeply impressed by a telenovela portrayal of a colonial marriage in which the wife was ordered by her husband never to move during intercourse, since he would be disturbed by any indication that she was experiencing pleasure.
10 During fieldwork patients generally seemed comfortable discussing surgeries,

but I never attempted to broach the topic of *plástica na intimidade*, "intimate plásticas," and here rely on media and marketing materials. See *Plástica & Beleza* (2006a, 2006b); and Clínica Vitalitá website (2006a, 2006b).

11 Another surgeon who operated on her maid, Dr. Berta, did not fit the usual profile of the plastic surgeon: *mulata*, female, and left-wing, formerly married to a communist (now remarried to an ex–air force officer who made his career during the military dictatorship). With kitsch objects in the waiting room, her office in the city center seems a world away from the chic Zona Sul clinics. She tells me she performed "various plásticas" on her maid, Lourdes. "She was once the *babá* of my husband and my son, and will be of my grandson. I proposed to her what I do to all my clients: the satisfaction of feeling pretty." Later, however, Dr. Berta confesses she worries about Lourdes: "She thinks she will be old and without a job. She has no family or children. It was a life of dedication to my own family. When she gets sad, I can't bear it." The charity of the gift of plástica seems to be tinged with concern about Lourdes' status as an empregada, with "no family of her own," suggesting emotional ambivalence underlying the relationship between mistress and maid.

12 Domestic work is more regulated since Congress officially recognized the occupation in 1973. Though servants have the right to some social benefits, many are unwilling or unable to obtain the signed work card, *carteira assinada*.

13 The corset is another historical example from industrializing Europe that suggests that demand for a beauty practice can reflect larger struggles over "female nature." The corset has become a symbol of women's social and physical confinement in Victorian patriarchy. But looking at female demand for this fashionable item tells a more complex story, David Kunzle (1981) argues. A corset was once prohibitively expensive, but mass production reduced costs, making it accessible to working women in nineteenth-century Britain. The "democratization" of the corset occurred during a time when there were new possibilities—and fantasies—of cross-class marriage. Whiles some critics worried about the corset's presumed threat to fertility, many instead were perturbed by the garment's erotic sculpting of the body, as "the most immediate visual effect of waist-compression is to enhance the secondary female characteristics of comparative breadth of bust and hips" (ibid.: 20). The corseted body was viewed as a potential disruption to the social order as "surplus millions of women" employed "extra attractions" in their "husband-hunting," in newspaper phrases of the day. The tight-laced body was also seen to threaten women's roles as mothers. "Tight-lacers" were presumed to use the corset in conjunction with, or even as, birth control and abortion. Alternatively, unmarried, working-class women wore corsets to conceal pregnancy—another threat to the unsuspecting gentleman suitor (ibid: 45). Although the corset reflected patriarchal ideologies, this form of erotic body sculpting—like plástica—also seemed to reflect diverse social aspirations, including distance from a more traditional role of mother.

14  I rely on the detailed analysis by Simpson (1993) of Xuxa's career.

15  See DaMatta (1985) for a now classic analysis of the opposition between *rua*, street, and *casa*, house, in Brazilian social life.

16  One newspaper article portrayed Carla Perez in a bikini and high heels, posing on her hands and knees on a bed. Under the photo, copy asked readers whether they would "spend almost 30,000 reais to carlaperizar," referring to the make-over undergone by the celebrity (*Folha Online* 2000). The point that cash could be exchanged for sex appeal or fame was perhaps made more strongly because the reader would know that Perez comes from a humble background. Rather than wealth or talent (after all, samba dancing skills are not rare) her plástica-sculpted body is the vehicle of a spectacular transformation from one of thousands of ordinary women aspiring to "enter TV" into a national sex symbol.

17  *Mulata* is here not a racial identity, but a job position. The slang expression— *mulata pra exportação*—refers to dancers who earn a living performing overseas.

18  Another surgeon asked rhetorically: "Who says plástica is only indicated for people who are not satisfied with their body?" His ads explicitly suggest he can help the patient achieve the redundant "more than perfect forms" (*Plástica & Beleza* 2002).

19  I borrow the phrase from a Brazilian journalist who used it to refer to the radical body modifications of male *travestis* (Denizart 1998).

20  Change in gender roles is a complex phenomenon difficult to capture in statistics. But, as Manuel Castells (1997) points out, new patterns in household composition and relationships are highly significant because aggregate change happens at a slow pace.

21  Historians have pointed out that a diversity of family structures could be found in colonial and monarchical Brazil. Nevertheless, sexual, economic, and political forms of domination were exercised to a remarkable extent within the clan relationships of the patriarchal family (de Almeida 1982, Kuznesof 1993).

22  As Antônio Cândido (1951: 304) put it: "The history of the Brazilian family during the last 150 years consists essentially of an uninterrupted series of restrictions upon its economic and political functions and the concentration upon . . . procreation and the disciplining of the sex impulse."

23  Reform of alimony laws freed them of notions of female sexual propriety. Before the legalization of divorce, the right to receive child support required that a mother separated from her husband refrain from sexual relationships (Alves and Barsted 1987). As late as 1989, a court ruled in favor of suspending alimony for reasons of "conduct." Four years later, however, the Superior Tribunal de Justiça found that ex-spouses should not be "impeded from forming new relations and to search for new partners, affinities and sentiments" (Guimarães 1997).

24  For example, the husband of a plástica patient felt a duty to economically support his wife. But if she had a namorado (boyfriend), then his response was "*Comeu, pagou*" ([if he] eats her, [then he] pays). That is, if another man had sex

with her, then the financial responsibility for her would be transferred to her lover.

25 See Thales de Azevedo (1986) for further discussion of older "rules of love."

26 It is of course difficult to measure changes in sexual experience. Castells (1997: 238) argues that the growing popularity of some practices, such as oral sex, indicates a rise in a "recreational type" of sexuality, oriented explicitly to female sexual satisfaction and untied from reproduction. In the United States, he points out, the number of women receiving oral sex has sharply risen over the twentieth century, from 40 percent for a 1933–37 cohort to between 75 and 80 percent of those born after 1960.

27 The critique of the "wolf whistle" as emblematic of patriarchal domination (Bartky 1990, Jeffreys 2005: 8), for example, might not resonate well in Brazil. With some exceptions, much organized Brazilian feminism has stressed labor and class issues, legal reform, racism, domestic violence, and health (plástica to date has not been seen as a major health risk), and "bracketed" (Warner 2002) non-nonviolent sexual relationships as a private domain (Goldstein 2003). Important exceptions include critiques of the media's role in sexualizing children at an early age as well as critiques of sexualized representations of the mulata by some activists and scholars in the black movement.

## CONCLUSION

1 Nose jobs that aim to "correct" ethnic traits, however, have a quite different logic that has nothing to do with youth.

2 The rising mainstream acceptance of homosexuality, for example, arguably reflects not just an increase in tolerance toward stigmatized minorities, but an emerging attitude toward sexuality as a form of self-expression, experimentation, or leisure activity untied from reproductive ends (Castells 1997).

3 Travestis also seem to have an ambivalent relationship with pleasure: unlike virtually all prostitutes (according to most studies), they say they enjoy commercial sex, though some become anorgasmic from taking female hormones.

# References

## BOOKS AND ARTICLES

"Abrindo caminhos." 2001. *Sociedade Brasileira de Pesquisa de Mercado* no. 13 (January–March).

ACOG. 2007. "ACOG Advises against Cosmetic Vaginal Procedures due to lack of Safety and Efficacy Data." American College of Obstetricians and Gynecologists. Press release, September 1.

Agamben, Giorgio. 1998. *Homo Sacer: Sovereign Power and Bare Life.* Translated by Daniel Heller-Roazen. Stanford, Calif.: Stanford University Press.

Althusser, Louis, 1971. "Ideology and Ideological State Apparatuses." In *Lenin and Philosophy and Other Essays.* Translated by Ben Brewster. New York: Monthly Review Press.

Alvarez, Sonia. 1990. *Engendering Democracy in Brazil: Women's Movements in Transition Politics.* Princeton: Princeton University Press.

Alves, Branca Moreira, and Leila Linhares Barsted. 1987. "Permanência ou mudança: A legislação sobre família no Brasil." In *Sociedade brasileira contemporânea: Família e valores,* edited by I. Ribeiro. São Paulo: Edições Loyala.

Andrews, G. R. 1991. *Blacks and Whites in São Paulo, Brazil: 1888–1988.* Madison: University of Wisconsin Press.

Angier, Natalie. 2000. *Woman: An Intimate Geography.* New York: Anchor Books.

Appadurai, Arjun. 1988. "Commodities and the Politics of Value." In *The Social Life of Things: Commodities in Cultural Perspective,* edited by A. Appadurai. Cambridge: Cambridge University Press.

Aragão, Luiz Tarlei de. 1983. "Em nome da mãe: posição estrutural e disposições sociais que envolvem a categoria mãe na civilização mediterrânea e na sociedade brasileira." In *Perspectivas Antropológicas da Mulher,* edited by B. Francheto et al. Rio de Janeiro, Zahar.

ASPS 2006. "Statistical Trends." Web pages of American Society of Plastic Surgeons, accessed 14 July 2006, www.plasticsurgery.org.

Babb, Florence. 2001. *After Revolution: Mapping Gender and Cultural Politics in Neo-liberal Nicaragua*. Austin: University of Texas Press.

Badinter, Elisabeth. 1980. *Mother Love: Myth and Reality*. New York: Macmillan.

Bakhtin, Mikhail M. 1994. "'Folk Humor and Carnival Laughter' from *Rabelais and His World*." In *The Bakhtin Reader*, edited by Pam Morris. London: Edward Arnold.

Balsamo, Anne. 1999. *Technologies of the Gendered Body: Reading Cyborg Women*. Durham, N.C.: Duke University Press.

Baran, Michael. 2007. "'Girl, You Are Not Morena. We Are Negras!': Questioning the Concept of 'Race' in Southern Bahia, Brazil." *Ethos* 35, no. 3: 383–409.

Bartky, Sandra. 1990. *Femininity and Domination: Studies in the Phenomenology of Oppression*. New York: Routledge.

Baudelaire, Charles. 1995. *The Painter of Modern Life and Other Essays*. Translated by Jonathan Mayne. London: Phaidon.

Baudrillard, Jean. 1990. *Seduction*. Translated by Brian Singer. Montreal: New World Perspectives.

———. 2005. *The System of Objects*. New York: Verso.

Béhague, D. 2002. "Beyond the Simple Economics of Caesarean Section Birthing: Women's Resistance to Social Inequality." *Culture, Medicine and Psychiatry* 26:473–507.

Béhague, D., C. Victora, and F. Barros. 2002. "Consumer Demand for Caesarean Sections in Brazil: Informed Decision Making, Patient Choice, or Social Inequality?" *BMJ* 324:942.

Benjamin, Walter. 1999. *The Arcades Project*. Translated by Howard Eiland and Kevin McLaughlin. Cambridge: Belknap Press.

Berman, Marshall. 1982. *All That Is Solid Melts in the Air: The Experience of Modernity*. New York: Simon and Schuster.

Besse, Susan. 1996. *Restructuring Patriarchy: The Modernization of Gender Inequality in Brazil, 1914–1940*. Chapel Hill: University of North Carolina Press.

Biehl, João. 1999. "Other Life: AIDS, Biopolitics, and Subjectivity in Brazil's Zones of Social Abandonment." Ph.D. diss., University of California, Berkeley.

———. 2004. "The Activist State: Global Pharmaceuticals, AIDS, and Citizenship in Brazil." *Social Text—80* 22, no. 3 (fall): 105–32.

———. 2005. *Vita: Life in a Zone of Social Abandonment*. Berkeley: University of California Press.

———. 2007. *Will to Live: AIDS Therapies and the Politics of Survival*. Princeton: Princeton University Press.

Biehl, João, with D. Coutinho and A. L. Outeiro. 2001. "Technology and Affect: HIV/AIDS Testing in Brazil." *Culture, Medicine, and Psychiatry* 25, no. 1: 87–129.

Bocayuva, Helena. 2001. *Erotismo à brasileira*. Rio de Janeiro: Garamond.

Bordo, Susan. 1993. *Unbearable Weight: Feminism, Western Culture, and the Body*. Berkeley: University of California Press.

————. 1999. *The Male Body: A New Look at Men in Public and in Private*. New York: Farrar, Straus and Giroux.

Borges, Dain. 1992. *The Family in Bahia, Brazil, 1870–1945*. Stanford, Calif.: Stanford University Press.

Bourdieu, Pierre. 1977. *Toward a Theory of Practice*. Oxford: Oxford University Press.

————. 1984. *Distinction: A Social Critique of the Judgment of Taste*. Cambridge, Mass.: Harvard University Press.

Bourdieu, Pierre, and Loïc Wacquant. 1999. "On the Cunning of Imperial Reason." *Theory, Culture, and Society* 16, no. 1: 41–58.

Buck-Morss, Susan. 1989. *The Dialectics of Seeing: Walter Benjamin and the Arcades Project*. Cambridge, Mass.: MIT Press.

Burdick, John. 1998. *Blessed Anastácia: Women, Race, and Popular Christianity in Brazil*. New York: Routledge.

Caetano, André, and Joseph Potter. 2004. "Politics and Female Sterilization in Northeast Brazil." *Population and Development Review* 30, no. 1: 79–109.

Caldeira, Teresa. 2000. *City of Walls: Crime, Segregation, and Citizenship in São Paulo*. Berkeley: University of California Press.

Caldwell, Kia Lilly. 2007. *Negras in Brazil: Re-envisioning Black Women, Citizenship, and the Politics of Identity*. New Brunswick, N.J.: Rutgers University Press.

Campbell, Colin. 1987. *The Romantic Ethic and the Spirit of Modern Consumerism*. Oxford: Blackwell.

Cândido, Antônio. 1951. "The Brazilian Family." In *Brazil: Portrait of Half a Continent*, edited by L. Smith and A. Marchant. New York: Dryden Press.

Canguilhem, Georges. 1989. *The Normal and the Pathological*. New York: Zone books.

Carranza, Maria. 1994. "Saúde reprodutiva da mulher brasileira." In *Mulher brasileira é assim*, edited by S. Heleieth and M. Muñoz-Vargas. Rio de Janeiro: Rosa dos Tempos.

Castells, Manuel. 1997. *The Information Age: Economy, Society and Culture*. Vol. 2: *The Power of Identity*. Cambridge, Mass.: Blackwell.

Caulfield, Sueann. 1997. "The Birth of Mangue: Race, Nation, and the Politics of Prostitution in Rio de Janeiro, 1850–1942." In *Sex and Sexuality in Latin America*, edited by Daniel Balderston and Donna J. Guy. New York: New York University Press.

————. 2000. *In Defense of Honor: Sexual Morality, Modernity, and Nation in Early Twentieth-Century Brazil*. Durham, N.C.: Duke University Press.

Caulfield, Sueann, and Martha de Abreu Esteves. 1993. "50 Years of Virginity in Rio de Janeiro: Sexual Politics and Gender Roles in Juridical and Popular Discourse, 1890–1940." *Luso-Brazilian Review* 30, no. 1, (summer): 47–74.

Chernin, K. 1981. *The Obsession: Reflections on the Tyranny of Slenderness*. New York: Harper and Row.

Cícero, Antônio. 1995. *O mundo desde o fim*. Rio de Janeiro: Francisco Alves.

Cohen, Colleen, Richard Wilk, and Beverly Stoeltje, eds. 1996. *Beauty Queens on the Global Stage: Gender, Contests, and Power*. New York: Routledge.

Collins, John. 2007. "Recent Approaches in English to Brazilian Racial Ideologies: Ambiguity, Research Methods, and Semiotic Ideologies. A Review Essay." *Comparative Studies in Society and History* 49:997–1009.

Costa, Jurandir Freire. 1979. *Ordem médica e norma familiar*. Rio de Janeiro: Graal.

Cruikshank, Barbara. 1996. "Revolutions from Within: Self-government and Self-esteem." In *Foucault and Political Reason*, edited by Andrew Barry, Thomas Osborne, and Nikolas Rose. London: University College London Press.

DaMatta, Roberto. 1985. *A casa & a rua: Espaço, cidadania, mulher e morte no Brasil*. São Paulo: Brasiliense.

———. 1986. "O corpo brasileiro." In *De corpo e alma*, edited by I. Strozenberg. São Paulo: Espaço e Tempo.

———. 1991. *Carnivals, Rogues, and Heroes: An Interpretation of the Brazilian Dilemma*. Notre Dame, Ind.: University of Notre Dame Press.

Davis, Kathy. 1995. *Reshaping the Female Body: The Dilemma of Cosmetic Surgery*. New York: Routledge.

de Andrade, Oswald. 1967. *Trechos escolhidos*. Rio de Janeiro: AGIR.

de Azevedo, Thales. 1986. *As regras do namoro à antiga*. São Paulo: Editora Ática.

de Certeau, Michel. 2002. *The Practice of Everyday Life*. Berkeley: University of California Press.

Deleuze, Gilles. 1993. *The Deleuze Reader*, edited by C. Boundas. New York: Columbia University Press.

Deleuze, Gilles, and Felix Guattari. 1983. *Anti-Oedipus: Capitalism and Schizophrenia*. Minneapolis: University of Minnesota Press.

Del Priore, Mary. 2000. *Corpo a corpo com a mulher*. São Paulo: Senac.

DeMott, Benjamin. 1990. *The Imperial Middle: Why Americans Can't Think Straight about Class*. New York: Morrow.

Denizart, Hugo. 1998. *Engenharia erótica: Travestis no Rio de Janeiro*. Rio de Janeiro: Jorge Zahar.

Douglas, Mary. 1970. *Natural Symbols: Explorations in Cosmology*. London: Barrie and Rockcliff.

Douglas, Mary, and Baron Isherwood. 1980. *The World of Goods: Toward an Anthropology of Consumption*. Suffolk: Penguin Books.

Downie, Andrew. 2000. "Brazil Reexamines Birth Options." *Christian Science Monitor*, November 7.

Dressler, William, Mauro Campos Balieiro, and José Ernesto dos Santos. 1998. "Culture, Socioeconomic Status, and Physical and Mental Health in Brazil." *Medical Anthropology Quarterly* 12, no. 4: 424–46.

Duarte, Luiz Fernando. 1986. *Da vida nervosa (nas classes trabalhadoras urbanas)*. Rio de Janeiro: Jorge Zahar Editor.

Dunn, Christopher. 2001. *Brutality Garden: Tropicália and the Emergence of a Brazilian Counterculture*. Chapel Hill: University of North Carolina Press.

Dweck, Ruth. 1999. "A beleza como variável económica: Reflexo nos mercados de trabalho e de bens e serviços." Texto para Discussão No. 618. Rio de Janeiro: IPEA.

Eriksen, Thomas Hylland. 2006. *Engaging Anthropology: The Case for a Public Presence*. Oxford: Berg.

Etcoff, Nancy. 2000. *Survival of the Prettiest: The Science of Beauty*. New York: Anchor Books.

Etcoff, Nancy, S. Orbach, J. Scott, and H. D'Agostino. 2004. *The Real Truth about Beauty: A Global Report*. Web pages of Campaign for Real Beauty, accessed September 2009, www.campaignforrealbeauty.com.

Faludi, Susan. 1992. *Backlash: The Undeclared War against American Women*. Garden City, N.Y.: Anchor Books.

Farias, Patrícia. 2002. "Corpo e classificação de cor numa praia carioca." In *Nu & vestido: Dez antropólogos revelam a cultura do corpo carioca*, edited by Mirian Goldenberg. Rio de Janeiro: Editora Record.

Farrer, James. 2002. *Opening Up: Youth Sex Culture and Market Reform in Shanghai*. Chicago: University of Chicago Press.

Faveret, F., and P. J. Oliveira. 1990. "A universalização excludente: Reflexões sobre as tendências do sistema de saúde." *Dados* 33, no. 2: 257–83.

Felski, Rita. 1995. *The Gender of Modernity*. Cambridge, Mass.: Harvard University Press.

Figueira, S. 1996. "O 'moderno' e o 'arcaico' na nova família brasileira: Notas sobre a dimensão invisível da mudança social." In *Uma nova família?*, edited by S. Figueira. Rio de Janeiro: Jorge Zahar.

Filet-Abreu de Souza, Julia. 1980. "Paid Domestic Service in Brazil." *Latin American Perspectives* 7, no. 1 (winter): 35–63.

Filho Dias, Antônio Jonas. 2000. "Ebonização estética e cosmética. Auto-estima, mídia, mercado consumidor e a opção fashion do resgate da cidadania em magazines para afro-brasileiros (1990–1999)," accessed April 21, 2010, www.desafio.ufba.br.

Fishlow, Albert. 2000. "Brazil and Economic Realities," *Daedalus*, Spring, 339–56.

Flores, William V., and Rina Benmayor, eds. 1997. *Latino Cultural Citizenship: Claiming Identity, Space, and Rights*. Boston: Beacon Press.

Foster Wallace, David. 2005. "Big Red Son." In *Consider the Lobster*. New York: Little Brown.

Foucault, Michel. 1973. *The Birth of the Clinic: An Archaeology of Medical Perception*. New York: Pantheon Books.

———. 1978. *The History of Sexuality*. Vol. 1. New York: Pantheon.

———. 1980. *Power/Knowledge: Selected Interviews and Other Writings, 1972–1977*. New York: Pantheon.

————. 1986. *The Care of the Self*. New York: Pantheon.

Freud, Sigmund. 1953 [1905]. *Three Essays on the Theory of Sexuality*. Vol. 7. Standard ed. London: Hogarth Press and the Institute of Psycho-Analysis.

————. 1957. "On Narcissism: An Introduction." In *General Selections from the Works of Sigmund Feud*. New York: Doubleday.

————. 1961. *Civilization and Its Discontents*. New York: W. W. Norton.

Freyre, Gilberto. 1933. *Casa-grande e senzala*. Rio de Janeiro: Maia & Schmidt.

————. 1956. *The Masters and the Slaves: A Study in the Development of Brazilian Civilization*. New York: Knopf.

————. 1984. "Uma paixão nacional." *Playboy*, no. 113 (December). Text available at www.releituras.com.

————. 1986. *Modos de homen & modas de mulher*. Rio de Janeiro: Record.

Fritsch, Peter. 1999. "Generics Break Brand Names' Hold on Brazil." *Wall Street Journal*, November 8, A33.

Fry, Peter. 1982. *Para inglês ver: Identidade e politica na cultura brasileira*. Rio de Janeiro: Zahar.

————. 2000. "Politics, Nationality, and the Meanings of 'Race' in Brazil." *Daedalus* 129 (spring): 83–118.

————. 2002. "Estética e política: Relações entre 'raça,' publicidade e produção da beleza no Brasil." In *Nu & vestido: Dez antropólogos revelam a cultura do corpo carioca*, edited by Mirian Goldenberg. Rio de Janeiro: Editora Record.

————. 2005. *A persistência da raça: Ensaios antropológicos sobre o Brasil e a África Austral*. Rio de Janeiro: Civilização Brasileira.

Fukuyama, Francis. 2004. "Transhumanism." *Foreign Policy*, Sept./Oct. 2004, Issue 144, 42–43.

Gacitúa-Marió, Estanislao, and Michael Woolock. 2008. "Overview: Assessing Social Exclusion and Mobility." In *Social Exclusion and Mobility in Brazil*, edited by E. Gacitúa-Marió and M. Woolock. Washington, D.C.: World Bank.

García Canclini, Néstor. 2001. *Consumers and Citizens: Globalization and Multicultural Conflicts*. Minneapolis: University of Minnesota Press.

Gask, Linda. 2004. *A Short Introduction to Psychiatry*. London: Sage.

Geertz, Clifford. 1973. *The Interpretation of Culture*. New York: Basic Books.

Georges, Isabel. 2003. "Gender, Class, and the Social Sense of Work." Paper presented at the Third Critical Management Studies Conference, (Re)Investigating Class in Service and Consumer Society (Farewell to the Working Class?). Lancaster, July 7.

Giddens, Anthony. 1993. *The Transformation of Intimacy: Sexuality, Love, and Eroticism in Modern Societies*. Stanford, Calif.: Stanford University Press.

Gilman, Sander. 1998. *Creating Beauty to Cure the Soul: Race and Psychology in the Shaping of Aesthetic Surgery*. Durham, N.C.: Duke University Press.

————. 1999. *Making the Body Beautiful: A Cultural History of Aesthetic Surgery*. Princeton: Princeton University Press.

Girard, Rene. 1966. *Deceit, Desire and the Novel: Self and Other in Literary Structure.* Baltimore: Johns Hopkins University Press.

Goldenberg, Mirian. n.d. "Laços da família." Unpublished manuscript.

———. 2000. "De amelias a operarias: Um ensaio sobre os conflitos femininos no mercado de trabalho e nas relações conjugais." In *Os novos desejos*, edited by M. Goldenberg: Rio de Janeiro: Record.

Goldstein, Donna. 2003. *Laughter out of Place: Race, Class, Violence, and Sexuality in a Rio Shantytown.* Berkeley: University of California Press.

Gonçalves, Isabela Lopes. 2001. "Cortes e costuras: Um estudo antropólogico da cirurgia plástica no Rio de Janeiro." M.A. thesis, Department of Cultural Anthropology, Museu Nacional, Rio de Janeiro.

Goodman, Joshua 2006. "Breast Obsessed TV Show a Colombian Hit." Associated Press, September 19, 2006.

Gould, Steven Jay. 1981. *The Mismeasure of Man.* New York: Norton.

Green, James. 1999. *Beyond Carnival: Male Homosexuality in Twentieth-Century Brazil.* Chicago: University of Chicago Press.

———. 2000: "Introduction." *Latin American Perspectives* 27:5.

Gregg, Jessica. 2003. *Virtually Virgins: Sexual Strategies and Cervical Cancer in Recife, Brazil.* Palo Alto, Calif.: Stanford University Press.

Guillermoprieto, Alma. 1990. *Samba.* New York: Knopf.

Guimarães, Marilene Silveira. 1997. "A igualdade jurídica da mulher." In *Mulher: Estudos de género*, edited by Marlene Neves Strey. São Leopoldo: Editora Unisinos.

Haberly, David T. 1983. *Three Sad Races: Racial Identity and National Consciousness in Brazilian Literature.* Cambridge: Cambridge University Press.

Hacking, Ian. 1995. *Rewriting the Soul: Multiple Personality and the Sciences of Memory.* Princeton: Princeton University Press.

———. 2006. "Making People Up." *London Review of Books*, August 17.

Haiken, Elizabeth. 1997. *Venus Envy: A History of Cosmetic Surgery.* Baltimore: Johns Hopkins University Press.

Hamburger, Esther. 1998. "Diluindo fronteiras: A televisão e as novelas no cotidiano." In *História da vida privada no Brasil.* Vol. 4, edited by L. Schwarcz. São Paulo: Companhia das Letras.

Hamermesh, D., and J. Biddle. 1994. "Beauty and the Labor Market." *American Economic Review* 84, no. 5: 1174–94.

Hanchard, Michael G. 1994. *Orpheus and Power: The "Movimento Negro" of Rio de Janeiro and São Paulo, Brazil, 1945–1988.* Princeton: Princeton University Press.

———. 1999, "Black Cinderella? Race and the Public Sphere in Brazil." In *Racial Politics in Contemporary Brazil*, edited by M. Hanchard. Durham, N.C.: Duke University Press.

Hasenbalg, C., and N. V. Silva. 1999. "Notes on Racial and Political Inequality in Brazil." In *Racial Politics in Contemporary Brazil*, edited by M. Hanchard. Durham, N.C.: Duke University Press.

Hau, Michael. 2003. *The Cult of Health and Beauty in Germany: A Social History, 1890–1930*. Chicago: University of Chicago Press.

Hegel, Georg Wilhelm Friedrich. 1920 [1835]. *The Philosophy of Fine Art*. Translated by Francis Plumptre Beresford Osmaston. London: G. Bell and Sons.

Hesse, David. 1994. *Samba in the Night: Spiritism in Brazil*. New York: Columbia University Press.

Hollander, Anne. 1993. *Seeing through Clothes*. Berkeley: University of California Press.

Holston, James. 1989. *The Modernist City: An Anthropological Critique of Brasília*. Chicago: University of Chicago Press.

———. 2008. *Insurgent Citizenship: Disjunctions of Democracy and Modernity in Brazil*. Princeton: Princeton University Press.

Hopkins, K. 2000. "Are Brazilian Women Really Choosing to Deliver by Cesarean?" *Social Science and Medicine* 51:725–40.

Htun, Mala. 2004. "From 'Racial Democracy' to Affirmative Action: Changing State Policy on Race in Brazil." *Latin American Research Review* 39, no.1 (2004): 60–89.

Ivy, Marilyn. 1995. *Discourses of the Vanishing: Modernity, Phantasm, Japan*. Chicago: University of Chicago Press.

Jeffreys, Sheila. 2005. *Beauty and Misogyny: Harmful Cultural Practices in the West*. London: Brunner.

Jensen, Tina Gudrun. 1999. "Discourses on Afro-Brazilian Religion: From De-Africanization to Re-Africanization." In *Latin American Religion in Motion*, edited by Christian Smith and Joshua Prokopy. New York: Routledge.

Karam, John Tofik. 2007. *Another Arabesque: Syrian-Lebanese Ethnicity in Neoliberal Brazil*. Philadelphia: Temple University Press.

Kaw, Eugenia. 1993. "Medicalization of Racial Features: Asian American Women and Cosmetic Surgery." *Medical Anthropology Quarterly* 7, no. 1: 74–89.

Kleinman, A., and A. Becker. 1998. "Sociosomatics: The Contributions of Anthropology to Psychosomatic Medicine." *Psychosomatic Medicine* 60, no. 4: 389–93.

Knauft, Bruce. 1989. "Bodily Images in Melanesia: Cultural Substances and Natural Metaphors." In *Fragments for a History of the Human Body*. Pt. 3, edited by M. Feher. New York: Zone Books.

Kottak, Conrad. 1990. *Prime Time Society: An Anthropological Analysis of Television and Culture*. Belmont, Calif.: Wadsworth.

Kramer, Peter. 1994. *Listening to Prozac*. London: Fourth Estate.

Kuczynski, Alex. 2006. *Beauty Junkies: Inside Our $15 Billion Obsession with Cosmetic Surgery*. New York: Doubleday.

Kulick, Don. 1998. *Travesti: Sex, Gender and Culture among Brazilian Transgendered Prostitutes*. Chicago: University of Chicago Press.

Kunzle, David. 1981. *Fashion and Fetishism: A Social History of the Corset, Tight-Lacing, and Other Forms of Body-Sculpture in the West*. London: Rowan and Littlefield.

Kuznesof, Elizabeth Anne. 1993. "Sexuality, Gender and the Family in Colonial Brazil." *Luso-Brazilian Review* 30, no. 1: 119–32.

———. 2003. "Sexual Politics, Race and Bastard-Bearing in Nineteenth-Century Brazil: A Question of Culture or Power?" *Journal of Family History* 16, no. 3: 241–60.

Lakoff, Andrew. 2005. *Pharmaceutical Reason: Knowledge and Value in Global Psychiatry*. Cambridge: Cambridge University Press.

Lancaster, Roger. 2003. *The Trouble with Nature: Sex in Science and Popular Culture*. Berkeley: University of California Press.

Larkin, Brian. 2002. "Indian Films and Nigerian Lovers: Media and the Creation of Parallel Modernities." In *The Anthropology of Globalization: A Reader*, edited by J. X. Inda and R. Rosaldo. Oxford: Blackwell Books.

Lasch, Christopher. 1979. *The Culture of Narcissism*. New York: W. W. Norton.

Larvie, Sean Patrick. 1997. "Personal Improvement, National Development: Theories of AIDS Prevention in Rio de Janeiro, Brazil." In *The Medical Anthropologies in Brazil*, edited by Annette Leibing. Berlin: Verlag für Wissenshcaft Und Bildung.

Lauerhass, Ludwig, Jr. 2006. "Introduction." In *Brazil in the Making: Facets of National Identity*, edited by C. Nava and L. Lauerhass Jr. Lanham, Md.: Rowman and Littlefield.

Lehmann, David. 1996. *Struggle for the Spirit: Religious Transformation and Popular Culture in Brazil and Latin America*. Cambridge: Polity Press.

Leibing, Annette. 2005. "The Old Lady from Ipanema: Changing Notions of Old Age in Brazil. *Journal of Aging Studies* 19:15–31.

Levine, Robert. 1997. *Brazilian Legacies*. Armonk, N.Y.: M. E. Sharpe.

Levine, Robert, and John Crocitti, eds. 1999. *The Brazil Reader*. Durham, N.C.: Duke University Press.

Lévi-Strauss, Claude. 1973. *Tristes Tropiques*. Translated by John and Doreen Weightman. New York: Penguin.

———. 1983. *The Raw and the Cooked: Mythologiques (Volume One)*. Translated by John and Doreen Weightman. Chicago: University of Chicago Press.

Lichtenstein, Jacqueline. 1987. "Making up Representation: The Risks of Femininity." *Representations* 20:77–86.

Lipovetsky, Gilles. 1994. *The Empire of Fashion: Dressing Modern Democracy*. Princeton: Princeton University Press.

Lloyd, Sheldon Mark. 2005. "An Elective with a Top Plastic Surgeon in Brazil." *BMJ Careers*, May 5; doi:10.1136/bmj.330.7499.s190.

Lock, Margaret. 1993. *Encounters with Aging: Mythologies of Menopause in Japan and North America*. Berkeley: University of California Press.

Lovell, Peggy. 1999. "Women and Racial Inequality at Work in Brazil." In *Racial Politics in Contemporary Brazil*, edited by M. Hanchard. Durham, N.C.: Duke University Press.

Lyotard, Jean-François. 1993. *Libidinal Economy.* Translated by Iain Hamilton Grant. Bloomington: Indiana University Press.

Maggie, Yvonne. 1992. *Medo do feitiço: Relações entre magia e poder no Brasil.* Rio de Janeiro: Arquivo Nacional, Ministério da Justiça.

Mariani, Maria Clara, and Ilana Strozenberg. 1976. *O sentido da ilusão: Um estudo sobre famílias e empregadas domésticas.* Rio de Janeiro: Museu Nacional.

Martin, Emily. 1987. *The Woman in the Body.* Boston: Beacon University Press.

Martín-Barbero, Jesus. 1993. *Communication, Culture and Hegemony: From the Media to Mediations.* London: Sage.

Martine, George. 1996. "Brazil's Fertility Decline, 1965–1995." *Population and Development Review* 22, no. 1: 47–75.

Marwick, Arthur. 1988. *Beauty in History: Society, Politics and Personal Appearance c. 1500 to the Present.* London: Thames and Hudson.

Mauss, Marcel. 1990. *The Gift: Forms and Functions of Exchange in Archaic Societies.* London: Routledge.

McCallum, Cecilia, and Ana Paula dos Reis. 2005. "Childbirth as Ritual in Brazil: Young Mothers' Experiences." *Ethnos,* 70, no. 3: 335–60.

Meade, T. 1996. *"Civilizing" Rio: Reform and Resistance in a Brazilian City, 1889–1930.* University Park: Penn State Press.

Mello, J. M. C., and F. Novais. 1998. "Capitalismo tardio e sociabilidade moderna." In *História da Vida Privada no Brasil.* Vol. 4, edited by L. Schwarcz. São Paulo: Companhia das Letras.

Meneguello, Cristina. 1996. *"Poeira de estrelas": O cinema hollywoodiano na mídia brasileira das décadas de 40 e 50.* Campinas, Brazil: Editora da Unicamp.

Midgley, Mary. 1988. "Beasts, Brutes, and Monsters." In *What is an Animal?,* edited by Tim Ingold. London: Routledge.

Miller, Daniel. 1995. "Consumption as the Vanguard of History." In *Acknowledging Consumption: A Review of New Studies,* edited by D. Miller. New York: Routledge.

Miller, Geoffrey. 2000. *The Mating Mind: How Sexual Choice Shaped the Evolution of Human Nature.* New York: Anchor Books.

Miller, Laura. 2006. *Beauty Up: Exploring Contemporary Japanese Body Aesthetics.* Berkeley: University of California Press.

Moors, Annelies, and Emma Tarlo. 2007. "Introduction" *Fashion Theory* 11, no. 2/3: 133–43.

Morgan, Kathryn Pauly. 1991. "Women and the Knife: Cosmetic Surgery and the Colonization of Women's Bodies." *Hypatia* 6:25–53.

Needell, Jeffrey. 1987. *A Tropical Belle Epoque: Elite Culture and Society in Turn-of-the-Century Rio de Janeiro.* Cambridge: Cambridge University Press.

Netto, Gisele. 2003. "Lente no futuro." Web document, accessed April 22, 2010, www.belezapura.org.br.

Novaes, Joana de Vilhena. 2004. "Sobre o intolerável peso da feiúra: Corpo, sociabilidade e regulação social." Ph.D. diss., clinical psychology, PUC, Rio de Janeiro.

Novelli J. M. N., and A. Galvão. 2004. "The Political Economy of Neoliberalism in Brazil in the 1990s," *International Journal of Political Economy*, 31, no. 4: 3–52.

O'Dougherty, Maureen. 2002. *Consumption Intensified: The Politics of Middle-Class Daily Life in Brazil*. Durham, N.C.: Duke University Press.

Oliven, George Ruben. 2000. "Brazil: The Modern in the Topics." In *Through the Kaleidoscope: The Experience of Modernity in Latin America*, edited by Vivian Schelling. London: Verso.

Ortiz, Renato. 2000. "Popular Culture, Modernity and Nation." In *Through the Kaleidoscope: The Experience of Modernity in Latin America*, edited by Vivian Schelling. London: Verso.

Ortner, Sherry. 1974. "Is Female to Male as Nature is to Culture?" In *Woman, Culture, and Society*, edited by M. Z. Rosaldo and L. Lamphere. Stanford, Calif.: Stanford University Press.

Ossman, Susan. 2002. *Three Faces of Beauty: Casablanca, Paris, Cairo*. Durham, N.C.: Duke University Press.

Owensby, Brian. 1999. *Intimate Ironies: Modernity and the Making of Middle-Class Lives in Brazil*. Stanford, Calif.: Stanford University Press.

Parker, Richard. 1991. *Bodies, Pleasures, and Passions: Sexual Culture in Contemporary Brazil*. Boston: Beacon Press.

———. 1999. *Beneath the Equator: Cultures of Desire, Male Homosexuality, and Emerging Gay Communities in Brazil*. New York: Routledge.

Peard, Julyan. 1999. *Race, Place, and Medicine: The Idea of the Tropics in Nineteenth-Century Brazilian Medicine*. Durham, N.C.: Duke University Press.

Peiss, Kathy. 1998. *Hope in a Jar: The Making of America's Beauty Culture*. New York: Metropolitan Books.

Pereira, Cláudia da Silva. 2008. "Gisele da favela": uma análise antropológica sobre a carreira de modelo" Ph.D. diss., anthropology, UFRJ/IFCS, Rio de Janeiro.

Pfeffer, Naomi. 1993. *The Stork and the Syringe: A Political History of Reproductive Medicine*. Cambridge: Polity Press.

Ping, Wang. 2000. *Aching for Beauty: Footbinding in China*. Minneapolis: University of Minnesota Press.

Pitanguy, Ivo. 1976. "Aspectos filosóficos e psicológicos em cirurgia plástica." *Boletim de Cirurgia Plástica* 66, no. 3/4 (March–April): 115–25.

———. 1983. "Aspectos filosóficos e psicológicos da cirurgia do contorno facial." *Sociedade Brasileira de Cirurgia Plástica Regional São Paulo*, September 24 and 25.

———. 1992. "Aspectos filosóficos e psicosociais da cirurgia plástica." In *Psicosomatica hoje*, edited by Julio de Mello Filho. Pôrto Alegre: Editora Artes Médicas.

———. 1993. "Philosophy and Contributions in Body Contouring Surgery." Naples: IX Congresso Mondiale, Società Italiana di DermoEstetica e Chirurgia Estetica.

———. 1997. *Perspectivas filosóficas e psicosociais da harmonia facial*. In *Ortodontia Clínica I*, edited by C. Cabrera. Curitiba: Ed. Produções.

———. 2008. Clinic website, accessed April 23, 2008, www.ivopitanguy.com.

Pitanguy, Jacqueline. 2002. "Bridging the Local and the Global: Feminism and the Human Rights Struggle in Brazil." *Social Research* 69, no. 3 (Fall): 805–20.

Popenoe, Rebecca. 2004. *Feeding Desire: Fatness, Beauty, and Sexuality among a Saharan People*. London: Routledge.

Potter, Joseph. 1999. "The Persistence of Outmoded Contraceptive Regimes: The Cases of Mexico and Brazil." *Population and Development Review* 25, no. 4 (December): 703–39.

Prado, Paulo. 1944. *Retrato do Brasil: Ensaio sobre a tristeza brasileira*. São Paulo: Editora Brasiliense Limitada.

Queiroz, Renato da Silva, and Emma Otta. 2000. "A beleza em foco: Condicionantes culturais e psicobiológicos na definição da estética corporal." In *Corpo do Brasileiro: Estudos de estética e beleza*, edited by R. Queiroz. São Paulo: Senac.

Rabinow, Paul, and Nikolas Rose. 2006. "Biopower Today." *Biosocieties* 1:195–217.

Rankin, C. 2005. "Prescribing Beauty: Women and Cosmetic Surgery in Postmodern Culture." Paper presented at "Body Modification: Mark II Conference," April 21–23, Macquarie University, Sydney, Australia.

Rebhun, L. A. 1999. *The Heart Is Unknown Country: Love in the Changing Economy of Northeast Brazil*. Stanford, Calif.: Stanford University Press.

Reis, Elisa 2000. "Modernization, Citizenship, and Stratification: Historical Processes and Recent Changes in Brazil." *Daedalus* 129 (Spring).

Ribeiro, C. A. C., and M. C. Scalon. 2001. "Class Mobility in Brazil from a Comparative Perspective." *Dados— Revista de Ciências Sociais* 44, no. 1: 53–96.

Ribeiro, C. A. C., and J. H. Aboudib. 1997. *Você e a cirurgia plástica: Tudo o que você precisa saber sobre cirurgia plástica*. Rio de Janeiro: Record.

Ribeiro, Yvonne Maggie de Leers Costa. 2006. "Uma nova pedagogia racial?" *Revista USP, São Paulo* 68, no. 22: 112–29.

Ricoeur, P. 1970. *Freud and Philosophy: An Essay on Interpretation*. Translated by D. Savage. New Haven, Conn.: Yale University Press.

Rieff, Philip. 1966. *The Triumph of the Therapeutic: Uses of Faith after Freud*. New York: Harper and Row.

Rojek, Chris. 2001. *Celebrity*. London: Reaktion Books.

Rowe, William, and Vivian Schelling. 1991. *Memory and Modernity: Popular Culture in Latin America*. London: Verso.

Russell-Wood, A. J. R. 1982. *The Black Man in Slavery and Freedom in Colonial Brazil*. New York: St. Martin's Press.

Russo, Jane. 2000. "A psicanálise enquanto processo civilizador: Um projeto para a nação brasileira." In *Cadernos IPUB* 6, no.18: 10–20.

Sabino, César. 2000. "Musculação: Expansão e manutenção," In *Os Novos Desejos*, edited by Mirian Goldenberg. Rio de Janeiro: Editora Record.

———. 2002. "Anabolizantes: Drogas de apolo." *Nu & vestido: Dez antropólogos revelam a cultura do corpo carioca*, edited by Mirian Goldenberg. Rio de Janeiro: Editora Record.

Sansone, Lívio. 2003. *Blackness without Ethnicity: Constructing Race in Brazil*. New York: Palgrave MacMillan.

Sant'Anna, Denise Bernuzzi. 1995. "Cuidados de si e embelezamento feminino: Fragmentos para uma historia do corpo no Brasil." In *Politicas do corpo: Elementos para uma história das práticas corporais*, edited by D. Sant'Anna. São Paulo: Estação Liberdade.

Santos, Cecília MacDowell. 2005. *Women's Police Stations: Gender, Violence and Justice in São Paulo, Brazil*. New York: Palgrave Macmillan.

SBCP (Sociedade Brasileira de Cirurgia Plástica). 2005. Brazilian Society of Plastic Surgery, press release obtained by personal communication.

Scarry, Elaine. 2001. *On Beauty and Being Just*. Princeton: Princeton University Press.

Scheper-Hughes, Nancy. 1992. *Death without Weeping: The Violence of Everyday Life in Brazil*. Berkeley: University of California Press.

Schneirov, Mathew, and Jonathan Geczik. 1998. "Technologies of the Self and the Aesthetic Project of Alternative Health." *Sociological Quarterly* 9, no. 3: 435–51.

Schwarcz, Lilia Moritz. 1998. "Nem preto nem branco, muito pelo contrário: Cor e raça no intimidade." In *História da vida privada no Brasil*. Vol. 4, edited by L. Schwarcz. São Paulo: Companhia das Letras.

———. 1999. *The Spectacle of the Races: Scientists, Institutions, and the Race Question in Brazil, 1870–1930*. New York: Hill and Wang.

Schwarz, Roberto. 1992. *Misplaced Ideas: Essays on Brazilian Culture*. London: Verso.

SGPR. 2006. Secretaria-Geral da Presidência da República. Personal communication via e-mail with the Subsecretaria de Comunicação Institucional. May.

Sedgwick, Eve Kosofsky, and Adam Frank. 1995. "Shame in the Cybernetic Fold: Reading Silvan Tompkins." In *Shame and Its Sisters: A Silvan Tompkins Reader*, edited by E. K. Sedgwick and A. Frank. Durham, N.C.: Duke University Press.

Segato, Rita L. 1998. "The Color-Blind Subject of Myth; Or, Where to Find Africa in the Nation." *Annual Review of Anthropology* 27:129–51.

Sevcenko, Nicolau. 2000. "Peregrinations, Visions and the City: From Canudos to Brasília. The Backlands Become the City, and the City Becomes the Backlands." In *Through the Kaleidoscope: The Experience of Modernity in Latin America*, edited by Vivian Schelling. London: Verso.

Severiano, Jairo, and Zuza Homem de Mello. 1997. *A canção no tempo: 85 anos de músicas brasileiras*. São Paulo: Editora 34.

Sharp, Lesley. 2000. "The Commodification of the Body and Its Parts." *Annual Review of Anthropology* 29:287–328.

Simmel, G. 1990 [1902]. *The Philosophy of Money*. London: Routledge.

Simpson, Amelia. 1993. *Xuxa: The Mega-Marketing of Gender, Race, and Modernity*. Philadelphia: Temple University Press.

Skidmore, Thomas. 1974. *Black into White: Race and Nationality in Brazilian Thought*. New York: Oxford University Press.

———. 1988. *The Politics of Military Rule in Brazil, 1964–1985*. New York: Oxford University Press.

Sodré, Muniz. 1999. *Claros e escuros: Identidade, povo e mídia no Brasil*. Petrópolis, Brazil: Editora Vozes.

Steele, Valerie. 1996. *Fetish: Fashion, Sex, and Power*. New York: Oxford University Press.

Stepan, Nancy Leys. 1991. *"The Hour of Eugenics": Race, Gender, and Nation in Latin America*. Ithaca, N.Y.: Cornell University Press.

Stoller, Ann Laura. 1995. *Race and the Education of Desire: Foucault's* History of Sexuality *and the Colonial Order of Things*. Durham, N.C.: Duke University Press.

Strong, Thomas. 2008. "Infection as a Social Relation: Serosorting in San Francisco." Paper presented at the American Anthropological Association annual conference, San Francisco, November 19–23.

Taylor, Charles. 1989. *Sources of the Self: The Making of the Modern Identity*. Cambridge, Mass.: Harvard University Press.

Telles, Edward. 2004. *Race in Another America: The Significance of Skin Color in Brazil*. Princeton: Princeton University Press.

Turner, Terence. 1980. "The Social Skin." In *Not Work Alone: A Cross-Cultural View of Activities Superfluous to Survival*, edited by J. Cherfas and R. Lewin. London: Temple Smith.

Twine, France Winddance. 1998. *Racism in a Racial Democracy: The Maintenance of White Supremacy in Brazil*. New Brunswick, N.J.: Rutgers University Press.

Vainfas, Ronaldo. 1989. *Trópico dos pecados: Moral, sexualidade e inquisição no Brasil*. Rio de Janeiro: Editora Campus.

Velho, Gilberto. 1998. *Nobres & anjos: um estudo de tóxicos e hierarquia*. Fonte: Rio de Janeiro.

Vianna, Hermano. 1988. *O mundo funk carioca*. Rio de Janeiro: Jorge Zahar.

———. 1999. *The Mystery of Samba: Popular Music and National Identity in Brazil*. Chapel Hill: University of North Carolina Press.

Villaça, Nizia. 2005. "As She Walks to the Sea: A Semiology of Rio de Janeiro." In *The Latin American Fashion Reader*, edited by Regina Root. Oxford: Berg.

Viveiros de Castro, Eduardo. 1998. "Cosmological Deixis and Amerindian Perspectivism." *Journal of the Royal Anthropological Institute* 4:469–88.

———. 2004. "Exchanging Perspectives: The Transformation of Objects into Subjects in Amerindian Ontologies." *Common Knowledge* 10, no. 3: 463–84.

Ward, Steven. 1996. "Filling the World with Self-Esteem: A Social History of Truth-Making." *Canadian Journal of Sociology* 21, no. 1: 1–23.

Warner, Michael. 2002. *Publics and Counterpublics*. New York: Zone Books.

Wolf, Naomi. 1991. *The Beauty Myth: How Images of Beauty Are Used against Women*. New York: William Morrow and Company.

Yalom, Marilyn. 1997. *A History of the Breast*. New York: Ballantine Books.

Young, Iris Marion. 1990. *Throwing like a Girl and Other Essays in Feminist Philosophy and Social Theory*. Bloomington: Indiana University Press.


## POPULAR MEDIA

*Brazzil Mag* (Brazzil Magazine).
2008. "Brazil Cosmetic Industry Hoping to Rake in us$12 Billion This Year." Geovana Pagel. Friday, September 26. Web pages, accessed September 15, 2009, www.brazzilmag.com.

Clínica Vitalitá website
2006a. "Cirurgia íntima feminina." Web pages, accessed January 20, 2006, www.vitalita.med.br.
2006b. "Cirurgia plástica estética e andrologia." Web pages, accessed January 20, 2006, www.sortimentos.com.

*Corpo à Corpo*
2001. "Dê um Up em seu Bumbum." December 30.

*Época*
1999a. "Sem medo dos 40." September 27.
1999b. "A serviço da beleza." November 29.
2000. "Reino das formas perfeitas." June 19.

*Folha Online*
2000. "Brasil fecha ano 2000 com 390 mil cirurgias plásticas." December 15.
2001. "Cirurgia plástica lidera ranking de queixas médicas." October 17.

*Folha de São Paulo*
1995. "Brasil quer ser chamado moreno." June 25.

*Globo Repórter*
1999. Indústria do rejuvenescimento. Television program aired April 16.

Gonzalez, Raul
2007. "Bumbums brasileiras." Web page of plastic surgeon Raul Gonzalez, www.raulgonzalez.com.br, accessed September 2009.

*Guardian, The*
2002. "Miss World's Nigerian Odyssey Abandoned after Three Days of Rioting Leave 100 Dead." James Astill, Saturday, November 23.

*Istoé*
1999. "Seios em alta." March 31.

*Istoé Gente*

1999. "Estrelas reformadas." December 13.

2001a. "A escultora de corpos famosos." April 9.

2001b. "Silicone no bumbum só existe no Brasil." February 9.

*Istoé Online*

2000. "Comissão de frente." March 8.

*Jornal do Brasil*

1986. "Cirurgia entorta busto e separa casal." November 14.

2001. "Miss Silicone." March 26.

*Los Angeles Times*

1987. "War on Fat: Rio Cultists: Good Looks at the Beach." August 15.

*O Dia*

1999. "Brasileiras queriam esculpir bumbum." Sunday, May 2.

2004. "Cirurgia plástica no sus: Portadores de hiv que sofrem de lipodistrofia vão poder passar por procedimento estético." December 4.

*O Estado de São Paulo*

1997. "Setor de beleza factura us$4 bilhões: Segmento triplicou nos últimos cinco anos e atrai pequenos investidores." June 24.

*O Globo*

2001. "Clínicas de cirurgia plástica não tem uti." *O Globo, Caderno Rio*, August 26.

2002. "O teste da plástica." March 24.

*Plástica & Beleza*

2000. "Ocidentalização: A plástica dos olhos puxados." Ano II, No. 20.

2001a. Plastic surgery clinic advertisement. Ano III, No. 24.

2001b. Plastic surgery clinic advertisement. Ano III, No. 25.

2002a. "Xuxa, rainha de todos os tempos." Ano IV, No. 35.

2002b. "Formas mais que perfeitas." Web pages, accessed January 20, 2006, plásticaebeleza.terra.com.

2006a. "Cirurgia plástica íntima: Cai o último preconceito." Web pages, accessed January 20, 2006, plásticaebeleza.terra.com.

2006b. "Plástica da intimidade: Acabou o tabu." Web pages, accessed January 20, plásticaebeleza.terra.com.

*Valor Económico*

2000. "Como o brasileiro encara a 'Vénus' de fim de século." July 25.

*Veja*

1992. "Menor aqui é melhor: Brasileiras cada vez mais jovens enfrentam a cirurgia plástica para diminuir tamanho dos seios." June 1.

1996a. "Festival de erros e mentiras." October 16.

1996b. "O preço da vaidade." October 16.

1998. "No tom certo: Fabricantes de cosméticos descobrem o filão dos produtos para negras e mulatas." December 2.

1999a. "Os meus, os seus, os nossos: Como divórcios, separações e novos casamentos estão mudando a família brasileira." March 17.

1999b. "Ursinho e salto alto." July 14.

2000a. "Os pais estão confusos." January 1.

2000b. "Sexo depois dos 40." May 24.

2000c. "Todos querem ser Zulu." September 6.

2001a. "Brasil, império do bisturi." January 10.

2001b. "Entrevista: Ivo Pitanguy." May 2.

2001c. "Silicone sem juros: Consórcios querem cobrir plásticas e curso superior." March 14.

2002. "Corpos à venda." March 6.

2004. "É de lei: O direito à beleza." January 7.

# Index

Page numbers in italics refer to illustrations.

Baker, Josephine, 25
Bakhtin, Mikhail, 97
Barata Ribeiro hospital, 55
Barbosa, Ruy, 224
bare sex. *See* biologized selves
Baudelaire, Charles, 242
Baudrillard, Jean, 249, 257n7
beauty culture, 23, 57–61, 246–47,
257n4; agency and choice in, 183; in
consumer capitalism, 31–33, 246–50;
corporeal ideals of, 13, 42, 68–69,
133–43, 202; facial ideals of, 142–50,
262n12; national identity in, 24–28,
41–44, 68–70. *See also* popular culture
beauty industry, 25–26, 28–29, 246–
50, 257n4
beauty pageants, 72–73, 230, *Plate 3*
beauty salons, 173
beauty work, 16–24, 173, 257n4; commodification and, 27–29, 31–33, 233–
34, 247–50, 257n7; internal logic
of, 20–21; moral field of, 16–17; as
realm of praxis, 20–21; scholarly approaches to, 17–21; in sexual culture,
28–33, 257n6. *See also* class aspects
of beauty work; racial identity; therapeutic rationale for beauty work
Benjamin, Walter, 59–60, 73
Dr. Berta, 265n11
Biehl, João, 87, 100, 243
biologized selves (bare sex), 32–33, 178,
239–52
biomedicine, 114–20
biopolitics, 56, 116, 177
biopower, 116–18, 234
bios (qualified life), 240
Black Brazilian Front (FNB), 171
black music, 167, *168*
blackness, black activism, 26–28, 150–
62; adoption of negro identity in,
150–52, 166, 262n13; celebrity role

models of, 162–67, 262nn19–21;
confrontation of racism in, 152–53,
172–74; consumption of beauty in,
153–62, 262nn15–17; cultural aesthetics of, 167–74, 263nn25–27; of
Preta Gil, 123–27, 129, *170*; working
self-esteem in, 151, 165. *See also* Afro-
Brazilians; racism
*Black Orpheus*, 24
*Black People* (magazine), 169
Boas, Franz, 129
body sculpting, 136, 231–32
Bordo, Susan, 234
Borges, Juliana, 72–73, *Plate 3*
bottom, the: Africanist ideals of, 13, 42,
68–69, 133–39, 261nn7–8; prosthet-
ics for, 261n8; surgical enhancement
of, 137–39, 261–62nn9–10; terminology for, 136
Bourdieu, Pierre, 26; on class body,
248–50; on multiculturalism, 172–
73; on social theory, 123
Brasília, 66
Brazil. *See* national identity
Brazilian Foreign Service, 263n24
Brazilianization, 118
Brazilian Ministry of Communications,
170
Brazilian Ministry of Education,
263n24
Brazilian Society of Market Research,
68, 154
Brazilian Society of Plastic Surgery, 95
breast augmentation, 41–44, 219–26,
243–44; risks and complications of,
94; scarring in, 12–13; in *Sin tetas
no hay paraíso*, 58–59; slang terminology for, 67, 71–72; therapeutic
rationale for, 46
breast competitions, 91
breastfeeding, 32, 184, 189, 202–4,
243. *See also* female reproduction

breast reductions and lifts, 42, 195, 243–44, 264n4, *Plate 5*; Pitanguy's methodology of, 53, 264n5; popularity of, 137–41; therapeutic rationale for, 52–54

brownness. See *morenidade*; mulatas, mulata culture

bunda, the. *See* bottom, the

*Bundas* (magazine), 136

Bündchen, Gisele, 209, 210

Burdick, John, 263n27

burns, 48

Bush (George H. W.) administration, 105

Busto, Norberto, 70, 71, 259n10

buttocks implants, 137–39

Cabral, Pedro Álvarez, 61

Caesarean deliveries, 113, 119, 182, 187–90, 259n12, 264n8. *See also* female reproduction

Caetano, André, 187

Campbell, Colin, 235–36, 258n9

Campbell, Naomi, 213, 218

Cândido, Antônio, 266n22

Candomblé, 40, 167, 263n22

Canguilhem, Georges, 115

capitalism of beauty, 28–33, 235–36, 246–50. *See also* consumer culture

*Caranaval em Madureira* (Amaral), 65

Cardoso, Fernando Enrique, 104–5, 151–52, 200, 258n7, 260n19, 263n24

Carnaval, 41–44, 50, 65, 207

Carranza, Maria, 188

*Casa-grande e senzala* (The Masters and the Slaves) (Freyre), 129–30, 261n3

Castells, Manuel, 223, 266n20, 267n26

Catholicism, 40, 186, 224, 226–27, 230–31

Cavalcanti, Emiliano di, 65

celebrities, 57–61; Carnaval presence

of, 42, 44; fashion models as, 205–11; media focus on, 70–72; popular imitation of, 18, 23, 25, 37–41, 204–19, 266n16

Cendrars, Blaise, 64

Chico Science & Nação Zumbi, 134

Chinese foot-binding, 242

Cícero, Antônio, 123

cinema, 208

citizenship, 111–13; consumption and; human rights and, 173; labor and work cards and, 108, 112, 260n20, 267n27; right to beauty and, 14–16, 18–20, 102–4, 109–14, 250

class aspects of beauty work, 20–22, 110–11, 251–52; in Caesarian section deliveries, 188; celebrities and, 18, 23, 25, 37–41, 57–61; income disparity and, 260nn22–23; for middle class, 260–61nn24–25; for poor and working-class women, 44–46, 195–204, 265nn11–13; right to beauty and, 14–16, 18–20, 102–4, 109–14, 250; self-esteem and, 21–22, 88–89, 235; socialites and, 7–10; social mobility and, 112, 129, 141–42, 147–48, 154, 166, 181–82, 246–50, 264nn1–2

Dr. Claudio, 55–56, 115

cleft palate, 79–80

clinical practice of beauty. *See* plastic surgery

Clínica Vitalitá, 192

Collor de Mello, Fernando, 19, 105, 260n19

color. *See* racial identity

Comando Vermelho, 111

companionate love, 227

complications. *See* risks and complications of surgery

Comte, Auguste, 63, 65

consumer culture: black beauty in, 153–62, 170–72, 262nn15–17; commodi-

ception and, 186–87, 231, 245–46; non-clinical Caesarean deliveries in, 113, 119, 182, 187–90, 259n12; plástica milestones associated with, 182, 183–86, 225–26, 264n4; political economy of, 29–34, 259n12; role of sexual pleasure in, 185, 188–94, 213, 227–29, 264n9; sterilization and, 182, 187–88; of teens, 213, 231. *See also* sexual culture

feminism: focus in, on women's rights, 224, 233, 267n27; liberal ideal in, of sex, 235; theory of beauty of, 29–31

fetishism, 59–61, 67–69, 72–74, 135–37

Figueira, S., 224–25

Dona Firmina, 47–49, *Plate 4*

Flávia, 52–54, 139, 204, 225–27, 237

Foucault, Michel: on biopower, 116, 117–18, 234; on sexual culture, 235–36

Fouquet, Jean, 239

Frank, Adam, 267n28

Freud, Sigmund: on fetish, 59; on genital ugliness, 192–93; on neurosis, 79

Freyre, Gilberto, 63, 65, 129–37, 141–42, 147–49, 261n4. See also *mestiçagem*

Fry, Peter, 167, 262n17

Fukuyama, Francis, 73

funk, 136, 261n7

*futebol*, 25, 65

Gabriel o Pensador, 136–37

Gauguin, Paul, 25

gay culture, 247–50, 267nn2–3

Geertz, Clifford, 57

gender norms, 48, 264n7; in creation of perfect bodies, 215–19; in distinctions between reconstructive and cosmetic surgery, 48, 219; fetishiza-

tion of beauty and, 60–61, 67–69; genital surgery and, 185, 188–94, 213, 264n9; in patriarchal families, 223–25, 266nn20–24; in surgeon-patient relationships, 32–33, 183, 185, 264n3; for travestis, 98, 248, 267n3. *See also* female reproduction; modernity

genital surgery, 185, 188–94, 213, 264n9

Giddens, Anthony, 118

Gil, Gilberto, 37, 38, 124–26, 258n1

Gil, Maria, 37–38

Gil, Preta, 37–41, 123–27, 129, 170, 258n1

Gillies, Harold Delf, 51, 78

Gilman, Sander, 78–79, 116, 221

Girard, René, 223

Gláucia, 9

global technologies, 59–61

Globo network, 66

gluteal prostheses, 137–39

Goldstein, Donna, 249

Gonzalez, Raul, 137

Guattari, Felix, 201

hair, 142–43, 150–51, 173, 262n11

Hakme, Farid, 147

Hanchard, Michael, 135–36, 137, 202, 263n26

health benefits of cosmetic surgery, 56–57, 114–20. *See also* therapeutic rationale for beauty work

Hegel, Georg, 241–42

Hippocratic oath, 77

*History of Sexuality* (Foucault), 234

Hollander, Anne, 239

Holston, James, 62, 111

homosexuality. *See* queer beauty

hormone replacement therapy, 230

Humberto, José, 92, 94

hybridity. See *mestiçagem*
hygiene promotion, 84–85, 267n27
hymen reconstruction, 194

Iberian bodies, 141–42
ideology of credit, 110
import substitution, 66, 104–5
Indian bodies, 141
inferiority complex, 78–80
insurance fraud, 95, 260n16
"In the Universe of Beauty," 15, 18–19,
  83
intimate plástica. *See* genital surgery

Jackson, Michael, 146
Jobim, Tom, 252
Jorge, Seu, 72, 137

Kama Sutra, 236
Kaw, Eugenia, 145
Kramer, Peter, 83
Kubitschek, Juscelino, 66
Kulick, Don, 248
Kunzle, David, 265n13
Kuznesof, Elizabeth, 226

labor and work: citizenship based in,
  108, 112, 260n20, 267n27; class
  polarization in, 105; of domestic
  workers, 2–3, 22, 44–46, 195–204,
  265nn11–12; of models and actors,
  161–62, 205–11; privatization and,
  108; racial implications in, 199–201;
  role of appearance in, 106–9, 114,
  215–19, 260n21; of wet nurses, 203
Lacan, Jacques, 87
*Laços da família* (Family Ties) (novela),
  227
Lens of Dreams (Lente de Sonhos),
  169, 208, *Plate 8*
Lévi-Strauss, Claude, 7–8, 29, 55
liberation theology, 40

*lipoescultura*, 137, 139, 221–22
liposuction, 97–98, 139, 221–23; costs
  of, 259n14; for HIV patients, 92, 119;
  Pitanguy's methodology of, 53; for
  pregnancy repairs, 182, 264n4; risks
  and complications of, 94, 260n15
liquid silicone, 21, 97–98, 139, 219,
  248
Dr. Lívia, 95, 222
Lobato, Monteiro, 135
Lula da Silva, Ignácio, 86
Lux soap ads, 156–58

*Macunaíma* (Andrade), 128
*Madonna and Child* (Fouquet), 239
maids. *See* domestic workers
male contraception, 187, 264n7
male estética patients, 109, 183, 231–33,
  248
male sexuality, 228
malpractice cases, 95
"Mania de peitão," 72
Dr. Marcelo, 89–92, 146
Dr. Márcio, 93
Mariani, Maria Clara, 200–201
marketing of beauty, 59, 156–62,
  262n17; in gay culture, 247–48;
  ideals of progress in, 185–86
Martins, Luiz Carlos, *138*
Martins, Wilson, 25
Marx, Karl, 31, 59, 246
mass media, 22–23, 66, 70–72; advertisements for beauty in, 67–70;
  celebrity beauty in, 57–61; images of
  female glamour in, 30–31, 208–11;
  lifestyle promotion in, 110–11; *Plástica & Beleza* magazine, 23, 44, 61,
  89, 90, 259n10. *See also* popular culture
Master Health, 108–9
Mauss, Marcel, 32–33
McIndoe, Archibald, 51

media. *See* mass media

medicalization of human experience, 115–18

medical practice. *See* plastic surgery

medical tourism, 15, 101

*medicina estética*, 185, 264n6. *See also* female reproduction

Menem, Carlos, 260n24

menopause, 230

*mestiçagem*, 126–28, 147, 261n6; Africanist corporeal ideals in, 133–43, 202; contrast of, with multiculturalism, 148–53, 170–74, 263n24; emergence of concept of, 129–30; eroticism inherent in, 130–31, 133–34; relation of, to morenidade, 131–33, 142–43, 171–72. *See also* racial identity

methodological nationalism, 41

Midgley, Mary, 245

miscegenation, 129–30, 149, 261nn3–5. *See also* mestiçagem

Miss Brazil pageant, 72–73, *Plate 3*

"Miss Third Age" beauty contest, 230

modeling, 161–62, 205–11, 217, 266n16, *Plates 7–8*

modernity, 31–34, 64–67; dilemmas of ideology in, 173; fungibility of capital in, 245–50; gaze on female body in, 65–66; media images of women in, 208–11; mestiçagem in, 128–31, 135; personal transformation fantasies in, 67–74; povão (common people) in, 64–66; rational sexuality of, 186–87

Moraes, Vinícius de, 252

*morenidade*, 131–33, 142–43, 152, 171

motherhood. *See* female reproduction

Motta, Zezé, 162–66, 262n21

mulatas, mulata culture, 24–26, 30; in Brazil's modern identity, 65–66; dancers as embodiment of, 42–44,

108, 266n17; in discourses of sexual desirability, 63–64, 163; valorization of, 68–70, 141, 152. *See also* mestiçagem

multiculturalism, 26–27, 127–35, 148–53, 170–74, 263n24

"Nádegas a declarar" (Buttocks/Nothing to Declare), 136–37

national health insurance, 85–87, 92, 96, 115, 260n18

national identity, 60–67; corporeal ideals in, 24–28, 41–44, 68–70, 135–43, 202; dyads of violence and beauty in, 61–64; erotic ideals of, 221–37; inclusive model of citizenship in, 62; links of, with gender and sexuality, 60–61; modernist approaches to, 64–67; role of mestiçagem in, 127–35, 148–50

Needell, Jeffrey, 63

negro identity. *See* blackness, black activism

Negroid nose, 109, 143–50, 260n21, 262n12, 267n1

*Negro 100%* (magazine), 169

neoliberalism, 105–6, 111–13; multiculturalist approach of, 172–73, 263nn25–27; valuation of appearance in, 114. *See also* political economy

Nietzsche, Friedrich, 17–20, 130

non-clinical Caesarean deliveries. *See* Caesarean deliveries

normalizing function of medicine, 115–16

nose jobs. *See* rhinoplasty

novelas, 162–67, 252

O Boticário, 155

O'Dougherty, Maureen, 67

Oliveira, P. J., 85

oral sex, 267n26
organ theft, 72
Oriental eyes, 145
Ossman, Susan, 173
Ovalle, Eliana, 70–71
Dr. Ox, 198–99, 215–18

patriarchal families, 223–25, 231, 246, 266nn20–24
Patrulha do Samba dancers, 71
Paul, Saint, 242
Dr. Paulo, 199
Peixoto, Afrânio, 193
Pentacostalism, 263n27. *See also* evangelical Christianity
Perez, Carla, 42, *43*, 136, 266n16
Petrobras, 150, 171
philosophy of plastic surgery, 49–57, 258n4
pill, the, 245–46
Pitanguy, Gisele, 81
Pitanguy, Ivo, 10–12, 19–20, 49; celebrity of, 15, 50, 61, 70, 96; clinic of, 66; philosophy of plastic surgery of, 14–15, 51–57, 80, 199, 250, 258n4; surgical methodologies of, 53, 264n5; on therapeutic rationale for surgery, 81–83, 89, 116, 120, 259n11
*plástica. See* plastic surgery
*Plástica & Beleza* (magazine), 23, 44, 61, 70–71, 89, 90, 191–92, 259n10
*Plástica & Corpo* (magazine), 61
*Plástica & Você* (magazine), 23, 259n10
plastic surgery, 10–16, 93; acceptance of, as medical specialty, 77–80; compensation in, 259n13; continuing education in, 68; embodied subjectivity in, 51–52, 99–101; experimental nature of, 97–98, 101; free and discounted cosmetic surgery in, 2, 14–16, 54; gendered surgeon-patient relationships in, 32–33, 183, 185,

264n3; origins and growth of, 7–10, 77–84, 115–16; rates of cosmetic surgeries in, 15–16, 54, 92, 139, 183, 257n3; residency programs in, 10–15, 51–52, 56, 93–94, 96, 101, 260n17; therapeutic rationale of, 89–101, 259n11. *See also* reconstructive surgery; surgical procedures; therapeutic rationale for beauty work
political economy: aesthetic health and, 34, 114–20; of female reproduction, 29–34, 259n12; of public health systems, 84–88; right to beauty in, 14–16, 18–20, 102–4, 109–14; of self-esteem, 21–22, 75–76, 84, 88–89, 116–17, 235. *See also* class aspects of beauty work; *povão, povo*
polygamy, 226–27
poor, the. See *povão, povo*
popular culture, 22–28, 57–59, 70, 259n10; black celebrities in, 162–67, 262nn19–21; black culture in, 167–74, 263nn26–27; double connotations of, 60–61; fetishization in, of female bodies, 135–37; imitation in, of celebrity beauty, 18, 23, 25, 37–41, 204–19, 266n16; imported nature of, 59–64, 67, 74, 167–74, 258–59nn7–8; prevalence in, of lighter-skinned people, 26, 142, 158–62. See *also* mass media
Pornochancada cinema, 163
pornography, 31–32
*Portrait of Brazil* (Prado), 131
Potter, Joseph, 187
*povão, povo*, 19; as barrier to modernization, 60; as candidates for plastic surgery, 103; elite views of, 87; in modernist art, 64–65. *See also* class aspects of beauty work
power, 116–18, 234, 246–52
Prado, Paulo, 131

pregnancy. *See* female reproduction
preventive plástica, 222–23
private clinics, 10–11, 66
production of beauty. *See* beauty work
projection, 81
prostitution, 31–32, 58–59, 217; artificiality and, 242; Europeanization in, 63–64; of travestis, 98, 248, 267n3
Prozac, 83
psychoanalysis, 76–83, 88–89
psychological rationale for beauty work. *See* therapeutic rationale for beauty work
public health campaigns, 84–85, 259n12
public hospitals, 85–87, 92–101, 258n5, 260n18. *See also* residency programs in plastic surgery; Santa Casa de Misericórdia

qualified sex, 240–41
queer beauty, 38, 98, 247–50, 267nn2–3

*Raça* (magazine), 38, 169, *170*
racial identity, 25–28, 170–73; aesthetics of race in, 123–27, 130–31, 263n25, 263n28; Brazil's inclusive continuum of, 34, 62, 123, 126–35, 261n6; in census categories, 132; color implications for, 158–62; corporeal ideals in, 13, 42, 68–69, 133–43, 202; in domestic work, 199–201; hair and facial features in, 142–51, 262n11; hierarchies of light and dark in, 24–27, 30, 109, 129, 135, 142–43, 149–50, 260n21, 261n6; market targeting of, 153–62; morenidade in, 131–33, 142–43; in public health campaigns, 84–85; in sexual desirability, 63–64, 130–31, 133–34; stereotyping of, 262n16; terminology of, 26–27, 123, 126–27. *See also* blackness, black

activism; *mestiçagem*; mulatas, mulata culture
racism, 27–28, 134, 147–53; black activist confrontations of, 172–74; official recognition of, 169–72, 263n24; scientific racism, 123, 141
Dr. Rafaela, 2
*Raizes* (Roots) (magazine), 169
rates of cosmetic surgeries, 15–16, 54, 92, 93, 139, 183, 257n3
Rebhun, L. A., 227
reconstructive surgery, 14–15, 18, 48–49, 219; for cleft palate, 79–80; philosophical union of, with cosmetic surgery, 55–57, 115, 258n4; psychological rationale for, 50–51; rates of, 54
Reis, Elisa, 104
religious practice, 40; black syncretic forms of, 167, 263n22, 263n27; of Catholicism, 186, 224, 226–27, 230–31; of evangelical Christianity, 39, 70–71; healing practices in, 84–85
residency programs in plastic surgery, 10–15, 51–52, 56, 93–94, 96, 101, 260n17
rhinoplasty, 244; as coming-out present, 183–84; racial contexts of, 109, 143–50, 260n21, 262n12, 267n1
Dr. Ribeiro, 196
right to beauty, 14–16, 18–20, 102–4, 109–14, 250
Rio de Janeiro, 4–7; beach culture of, 133; Carnaval of, 41–44; public health systems in, 84–89; suburbs of, 165; urban rainforests of, 37
risks and complications of surgery, 40, 70, 77, 94–101, 259–60nn14–16
Rivers, W. H. R., 78–79
Dr. Roberto, 86–87
Rocha, Marta, 72–73
Rodrigues, Debora, 71

Rodrigues, Nelson, 9
Rodrigues, Nina, 84

samba, 25, 44, 55, 61, 72; African roots
of, 167; as emblem of Brazilian identity, 64–65, 259n9; schools for, 65,
207–8
*Samba* (Cavalcanti), 65
Sansone, Livio, 108
Santa Casa de Misericórdia, 10–16,
258n5, *Plate 2*; discounted fees at,
2, 54, 107, 260n17; psychological
screenings at, 81, 88–89; residency
program of, 93, 260n17; surgical
plan process in, 102–3
scarring, 139–41
Scheper-Hughes, Nancy, 72, 188
Schwartz, Roberto, 63
scientific racism, 123, 141
Sedgwick, Eve Kosofsky, 267n28
Segato, Rita, 147, 263n26
self-esteem, 21, 33–34, 40–41, 46,
56–57, 75–89, 109–14, 235; in black
identity work, 151, 165, 169; emergence of concept of, 78; political
economy of, 75–76, 88–89, 116–17;
right to beauty in, 102–4; vanity as,
197–201. *See also* therapeutic rationale for beauty work
self-governance. *See* political economy
sex tourism, 178
sexual culture, 28–34, 219–37, 257n6;
of adolescents, 213, 230–31; biologized selves (bare sex) in, 32–33, 178,
239–52; of domestic workers, 200–
201; female autonomy in, 228–29;
fetishization of beauty in, 60–61,
67–69; homosexuality in, 247–50,
267nn2–3; ideal male bodies in,
231–33; management of aging in,
223, 225–26, 229–33, 245, 251–52,

267n26; pleasure in, 177, 185, 188–
94, 213, 221–37, 262n18, 264n9;
racial and class dynamics of, 63–64,
130–34, 233, 248–50, 267n27; of
rational modernity, 186–87. *See also*
female reproduction; prostitution
sexually transmitted diseases (STDS),
231
Sharp, Lesley, 233
*siliconada*, 4, 72–73
silicone: for buttocks implants, 137–39;
liquid injections of, 21, 97–98, 139,
219, 248. *See also* breast augmentation
Silimed, 2
Simmel, Georg, 246
Simpson, Amelia, 210
*Sin tetas no hay paraíso* (telenovela),
58–59, 217
slavery, 26, 110, 167, 199; abolition of,
149; bodies as property in, 198; location of patriarchal structures in, 224,
266n21; miscegenation associated
with, 133–34, 261nn3–5; period
drama portrayals of, 163–64
soap operas, 162
soccer, 25, 65
social class hierarchies. *See* class aspects of beauty work
socialites, 7–10
Society of Ex-Students of Prof. Pitanguy, 51, 93–94
Sodré, Muniz, 263n25
sterilization, 182, 187–88, 264n7
Stratz, Carl Heinrich, 130
Strozenberg, Ilana, 200–201
subjectivation, 243
suntanning, 132–33
surgical procedures: observations of,
52–54; photographic documentation
of, 53, 68, 258n3; risks and com-

plications of, 40, 70, 77, 94–101, 259–60nn14–16; surgical plan process for, 86, 102–3; for touch-ups and corrections, 95–96, 99. *See also* plastic surgery; *under specific types of procedures*

Tatiana, 8–9, 189
television, 66; mass-mediated glamour on, 208–11; prime-time novelas on, 162–67, 252, 262nn19–21
testosterone, 230
therapeutic rationale for beauty work, 51–57; in aesthetic health, 114–20; building of self-esteem as, 21, 33–34, 40–41, 46, 75–89, 113–14, 221, 235; class contexts of, 84, 88–89, 102–14, 116–17; clinical application of, 89–101, 259n11; personal transformation fantasies in, 67–73; in Pitanguy's philosophy of plastic surgery, 81–83, 199, 258n4; subjectivity of aesthetic defects and, 99–101
touch-ups, 95–96, 99
transference, 81–83
transhumanism, 73
*travestis*, 98, 248, 267n3
tubal ligations, 182, 187–88
Twine, France Winddance, 142

universal right to healthcare, 85–87, 260n18

vaginal tightening, 185, 188–94, 193
vanity, 197–98
Vargas, Getúlio: formation of national identity under, 65, 66, 108, 112; state-directed industrialization under, 66, 104–5; suppression of Black Brazilian Front by, 171
vasectomy, 187, 264n7
*Veja* magazine, 15–16, 80, 182
Vianna, Hermano, 64, 129
Vinícius dos Santos, Marcos, 71
virginity, 193–94, 224, 230–31, 244
Vivieros de Castro, Eduardo, 20

Wacquant, Loïc, 26, 172–73
weight lifting, 136, 231–32
wet nursing, 203
white bodies, whitening, 26, 129, 141–42, 147–48
wife killing, 224
Wilde, Oscar, 9
Wolf, Naomi, 30
work. *See* labor and work
World Health Organization, 55, 114

*Xica da Silva* (film), 163–64
*Xou da Xuxa* (show), 209–10
Xuxa, 209–10, 249

Young, Iris Marion, 191, 194

zoë (bare life), 240

ALEXANDER EDMONDS IS ASSISTANT PROFESSOR OF

ANTHROPOLOGY AT THE UNIVERSITY OF AMSTERDAM.

: : :

Library of Congress Cataloging-in-Publication Data

Edmonds, Alexander

Pretty modern : beauty, sex, and plastic surgery in

Brazil / Alexander Edmonds.

p. cm.

Includes bibliographical references and index.

ISBN 978-0-8223-4785-9 (cloth : alk. paper)

ISBN 978-0-8223-4801-6 (pbk. : alk. paper)

1. Surgery, Plastic—Social aspects—Brazil.  2. Beauty,

Personal—Social aspects—Brazil.  I. Title.

RD119.E366 2010

391.60981—dc22    2010028795